A History of World Litera

A History of World Literature is a fully revised and expanded edition of *The Routledge Concise History of World Literature* (2012). This remarkably broad and informative book offers an introduction to "world literature."

Tracing the term from its earliest roots and situating it within a number of relevant contexts from postcolonialism, decoloniality, ecocriticism, and book circulation, Theo D'haen in ten tightly-argued but richly-detailed chapters examines:

- the return of the term "world literature" and its changing meaning;
- Goethe's concept of *Weltliteratur* and how this relates to current debates;
- theories and theorists who have had an impact on world literature; and
- how world literature is taught around the world.

By examining how world literature is studied around the globe, this book is the ideal guide to an increasingly popular and important term in literary studies. It is accessible and engaging and will be invaluable to students of world literature, comparative literature, translation, postcolonial and decoloniality studies, and materialist approaches, and to anyone with an interest in these or related topics.

Theo D'haen is Emeritus Professor of English and Comparative Literature at Leuven University and Emeritus Professor of English and American Literature at Leiden University. He has published widely on (post)modernism, (post)colonialism, and world literature. His publications include *World Literature in an Age of Geopolitics* (2021) and *The Routledge Companion to World Literature, Second Edition* (co-edited with David Damrosch and Djelal Kadir; Routledge, 2022).

A History of World Literature

Theo D'haen

Routledge
Taylor & Francis Group
LONDON AND NEW YORK

Designed cover image: simonidadjordjevic, Getty

Previously published as *The Routledge Concise History of World Literature*, 2012

First published 2024
by Routledge
4 Park Square, Milton Park, Abingdon, Oxon OX14 4RN

and by Routledge
605 Third Avenue, New York, NY 10158

Routledge is an imprint of the Taylor & Francis Group, an informa business

© 2024 Theo D'haen

The right of Theo D'haen to be identified as author of this work has been asserted in accordance with sections 77 and 78 of the Copyright, Designs and Patents Act 1988.

All rights reserved. No part of this book may be reprinted or reproduced or utilised in any form or by any electronic, mechanical, or other means, now known or hereafter invented, including photocopying and recording, or in any information storage or retrieval system, without permission in writing from the publishers.

Trademark notice: Product or corporate names may be trademarks or registered trademarks, and are used only for identification and explanation without intent to infringe.

British Library Cataloguing-in-Publication Data
A catalogue record for this book is available from the British Library

Library of Congress Cataloging-in-Publication Data
Names: D'haen, Theo, author.
Title: A history of world literature / [Theo D'haen].
Other titles: Routledge concise history of world literature
Description: Abingdon, Oxon ; New York, NY : Routledge, 2024. | "Previously published as the Routledge concise history of world literature, 2012." | Includes bibliographical references and index. |
Identifiers: LCCN 2023054603 (print) | LCCN 2023054604 (ebook) | ISBN 9781032433059 (hardback) | ISBN 9781032433042 (paperback) | ISBN 9781003366713 (ebook)
Subjects: LCSH: Literature--History and criticism. | Comparative literature.
Classification: LCC PN86 .H25 2024 (print) | LCC PN86 (ebook) | DDC 801.95--dc23/eng/20240220
LC record available at https://lccn.loc.gov/2023054603
LC ebook record available at https://lccn.loc.gov/2023054604

ISBN: 978-1-032-43305-9 (hbk)
ISBN: 978-1-032-43304-2 (pbk)
ISBN: 978-1-003-36671-3 (ebk)

DOI: 10.4324/9781003366713

Typeset in Times New Roman
by Taylor & Francis Books

Contents

Acknowledgements		vi
	Introduction: The (Re)Turn of World Literature	1
1	Naming World Literature	5
2	Goethe's *Weltliteratur* and The Humanist Ideal	28
3	World Literature and Comparative Literature	48
4	World Literature as an American Pedagogical Construct	81
5	World Literature in European Academe	104
6	World Literature as System	123
7	World Literature and Translation	145
8	World Literature, (Post)Modernism, (Post)Colonialism, Littérature-Monde, Decoloniality	167
9	Asian, African, and Oceanian Perspectives on World Literature	198
10	World Literature and Planetary Materialities	218
	Bibliography	238
	Index	276

Acknowledgements

For the first version of the present book, published in 2012 as *The Routledge Concise History of World Literature*, it was a real pleasure to thank some of the many people who, over the years, had offered me advice, suggestions, information, or simply the opportunity to bore them with my questions. What followed was a very incomplete list, and apologies were and are still due to those whose names should have figured there but which, for one reason or another, but most probably through sheer forgetfulness on my part, did not. I want again to thank, then, Carlos Álvar (Alcalá and Geneva), Hans Bertens (Utrecht), Jean Bessière (Sorbonne), Tomasz Bilczewski (Cracow), Helena Buescu (Lisbon), Paul Cornea (Bucharest), David Damrosch (Harvard), César Domínguez (Santiago de Compostela), Oana Fotache (Bucharest), Djelal Kadir (Pennsylvania State University), Svend Erik Larsen (Aarhus), Sarah Lawall (Massachusetts at Amherst), Gunilla Lindberg-Wada (Stockholm), Saiyma Masood (International Islamic University at Islamabad), Liviu Papadima (Bucharest), Anders Pettersson (Umeå), Monika Schmitz-Emans (Bochum), Manfred Schmeling (Saarbrücken), Monica Spiridon (Bucharest), Mads Rosendahl Thomsen (Aarhus), and Bo Utas (Uppsala).

For this revised and expanded version, under a different title, I again owe thanks to some of the same colleagues, and to some new ones. I want to thank, then, next to those already mentioned, Marie Thérèse Abdelmessih (Cairo), Omid Azadibougar (Hunan Normal University), Stefan Helgesson (Stockholm), José Luís Jobim (Rio de Janeiro), Galin Tihanov (Queen Mary College of London), and Longxi Zhang (City University of Hong Kong and Hunan Normal University).

I apologize that, in the end, I have not used the information, nor taken up the advice, that some of those mentioned have so generously given. The reason for this is to be found in limitations of space on the one hand, and on the other because I did not want to present too disparate a "story" of world literature. The latter meant that, regardless of some of the material kindly offered being extremely interesting, I had to discard it. Of course, any errors in the text that follows are exclusively my own.

Finally, thanks to all those who are dear to me for their patience and forbearance during the time it took me to write this book.

Introduction
The (Re)Turn of World Literature

To begin with, a word of warning: this is not a history of the literary works that in some way or other are deemed part of world literature. Rather, it is a history of what has been written *about* world literature.

No other approach to literary studies has known as spectacular a success in the new millennium as that which goes by the name of "world literature." Still, both the term and the study of what it covers have a long history. Until roughly the turn of the twenty-first century, though, these led a rather hidden existence. Most students of literature were aware, even if often only vaguely, that Goethe, somewhere rather early in the nineteenth century, had used the term *Weltliteratur*. Beyond the rather narrow circle of comparative literature scholars the concept had never really gained much currency until recently.

Even within comparative literature, the subject for a long time remained a minority concern at best, for much of its history restricted to a small elite of European academics, or European-born literary scholars exiled or self-exiled in the United States. Moreover, regardless of its "global" claim, world literature in its orthodox guise largely limited itself to the comparative study of some major, and occasionally some minor, European literatures. In the 1970s to early 1990s the subject seemed almost dead and buried. In the early 2000s world literature rather suddenly resurfaced. In fact, it rapidly established itself as the new paradigm for the study of literature in the United States, and then increasingly also around the world, not only in Europe but also in the fast-developing academic environments of for instance East- and South-Asia.

The return of interest in the subject was heralded in 1994 by the collective volume *Reading World Literature: Theory, History, Practice*, edited by Sarah Lawall. In 1999 there followed Pascale Casanova's *République mondiale des lettres*, quickly translated into *English as The World Republic of Letters* (2004). Franco Moretti in 2000 published "Conjectures on World Literature" in the *New Left Review*. This article immediately drew heavily critical fire and became the focus of much vigorous debate, mostly in English. The various reactions to his article by Christopher Prendergast, Jonathan Arac, Emily Apter, and others provoked Moretti to "More Conjectures on World Literature," published in the *New Left Review* again in 2003. Prendergast in 2004 collected a number of articles, some of them, like his own leading off the volume, reactions to

DOI: 10.4324/9781003366713-1

Casanova and Moretti, in *Debating World Literature*. Moretti continued the debate with *Graphs, Maps, Trees: Abstract Models for Literary Study* (2005) and "Evolution, World Systems, *Weltliteratur*" (2009a [2006]). These texts, along with others on the subject, were collected in *Distant Reading* (2013a). In the meantime, David Damrosch's 2003 *What is World Literature* had appeared. This quickly became the reference for most further discussions of the subject.

The 2004 American Comparative Literature Association report on the state of the discipline, prepared by Haun Saussy, with reactions by a number of leading American comparatists, among whom Damrosch, Apter, Djelal Kadir, and Françoise Lionnet, largely concentrated on the question of world literature. The expanded version, published in 2006 as *Comparative Literature in an Age of Globalization*, added further reactions from the likes of the eminent structuralist scholar Jonathan Culler and the postmodern specialist Linda Hutcheon. John Pizer in 2006 gave *The Idea of World Literature*. The same year also saw the publication of Apter's *The Translation Zone: A New Comparative Literature*, which, even though its title makes no mention of it, is also heavily concerned with world literature. Mads Rosendahl Thomsen's *Mapping World Literature* appeared in 2008. Meanwhile, most leading journals in the field of comparative literature had also jumped on the world literature bandwagon. The British comparative literature journal *Comparative Critical Studies* devoted a whole issue to "Comparative Literature and World Literature" in 2006, with contributions by Damrosch, Susan Bassnett, Culler, Thomas Docherty, Kadir, and Hutcheon. Many other journals carried important articles on world literature too, as did for instance *Comparative Literature Studies*. And the pace kept accelerating. In 2009 Damrosch, who had quickly established himself as the most productive scholar in the field, published a small booklet on *How to Read World Literature* (2009b), for use in class, or by students. That very same year he followed up with an edited volume, *Teaching World Literature*. In 2012 there appeared *The Routledge Concise History of World Literature*, a much leaner version of the book you are now holding. The same year saw the publication of *The Routledge Companion to World Literature*, edited by Theo D'haen, David Damrosch, and Djelal Kadir. *World Literature: A Reader*, edited by Theo D'haen, César Domínguez, and Mads Rosendahl Thomsen, came out in 2013. Since then, work on world literature has not only proliferated but has also moved in new directions. These developments were charted in the second, revised edition of *The Routledge Companion to World Literature* (2022), curated by the same editors as the first edition. The four-volume *Literature: A World History*, under the general editorship of Damrosch and Gunilla Lindberg-Wada, likewise appeared in 2022. All this warranted revising, updating, and expanding the 2012 *Routledge Concise History of World Literature* into the more substantial *A History of World Literature* upon which you are about to embark.

Yet how did this revival of interest in world literature come about so suddenly, and where did it all start? What does it mean for how literature is read, taught, studied, and thought about worldwide in the third decade of the twenty-first century?

Although the term "world literature," or more accurately *Weltliteratur*, may not have quite originated with Goethe, his use of it certainly made all the difference as from his mention of it in 1827 it spread like wildfire all over Europe. Unfortunately, though, Goethe never clearly defined what he meant by the term, and consequently it assumed various guises as the nineteenth and twentieth centuries wore on. Goethe probably simply meant the term to refer to the increased circulation of works of literature among European writers and intellectuals. Very rapidly, though, it also came to stand for the totality of all works of literature in the world, past and present. Hence, the nineteenth century saw the rise of comprehensive, at least so in intention, histories of world literature. In the beginning this was a German specialty, but the German example was widely followed almost everywhere, and this down to the present. Most of these works paid scant attention to developments outside of Europe. Some paid them no attention at all. Many of these histories gave their own national literature disproportionate space. Almost all concentrated, besides, on a few "major" European literatures. Chapter 1 treats the early history of *Weltliteratur*, discusses the various translations of the term in a few European languages and literatures, and briefly preludes upon the discussion of its relationship with comparative literature to follow in a later chapter.

Alternatively, over the nineteenth century there also arose the interpretation of world literature as the canon of the world's literary masterpieces. This canon was largely confined to European works. The aesthetic ideal largely determining the criteria for the selection of the canon was heavily indebted to humanism. Goethe himself, moreover, was heavily influenced by the classical tradition underlying humanism. All this has led to the charge that world literature is inherently Eurocentric. Chapter 2 examines this charge.

Almost concurrently with the spread of the term and idea of world literature there also emerged the beginnings of the discipline of comparative literature. In Chapter 1 I already briefly review how within comparative literature the issue of world literature led to a quest for terminological precision. In Chapter 3 I discuss how comparative literature over the course of its history has dealt with world literature. The first half of the chapter concentrates on the period up to, roughly, World War II and the continental European tradition, or on what is commonly labelled the "French" school of comparative literature. The second half focuses on the so-called "American" school rising to dominance after World War II. Recently, there has also emerged a self-styled "Chinese" school – I go into some detail on this in Chapter 9.

A major difference between European and American ways of dealing with world literature lies in how research in, and the teaching of, world literature have been incorporated into university curricula. Until recently, in Europe interest in the subject was mostly limited to research. In contrast, in the United States it has from very early on informed course work on all levels of university education, and most particularly undergraduate survey courses. The specifically American pedagogical investment in world literature is the subject of Chapter 4.

As of the turn of the millennium, interest in the teaching of world literature mounted in Europe too. Some of the developments this led to are discussed in Chapter 5.

As mentioned, European interest in world literature until recently mostly focused on research rather than teaching. This focus led to systemic, rather than, as in the US, pedagogical approaches to world literature. Chapter 6 discusses a number of these systemic approaches, briefly stopping at some Central and Eastern European theories from the middle of the twentieth century, and then quickly proceeding to more recent theories of French and Italian origin. The latter have significantly re-invigorated the debate on the subject. Over the last ten years however, interest in systemic theories has also been on the rise in the US.

Chapter 7 is devoted to the question of translation in relation to world literature. Already for Goethe, translation was an essential ingredient of *Weltliteratur*. Much neglected in most earlier studies of literature, including comparative literature, translation since the last quarter of the twentieth century has developed into a major field of study of its own. With the renewed interest in world literature, translation studies has come to occupy a central position in literary studies.

Chapters 1 through 7 are mostly concerned with theories, methods, and approaches to world literature that have come to fruition in Europe and the US, and that were – at least originally – designed with European or Western literature in mind. In Chapters 8 through 10 the scope widens.

Postcolonialism, riding high in the 1990s, originally took a deep dislike to world literature, accusing it of glossing over the politics of locality it insisted upon itself. As of the 2010s, though, we see postcolonialism operationalizing the "world" in "world literature" via what Edward Said called "worlding," away from the passive description of an international body of literary works toward a militant agent for political change. This development, along with parallel movements sharing the same concerns, such as decoloniality, are the subject of Chapter 8.

In Chapter 9 I turn to how Asian, African, and scholars from Oceania have joined the discussion on world literature. As promised earlier, then, I take a closer look at world literature in China, but I also stop off in other parts. Here again the question of how to "world" world literature plays a major role.

Finally, Chapter 10 looks at world literature from the materialist perspective of market conditions and circulation, both with respect to matters of ecology, the popularity of certain genres, and the dissemination modalities of texts.

Throughout it will become clear that world literature is not an arcane subject for ivory tower scholars. On the contrary, the debate over world literature as it has developed, and sometimes raged, over the last two centuries closely reverberates with the changes taking place in the world itself over that same period. What constitutes world literature, for whom, and when, and how one should describe it, study it, and teach it, reflect changing constellations of power around the world: literary, intellectually, but also, and perhaps even foremost, economically and politically. That is why world literature is such an interesting subject and its study such a fascinating field.

1 Naming World Literature

Overview

In this first chapter we take a look at how "world literature" got its name, and at some of the fluctuations that name, and the idea or ideas it has stood for, have undergone over the past two centuries or so. Put at its simplest, we see the story of world literature coming full circle over these two centuries, with the more recent and most influential commentators adopting a position that is close to that of the man who first made the term popular, Johann Wolfgang (von) Goethe (1749–1832). Goethe gained fame very early with a tragedy, *Götz von Berlichingen* (1773), and even more so with his epistolary novel *Die Leiden des jungen Werthers* (1774; The Sorrows of Young Werther) about an unhappy love affair that had all of Europe in tears. Other important works include the plays *Faust I* and *II* (1808, 1832), the two-part novel of education *Wilhelm Meisters Lehrjahre* (1795–1796; Wilhelm Meister's Apprenticeship) and *Wilhelm Meisters Wanderjahre* (1829; Wilhelm Meister's Journeyman Years), and the volume of poems *West-östlicher Diwan* (1819; West-Eastern Divan), inspired by the poetry of the fourteenth-century Persian poet Hafez or Hafiz. Next to the most important German, and many would say European or even world, writer of his age, Goethe was also a noted scientist. His novel *Die Wahlverwandtschaften* (1809; Elective Affinities) looks at marriage, and the relationships between men and women, as analogous to chemical reactions. Goethe also was active as a geologist and botanist, and he elaborated a theory of colours that drew a lot of attention at the time.

Until recently it has been commonplace to assert that Goethe coined the term "*Weltliteratur.*" We now know that this is not correct. Thomas Bleicher (1979) has shown how the idea, if not the term, had a long prehistory before Goethe. As to the term itself, August Ludwig von Schlözer (1735–1809), a German historian who also wrote a world history, already used it in print in his 1773 *Isländische Literatur und Geschichte* (Icelandic Literature and History) (Schamoni 2008; Gossens 2010; Gossens 2011: 12). Yet another German, the writer Christoph Martin Wieland (1733–1813), certainly used it early in the nineteenth century (Weitz 1987; Pizer 2006; Tihanov 2011, 2019). None of these earlier uses have had the impact that Goethe's has had, though. Goethe first recorded the term in his diary on 15 January 1827. In his *Gespräche mit Goethe* (1836–1848; Conversations with Goethe) Johann Peter Eckermann (1792–1854) notes Goethe on 31 January of the same year as saying that "national literature has not much meaning nowadays: the epoch of world literature is at hand, and each must work to hasten its coming" (Strich 1949: 349), and he would regularly return to *Weltliteratur* over the next four years, almost up to his death in 1832. In all we have twenty-one rather brief passages from Goethe's own writings and his recorded conversation in which the term appears (Strich 1957: 369–372, 1949: 349–351). Ever since the publication of *Conversations with Goethe,* these passages have served as the inevitable point of departure for all further discussions on the topic. Yet nowhere in his voluminous writings does Goethe give a precise definition of *Weltliteratur*. In fact, Hendrik Birus (2000) details the notorious ambiguity or polysemy of Goethe's utterances on world literature. It is not surprising, then, that these utterances have given rise to ambiguities. These ambiguities, moreover, largely stem from Goethe's own historical situation. In what follows we enter into the twists and turns these ambiguities have led to with regard to "world literature."

Goethe's *Weltliteratur*

At the time of Goethe's taking an interest in "*Weltliteratur*" Europe had only relatively recently emerged from a period of violent warfare occasioned by the French Revolution and the Napoleonic Wars. Goethe had himself been actively involved in some of these events. Germany at the time was divided into numerous smaller, and a few larger, kingdoms, principalities, duchies, and the like. Goethe himself for the better part of his adult life had been living in Weimar, at the court of the Dukes of Saxe-Weimar. After the final defeat of Napoleon in 1815 Europe had entered upon a period of pacification and political restoration. Goethe noted that under these circumstances an increase in the production and circulation of periodicals facilitated the exchange of ideas across Europe. In his own journal *Über Kunst und Altertum* (On Art and Antiquity; Vol. 6, part 1), in an 1827 article on a French adaptation of his own play *Tasso*, he commented upon this as a sign of "the progress of the human race, of the wider prospects in world relationships between men," and it led him to the "conviction that a universal world literature is in process of formation in which we Germans are called to play an honourable part" (Strich 1949: 349). In an 1828 issue of *Über Kunst und Altertum* (On Art and Antiquity; Vol. 6, part 2), in an article on "Edinburgh Reviews," he elaborated:

> these journals, as they gradually reach a wider public, will contribute most effectively to the universal world literature we hope for; we repeat however that there can be no question of the nations thinking alike, the aim is simply that they shall grow aware of one another, understand each other, and, even where they may not be able to love, may at least tolerate one another.
> (Strich 1949: 350)

The "honourable part" Goethe saw reserved for the German language and its literature lay in German literature mediating between the world's literatures because of what he esteemed to be the German language's unique gift for translation. This, Goethe thought, would also enhance the prestige and standing of German literature in a Europe in which, contrary to the English and French cases, German literature did not enjoy the support of a strong nation state, and could not invoke a robust national identity. By the German language, then, and with German literature acting as a sort of arbiter for the dissemination of work in foreign languages throughout Europe, a transnational literature would come into being that would serve the cause of understanding and toleration among nations and peoples.

Weltliteratur, "Letters," and Literature

In an address to the Congress of Natural Scientists in Berlin, in 1828, Goethe further refined upon his earlier ideas. "In venturing to announce a European, in fact a universal, world literature," he said,

> we did not mean merely to say that the different nations should get to know each other and each other's productions; for in this sense it has long been in existence, is propagating itself, and is constantly being added to.
> (Strich 1949: 350)

"No, indeed! The matter is rather this" he claimed, "that the living, striving men of letters should learn to know each other, and through their own inclination and similarity of tastes, find the motive for corporate action" (Strich 1949: 350). In the original German, Goethe uses "Literatoren," which is a rather neutral term. Goethe's translator's use of the term "men of letters" in this passage, though, accurately points to the double frame of reference Goethe seems to invoke here, and hence perhaps to his own final indecision as to what precisely he meant with *Weltliteratur.*

On the one hand, the term "men of letters" suggests that Goethe while thinking of *Weltliteratur* may have been harking back to the concept, predating the French Revolution, of the "Republic of Letters." This term refers to the communities of writers, philosophers, and scientists, that during especially the seventeenth and eighteenth centuries kept in touch with one another, across Europe, by the exchange of, precisely, letters. What they corresponded about, more importantly, were "letters" in the sense of any writing about any kind of "knowledge," stretching from poetry to politics, from astronomy to astrology. The impact these writers had can best be gauged from the fact that it is their ideas, especially those of the so-called *lumières* or Enlightenment philosophers of the eighteenth century, that led to the French Revolution. In fact, they acted as a kind of independent "republic" next to, and often in disagreement with, the official state powers across Europe. In Goethe's day, periodicals had replaced letter writing as the main medium of intellectual exchange. The men writing and reading these journals in Goethe's view should assume the mantle of their earlier counterparts of the Republic of Letters, and they should strive for the same impact. *Weltliteratur* would then refer to an updated form of transnational communication among, in first instance, European, and in further instance "world," intellectuals, to use a term that in Goethe's days had not yet been coined.

Alternatively, the use of such a term as "men of letters" also hints at Goethe's unease with what he saw as unwelcome developments in his already increasingly "modern" and commercialized world, of which the enhanced circulation of journals and periodicals was in itself a telling instance. In an 1829 essay on a German translation of Thomas Carlyle's *Life of Schiller*, and after having mentioned the inevitability of the coming of world literature, Goethe writes that "what suits the masses will spread and will, as we can already see now, give pleasure far and wide … but what is really worth-while will not be so popular" (Strich 1949: 25). So, "the serious-minded will form a quiet, I might almost say an oppressed community" and find their main consolation, "in fact the greatest encouragement," in the fact that "Truth has its function and performs it … if they discover this for themselves and can point it out to others, they will have a profound effect on their generation" (Strich 1949: 25; for a slightly different version of the same passage see Goethe, ed. John Gearey, 1986: 227).

Weltliteratur here assumes the double guise of on the one hand signaling, positively, the intimate "commerce" or exchange of ideas between likeminded writers around Europe and on the other hand, negatively, that of the ever faster and ever-increasing commercialization, including in the province of "letters," that Goethe saw taking place all around him. Later ages would rephrase this distinction as the opposition between *Literatur* and *Lektur*, or *Unterhaltungsliteratur* (Schneider 2004), that is to say: between literature and popular literature. Goethe's aversion to the latter would eventually translate into the rejection of mass culture by, for instance, Theodor Adorno (1903–1969) and most of the Frankfurt School, as well as their American followers, foremost Fredric Jameson.

The "commercial" reference of *Weltliteratur* is picked up by Karl Marx (1818–1883) and Friedrich Engels (1820–1895) in their *Communist Manifesto* (1848), where they posited that

> in place of the old wants, satisfied by the productions of the country, we find new wants, requiring for their satisfaction the products of distant lands and climates. In place of the old local and national seclusion and self-sufficiency, we have intercourse in every direction, universal interdependence of nations. And as in material, so also in intellectual production. The intellectual creations of individual nations become common property. National one-sidedness and narrow-mindedness become more and more impossible, and from the numerous national and local literatures, there arises a world literature.
>
> (Marx 2010: 16)

In essence, the opposition between these two concepts of "world literature," the one referring to the circulation of what are in essence "high" cultural goods among an international elite of "connaisseurs," the other embracing all works of literature everywhere, keeps running through the subject's further history. (For a detailed account of Marx and world literature see Prawer 1976 and David 2011.)

The use of the word "literature" in the final sentence of the previous paragraph points to a further ambiguity in Goethe's various pronouncements on world literature, namely that related to the uses of "letters" and "literature." Discussion of Goethe's *Weltliteratur* almost from the very beginning became caught up in a more general discussion about the concept of "literature" raging at the beginning of the nineteenth century (Hoesel-Uhlig 2004). In fact, it is only at that moment that "literature" gained its present meaning, at least as used in Europe and by extension in the West, or in Western-inspired thinking on the issue. Until the end of the eighteenth century, the term "letters" covered all forms of written knowledge. At the end of the eighteenth century, largely as a result of the German philosopher Emmanuel Kant's intervention, "literature" comes to designate only that part of the overall mass of written material that is ruled by the aesthetic sense, or "taste," and not by any objectively verifiable claim to "truth." Implicitly, the question then shifts to what is "good" literature and what is not? Goethe's own unease with *Weltliteratur* in his 1829 essay on Carlyle's *The Life of Schiller* quoted above as possibly designating all "literature" regardless of "quality" reflects this shift. At the same time, the rise of literary historiography as a branch of the newly emerging "science" of history at the end of the eighteenth and the beginning of the nineteenth centuries redirected attention to "literature" as the archive of everything ever written that fit the category of literature newly defined. Consequently, after Goethe the interpretations put upon *Weltliteratur* have mostly tended to vacillate between the aesthetic and the archival, between an exclusive canon of what is deemed aesthetically most valuable in, and as comprehensive a coverage as possible of, "all" literature. Only recently has there been a return to Goethe's original concept of *Weltliteratur* as a form of circulation, albeit, of course, with a difference.

World Literature Versus National Literature

At first sight the greatest ambiguity of all is that Goethe pushed the idea of world literature in an age of intense nationalism. In Germany as in the rest of Europe, and later also in the Americas, during the nineteenth and twentieth centuries most effort would go into the writing of national literary histories. This was the logical cultural counterpart to the relentless process of political nation-building or consolidation going on across Europe. According to the tenets of Romanticism, each nation strove to ground its legitimacy in its own literary antecedents. Consequently, we see the first systematic histories of Europe's various national literatures appearing in the first part of the nineteenth century. This is not to say that there had been no earlier national literary histories. Italy until beyond the middle of the nineteenth century remained subdivided into a motley quilt of larger and smaller political entities, with no hope of political unification in sight. The unity of a political "patria" or "fatherland" thus lacking was sought for in literature, and particularly in what Claudio Guillén (1924–2007) (1993: 27) calls a "common poetic patrimony." Guillén cites Giaconto Gimma's *Idea della storia dell'Italia letterata* (1723; The Idea of the History of Literary Italy) and Marco Foscarini's *Storia della letteratura veneziana* (1752; History of Venetian Literature) as the earliest examples of such histories. In France a multivolume *Histoire littéraire de la France* (Literary History of France) started appearing in 1733. The latter, an encyclopedia rather than a proper "history," was inaugurated by the Benedictine monks of Saint Maur, continued by the Institut de France in 1814, and still later by a French academy, and continues until today. Invoking the authority of the *Histoire* of the Benedictines, next to that of for instance the French sixteenth-century writer and philosopher Michel de Montaigne, the early nineteenth-century author René de Chateaubriand, and others, Matthieu Richard Auguste Henrion (1805–1862) published a one-volume *Histoire littéraire de la France au moyen âge* (Literary History of France During the Middle Ages) in 1827, with a second edition in 1837. Henrion was a French lawyer, royalist, supporter of Napoleon III, and a Catholic Ultramontanist – which is to say a supporter of the authority of the Pope over that of the local or national clergy. He frequently contributed to Catholic periodicals and wrote numerous works on religion in France. In his foreword to his *Histoire littéraire de la France au moyen âge*, Henrion justifies his enterprise by saying that whereas French youth during their studies are familiarized with Greek and Latin letters, they remain strangers to the various phases of "our country's civilisation" (1827: i; civilisation de notre pays). Similarly, he claims, whereas "the better kind of people" (les gens du monde) are well up on matters political, they "barely know anything about our literary history" (Henrion 1827: i; connaissent à peine notre histoire littéraire). The very first pages of Henrion's *Histoire* set the tone for much of what is typical of nineteenth-century national literary historiography. He immediately starts by claiming for French literature the succession to the giants of Greek and Latin literature. In a similar vein, albeit perhaps not always with the same *aplomb*, all national literary histories glorified their own literature. Henrion qualifies his work as an *Essai,* "sufficiently brief not to lay claim to the attention for too long, yet sufficiently thorough to cover all essentials" (Henrion 1827: i; assez rapide pour ne pas détourner trop longtemps l'attention, assez détaillé pour qu'il renfermât les notions les plus essentielles).

The *Geschichte der poetischen Nationallitteratur der Deutschen* (1835–1842, five volumes; History of the National Literature of the Germans) by Georg Gottfried Gervinus (1805–1871) is a totally different affair in its comprehensiveness as well as thoroughness. Not for nothing does Michael S. Batts choose the date of appearance of the first volume of Gervinus's history (as of the fifth edition, by Karl Bartsch, renamed *Geschichte der deutschen Dichtung*, 1871–1874; History of German Literature) as the starting date for his own *A History of Histories of German Literature, 1835–1914* (1993). For Batts, Gervinus's *Geschichte* is "quite different from anything that had appeared before and ... set a standard for the future" (Batts 1993: 1). In fact, Batts situates Gervinus's work as at the start of "Germanistik," the academic discipline of the study of German language and literature. Most other, at least Western, European countries followed suit over the nineteenth century. In Holland, for instance, we have W.J.A. Jonckbloet's (1817–1885) multivolume *Geschiedenis der Nederlandsche letterkunde* (1868–1870; History of Dutch Literature). Although, as we briefly saw earlier, Goethe himself wanted to propagate world literature at least partially because he thought that German letters would be enhanced if they should succeed in playing a central role in the circulation of the world's literatures, and because in this way the relative inconsequence of the numerous but mostly small German entities in the political realm would be somewhat offset by the increased weight of German literature in the cultural realm, Goethe's aims in all this were cosmopolitan rather than narrowly nationalistic. In fact, for at least a number of commentators Goethe would have insisted upon his ideas on world literature in reaction to what he perceived as the narrowly patriotic concerns of his Romantic co-evals. Perhaps it is more correct to say that he did so in a limited "window of opportunity," when Europe was still in recoil from the excesses of the Napoleonic period, and before the onset of the nationalist movements that would erupt across Europe as of about 1830, with the Greek rising of the early 1820s serving as ignitor.

Goethe so to speak by-passes the level of the nation because "Germany" in his day is not a unified country, and therefore in the eyes of Goethe German literature is at a disadvantage in comparison to English and French literature, both of which can count with the backing of a powerful national identity to which they can and do give expression. Understandably then, Goethe concentrates on the complementarity of the local and the universal, of the regional, expressive of the kind of identitarian realities operative in his own immediate context, with the universal, which in his case is primarily the European, level. In this he was partially undoubtedly also inspired by the early forms of Romanticism that emphasized the local or regional as the expressions of a genuine popular sense of "belonging," inspired by the rising nostalgia for a "home" in time and space brought about by accelerating modernity in the form of the twin forces of industrialization and increased mobility, or in other words precisely the increased "commerce" that Goethe saw as facilitating the advent of *Weltliteratur*. To use the terminology of Aleida Assmann (2010), Goethe lived in an age when Romanticism, in the figures of the brothers Schlegel and Grimm, building on the work of Herder, could still combine short-term individual and social memory alive in "folk-culture" with long-term cultural memory as embodied or enshrined in the works of artists and scholars built upon this folk-culture. After Goethe national literary histories would start to serve as institutionalized forms of national memory.

Heine and World Literature in Nineteenth-Century Germany

What are the various offshoots, then, to which Goethe's thoughts on world literature, and particularly the ambiguity imbued in them, gave rise? For John Pizer, in his *The Idea of World Literature: History and Pedagogical Practice* (2006), only one German writer active in Goethe's own lifetime practiced anything resembling Goethe's own original idea of world literature as signaling and at the same time promoting an intensified cultural exchange among nations. Heinrich Heine (1797–1856) was one of the most important German poets of the first half of the nineteenth century. He was born in Düsseldorf, then a small town, of Jewish parents. He later converted to Protestantism. Most of his adult life was spent in Paris, where he moved permanently in 1831. Witty and ironical, Heine criticized not only fellow poets and writers, but also the German authorities, for which his work often fell victim to censorship. His move to Paris was inspired by a search for greater political and poetic freedom. Many of Heine's poems were put to music by famous composers such as Robert Schumann and Franz Schubert. In a number of essays written during his Parisian years, in German and French, Heine strove to make German culture better known to the French, and French culture to the Germans. He thus sought to update Mme De Staël's (1766–1817) *De l'Allemagne* (1813; On Germany). Anne Louise Germaine de Staël-Holstein was a Swiss writer and socialite who ran a famous literary salon in Paris, and at her Castle in Coppet, a village on Lake Geneva. Mme de Staël's father held important positions under King Louis XVI, and she herself was involved in politics during the period of the French Revolution and its aftermath. She published various poems and novels, the most famous being *Delphine* (1802) and *Corinne ou l'Italie* (1807; Corinne or Italy). Next to *De l'Allemagne* she also published essays such as *Sur la litérature considérée dans ses rapports avec les institutions sociales* (On literature considered in its relations to social institutions, 1800). *De l'Allemagne* is a philosophical and literary inquiry into German culture meant to further French understanding for its eastern neighbor. In many ways it can be seen as having preluded upon Goethe's *Weltliteratur*, but it also propagated the German Romantic nationalism Goethe shied away from and Heine abhorred. Although he formally had nothing to do with them, Heine in his ideas was close to *Junges Deutschland* (Young Germany), a German social and literary reform movement of the 1830s. Inspired by liberal ideas of French origin the writers making up the movement opposed nationalist and Romantic excesses. By the German authorities, and by conservative commentators, they were seen as dangerous revolutionaries, and their works were banned or censored. Several other members of *Junges Deutschland*, such as Ludolf Wienbarg (1802–1872) in an

1835 article, and Karl Gutzkow (1811–1878) in an 1836 book, defended Goethe and his *Weltliteratur*. With Gutzkow nevertheless there already emerges an emphasis on the national within world literature.

After Heine, if Goethe's *Weltliteratur* was invoked, it was either in the service of nationalism, or to reject it as a threat to national culture. The former we find with the already-mentioned Gervinus, who in his *Geschichte* praised Goethe for the important role the latter saw German language and literature play on the scene of world literature, but only in so far as it strengthened German nationalism and advanced German politics. A rejection of *Weltliteratur* as a threat to German national character we find in *Geschichte der Literatur der Gegenwart* (1840; History of Contemporary Literature) by Theodor Mundt (1808–1861) (Pizer 2006: 63). Mundt was yet another member of *Junges Deutschland*, the adherents of which, as nationalist fervor mounted in a Germany on the road to unification, finally achieved in 1871, increasingly turned against the cosmopolitanism of a Goethe and a Heine, in favor of a nationalist and patriotic stance. As Peter Gossens puts it,

> Drawing upon the ideas of Herder, Schlegel and Hegel, Mundt, in a series of literary histories, elaborates a concept of world literature in which literature becomes representative of a nation's development. Thus, Mundt actively contributes to a literary historical approach that sees a world literary canon as consisting of the cumulation of national canons. This approach heavily marked the world literary histories written in the second half of the nineteenth century and continues to be significant even for our contemporary views of the subject.
>
> (Unter Rückgriff auf Herder, Schlegel und Hegel entwickelt Mundt in einer Reihe von Literaturgeschichten ein Konzept von Weltliteratur, bei dem die Literatur zum Repräsentanten nationaler Entwicklung wird. Mundt trägt damit wesentlich zu einer literaturgeschichtlichen Fundierung eines additiven, national orientierten Weltliteraturkanons bei, der die Weltliteraturgeschichten in den zweiten Hälfte des 19. Jahrhunderts, aber auch noch unser heutiges Weltliteraturverständnis nachhaltig prägt.)
>
> (Gossens 2010: 15)

In *Weltliteratur: Modelle transnationaler Literaturwahrnehmung im 19. Jahrhundert*, a book he published the year after the 2010 article that I just quoted, Gossens (2011) gives a very thorough and detailed survey of nineteenth-century German thought on world literature.

Philarète Chasles and World Literature in Nineteenth-Century France

If in Germany, and in German, according to Pizer, only Heine can be taken to follow Goethe's lead in actively furthering *Weltliteratur* even without ever mentioning the term himself, in France the same can be said of Philarète Chasles (1798–1873). Chasles, because of his father's involvement with the Napoleonic regime, spent some of his youth in exile in England after the fall of Napoleon. Later, he would become a prolific literary critic and university lecturer in France, holding the prestigious chair of foreign literatures at the Collège de France from 1841 to his death. Chasles did much to further the understanding of foreign literatures, and particularly English literature, in France. His "Goethean" spirit can plainly be seen from the opening lecture to a course on "Foreign Literature Compared" he gave at the Parisian *Athénée* in 1835. "The entire idea of this course," he tells his audience, the "unique purpose of the studies with which [they] wish to associate [them]selves," is to demonstrate "the distant influence of one mind upon others, the magnetism of one thought for another" (Chasles 1973: 20). The "admirable study he is involved in," he announces, is "the intimate history of the human race, it is the drama of literature, for the drama is no more than the relationships of men with men; it is the exchange of intellectual feelings among all the nations of Europe" (Chasles 1973; 21). As such, he traces how Italy borrows from Greece and Rome, France and Spain from Italy, England and Germany from France, and all from each other, nor does he forget to mention the influence of Arab, Gothic, Byzantine, and Provençal antecedents. To each of the literatures mentioned Chasles ascribes specific characteristics, evocative of what today we would perhaps call national characters, Italy being associated with the senses and the passions, Spain with lyrical genius, Germany with the mind. Mentioning Goethe, next to Luther, Leibniz, and Kant, Chasles praises Germany, "this eminently critical country," for its "vast literary understanding," and its "magnificent comprehension of all the intellectual phases of the world" (Chasles 1973: 25). Still, Chasles says, he is going to "concern [him] self primarily with France," because France is "the center, but the center of sensitivity; she directs civilization, less perhaps by opening up the route to the people who border her than by going forward herself with a giddy and contagious passion" (Chasles 1973: 21). "What Europe is to the rest of the / world," he claims, "France is to Europe; everything reverberates toward her, everything ends with her" (Chasles 1973: 21–22). France, Chasles maintains, is "always influenced by the foreign, always mistress of the influences she receives" (Chasles 1973: 22). Goethe had already believed that in the final analysis France stood to gain most from the dawn of *Weltliteratur*. In his own present, however, he had seen German literature as mediator for the world's literatures, a position that Chasles in his lecture, and in the remainder of his course, claims for France as "*Grand-Sympathique* of the civilized world" past, present, and future (Chasles 1973: 22).

As the title of his lecture indicates, Chasles implicitly inspired himself upon the "comparative method" that in the nineteenth century came to dominate science, and that underpinned the findings of, for instance, the then new discipline of philology, but also of Charles Darwin later in the century. Although he himself never used the term, Chasles can therefore be considered one of the founding fathers of the discipline we now refer to as Comparative Literature. It is not a coincidence, then, that the opening lecture from his 1835 *Athénée* course from which I just quoted features as the first passage in Hans-

Joachim Schulz and Philip H. Rhein's 1973 anthology *Comparative Literature: The Early Years*. In fact, the relationship between World Literature and Comparative Literature has been an intimate yet tangled one from the start. I will come back to this in a later chapter. For the time being, I will continue with the vicissitudes the term and concept of world literature underwent between Goethe's time and our present one.

Toward the end of his 1835 lecture Chasles derides the study of "literature" as concerned with phrasing, metaphors, and style, and instead of the study of "literary history" advocates that of "intellectual history" and the "history of human thought" (Chasles 1973: 33 and 35). Potentially, this opens the door to all kinds of writing being included, and indeed Chasles mentions "the Koran of Mohammed and the proclamations of Bonaparte; a madrigal of the Marquis de Pézay and the laws of Zoroaster" (Chasles 1973: 33). He proposes however not to "follow a systematic synthesis," but rather to take "a pleasure trip, a random walk, not a geometric march bound by rigid cadence" (Chasles 1973: 36). During this "walk" he will concentrate upon the "great writers," Cervantes, Rabelais, Shakespeare, and others such, all "great men" (Chasles 1973: 36), whom, to use the term the American writer and philosopher Ralph Waldo Emerson in 1850 used for one of his books, he also saw as "representative men" for their times. Effectively speaking, then, this amounts to a canon, if not of "great works," then at least of "great writers." In the second half of the nineteenth century scholars and writers would more systematically work out what is only mooted with Chasles. By and large they abandoned the original Goethean concept of *Weltliteratur* as the transnational contemporary circulation of ideas among the authors and leading intellectuals of in first instance the nations of Europe. Instead, they interpreted world literature as meaning either the archive of all that had ever been written, even if often, in spite of Chasles's proposal, limited to *belles lettres* or "literature" in the more restrictive sense, or, more often, as the canon of "world masterpieces." Telling in this respect is *Great Writers: Cervantes, Scott, Milton, Virgil, Montaigne, Shakespeare*, a work published in 1907 by George Edward Woodberry (1855–1930), from 1891 to 1904 professor of Comparative Literature at Columbia University in New York. Moreover, although Chasles, while insisting on France being the "center" (Chasles 1973: 21), could also find fault with French literature, blaming it for sometimes having made mistakes and even of having misled other European literatures into following its own wrong turns, and thus expresses "complete contempt for narrow-minded and blind patriotism," which he likens to the "love of an idiotic mother who suffocates her child in the diapers she wraps him in" (Chasles 1973: 23), later scholars often have no such scruples and, as the example of Mundt cited earlier shows, use world literature as a vehicle to implicitly promote their own national literature.

Histories of World Literature

The center of world literary history writing throughout the nineteenth and early twentieth centuries undoubtedly was Germany. For Anders Pettersson,

Karl Rosenkranz's (1805–1879) *Handbuch einer allgemeinen Geschichte der Poesie* (Handbook General History of Poetry), published in 1832, is the "first completed history of world literature" (Pettersson 2005: 57). For Gossens (2010: 17), the literary historians Hermann Hettner (1821–1882), Johannes Scherr (1817–1886), and Adolf Stern (1835–1907) were mainly responsible for popularizing and developing thinking on world literature in nineteenth-century Germany. Instead of insisting on the utopian dimension of a Goethean concept of world literature furthering the intellectual exchange of ideas across Europe, all three basically follow a cumulative approach, describing the literary production of discrete countries from a chronological point of view and then simply adding one to the other the national literatures of the various countries or cultures to arrive at a description of the world's literary production. In practice, coverage did not extend to the entire globe, but usually remained focused on Europe, and even on a relatively limited part of Europe. In a series of works published from the mid-1850s through the early 1870s Hettner concentrates on the literatures of France, England, and Germany during the Enlightenment. For Hettner these play the central role in the development of European and world literature during the period that interests him. Stern in 1888 published the first literary history to carry *Weltliteratur* in its title: *Geschichte der Weltliteratur in übersichtlicher Darstellung* (History of World Literature Clearly Explained). Most interesting and influential, however, was Scherr, whose *Allgemeine Geschichte der Literatur von den ältesten Zeiten bis auf die Gegenwart. Ein Handbuch für alle Gebildeten* (1851; General History of Literature from Antiquity to the Present. A Manual for all Educated People) aimed at a comprehensive while at the same time geographically representative overview of "the achievements in poetry and literary prose" (Gossens 2010: 18; die Erzeugnisse der Poesie und schönen Prosa) of humanity, and this in a truly transnational approach, looking for structural and historical developments that transcended national and linguistic boundaries. Some years earlier, in 1848, Scherr had already published what in effect was an anthology of world literature with his *Bildersaal der Weltliteratur* (Picture Gallery of Literature). Revised editions of this work appeared in 1869 and 1885.

Scherr's History, regularly updated by later scholars, went through eleven editions, with the last of these appearing in 1921. As of the edition of 1895 the work bore the title *Illustrierte Geschichte der Weltliteratur* (Illustrated History of World Literature). As Scherr for obvious reasons had to be selective in his presentation of the world's literature, he had to institute a canon, which he did on aesthetic grounds. Stern's work, unlike that of Scherr, did not go through repeated editions. Still, together these two provided the examples upon which most subsequent histories of world literature would model themselves, in Germany but also elsewhere. In Germany, according to Gossens, this took the form of a whole series of similar histories, mostly written by one single author and targeted for specific audiences. These works could be differentiated according to levels of difficulty and scholarship, aimed at high school or university students. They might also be meant for the use of the so-called "interested layman." But they might also cater to the religious or philosophical orientation of the readership they aimed at. Thus, different histories might be used in protestant and catholic schools, for instance. Gossens insists that in most of these works "the foundational value of the ideas of transnationalism and cosmopolitanism needs qualification ... most often the aim is to foreground the special qualities of one's own nation" (Gossens 2010: 19; die Denkfiguren von Transnationalität und Kosmopolitismus ... nur bedingt grundlegend sind ... meist geht es darum, die qualitativen Besonderheiten der eigenen Nation hervorzuheben).

Beyond Germany, the genre of world literature histories, because such we can now call it, as described by Gossens and modeled specifically upon Stern rather than Scherr, knew a great vogue especially in the Scandinavian countries, the Netherlands, and Britain, but also in the United States. J.C. Brandt Corstius (1963) and Anders Pettersson (2005) enumerate and briefly discuss many of these histories. Interestingly, terminology often differs from one country or language to another, and "world literature" relatively rarely figures in the titles to these works. Earlier, we already saw that even in Germany *Weltliteratur* was used only late in the century in the title to such a work. In France, Chasles, while in effect writing what amounted to some sort of "world literature" history, preferred the word "comparaison" in his title. In Germany, the term used most often in the titles to such works was *allgemein* (general), stressing the comprehensiveness and general reach of the work in question.

Corstius (1963) signals that many of these works, although the ambition overtly was to write a history of the world's literatures, in fact, and in line with what Gossens suggests above, ended up giving inordinate room to their native literatures, at the expense of "foreign" and especially non-European literatures. To forestall this possibility, authors sometimes opted to by-pass discussions of their native literature altogether. In this respect Corstius (1963) mentions Otto von Leixner's (1847–1907) 1880–1882 *Illustrierte Geschichte der fremden Literaturen* (Corstius refers to the second edition of 1899; Illustrated History of Foreign Literatures) and Paul Wiegler's (1878–1949) 1913 *Geschichte der fremdsprachigen Literaturen* (History of Literatures in Foreign Languages). In 1911 von Leixner's work was translated and revised for a Dutch public as *Der Wereld Letterkunde voor Nederlanders bewerkt door P.A. M. Boele van Hensbroek* (The World's Literature Revised for the Use of the Dutch by P.A.M. Boele van Hensbroek). In his foreword, van Hensbroek (1853–1912) insists that he has very much changed Leixner's original version and justifies this from the extreme German chauvinism that speaks from it – therefore the need to revise it "in line with the endeavor to make a book for Holland" (in overeenstemming met het streven, een boek voor Nederland te maken; van Hensbroek 1911: vi). In fact, van Hensbroek is not less chauvinistic than von Leixner, of course. At the same time, the Dutch book does carry the term "world literature" in its title. Yet it excludes Dutch literature itself, while including the literatures of Holland's colonies.

World Literature and Comparative Literature

In France, Corstius (1963) mentions Frédéric Loliée's (1856–1915) 1903 *Histoire des littératures comparées*, translated in 1906 as *A Short History of Comparative Literature from the Earliest Times to the Present Day*. In fact, the change from Frédéric Loliée's "littératures comparées" to the English version's "comparative literature" is not a coincidence. Toward the end of the nineteenth century the term "comparative literature" had gained entrance in the English-speaking world first through a lecture course Charles Chauncey Shackford (1815–1891) gave at Cornell University in 1871, in the inaugural lecture to which he expatiated upon the discipline, and then through a book with the title *Comparative Literature* by Hutcheson Macauley Posnett (1855–1927) in 1886. In France, Germany, Italy, and other continental European countries the discipline of "littérature comparée," "vergleichende" or "allgemeine und vergleichende Literaturwissenschaft," or "letteratura comparata" had been building throughout the second half of the nineteenth century (Pichois and Rousseau 1967). In England, Matthew Arnold (1822–1888) translated the term, from the French, as "comparative literature" in 1848 (Pichois and Rousseau 1967: 19). From the very beginning, "world literature" almost inevitably became the province of this new discipline. This, however, was not Goethe's *Weltliteratur,* but rather that of Scherr and his contemporaries, and therefore in effect that of a representative canon. Moreover, as also indicated before, this canon largely was restricted to literatures in European languages, and even primarily in a few major European languages, foremost French, English, and German, with Italian and Spanish as distant seconds, and then the occasional other, smaller, European literature, often depending upon the provenance or linguistic skill of the discipline's practitioner in question. I will come back to the relationship between World Literature and Comparative Literature in a later chapter. For the time being I just want to point out that the systematization of the discourse on world literature occasioned by its assumption by Comparative Literature led to a distinction between various terms used to indicate some of the various offshoots to which Goethe's use of the term had given rise to begin with.

Shackford started off his 1871 lecture by positing that "literature is a vast subject, and what is called universal literature is not only vast, but too often vague" (Shackford 1973: 42). Later he also uses the term "general literature," without it being entirely clear whether he simply sees this as synonymous with universal literature, or rather as equivalent to the French "littérature générale." When he speaks of "structural affinities" (Shackford 1973: 43) this rather seems to indicate the latter, with its pursuit of the common traits of different literatures in their historical evolution and relations, a suspicion that is confirmed by his subsequent discussion of specific genres arising in comparable circumstances in different countries, or as passing from one country to another. Pichois and Rousseau warn that French "littérature générale" should not be confounded with American "General Literature" which, they say, should rather be likened to French "philosophie de la littérature" or German "Literaturwissenschaft" (Pichois and Rousseau 1967: 94). For them, the only valid French translation for Goethe's *Weltliteratur* is "littérature universelle," which in English translation for them becomes "World Literature" (Pichois and Rousseau 1967:102).

As we saw, for Shackford universal literature was the totality of literature, in fact, almost an oxymoron for "literature," regardless of language or location. Even if Claudio Guillén is not quite fair when in his *The Challenge of Comparative Literature* he says that for Pichois and Rousseau "littérature universelle" is reduced to the "*Who's Who* of the most illustrious authors" (Guillén 1993: 65), it is true that for them "world literature in essence aims to review and explain those masterpieces that are the patrimony of humankind" (Pichois and Rousseau 1967: 102; la littérature universelle … se propose au fond de recenser et d'expliquer les chefs-d'oeuvre qui forment le patrimoine de l'humanité). Richard Moulton (1849–1924), in his 1911 *World Literature and Its Place in General Culture*, gives yet a further twist to the discussion. Admitting that the term "world literature" may "legitimately be used in more than one sense," he stipulates that he himself is "throughout attaching to it a fixed and special significance" (Moulton 1921: 6). "Universal Literature" he takes to mean "the sum total of all literatures," whereas "world literature," as he uses the term, "is this Universal Literature seen in perspective from a given point of view, presumably the national standpoint of the observer" (Moulton 1921: 6) which, as far as his own position is concerned, he somewhat later defines as "the English-speaking peoples" (Moulton 1921: 9). Albert Guérard (1880–1959) systematized all this, at least in English, in his 1940 *Preface to World Literature* as follows:

> Certain authorities choose to establish a four-fold division: Universal Literature, World Literature, Comparative Literature, General Literature. *Universal Literature*, in this scheme, stands for the fullest possible expansion of our field: it embraces all literatures, of all ages, in all languages, without insisting on their unity or their relations. *World Literature* is limited to those works which are enjoyed in common, ideally by all mankind, practically by our own group of culture, the European or Western. In both these cases, the word *Literature* applies to a body of literary works, not to their critical study. *Comparative Literature* and *General Literature*, on the contrary, are methods of approach. The first is concerned with the mutual influences between various national literatures; the second with those problems which are present in the literature of every epoch and every country.
>
> (Guérard 1940: 15)

Guérard's "Comparative" and "General" Literature neatly correspond with the German *vergleichende* and *allgemeine Literaturwissenschaft*. Corstius (1963: 11) points out that already around 1920 the French comparatist Paul van Tieghem (1871–1948) had called for a "littérature générale" in the sense meant by Guérard. In English, what Guérard calls General Literature we would now probably sooner call Theory of Literature, as Guillén also argues (Guillén 1993: 66). Without reference to Guérard or any other predecessor in the matter, A. Owen Aldridge (1915–2005) in 1986 largely reiterated Guérard's classification, with this difference that he defined world literature as comprising "the great works or classics of all times selected from all of the various national literatures," and Universal Literature as comprising, "in a restricted and more practical sense ... all works that contain elements cosmopolitan enough to appeal to the average person in any literate culture" (Aldridge 1986: 55–56).

World Literature, European Literature

The almost exclusive concentration upon European or Western literature which Guérard signals can be seen as extending the national bias signaled by Moulton and his contemporaries to a wider cultural perspective, while still usefully bracketing literatures other than European or Euro-American. Already in 1901, in his inaugural lecture upon accepting the Chair of Comparative Literature at the University of Lyon, Fernand Baldensperger (1871–1958) ironically commented: "European literature! – or, with the more ambitious term our neighbors use, world, or universal literature" (quoted in Corstius 1963: 7; la littérature européenne! – ou encore, selon la désignation plus ambitieuse qu'emploient nos voisins, la littérature mondiale, ou universelle). Although Baldensperger and Guérard were stating what was undoubtedly received practice in their days, Posnett as well as a number of German scholars had paid at least some attention to non-European literatures, albeit usually limited to (much) earlier periods, and often concentrating almost exclusively on works with a religious or mythological content. Still, the Dutch-language *Der wereld Letterkunde* that I mentioned earlier opens with a 90-plus page section devoted to "Oostersche letteren" (Oriental literatures), chronicling Egyptian, Babylonian and Assyrian, Chinese, Japanese, Hebrew, Arab, Persian, and Indian literature, as well as that of the then Dutch colonial East Indies, that is to say present-day Indonesia, and this up to the nineteenth century, albeit of course in summary form. Peter Ulf Møller mentions that Francis Bull's 1940 Danish *Verdens litteraturhistorie* (World Literary History) "deals exclusively with European writers, in spite of its title" (Møller 1989: 20).

Pretty much the same thing applied to most other histories of world literature written in Western languages during most of the remainder of the twentieth century, according to Corstius who in his 1963 article briefly reviews the Argentinian Ezequiel Martínez Estrada's *Panorama de las literaturas* (1946; Panorama of Literatures), the Dutch F.W. van Heerikhuizen's *Gestalten der Tijden* (1951 and 1956; Figures of the Ages), the Swiss Robert Lavalette's *Literaturgeschichte der Welt* (1948, 1956; Literary History of the World), the latter's compatriot Eduard von Tunk's *Illustrierte Weltliteraturgeschichte* (1954–1955; Illustrated

History of World Literature), the German Erwin Laath's *Geschichte der Weltliteratur* (1953; History of World Literature), and the Spanish Martín de Riquer and José María Valverde's *Historia de la literatura universal* (1957–1959; History of World Literature). Slightly better when it comes to including non-Western literatures are, still according to Corstius (1963), G. Prampolino's *Storia universale della letteratura* (seven volumes, 1948–1953; World History of Literature) and the French three-volume Pléiade *Histoire des littératures* (1955–1958; History of Literature) edited by Raymond Queneau. Typical for most of these histories continues to be that they pay a disproportionate amount of attention to their own national literature. Queneau, for example, devotes one of the three sizeable volumes of his history to (overwhelmingly) French literature and (some) other francophone literatures.

Nor do things outside of the Euro-American ambit seem to have been much different.

The Indian scholar Krishna Chaitanya (pseudonym of K.K. Nair, 1918–1994) wrote what is variously referred to as a nine-volume or a ten-volume *History of World Literature* (Bombay-Calcutta-Madras-New Delhi: Orient Longmans). I have only been able to consult the three volumes in the Harvard Library, published in 1964, 1965, and 1966, and which deal, respectively, with Ancient Mesopotamian and Ancient Egyptian, Ancient Greek, and Ancient Roman Literature. A fourth volume, published in 1968, deals with Ancient Jewish Literature. From what I have seen, these volumes follow the traditional pattern of earlier twentieth-century such English-language overviews. In fact, Chaitanya explicitly refers to the example of *The Outline of Literature* (1923) by John Drinkwater (1882–1937). Drinkwater's *Outline* also served as an example for publications on world literature in China.

Rabindranath Tagore and Maxim Gorky on World Literature

Closer to Goethe's original ideas on *Weltliteratur*, yet inflected by their specific situations, were those of Rabindranath Tagore and Maxim Gorky early in the twentieth century. On 9 February 1907 Rabindranath Tagore gave a lecture on "World Literature" to the Indian National Council of Education in which he explicitly stated that "Comparative Literature is the English title you [those that invited him] have given to the subject I have been asked to discuss ... in Bengali I shall call it world literature" (Tagore 2001: 148). In their note to this piece the editors of *Rabindranath Tagore: Selected Writings on Literature and Language* say that in this "he was probably influenced by Goethe's term *Weltliteratur*" (Tagore 2001: 376). In his lecture, Tagore went to great lengths to claim literature as the expression of all of humanity. "If we realize that universal humanity expresses itself in literature," he said, "we shall be able to discern what is worth viewing in the latter" (Tagore 2001: 148). Drawing upon Indian mythology, and extensively metaphorizing, Tagore construes literature as a "second world around the material one," in which humankind extends itself "through the creation of feelings and ideas" (Tagore 2001: 150). "It is time," he finds, that we pledged that our goal is to view universal humanity in universal literature by freeing ourselves from rustic uncatholicity; that we shall recognize totality in each particular author's work, and that in this totality we shall perceive the interrelations among all human efforts at expression.

(Tagore 2001: 150; see also Chaudhuri 2021)

In 1919 the Moscow-based Soviet publishing house "World Literature" inaugurated, in Russian translation, a series comprising more than 1500 book-length works dating from the French (1789) to the Russian (1917) Revolutions. The occasion led Maxim Gorky (pseudonym of Aleksey Maximovich Peshkov [1868–1936]) to write a celebratory essay. From his explicit mention that within the People's Commisariat for Culture a number of people have been appointed "to publish the works of the most important writers from England, America, Hungary, Germany, Italy, Spain, Portugal, the Scandinavian countries, France, etc" (Gorky 1969: 37; um die Bücher der bedeutendsten Schiftsteller Englands, Amerikas, Ungarns, Deutschlands, Italiens, Spaniens, Portugals, der skandinavischen Länder, Frankreichs usw. Herauszugeben), one might perhaps conclude that the publishing venture under consideration would in essence be Eurocentric. Gorky states, though, that a further aim is to acquaint the Russian people also with "the literary achievements of the East – the literature of India, China, Japan, and of the Arabs" (Gorky 1969: 38; dem literarischen Schaffen des Ostens – der Belletristik Indiens, Chinas, Japans und der Araber). What mattered most for Gorky, of course, was to recuperate the idea of world literature for the ideology of the newly created Soviet state in the interest of which he labored. This recuperation ran along two lines. First, he claimed,

We notice, and we believe, that it is the aim of that powerful flood of creative energy embodied in images and words to wash away forever all distinctions between races, nations and classes, to liberate all peoples from the heavy yoke of having to struggle with each other, and to link all their powers in the struggle against the mysterious forces of nature ... and then it appears that the art of the word and of the image is the religion of all mankind, a religion that comprises all that is written in the sacred books of ancient India, in the Zand-Awesta, in the New Testament, and in the Quran.

(Angesichts des machtvollen Stroms der in Gestalten und Worten verkörperten schöpferischen Energie spürt und glaubt man, dass es das Ziel dieses Stromes ist, für immer alle Unterschiede der Rassen, Nationen und Klassen hinwegzuspülen, die Menschen von dem schweren Joch des Kampfes gegeneinander zu befreien und danach alle ihre Kräfte auf den Kampf gegen die geheimnisvollen Naturgewalten zu lenken ... Und dann scheint es, als sei die Kunst des Wortes und des Bildes die Religion der ganzen Menschheit, eine Religion, die alles in sich aufnimmt, was in der Heiligen Schrift des alten Indiens, in Zand-Awesta, im Evangelium und im Koran geschrieben steht.)

(Gorky 1969: 37)

Next to this more general, vague, and quasi-religious motivation (fitting at least one strain of Gorky's thought, aiming to recapture the power of religion for the purpose of a secular commonality of all people) there is however also a more direct aim, especially as related to a series of shorter paperbound editions aiming at the widest possible distribution among the masses:

> the paperbound editions aim to acquaint the widest possible readership as extensively as possible with the living conditions of the peoples of Europe and America, to show them which ideas, wishes and habits they share, and in which they differ, and to prepare the Russian reader for the absorption of that knowledge of the world and its peoples that literature so richly and vividly mediates, and that greatly facilitates mutual understanding between people using different languages.
>
> (Die broschierten Ausgaben haben das Ziel, breiteste Leserkreise so allseitig wie möglich mit den Lebensbedingungen der Völker Europas und Amerikas bekannt zu machen, ihnen die Gemeinsamkeit und die Unterschiede der Ideen, Wünsche und Gewohnheiten zu zeigen und den russischen Leser für die Aufnahme jener Kentnisse über Welt und Menschen vorzubereiten, die die Belletristik so reichlich und lebendig vermittelt und die das gegenseitige Verständnis der verschiedensprachigen Völker sehr erleichtern.)
> (Gorky 1969: 39)

Obviously, the kind of world literature here referred to answers to Gorky's socialist-realist desiderata under the guise of a Goethean "Verständniss" (understanding) between Europe's, and later the world's, various peoples.

In *Eurasia Without Borders: The Dream of a Leftist Literary Commons 1919– 1943* (2021) Katerina Clark details how during the interbellum the new-born Soviet Republic nourished the ideal of a Eurasian supercontinent, united by a Marxist-Leninist ideology with Moscow at its center, via the promotion of a "world literature" propagating the ideas of the October revolution. With as road markers a series of international writers' conferences under the auspices of the Soviet Union she traces how between 1919 and 1943 (the period of the Comintern, the Third International) writers from across Europe and Asia (and some from North America) were invited to spread socialism and communism. Clark makes clear that the world literature propagated by the Soviet Union is very different from that usually taken as such in Western countries. Jack London, Upton Sinclair, and Bertolt Brecht were applauded for their commitment to the proletariat, while Ernest Hemingway and Thomas Mann were branded as illustrating the decay of capitalist society. Authors with outspoken communist sympathies such as the Americans Josephine Herbst and Max Eastman were highly regarded, as were anti-colonial writers such as the South African Peter Abrahams. Whereas in the beginning the emphasis was on anti-imperialism this later shifted to anti-fascism and, in accordance with a hardening ideological line, on socialist realism and the celebration of "heroes" of the Soviet Union such as Stakhanov.

Peter J. Kalliney in *The Aesthetic Cold War* (2022) picks up where Clark (2021) stops. He demonstrates how after World War II and during the entire Cold War era both the Soviet Union and the United States and some of its allies, foremost the United Kingdom, via financial support, publication venues, and writers' gatherings catered to what then would have been called "Third World" authors. This effectively gave rise to a literature that was both anti-colonial and fiercely jealous of its independence from its nominal benefactors, with some authors successfully playing off both sides against one another. The United States and the United Kingdom fostered what in retrospect, especially after the end of the Cold War with the Fall of the Berlin Wall in 1989, we have come to call postcolonial literature, especially anglophone, but which at the time passed variously as Commonwealth Literature or Literature(s) in English. In French this was the literature of the "francophonie," which since the 1990s has also increasingly been subsumed under the postcolonial label. The Soviet Union rather promoted literature in local languages.

World Literature Beyond Europe

Gorky's name would later be given to a Moscow institute explicitly dedicated to the study and propagation of world literature along Soviet lines. It is under the auspices of the Gorky Institute of World Literature that the multivolume *Istorija vsemirnoj literatury v devjati tomach* (The History of World Literature in Nine Volumes) started appearing as of 1983 in Moscow. The project never reached its full nine volumes. The Soviet Union imploded after volume eight had appeared and the enterprise was discontinued. Nevertheless, the ambition was to produce a history in which all literatures would be "at home." Møller quotes R.M. Samarin, one of the early leaders of the project, as explicitly contrasting the endeavor he and his colleagues are engaged in with customary Western Comparative Literature practice privileging Western literature. Instead, he proclaims,

> the Soviet History of World Literature will tell the story of how in the course of the centuries there arose a house of the literature of mankind, unified and miraculously diversified, embodying the creative genius of all the peoples of the world.
>
> (Møller 1989: 21)

Especially in Scandinavia, where there is a long tradition of world histories of literature, some such histories published over the past few decades have explicitly aimed at presenting a non-Eurocentric picture of the world's literatures, but as Møller demonstrates by a simple tally of pages, neither the Danish twelve-volume *Verdens Litteraturhistorie* (Literary History of the World) of 1971–1973, edited by Edvard Beyer, F.J. Billeskov Jansen, Hakon Stangerup, and P.H. Traustedt, nor the later joint Scandinavian, though in fact mostly Danish, seven-volume *Verdens Litteraturhistorie* (Literary History of the World) of 1985–1994, edited by Hans Hertel, devote as much space to non-European literatures as does the Soviet History (Møller 1989: 27–28). The Soviet *History of World Literature*, then, remains an early example of the rejection of Eurocentrism in literary history. Of course, after World War II the call for a wider and fairer representation of the world's literatures has sounded ever louder as we approach the present, also in "the West." One of the most vocal advocates of enlarging the canon of world literature to include non-Western works was the French comparatist René Etiemble (1909–2002), who as of the 1960s in numerous works and essays ridiculed the narrowness of a Western canon of world literature and in often provocative terms called for the inclusion of Asian and African works, not just from the remote past but also contemporary ones. However, it would take some time before Etiemble's injunctions were taken up. In 2022 there appeared, under the general editorship of David Damrosch and Gunilla Lindberg-Wada, a four-volume *Literature: A World History* that gives equal representation to the various parts of the globe. The four volumes are arranged chronologically, covering, respectively, from the beginnings of literature to CE 200, 200–1500, 1500–1800, and 1800–present. Each volume features six macro-regions: East Asia, Central and West Asia, South and South-East Asia (and also covering Australia, New Zealand, and the Pacific), Africa, the Americas, and Europe.

Eurocentrism would of course come fully under attack in postcolonialism. Inspired by the work of Edward Said (1979 and 1993), himself building upon the theories of, primarily, Michel Foucault, but later also Gilles Deleuze and Félix Guattari, postcolonialism, emerging in the 1980s and reaching its peak in the 1990s, endeavored to widen the geographical scope of world literature, while the advocates of multiculturalism, gaining ground around the same time as postcolonialism, strove for a fairer representation of all kinds of minorities, also from, but of course not limited to, Western literatures. Perhaps less immediately related to developments in literary studies as seen from the West, but in fact closely related to postcolonialism, were subaltern studies, initiated in India, and dependency theory and decoloniality, primarily arising in Latin America. Somewhat later, as of the beginning of the twenty-first century, there also arose a self-styled "Chinese" school of comparative literature with its own specific views on world literature. Jointly, all these led to the concept of a Global South as opposed to a Global North, identifiable with the West and perceived as dominant, in first instance economically and politically, but ultimately also culturally. Concurrently, in the West itself postmodernism sought to do away with all hierarchical distinctions altogether, and hence argued either the impossibility of a canon, including of world literature, or its individual and as it were coincidental nature.

Whereas postmodernism, postcolonialism, and multiculturalism, while of course not unrelated to political and social developments beyond the realm of literature, were primarily phenomena of a cultural nature that sought to recalibrate particularly the canon of world literature each from its own perspective, in the 1990s the primarily economics-driven advent of globalization led to a novel approach to world literature. In *La République mondiale des lettres* (1999; The World Republic of Letters 2004) Pascale Casanova, extrapolating Bourdieu's theories on social and cultural "capital" to the world market of literature, saw France, and particularly Paris, as the crucible where, at least between the seventeenth and the middle of the twentieth century, world literature was "made" in an ongoing process of critical recognition, translation, reception, and canonization. Meanwhile, Franco Moretti, Italian but working in the United States, in "Conjectures on World Literature" (2000), "Further Conjectures on World Literature" (2003) and *Graphs, Maps, Trees* (2005) picked up on earlier work of his in *Atlas of the European Novel 1800–1900* (1998), using a combination of metaphors borrowed from the sciences with the world systems approach pioneered since the 1970s by the economic historian Immanuel Wallerstein to study, both synchronically and diachronically, the origin and spread of literary forms, motifs, and styles from Europe, and in first instance Paris and London, throughout the world. These takes on world literature were quickly contested as Eurocentric by postcolonial, subaltern studies, dependency theory, decoloniality, and Chinese scholars. At the same time, the "world" in world literature started assuming, next to a purely geographical meaning, an ontological-moral one. "Worlding" became a key term in discussions about world literature.

In the United States, the shock of 9/11, and the awareness this induced of how in the newly "global" world not just of the economy but also of politics, ethics, and religion, and of terrorism even, the US could no longer take cover behind its exceptionalism, gave rise to an increased awareness also of the need to better understand the world beyond the nation's borders, and that nation's interconnectedness with the world. One form this need assumed was a sudden and sharp increase in interest in world literature as a conduit through which to get in touch with the world's cultures. A first requirement to make the world, or more of it than had hitherto been the case, accessible to the US, was a greater emphasis on translation into (American) English, and on seeing American literature and culture in relation to this new world constellation, both synchronically and diachronically. These various needs, and the solutions proposed, were explored in a number of books published shortly after 9/11, most of them building on earlier articles. Emily Apter argues the case for translation, primarily synchronically, in *The Translation Zone: A New Comparative Literature* (2006b). In *What Is World Literature?* (2003) David Damrosch puts the case for translation as a necessary instrument for, and at the same time an agent in, what he takes world literature to be, viz. "all literary works that circulate beyond their culture of origin, either in translation or in their original language" and this at any given moment, so both synchronically and diachronically (Damrosch 2003: 4). As Damrosch puts it: "a work only has an effective life as world literature whenever, and wherever, it is actively present within a literary system beyond that of its original culture" (Damrosch 2003: 4). In this definition there are clear echoes of the idea of the German writer and philosopher Walter Benjamin (1892–1940) that foreign translation constitutes a work's "afterlife" (Benjamin 2000). At the same time Damrosch here also comes close again to the original Goethean idea of *Weltliteratur* as an active principle in the world, rather than a list or series of "great works" or as a summary of all literature in all the world.

Conclusion

- Though Goethe was not the first to use the term "world literature," his use of it has had the greatest impact.
- Whereas Goethe meant world literature to refer to the increased circulation of literary works among European writers and intellectuals in order to promote a better understanding of each other's cultures, after Goethe the term variously also came to stand for the totality of all the world's literature and for a selection of "the best" of the world's works of literature, in effect a world literature canon.
- Almost from the very beginning World Literature had to enter into competition with the rising tide of national literature studies, and it was often recuperated by the latter to implicitly glorify some national literature or other.
- Though Goethe himself had a lively interest in non-European literatures, World Literature for most of its history has meant the literatures of Europe, and often only of some major European literatures.
- Since the turn of the third millennium, we notice a return to Goethe's original concept of world literature, now enlarged to the entire world.
- Over the last two decades there has been a strong non-European input into world literature studies or World Literature.

2 Goethe's *Weltliteratur* and The Humanist Ideal

Overview

For most of its history – that is, the history of the term, the concept, and the practice – "world literature" has been an exclusively European, or Euro-American, concern. Only in the last two decades or so has the discussion really broadened to voices from beyond Europe and the Americas. The instigator of the concept, if not of the term, Goethe himself, has been accused of Eurocentrism because of three passages that seem to specifically conflate world literature and European literature. Fritz Strich defends Goethe against these charges by arguing that the latter was speaking on behalf of all, and not just European, humanity. Still, the fact that Goethe in his views of humanity was strongly influenced by his adulation of ancient Greece and Rome as interpreted by the Renaissance humanists and their more recent eighteenth-century followers in the eyes of his detractors proves that his ideas on *Weltliteratur* were pre-determined by a European "classical" norm, and hence inevitably Eurocentric. None less than Edward Said, trailblazer of postcolonialism and severe critic of European exclusionism, though, rushed to Goethe's, and humanism's, defense. Said sees humanism, in its Renaissance form, as grounded in philological research, and hence in the critical reading of texts, and particularly those texts that underpin Europe's own foundations. Humanism for Said is therefore inherently self-questioning. Said sees the philological method embodied in exemplary form in the work of the German scholar Erich Auerbach. Emily Apter, though, defends the case of another German philologist – Leo Spitzer – claiming that he, like Auerbach but even more pronouncedly, opened up the philological method to reach beyond Europe and its literature(s). A third German philologist, Ernst Robert Curtius, forms a useful contrast to Auerbach and Spitzer.

Humanität and Humanism

In an address to the Congress of Natural Scientists in Berlin, in 1828, Goethe referred to "a European, in fact a universal, world literature." The second passage appeared in 1829 in *Kunst und Altertum*, Vol. 6, part 3, where Goethe

DOI: 10.4324/9781003366713-3

revised what first he had called "World Literature" as "European, in other words, World Literature." The final passage dates from 12 August of the same year, when in a conversation of Goethe's with the German historical novelist Willibald Alexis (pseudonym of Georg Wilhelm Heinrich Haring, 1798–1871) "there appeared references to a common European or World Literature." Fritz Strich, one of the most perceptive and thorough commentators on Goethe and world literature, and from whose book on Goethe I copied the three instances quoted (Strich 1949: 250–251; passages 12, 16, and 17 respectively), defends Goethe from any such charge of Eurocentrism. Writing in 1945, well before the invention of the very term "Eurocentrism," Strich in the first chapter of his *Goethe and World Literature* warns that "in present-day speech practically no distinction is made between world literature and European literature – and this is a serious error" (Strich 1949: 16). For Goethe, according to Strich:

> World literature is, to start with, European literature. It is in process of realising itself in Europe. A European literature, that is a literature of exchange and intercourse between the literatures of Europe and between the peoples of Europe, is the first stage of a world literature which from these beginnings will spread in ever-widening circles to a system which in the end will embrace the world. World literature is a living, growing organism, which can develop from the germ of European literature, and in his *West–Eastern Divan*, which was to throw a bridge from East to West, Goethe himself began the task of incorporating in it the Asiatic world.
> (Strich 1949: 16)

Notwithstanding Strich's spirited defense of Goethe, it has to be admitted that even if the latter may have ideally meant the term *Weltliteratur* to embrace the entire world, it is also true that Goethe's own ideas about what that world was like, and what the role of *Weltliteratur* in it would be, were colored by his own belonging to a particular time and place. For Strich, Goethe saw as the first, and highest, aim of world literature "to foster the / growth of a common humanity in its most perfect and universal form: to advance human civilisation" (Strich 1949: 12–13). Or, in another formulation: "It is in the idea of universal humanity that one finds the true source of world literature" (Strich 1949: 37). Inevitably, these ideals of "common humanity in its most perfect and universal form" and "universal humanity" reflected contemporary thinking on the subject – as, for instance, in the *Briefe zur Beförderung der Humanität* (1793–1797; Letters on the Promotion of Humanity) of Johann Gottfried Herder (1744–1803), or the writings of Immanuel Kant (1724–1804), who defined it as "the idea of the union of civility and virtue in one's relations with other people" (Eisler 1930; die Denkungsart der Vereinigung des Wohllebens mit der Tugend im Umgange, *Anthr.* 1. T. § 88 (IV 218)). In 1808, Friedrich Immanuel Niethammer (1766–1848), in his *Der Streit des Philanthropinismus und des Humanismus in der Theorie des Erziehungs-Unterrichts unserer Zeit*

(The Battle between Philanthropism and Humanism in Contemporary Educational Theory), coined the term "Humanismus" in German. Needless to say, these late eighteenth- and early nineteenth-century ways of conceiving "humanity" and "humanism" themselves drew from a long history, and particularly upon classical antiquity as mediated by Renaissance Humanism.

The Middle Ages, especially after the Carolingian restoration of something resembling the ancient Western Roman Empire, had largely inspired itself upon Roman antiquity and upon a relatively small selection of Latin classics. The fall of Constantinople to the Ottomans in 1453 caused a massive transfer of Greek knowledge in the form of manuscripts, but also of Byzantine scholars seeking refuge, especially to northern Italy, thus giving an enormous boost to the growing Renaissance movement there. The study of ancient Greek literature and philosophy renovated European learning and education and made the classical world into the example to be emulated. At the same time, the invention and spread of the printing press sped up the production and circulation of texts that until then had only been available in very limited numbers, and often in the form of collections of quotations and extracts rather than as complete texts. This led to the rise of philology in the comparative study of Latin, Greek, Hebrew, and, not much later, oriental languages such as Sanskrit. Partially, these studies served the ends of religion, of the established Church, and of imperial powers such as Habsburg Spain, as in the magnificent polyglot bibles produced for the Spanish crown by the Antwerp printing house of Christophe Plantin (1520–1589). However, they also served the more secular ends of smoothing the way for the beginnings of critical and empirical scientific investigation, and for redirecting attention from God to His creation, and especially to man and manmade things, or *humanitas*. Scholars and writers who followed the latter path generally referred to themselves as "humanists," with some of the most famous names being those of Desiderius Erasmus (1466–1536) and Thomas More (1478–1535).

By the middle of the eighteenth century, when Goethe was born, Enlightenment thinking had, at least in scientific and scholarly circles, further loosened the bonds between God and nature, including man. Deism enshrined God as a remote "first principle," without any direct or immediate effect upon the world in any of its outward guises. At the same time the Enlightenment also promoted concern for the individual and "common man." Together with a renewed interest in classical antiquity spurred by, for instance, the extensive writings on especially Greek art of the German art historian and archaeologist Johann Joachim Winckelmann (1717–1768), and also by the mid-century excavations at Herculaneum and Pompeii, this led to a renewed form of humanism – in German often referred to as "Neuhumanismus." This *Neuhumanismus* fed immediately into both romanticism and neo-classicism. As the Greeks were seen as the original fountainhead of European culture and civilization, creating as it were ex nihilo the arts, philosophy, and the sciences, they were also seen as proof of the creative power of "primitive" man, and hence also of the "folk." For Herder this legitimized his search for the "roots" of a "nation" in a people's language as embodied in its folk poetry. Goethe was also interested in folk poetry, and he discussed various instances of it in his writings. He saw such poetry, and folk literature in general, as expressive of a common core of humanity dressed up in a specific language or a specific people's particularities. However, this is not what he called "world literature." Rather, he termed it "world poetry." It only became world literature if it partook in the intellectual exchange among the nations and peoples.

Of course, similar interests flourished around Europe – for instance, with the so-called Scottish Antiquaries and James McPherson's Ossian poems. It is Herder, though, and after him the Grimm and Schlegel brothers, who systematized all this into the theoretical foundations of romanticism, and hence laid the foundations of the study and teaching of national literatures. At the same time, an emphasis upon a Greek and Latin curriculum in the most highly valued forms of education, particularly the *Gymnasium* in Germany and in most public schools in England, and a general adulation of the classical ideal of man underpinned the rise of neo-classicism which, instead of the spontaneity, originality, and novelty propagated by romanticism, favored measure, balance, and imitation, particularly of the classics. It is the combination of the qualities valorized by neo-classicism that constituted *Humanität*, if we are to follow Kant when he writes that,

> one part of philology is constituted by the humanities, by which we understand knowledge of the classics, which promotes the union of knowledge and taste, files away a person's raw edges, and furthers that communicative ability and urbanity of which *humanität* consists.
>
> (Einen Teil der Philologie machen die Humaniera aus, worunter man die Kenntnis der Alten versteht, welche die Vereinigung der Wissenschaft mit Geschmack befördert, die Rauhigkeit abschleift und die Kommunikabilität und Urbanität, worin Humanität besteht, befördert.)
>
> (Eisler 1930; *Log. Einl*. VI (IV 50))

The earlier quote from Kant, where he fills out his definition of humanism, clearly also refers to a classical ideal. Most romantic writers, of course, enjoyed a "classical" education.

Goethe in Italy

With his *Werther* (1774) in particular, along with his other *Sturm und Drang* (Storm and Stress) works published during the 1770s such as *Prometheus* (1773) and *Götz von Berlichingen* (1773), Goethe helped pave the way for romanticism throughout Europe. In some way or other these works are also anti-authoritarian, whether it is against prevailing morals and religion, as when Werther commits suicide for love, or when Prometheus defies the Gods, or Götz the emperor. After his move to Weimar at the invitation of the Duke of Saxe-Weimar, though, Goethe increasingly turned neo-classicist in art, although for much of his life he stayed non-conformist in morals and religion (see Boyle, passim). His reading of Winckelmann, and the latter's example, incited Goethe to undertake an extended stay in Italy in 1786–1788. During the two years he spent traveling the length of the peninsula and Sicily he closely acquainted himself with classical architecture, both Roman and Greek. Though Goethe published his *Italienische Reise* (Italian Journey) only in 1816–1817, his Italian experience clearly served as catalyst for his "conversion" from *Sturm und Drang* proponent to neo-classicist, and to figurehead of so-called Weimar classicism. This is especially clear in how he writes about the legacy of classical architecture in the South of Europe, represented by Italy, when compared to the medieval Gothic products of Northern Europe, and particularly Germany, as in the following passage, dated 27 October 1786:

> I walked up to Spoleto and stood on the aqueduct, which also serves as a bridge from one hill to the other. The ten brickwork arches which span the valley have been quietly standing there through all the centuries, and the water still gushes in all quarters of Spoleto. This is the third work of antiquity which I have seen, and it embodies the same noble spirit. A sense of the civic good, which is the basis of their architecture, was second nature to the ancients. Hence the amphitheatre, the temple, the aqueduct. For the first time I understand why I always detested arbitrary constructions, the Winterkasten on the Weissenstein, for example, which is a pointless nothing, a monstrous piece of confectionery – and I have felt he same about a thousand other buildings. Such things are still-born, for anything that does not have a true *raison d'être* is lifeless and cannot be great or ever become so.
> (Goethe 1970: 124–125)

Part of this legacy is its rediscovery, and imitation, in the Renaissance by artists/humanists such as Andrea Palladio (1508–1580), an Italian Renaissance architect active in and around Venice during the sixteenth century. Heavily influenced by Greek and Roman architecture, his buildings, and the precepts upon which he based them as laid down in his *I Quattro Libri dell'Architettura* (1570; The Four Books of Architecture), richly illustrated with engravings, remained the models for both public and private buildings all across Europe for the next few centuries. In Padua, Goethe buys a catalogue of the works of Palladio, and in Venice he goes in search of the buildings of the master. On 2 October 1786 he visits a monastery designed by Palladio. Although only part of the original design has been actually realized, Goethe still finds that:

> Jahrelang sollte man in Betrachtung so eines Werks zubringen. Mich dünkt, ich habe nichts Höheres, nichts Vollkommneres gesehen, und glaube, daß ich mich nicht irre. Denke man sich aber auch den trefflichen Künstler, mit dem innern Sinn fürs Große und Gefällige geboren, der erst

mit unglaublicher Mühe sich an den Alten heranbildet, um sie alsdann durch sich wiederherzustellen.

(Goethe 2007: 71–72)

Auden and Mayer translate this passage as: "I am convinced I am right when I say that I never saw anything more sublime, more perfect, in my life. One ought to spend years contemplating such a work" (Goethe 1970: 80). This much foreshortened version fails to catch the real import the view of this building has for Goethe, and particularly its autobiographical implications. A fuller translation would read:

> One ought to spend years contemplating such a work. I think I have never seen anything more elevated, more perfect, and I believe I am not mistaken in this. But also picture to yourself the accomplished artist, born with an innate sense of the great and the pleasing, who with an incredible effort first schools himself after the classics, and then proceeds to recreate them through his own art.
>
> (my translation)

For Goethe, Palladio's greatness results, first, from his study of and, second, his imitation/emulation of the classics – especially the Greeks. Not only does this process correspond to the classical rhetoric recipe of *translatio, imitatio, aemulatio* (translation, imitation, emulation), it also closely parallels Goethe's own ambitions with his Italian journey. In a passage dated the following day, 3 October 1786, Goethe generalizes upon his earlier remark:

> Palladio was strongly imbued with the spirit of the Ancients, and felt acutely the petty narrow-mindedness of his times, like a great man who does not wish to conform to the world but to transform it in accordance with his own high ideals.
>
> (Goethe 1970: 81)

The same thing applies for Goethe and his likeminded contemporaries, for Michelangelo, Raphaël, and most Renaissance artists. Of course, Goethe saw all this in relation to his own position. The link he makes between Palladio's imitation of the Greeks and the pettiness of his times obviously anticipates Goethe's own later yearning for *Weltliteratur* as a remedy for the fragmentation of his own times. The link with humanism in its classical and Renaissance variations and that of Goethe and his times is made in remarks such as that dated 3 December 1786, when during his extended first stay in Rome, he exclaims "the entire history of the world is linked up with this city, and I reckon my second life, a very rebirth, from the day when I entered Rome" (Goethe 1970: 148), where he actually uses the German equivalent, "*Wiedergeburt,*" for "Renaissance" for his own feelings when experiencing classical art first hand. Earlier, in an entry dated Foligno, 26 October 1786, Goethe had expressed the same idea in more general terms when, having gone to look at a small antique temple described by Palladio, he concludes with: "I cannot describe the sensations which this work aroused in me, but I know they are going to bear fruit for ever" (Goethe 1970: 121). From passages such as these it is evident that Goethe looks upon his Italian journey, and the exposure to the classics it brings, as an essential element in his own *Bildung*. From passages such as that quoted earlier, on the occasion of his visit to Spoleto, it is equally clear that when he lauds these same classics for having always aimed with their buildings at *bürgerlichen Zwecken* – that is to say, humanly practical and not god-centered purposes – he is highlighting their "humanity."

The rediscovery of the Roman and Greek antiquities in the eighteenth century, through the excavations at Pompeï, Herculaneaum, and Paestum, and through the writings of Winckelmann, especially the latter's *Gedanken über die Nachahmung der griechischen Werke in der Malerei und Bildhauerkunst* (1755; Reflections on the Imitation of the Greeks in Painting and Sculpture) and *Geschichte der Kunst des Altertums* (1764; History of Ancient Art), gave rise to Hellenism, an adulation and glorification of especially Greek antiquity in its more expansive phase and its prolonged afterglow under Rome. As Martin Bernal, in a critical-negative sense in *Black Athena* (1987), and others in a more positive sense have shown, eighteenth-century Hellenism also led to the Germanic and English-speaking peoples claiming for themselves the right of succession to the Greeks as the creators of a Europe *sui generis*. Small wonder then that the American nineteenth-century author and friend of Emerson's Margaret Fuller, in her "Translator's Preface" to *Conversations with Goethe in the Last Years of his Life, Translated from the German of Eckermann*, labels Goethe "of German writers the most English and most Greek" (Fuller 1839: xvii). It is certainly also not a coincidence that Goethe's first clearly neo-classicist work is his verse drama *Iphigenie auf Tauris* (1786; Iphigenia in Tauris), a re-working of earlier prose versions (1779 and 1781), and emphasizing human understanding, or *Humanität*, over the inhuman demands of the Gods.

From the very beginning, then, for Goethe *Weltliteratur* and humanism were closely linked. *Weltliteratur* was to fulfill the role that his own trip to Italy, and his exposure there to the revitalizing influence of classical antiquity, had played for him: to elevate the humanist individual, and the elite company of like-minded humanists and men of letters which he had in mind when speaking of *Weltliteratur*, to a higher awareness of what humanity was about, a form of both personal and collective *Bildung* (education), so to speak. In essence, then, his thinking about *Weltliteratur* was rooted in his humanist universalism which itself drew upon the Renaissance and Enlightenment thinking of the universal as an extension of the classical. That such a reasoning is at the heart of an important, and perhaps the dominant, strain in European thinking ever since the Renaissance, going back precisely to the latter's renewed engagement and interpretation of Greek thought, is argued by Rodolphe Gasché in *Europe, or the Infinite Task: A Study of a*

Philosophical Concept (2009). Gasché situates the thought of, respectively, the Austrian-German Edmund Husserl, the German Martin Heidegger, the Czech Jan Patočka, and the French Jacques Derrida, and without specifically referencing Goethe, in a European tradition that sees it as Europe's destiny to divest itself of its Europeanism precisely by spreading the idea of universalism to the rest of the world, that is to say the universalism of humanism, with the latter implying an awareness of the value of the individual – which complies with the Renaissance and Enlightenment interpretation of the classical idea of the human, and which needed this genealogy to firmly legitimate itself. Just as Husserl, Heidegger, Patočka, and Derrida rephrase this idea for the twentieth century, beginning to end, so Goethe does the same with regard to his own times and, making use of the historical "window of opportunity" offered to him by the period between the end of the Napoleonic wars and the onset of the ardent nationalisms of the second third of the nineteenth century referred to earlier, reformulates this idea in terms of world literature. That is also why Goethe, in contrast to a number of later theoreticians of world literature, particularly in the nineteenth century but partially well into the twentieth century, is not interested in drawing up a canon of world masterpieces, but rather in what world literature, as he conceives it to be, can contribute to the *Bildung* of humanity by fostering the circulation of what he sees as the right kind of ideas and forms. As his discussions of Serbian folk poetry and Chinese fiction demonstrate, what constitutes the right kind of ideas and forms for Goethe is determined by their proximity to what he sees as universal "humanity," and that in turn is determined by the yardstick of the classical ideal that he upholds for everything.

World Literature and Philology

In practice, the classical and universalist genealogy of the "human" underlying Goethe's conception of world literature for the longest time largely limited the latter's reach to European literature, or, by extension, Western man and Western literature. Both Moulton and Guérard, writing for an American public in 1911 and 1940 respectively, make no bones about this. In the first chapter I already mentioned that Moulton distinguished between what he called "universal" and "world" literature, with the former covering all literature written anywhere in the world, and the latter that part of the former that was significant from a certain perspective, which for him was that of the English-speaking peoples. Therefore, he starts from what he calls the literary pedigree of those English-speaking peoples and, predictably so at the time he is writing, finds it in the fusion of what the English writer, educator, and cultural critic Matthew Arnold in *Culture and Anarchy* (1869) had termed the Hebraic and the Hellenic elements brought about by the spread of Greek rule under Alexander the Great. From there on Moulton traces the developments leading to English literature through the various phases of European cultural history: classical antiquity, Christianity, the Middle Ages, and finally the age of nation states and national literatures. However, he sees the latter as integrally taking part in what he calls European civilization. World literature, for Moulton, then, is what he calls in the penultimate chapter of his book "The Autobiography of Civilization" – that is, European civilization.

Guérard, in his Foreword, invokes humanism as the ideal horizon of world literature, and clarifies that by humanism he means "simply our belief in the essential unity of the human race" (Guérard 1940: xii). Nevertheless, in his first chapter he resorts to the same distinction between universal and world literature that we also saw Moulton as making, and for him too "world literature is limited to those works which are enjoyed in common, ideally by all mankind, practically by our own group of culture, the European or Western" (Guérard 1940: 15). Moulton and Guérard were both Europeans, but they worked within the US academic system, and their books served a primarily educational purpose within that system. I will return to this in Chapter 4.

For the more recent discussions on world literature, humanism, and Eurocentrism as they have played especially in the United States as of the turn of the millennium, and particularly so after the events of 11 September 2001, Moulton and Guérard do not play a major role. That role is reserved for a number of European, and more precisely German, philologists of the first half of the twentieth century. Undoubtedly, the fact that two of these, Leo Spitzer (1887–1960) and Erich Auerbach (1892–1957), spent the final years of their lives and careers in the United States, where they exerted a powerful influence on the practice of Comparative Literature, is not without importance here. Neither is the fact that the writings of Auerbach particularly were taken up both early and late in his career by Edward Said (1935–2003), himself Professor of English and Comparative Literature at Columbia University in New York for most of his career, and a (many would say *the*) driving force in the emergence of postcolonial studies in the USA and the world with his groundbreaking *Orientalism* (1979). Said himself had American and Palestinian roots and was raised in the Middle East, mostly Egypt. All his life he remained a forceful spokesman for the rights of the Palestinians, and his interest in postcolonialism was undoubtedly fueled by his own family history of exile. This was a history which, originating from different yet related circumstances, was also shared by Erich Auerbach, a German Jew who, because of the Nazis coming to power in Germany in 1933, had to seek refuge in Turkey in 1935, the year of Said's birth. In Istanbul, Auerbach became Professor of Romance Philology as successor to Leo Spitzer, another Jewish scholar, born in Austria but working in Germany, who had moved to Istanbul for the same reason already in 1933. In 1969 Said, together with his wife, Maire, translated Auerbach's 1952 essay "Philologie der Weltliteratur" as "Philology and World Literature." It is in this essay that Auerbach, in words that recall Goethe's most famous statement on world literature, proclaims that "our philological home is the earth: it can no longer be the nation" (Auerbach 1969: 17).

In 2003, the year of his death, Said provided an "Introduction" to a new edition of Auerbach's *Mimemis: Dargestellte Wirklichkeit in der abendländischen Literatur*, a work written during the latter's stay in Istanbul while World War II was raging, published in German in 1947, and in an English translation (by Willard Trask) as *Mimesis: The Representation of Reality in Western Literature* in the USA in 1953. That introduction was republished in 2004 as part of what in effect would be Said's last, and posthumous, book: *Humanism and Democratic Criticism*. *Humanism and Democratic Criticism* contains the revised versions of three lectures Said gave in January 2000 at Columbia University in an annual series of lectures on aspects of American culture. In his "Preface" to the book Said stipulates that in 2003 he expanded and revised his original lectures, adding a fourth lecture on Auerbach's "humanist masterpiece" *Mimesis* (Said 2003: xv) and that later on he added yet another lecture on "The Public Role of Writers and Intellectuals." All changes, he insists, were made because of the "terrible events of 9/11" (Said 2003: xvii). The destruction of the twin towers in New York led to a "changed political atmosphere" in the USA and beyond, he argues, which sets "America" against the world, and the "West" versus "Islam." Yet, and with what I can only see as a submerged reference to Goethe's ideas on world literature, he contends that "far more than they fight, cultures coexist and interact fruitfully with each other" (Said 2003: xvi). And then he continues: "It is to this idea of humanistic culture as coexistence and sharing that these pages are meant to contribute" (Said 2003: xvi). Said finds the example for such a humanistic culture in Auerbach and to a lesser extent in Spitzer. The example of the latter will be taken up fervently by Emily Apter in her *The Translation Zone: A New Comparative Literature* (2006b).

Auerbach and Spitzer were both members of what Hans Ulrich Gumbrecht calls "the great Romance scholars" in *Vom Leben und Sterben der grossen Romanisten* (2002; Life and Death of the Great Romance Scholars), a book in which he takes a close look at the careers of five major German scholars who have marked the discipline of Romance philology in the first half of the twentieth century: Karl Vossler, Ernst Robert Curtius, Leo Spitzer, Erich Auerbach, and Karl Krauss. Next to Auerbach and Spitzer, Curtius (1886–1957) is also of interest for recent discussions on humanism and world literature. It should not surprise us that the relevant statements on these issues by Curtius, Spitzer, and Auerbach date from during or after World War II. These scholars had experienced first-hand the decline of "humanism" under Nazism, and they felt the need to re-affirm this ideal.

Even if World War II presented the stronger challenge to the humanist ideals of a European civilization, World War I had already shattered the (until then) rather complacent and essentially bourgeois idea of a great common European civilization regardless of national peculiarities. After all, the Europe of before 1914 still comprised a number of major multilingual and multiethnic empires, such as the Austro-Hungarian, the Russian, and the Ottoman. Germany, still divided into many smaller – and some larger – states in Goethe's time, had become a powerful empire under Prussia. Italy had been united by Garibaldi under the House of Savoy. Certainly, national pride ran high everywhere, but violent eruptions of nationalism had largely been "neutralized" ever since the numerous revolts of 1848, and the even earlier revolutions leading to the independence of Greece and Belgium. However, the Balkans seethed with ethnic resentment, and the outbreak of World War I (in 1914) following the assassination of the Austro-Hungarian crown prince in 1914 blew the lid off the system of military and political balances and alliances that, apart from the Franco–German war of 1870, had kept Europe largely peaceful since Napoleonic times.

Ernst Robert Curtius

Ernst Robert Curtius, in the preface to the English (American) translation of his *European Literature and the Latin Middle Ages*, starts out by saying that his own interest in literature, especially in Romance literatures, and even more specifically in first instance in French, and contemporary French at that, literature was spurred by World War I, and by his desire to make Germany's arch-enemy, France, more understandable to a German public.

In fact, Gumbrecht, in his discussion of Curtius, speculates that the latter switched from pursuing a career in law (he obtained a doctorate at law in 1913) to one in philology because of the horrors he encountered as a soldier in World War I. From the study of philology proper, Curtius soon also turned to the study of modern English literature, particularly T.S. Eliot and James Joyce.

Increasingly though, as he argues in the preface to *European Literature and the Latin Middle Ages*, he became interested in Virgil and Dante, and in "what the roads were that led from the one to the other?" The answer, he says, "could not but be found in the Latin continuity of the Middle Ages ... and that in turn was a portion of the European tradition, which has Homer at its beginning and at its end, as we see today, Goethe" (Curtius 1953: vii). It is this tradition that Curtius saw as uprooted by World War I and its aftermath, "especially in Germany," as he puts it, and that, in 1932, led him to write a polemical pamphlet called *Deutscher Geist in Gefahr* (The German Spirit Endangered), in which he pleaded for a "new Humanism." With the rise to power of the Nazis in 1933 Curtius abandoned the study of contemporary literature and turned to the study of the Latin Middle Ages, resulting in the publication, in German, in 1948, of the book for which he is now chiefly remembered. This book, he stresses, "is not the product of purely scholarly interests ... it grew out of a concern for the preservation of Western culture" (Curtius 1953: viii) and "it grew out of vital urges and under the pressure of a concrete historical situation" (Curtius 1953: x). "In order to convince," he says, "I had to use the scientific technique which is the foundation of all historical investigation: philology"; yet he also hopes that it is clear that "philology is not an end in itself ... what we are dealing with is literature – that is, the great intellectual and spiritual tradition of Western culture as given form in language" (Curtius 1953: x).

Several items deserve commenting on here. Said mentions Curtius only in passing in *Humanism and Democratic Criticism*, in the chapter on Auerbach. It is clear though that he writes from premises strikingly similar to those of Curtius: the pressure of a concrete historical situation, the concern with humanism to counter the rising tide of barbarism, and the turn to philology. Whereas Curtius wants his humanism to bolster a tradition limited to the West, and specifically to Europe, and perhaps even Western Europe, Said aims for his humanism to open out to the world. The continuity Curtius seeks is that of a particular idea of Western culture. The continuity Said strives for is that of philology as a scientific-investigative method. In doing so, Said returns to the original use and impact of philology as applied by the earliest, Renaissance, humanists – that is, as a critical method with which to probe all received ideas and all false continuities. From this perspective, and without Said ever mentioning as much, we might see the Renaissance not as continuous with the Latin Middle Ages but rather as breaking with them precisely because it questions all medieval doxa. The details of why Said found this use of philology with Auerbach rather than with Curtius we will come to in a minute – suffice to note for now that Gumbrecht draws a comparable parallel when it comes to Curtius' and Auerbach's attitudes toward the Western tradition as expressed in their respective masterpieces, *European Literature and the Latin Middle Ages* and *Mimesis*. When referring to Curtius' rationale, as given in the preface and as discussed above, for writing his *European Literature and the Latin Middle Ages*, Gumbrecht asks:

> As if in those days it would not have been possible to do a little better. I mean an analysis or approach that would have been more apt to recognize in National Socialism also the proof for the falling apart of the European cultural tradition, rather than preaching its untrammeled conservation. The latter was precisely the reaction of the emigrant Erich Auerbach, who until his very death never again succeeded in regaining faith in political expectations founded on cultural traditions.
> (Ob damals nicht auch Besseres am Horizont des Möglichen stand. Ich meine ein Denken, welches geeignet gewesen wäre, im Nationalsozialismus auch die Evidenz für das Scheitern der europäischen Kulturtradition zu erleben, statt deren unversehrte Bewahrung zu predigen. Das genau war die Reaktion des Emigranten Erich Auerbach, dem es bis zu seinem Tod nicht mehr gelang, die auf kulturelle Tradition gesetzten politische Hoffnungen zu erneuern …)
> (Gumbrecht 2002: 67–68)

Earlier I suggested that Said, in the very first paragraphs of his Preface to *Humanism and Democratic Criticism*, makes an oblique appeal to Goethe's ideas on world literature to plead the coexistence and fruitful interaction of cultures, and particularly to gainsay the supposed opposition between the West and, specifically, Islam, and beyond this "the rest." Implicitly, along with other recent critics who do so explicitly, he sees Goethe as being at the beginning of an opening up of European culture and literature toward the world. Curtius, as we saw earlier, sees Goethe as the endpoint of a homogeneous European tradition that Curtius himself seeks to restore. In "Fundamental Features of Goethe's World," published in 1949 and collected in *Essays on European Literature* (1973, 1950 in German as *Kritische Essays zur europäischen Literatur*), Curtius pictures Goethe as an advocate of "aristocratic individualism" who sought "connection only with the 'most excellent'" (Curtius 1973: 76), an elitist not in the political sense of the term, but rather in that of a select band of like-minded spirits past and present. Goethe, for Curtius, is "the final self-concentration of the western mind in a great individual" (Curtius 1973: 90). Therefore, he is:

> something more and something other than a German poet ... he is solidary with the spiritual heritage of Europe. He stands in the line of Homer, Sophocles, Plato, Aristotle, Virgil, Dante, and Shakespeare. The consciousness of his place in this series is very much alive in him. His piety towards the "fathers," his alliance with the "dignified men" of old and with the chorus of spirits of the past, his conviction that there is a realm of the "Masters," with whom he feels he belongs – this most characteristic and remarkable trait of his form of mind acquires its deepest sense only now. This consciousness of solidarity through the millennia Shakespeare could not have had, Dante only within the Latin tradition. To Goethe it was given as a legitimation and corroboration of his mission. It is a sign, so to speak, from "the alphabet of the universal spirit."
>
> (Curtius 1973: 90–91)

Curtius concludes his essay by reminding us that Goethe on occasion described himself as an "epigone poet," and that in a letter to Georg Friedrich Creuzer (1771–1858) in 1817 he wrote that epigone poets such as him "must revere the legacy of our ancestors" and "bow before these men whom the Holy Spirit has inspired and dare not ask, whence or whither." That attitude, Curtius says, "can today be the one that a 'small number' adopts towards Goethe" (Curtius 1973: 91). Obviously, he counts himself among this "small number." But I think his epigonism went further than mere reverence; he wanted to restore the tradition of the Master and re-establish the continuity of European culture.

Erich Auerbach

It is against the Goethe drawn by Curtius that Auerbach turns in chapter 17 of *Mimesis*, "Miller the Musician." *Mimesis* was written under the pressure of the same war as Curtius' *European Literature and the Latin Middle Ages*, not in Bonn, but in Istanbul. For Auerbach too it is philology, or what he calls the "method of textual interpretation," (Auerbach 1953: 556) that underpins his findings. Other than Curtius, though, Auerbach does not chronicle the continuity of an unchangeable Western humanist tradition but rather the relentless "humanization" of that tradition from the ancients, both Greek and Latin, as well as Judaic, through a progressive intermingling of styles high and low, to French realism in the nineteenth century, when there is no longer a distinction of styles and the only thing left to form the subject of literature is "man." This is humanism in its most bare and simple form – not heroes, not gods, but also not buffoons, the ones to be gloried or glorified, the others to be mocked and humbled, take center stage, but "man" pure and simple, and even "common" man at that. Goethe, Auerbach argues, could have played a major role in this development, and through him Germany. However, Goethe failed to fulfil the promise of his early work in this regard. And it wasn't just Goethe who failed in this respect. Friedrich Schiller, with an analysis of a passage from whose *Kabale und Liebe* (1782–1783; Luise Millerin) the chapter in question starts, failed to make good on the promise of nascent realism which this early work shows. The reason, Auerbach argues, is to be found in the political division of Germany at the end of the eighteenth century. The numerous petty potentates autocratically ruling often tiny territories did everything in their power to stem the rising tide of social and political revolution and maintain what was in effect a petty-bourgeois status quo. The youthful Goethe, as we have argued earlier, in his *Sturm und Drang* period, like Schiller in *Kabale und Liebe*, seemed poised to storm these bastions of privilege and immutability. However, after his conversion to neo-classicism and his move to Weimar it is precisely those qualities that Curtius most admires in Goethe – his aristocratic individualism, his elitism, his loyalty to tradition – that make him shy away from social and political changes tending toward the inclusion of larger parts of the population, rising social classes, and in short what we would call democracy. The inclusion and depiction of the common man, then, which the French and the English novel increasingly successfully achieved during the nineteenth century, did not happen until much later in German literature. With Goethe's immense influence on nineteenth-century German literature, next to Germany's political situation, acting as a brake, that literature never fully acceded to realism until, Auerbach argues, Thomas Mann's *Buddenbrooks* in 1901.

Edward Said

It is clear that Said recognizes in what he calls Auerbach's "humanist masterpiece" (Said 2003: xv) much of what he advocated himself over the course of his own career as a critic. Most of the relevant points are highlighted in the chapters, or lectures, preceding that on *Mimesis* in *Humanism and Democratic Criticism*. Most of them come down to how humanism and philology work hand in hand to constitute not only a continuous regime of investigation and critique, but also of self-critique. Said starts from the premise that

> the core of humanism is the secular notion that the historical world is made by men and women, and not by God, and that it can be understood rationally according to the principle formulated by Giambattista Vico in *New Science*, that we can really know only what we make or, to put it differently, we can know things according to the way they were made.
>
> (Said 2003: 11)

This implies what the American scholar Djelal Kadir, taking his cue from Said's plea for a "worldly" criticism in *The World, The Text, and the Critic* (1984 [1983]), has called the "worlding" (Kadir 2004) of both the work and the critic in the sense of a vivid awareness of their historicity, and particularly of the critic's self-awareness of their own relationship to their object of study and their discipline. This sensitivity Said recognizes in how Auerbach, starting from a close textual analysis, and along philological lines, relates each of the works he discusses to its historical setting not primarily by its content but by its use of language and structure. He also recognizes it in how Auerbach, at the end of *Mimesis*, stresses that each form of understanding is also a form of self-understanding at a particular time and in a particular place. This is clear in Auerbach's discussion of Goethe mentioned earlier when Goethe's reluctance to further the introduction of realism in German literature, and his conservatism in politics, or at least his refusal to actively uphold the causes of democracy and political unification in Germany in the post-Napoleonic era, are seen as possible causes for, or in any case as not having contributed to preventing, the unhappy fate that ultimately befell Germany, and Europe, at the time of Auerbach's writing of *Mimesis*.

In the conclusion to *Mimesis* Auerbach defends why he does not offer any totalizing view of the Western tradition (and one immediately thinks of Curtius's *European Literature and the Latin Middle Ages*) but rather works from almost random passages, and from works that Auerbach himself claimed were chosen equally at random, based on his own ready knowledge and from what he had to hand in Istanbul during the war. Instead of "one order and interpretation," Auerbach says, he offers "many," so that what emerges is a "synthesized cosmic view or at least a challenge to the reader's will to interpretive synthesis" (Auerbach 1953: 549; also quoted in Said 2003: 117). This resembles nothing so much as that contrapuntal approach that Said himself had unfolded in *Culture and Imperialism* (1993), and to which he returns in *Humanism and Democratic Criticism* when he notes that the term "canon" not only refers to a "law" but also to a musical piece in which various voices pursue and join each other (Said 2003: 25). Such contrapuntal reading then allows precisely for that permanent critique and self-critique that for Said are at the heart of humanism:

> that it is possible to be critical of humanism in the name of humanism and that, schooled in its abuses by the experience of Eurocentrism and empire, one could fashion a different kind of humanism that was

cosmopolitan and text-and-language-bound in ways that absorbed the great lessons of the past from, say, Erich Auerbach and Leo Spitzer and more recently Richard Poirier, and still remain attuned to the emergent voices and currents of the present, many of them exilic, extraterritorial, and unhoused, as well as uniquely American.

(Said 2003: 10–11)

To apply these lessons, for Said, is also to world oneself as a humanist critic:

It means situating critique at the very heart of humanism, critique as a form of democratic freedom and as a continuous practice of questioning and of accumulating knowledge that is open to, rather than in denial of, the constituent historical realities of the post-Cold War world, its early colonial formation, and the frighteningly global reach of the last remaining superpower of today.

(Said 2003: 47)

Especially in America, he argues, where so many people from so many traditions always have come and continue to mingle, such a "worldly" disposition is not only necessary, it is already inherent to the very make-up of the country:

American humanism, by virtue of what is available to it in the normal course of its own context and historical reality, is already in a state of civic coexistence, and, to the prevailing worldview disseminated by U.S. officialdom – especially in its dealings with the world outside America – humanism provides little short of stubborn, and secular, intellectual resistance.

(Said 2003: 49)

Resistance, of course, is the term Said used earlier in *Culture and Imperialism* to refer to anti- and what we would now call postcolonial literature. That literature, in turn, can be seen as accomplishing what Auerbach says – in a passage at the very end of *Mimesis* that to me seems clearly not only to echo Goethe's ideas on world literature but also to extend them from Europe to the entire world – in relation to Virginia Woolf's *To the Lighthouse*. In the final chapter of his book Auerbach discusses how Woolf's novel, like so many other modernist works, is anchored in what he calls "the random moment." "The more [this] is exploited," Auerbach argues, "the more the elementary things which our lives have in common come to light," or, in other words, the greater degree of reality is achieved.

In this unprejudiced and exploratory type of representation we cannot but see to what an extent – below the surface conflicts – the differences between men's ways of life and forms of thought have already lessened. ... There are no longer even exotic peoples. A century ago (in

Mérimée for example), Corsicans and Spaniards were still exotic; today the term would be quite unsuitable for Pearl Buck's Chinese peasants. Beneath the conflicts, and also through them, an economic and cultural levelling process is taking place. It is still a long way to a common life of mankind on earth, but the goal begins to be visible.

(Auerbach 1953: 552)

In our age of globalization, but also of a return to ethics in literary studies, the passage of Auerbach's just cited begins to sound very much like an anticipated ethics of world literature, one moreover to which Said would unreservedly have been able to subscribe. Small wonder then that precisely in his chapter on Auerbach, Said revises the former's negative judgment on Goethe, calling the latter a progenitor of the former and particularly of the "extraordinary attention to the minute, local detail of other cultures and languages" that the tradition of hermeneutical philology as embodied by Auerbach practices (Said 2003: 95). In a passage that may well reverberate with his prefatory remarks about the "much exacerbated conflict between what have been called 'the West' and 'Islam'," Said reminds us that Goethe "in the decade after 1810 became fascinated with Islam generally and Persian poetry in particular," and that it was during this period that he composed his *West-östlicher Diwan*. "During the 1820s," Said continues,

those earlier thoughts carried him toward a conviction that national literatures had been superseded by what he called *Weltliteratur*, or world literature, a universalist conception of all the literatures of the world seen together as forming a majestic symphonic whole.

(Said 2003: 95)

This sentence reminds us that Said was not only an insightful literary critic and theoretician, but also an accomplished musician. Robert Young comments in this regard that, "Said's writings on music were the one arena where he necessarily moved away from his chosen model of German philology, particularly the tradition of Auerbach" (Young 2010: 365). "The irony of Said's deep sense of affiliation to this tradition," Young adds,

was that its other branch, Oriental philology, was the very one that he attacked in *Orientalism* ... this constitutes the central contrapuntal paradox of Said himself, that he at once affirmed and placed himself in a tradition whose work also included that which he most vigorously denied.

(Young 2010: 365)

Looking back at the end of his life on his most influential book, *Orientalism*, Said called what he had tried to do in that book "humanistic critique" (Said 2003). He explicitated that by what he called "humanism" he meant first of all attempting to dissolve Blake's mind-forg'd manacles so as to be able to use one's mind historically and rationally for the purposes of reflective understanding ... moreover humanism is sustained by a sense of community with other interpreters and other societies and periods: strictly speaking therefore, there is no such thing as an isolated humanist.

(Said 2003)

Finally, let us also recall that Said, together with Daniel Barenboim, was the founder, in 1999, of the West–Eastern Divan Orchestra, bringing together young musicians from around the Near- or Middle-East, and most particularly including both Israelis and Palestinians.

Leo Spitzer

Like Said's *Humanism and Democratic Criticism*, Emily Apter's *The Translation Zone: A New Comparative Literature* "was shaped by the traumatic experience of September 11, 2001" (Apter 2006b: vii). Apter is more concerned with the issues of translation and comparative literature, and therefore I will return to her book in more detail in following chapters. Here, though, I will briefly discuss the first part of her book, entitled "Translating Humanism," which deals with how humanism has been adapted, or "translated," in the work of Leo Spitzer, the third "grosser Romanist" (great Romance scholar) in Gumbrecht's term, specifically in relation to Auerbach, and Said's reading of Auerbach. Discussing "Saidian Humanism" in the chapter of the same title, Apter voices her perplexity when reading Said's 2003 introduction to Auerbach's *Mimesis* at "what seemed to be a noticeable *lack* of attention to Auerbach's Eurocentrism" (Apter 2006b: 69). Later on she will say that on a second reading she realized that,

> Said was taking up the challenge of using Auerbachian humanism to fashion new humanisms, not merely because of a sober conviction that great books, on the grounds of their intrinsic merit, should continue to have traction in a global, increasingly mediatized culture industry, but more because of his belief that humanism provides futural parameters for defining secular criticism in a world increasingly governed by a sense of identitarian ethnic destiny and competing sacred tongues.
>
> (Apter 2006b: 72)

With reference to world literature and humanism, however, she contends that Said would have done better to use Spitzer as his *Ansatzpunkt* (Auerbach's own term for what provides the philological critic with an "entry" into the text) than Auerbach. Indeed, she claims that what she calls Said's "Welthumanism" in *Humanism and Democratic Criticism* "is indebted not so much to Auerbach as to Spitzer," and she cites Said commenting on Spitzer's statement in his famous 1948 essay "Linguistics and Literary History" that "the Humanist believes in the power of the human mind of investigating the human mind" with "Spitzer does not say the European mind, or only the Western canon ... He talks about the human mind *tout court*" (Apter 2006b: 70; Said 2003: 26). Beyond this statement, though, Apter also sees other grounds for foregrounding Spitzer rather than Auerbach as prefiguring Said's ideas on a humanism that transcends the European.

Apter rehearses how Said conducts a running debate with Auerbach from the very beginning of his career, with the translation (together with his wife Maire) of Auerbach's "Philology and World Literature" in 1969, over his use of him in *Orientalism* and *The World, The Text, and the Critic*, down to *Humanism and Democratic Criticism*. As I have done earlier, she also stresses the parallels between Said and Auerbach, and particularly how Said himself repeatedly returns to Auerbach's condition of exile in Istanbul from 1935 to 1947. In contrast, Spitzer spent only three years in Istanbul, from when he fled Cologne, where he was succeeded by Curtius, in 1933, to his further move to the United Sates in 1936. Yet, based on interviews with former students of Spitzer's and Auerbach's at Istanbul, Apter posits that Spitzer, when he arrived in Istanbul, quickly added Turkish to the dozen languages or so he already knew, while Auerbach apparently never learned the language. It was also in Spitzer's seminars that languages other than European ones featured. In fact, she argues, "the seminar also acted as a laboratory for working through what a philological curriculum in literary studies should look like when applied to non-European languages and literatures" (Apter 2006b: 55). For this reason, Apter credits Spitzer with "inventing" Comparative Literature in its modern guise during his stay in Istanbul. "In retrospect," she concludes, "Spitzer's invention of comparative literature in Istanbul transformed philology into something recognizable today as the psychic life of transnational humanism" (Apter 2006b: 64).

Finally, what of the question about humanism's alleged or necessary Eurocentrism? As we have seen, it all depends upon what one means with "humanism." If one means by that term a certain idea of a European tradition rooted in the classics and passed on from especially the Renaissance, but more likely from the eighteenth century to the present, especially in established forms of education, in the guise of a canon of great works, yes, it is Eurocentric and universalist in the worst sense – i.e. as projecting an ideal of European man as normative for the world at large. If, however, one means by it the marriage between philology as a critical method and a concern for the human, humanism becomes universalizing in Said's sense of critique and self-critique. The humanism of the Renaissance rests upon the re-discovery of classical civilization as the realm of the human instead of the divine, as was the case in medieval times. This is symbolized by the rediscovery of the human body as the legitimate and proper subject for art, as Kenneth Clark has convincingly shown in his celebrated study *The Nude* (1953), and by the philological study of texts not as divine revelation but as man-made. However, the adulation of the classics this initially implied also made them into a measure for conservatives to return to again and again, thus making humanism for this group a permanent state in the past from which the present could only be a falling off. This adulation was for students of literature, and particularly world literature, still reinforced by Goethe's own continuous return to the classics, particularly the Greeks. The emergence of humanism thus became for these conservatives the moment of fusion of classic/modern into a moment of stability, with Dante as the fulcrum of this meeting. This then also became the measure for Curtius who wanted to see continuity in European culture and literature, and hence of "eternal" Greek and Goethean values. His position, mutatis mutandis, was shared by other conservatives such as T. S. Eliot, a correspondent of Curtius'. The other camp stressed the evolving aspect of "humanity" in humanism. This is what Said sees Auerbach doing, and what he himself put into practice. This necessarily also implies a return to philology in the original spirit of humanism: as a critical instrument to analyze man-made texts and worlds; humanism not as the stabilization of Europe's past greatness but as Europe de-Europeanizing itself via self-critique; and in terms of world literature a Europe that, to use Dipesh Chakrabarty's (2000) apt term, "provincializes" itself by universalizing its critical method.

Conclusion

- Because of Goethe's humanistic infatuation with ancient Greek and Roman culture, a world literature taking its cue from him, and especially from his insistence on the validity of the classical as normative for universal humanity, has often been deemed inevitably Eurocentric.
- Goethe's humanism was confirmed and deepened by an extended trip to Italy he undertook while still a young man, during which he avidly went in search of ancient monuments.
- Humanism, however, is more than ancient monuments; the rise of humanism in the Renaissance also marks the rise of philology as investigative method to draw out the meaning of all kinds of texts.
- The postcolonial critic and theoretician Edward Said insists precisely on the value of humanistic philology as an instrument also for self-critically investigating the foundations of humanism itself, and of that European civilization it undergirds.
- Edward Said and Emily Apter draw on the examples of the German philologists Erich Auerbach and Leo Spitzer to argue that a world literature modelled upon Goethe's example and using humanistic philology as its instrument is not necessarily Eurocentric but is rather open to the world.

3 World Literature and Comparative Literature

Overview

The study and teaching of world literature have traditionally been seen as belonging to the province of the discipline of comparative literature. The Hungarian comparatist Arpád Berczik even calls comparative literature the "applied science of world literature" (Berczik 1972: 159; die angewandte Wissenschaft des Weltliteratur). In fact, the actual teaching of something called "world literature" until recently has mainly been confined to the United States, and we will return to it in Chapter 4. As to the actual study of world literature, if in most writings on comparative literature there is the obligatory, but often also perfunctory, nod to the term, just as often the possibility of actually "doing" world literature has been dismissed out of hand. This is especially true of the so-called "French" school of comparative literature, which from the mid-nineteenth to the mid-twentieth century practically commanded the field, and which heavily insisted on the "comparative" element in the discipline's practice. Moreover, in Europe or in the European tradition, comparative literature in practice was the domain of a cultured elite naturally schooled in a variety of languages, often because of the specific political or other conditions in which they found themselves. It is certainly no coincidence that many of the nineteenth-century forerunners of comparative literature, and of its earlier practitioners in the twentieth century, were Swiss or worked in that country. Additionally, the cultured elite in Europe during the nineteenth and early twentieth century as a matter of course understood, spoke, and wrote French, and was educated with Latin and Greek as self-evident parts of the high school curriculum, with Latin often being a prerequisite for admission to university. Finally, scholars working in languages and literatures until World War II were almost invariably philologists, who as a matter of course studied several European rather than single national literatures. In the United States circumstances were completely different, and when after World War II the lead in comparative literature passed from Europe to the USA this also had immediate consequences for the study of world literature. The scope of the literatures that could be studied broadened significantly, no immediate filiation between various works studied need be demonstrated, and more general topics could be

DOI: 10.4324/9781003366713-4

broached. For various reasons, though, from the 1970s through the 1980s comparative literature, and the study of world literature with it, were eclipsed by a rapid succession of theoretical movements that flourished in national literature, and particularly English departments, rather than comparative literature departments, at least in the United States. The recent renewed interest in world literature, though, has returned comparative literature to the center of American academe. However, this is a much-changed comparative literature from its earlier days. Interestingly, the recent upswing of interest in world literature as fueled by comparative literature goes hand in hand with a re-discovery, or in any case a re-reading and re-interpretation, of a number of pioneers in the field of comparative literature that are being re-appropriated for present-day concerns. In what follows I sketch the intricate, though until recently not necessarily very intimate, relationship between comparative literature, especially in its "French" and "American" guises, and world literature.

Intimations of Comparative Literature

The birth of comparative literature coincides with Goethe's observations on *Weltliteratur*. It also coincided, as we have seen in the first chapter, with the emergence of a clear consciousness of national literatures and with the writing of their histories. It is not that histories of literature spanning a wider reach than a single country or one single language had not been written before. Guillén (1993: 27) mentions several eighteenth-century such histories which, like the first national histories he also mentions, and which I cited in the first chapter, were all written in Italy: *Della storia e della ragione d'ogni poesia* (1739; On the History and Reason of All Poetry) by Francesco Saverio Quadrio (1695–1756), the *Discorso sulle vicende d'ogni letteratura* (1760; Discourse on What Happened in All Literature) of Carlo Denina (1731–1813), and especially the seven-volume *Dell'origine, dei progressi e dello stato attuale d'ogni letteratura* (1782–1799; On the Origin, Development and Contemporary Situation of All Literature) by Juan Andrés (1740–1817), a Spanish Jesuit who worked most of his life in Italy. The Swiss-American comparatist François Jost, in his *Introduction to Comparative Literature* (1974), adds an even earlier Italian example to Guillén's: *Storia della vulgar poesia* (1698; A History of Poetry in the Vernacular) by Giovanni Mario Crescimbeni (1663–1728). Jost also mentions a number of examples from England and France. John Dryden (1631–1700), Jost points out, wrote a number of essays on various genres, as well as on comparisons between poetry and painting, in which he addressed more than one literature. In 1785, John Andrews (1736–1809) published a *Comparative View of the French and English Nations in Their Manners, Politics, and Literature*. In 1727 Voltaire (1694–1778) had already written an *Essai sur la poésie épique* (Essay on Epic Poetry) and in 1762 Jean-Baptiste-René Robinet (1735–1820) offered his *Considérations sur l'état présent de la littérature en Europe* (Considerations on the Present State of Literature in Europe). Most of these, however, do not correspond to what as of the nineteenth century we would normally consider "histories" in that they do not offer a continuous and reasoned narrative relating to people, works, and events.

The transnational study of literature as practiced by comparative literature, Guillén (1993: 27) argues, could only come into being "when two events occur: one, when a large number of modern literatures – literatures that recognize themselves as such – come into existence; and two: when a unitary or absolute poetics ceases to be an accepted model." Indeed, the older transnational literary histories that Guillén mentions start from the assumption of an accepted neo-classical model of a unitary or absolute poetics stretching back from their own times to the Greek and Roman classics, and from a sense of community over such poetics shared in the Republic of Letters mentioned in the first chapter. We might speak here, with the American comparatist Alexander Beecroft (2008: 95; 2015), who takes his cue from the Indologist Sheldon Pollock (1996) on the Sanskrit "Cosmopolis," of a cosmopolitan system in which, at variance with what Beecroft calls a "panchoric system," in which "a literary language allows literature to circulate among a set of political entities sharing a native language (but likely not a political regime)." In a cosmopolitan system

> a cosmopolitan literary language creates a cross-cultural system, in which speakers of many languages share a common literary idiom ... this language may be the cultural expression of a world-empire, or a nostalgic reminiscence of a former empire, or it may constitute a cultural world-empire without political ramifications.

Writers, readers, and all men (and women) of letters before the end of the eighteenth century shared in such a cosmopolitan system on the basis of first Latin, later complemented by French, as commonly shared languages, as well as on the basis of a common understanding of what "letters" stood for. One of the ironies of history is that the German philosopher Immanuel Kant (1724–1804), who in his *Perpetual Peace: A Philosophical Sketch* (1795) defended cosmopolitanism and is still valued as one of the most important philosophers on the issue, with his *Critique of Judgment* (1790), as briefly argued in the first chapter, also paved the way for the conception of "literature" as the new name for what until then had been known as "belles-lettres" within the general category of "letters" as an autonomous domain ruled by taste (judgment) and not by "truth," like science, and hence also for the separation of the unitary realm of "letters," as shared around Europe, into distinct national "literatures."

Once the new national literatures came into their own, they also called forth, in an almost Hegelian dialectic, a new internationalism in the form of both Goethe's *Weltliteratur* and the early stirrings of comparative literature. Guillén cites Joseph Texte (1865–1900), one of the earliest official comparative literature scholars, when looking back in 1898 at the birth of the discipline, as concluding that romantic criticism had been "in one sense, an agent of *concentration*, and in another, an agent of *expansion*" (Guillén 1993: 28). It had been an agent of concentration in furthering national literatures; an agent of expansion by furthering the transnational dimension of literature. We can already see the combination of this twofold process in *De la littérature considérée dans ses rapports avec les institutions sociales* (1799; On Literature Considered in Relation to Social Institutions) and *De l'Allemagne* (1810; On Germany) by the Swiss Madame (Anne Louise Germaine) de Staël (1766–1817), and *Littérature du midi de l'Europe* (1813; Literature from the South of Europe) by the equally Swiss Jean-Charles-Léonard Simonde de Sismondi (1773–1842). These works, as I have also argued with regard to Goethe on *Weltliteratur*, simultaneously look back at the Republic of Letters and forward to the new romantic era of national literatures.

Mme de Staël was the center of a cosmopolitan circle at her salon in Paris and her estate in Coppet, Switzerland, with as regular members, among others, Sismondi, the also Swiss Benjamin Constant (1767–1830), and the German writer and philologist August Wilhelm (von) Schlegel (1767–1845). The celebrated British-Scots poet Byron (1788–1824) was also, during certain periods, a frequent visitor. Together, along with like-minded writers and thinkers across Europe, they can be considered as part of what the French critic Paul van Tieghem (1871–1948) in one of the earliest systematic treatments of comparative literature as a discipline calls the fourth cosmopolitan age in European letters:

> After the Christian and Chivalresque cosmopolitanism of the middle ages, after the humanist cosmopolitanism of the Renaissance, after the classicist and philosophical cosmopolitanism of the Age of Enlightenment, there appears a romantic and historical cosmopolitanism that, much more than its predecessors, takes into account national differences, deigns to accept them and does its best to understand them.
>
> (Apres le cosmopolitisme chrétien et chevaleresque du moyen âge, apres le cosmopolitisme humaniste de la renaissance, apres le cosmopolitisme classique et philosophique de l'âge des lumières, paraît un cosmopolitisme romantique et historique qui tient compte, beaucoup plus que ses prédécesseurs, des différences nationales, qui se plaît à les accepter et s'efforce de les comprendre.)
>
> (Van Tieghem 1931: 27–28)

It is in this context that Van Tieghem refers to Goethe and *Weltliteratur*: "That is why Goethe, in 1827, spoke to Eckermann about world literature (*Weltliteratur*) as the totality of all singular literatures, a totality that one should take into account so as not to fall victim to national prejudices" (Van Tieghem 1931: 27; C'est ainsi que Goethe, en 1827, parlait à Eckermann de la "littérature universelle" [*Weltliteratur*] comme de l'ensemble des littératures particulières, ensemble qu'il faut savoir considérer pour ne pas être dupe de préjugés nationaux).

The works of De Staël and Sismondi are often cited as forerunners to comparative literature proper, as is the *Geschichte der Poesie und Beredsamkeit seit dem Ende des 13. Jahrhunderts* (1801–1819; a twelve-volume History of Poetry and Eloquence since the End of the Thirteenth Century), by the German philosopher and critic Friedrich Bouterwek (1766–1828). August Wilhelm Schlegel used the word "comparison" in his *Comparaison entre Phèdre de Racine et celle d'Euripide* (1807; A Comparison between the Phèdre of Racine and that of Euripides). Certainly, "comparison" was a buzzword at the turn of the nineteenth century, though initially in the sciences rather than in literature. It indicated a scientific method that had become very popular especially in anatomy and philology. In the former field its main proponent was the French naturalist Georges Cuvier (1769–1832) who in 1800 had published his *Leçons d'anatomie comparée* (Lessons in Comparative Anatomy) and which had met with great success across Europe. In philology, the name of the English legal scholar, judge, and orientalist William Jones (1746–94) stands out. With his work on Sanskrit, relating it to most of Europe's languages as well as to Persian, and positing a common Indo-European ancestry for them all, Jones is usually seen as the founder of comparative linguistics.

Comparative Literature: The Early Years

The birth of comparative literature as a discipline proper is to be situated in France. Jost (1974) mentions as the earliest instance of the documented use of "littérature comparée" a *Cours de littérature comparée*, comprising a series of textbooks published in 1816 by Jean-François-Michel Noël (1755–1841) and several collaborators. As Jost hastens to point out, though, Noël's collection merely consisted of an assemblage of texts, without any truly comparative framework. The true origins of the discipline are to be found with Abel François Villemain (1790–1870), Philarète Chasles (1798–1873), and Jean-Jacques Ampère (1800–1864). In the 1820s, Villemain, professor of Eloquence at the Sorbonne, presented a series of lectures that resulted in a number of volumes published in 1828, 1829, and 1830 under the titles *Tableau de la littérature au XVIIIe siecle* (Survey of Eighteenth-Century Literature) and *Tableau de la littérature au Moyen Age en France, en Italie, en Espagne et en Angleterre* (Survey of Medieval Literature in France, Italy, Spain and England), addressed to the "amateurs de la littérature comparée" (Guillén 1993: 24; amateurs of comparative literature). Ampère, after first having published on German and Scandinavian folk poetry, introducing his French public to these subjects, turned to the history of French literature, which he taught at the Sorbonne and the Collège de France. He also developed an interest in Dante, visited the United States in 1851, and eventually became a member of the Académie Française. In 1830 he delivered his inaugural lecture to the Marseilles *Athénée* discourses on the "comparative history of arts and of literature" (histoire comparative des arts et de la littérature). Two years later he was appointed to the University of the Sorbonne in Paris, where in his inaugural lecture he again referred to "this comparative study, without which literary history is not complete" (cited in Pichois and Rousseau 1967: 16; cette étude comparative, sans laquelle l'histoire littéraire n'est pas complète). Finally, Philarète Chasles, whom I already dealt with in some detail in the first chapter, dedicated his inaugural lecture at the Parisian *Athénée* in 1835 to "la littérature étrangère comparée" (foreign literatures compared).

The new discipline received its popular consecration in France when the celebrated critic Charles-Augustin Sainte-Beuve (1804–1869) in two articles on Jean-Jacques Ampère, in 1840 and in 1868, talks of "l'histoire littéraire comparée" and "littérature comparée," respectively. Though the importance of Ampère for the early development of comparative literature has always been recognized, until recently his work had not drawn any particular attention from the point of view of world literature. Now, however, and along the lines of what we will also see happening further on with such figures as Hugo Meltzl and Georg Brandes, Ampère is in the process of being reclaimed as an alternative starting point for the actual discipline of comparative literature – alternative, that is, to what toward the end of the nineteenth century hardened into the "orthodox" form of comparative literature practiced in France, and under French influence in most of the Western academic world. Françoise Lionnet (2012: 328, 2022: 269), in her contribution to *The Routledge Companion to World Literature* sees Ampère as "an early advocate of a global approach to French literature, and a believer in its fundamental heterogeneity."

In 1847 Charles Louandre (1812–1882), with a reference to Chasles, proclaims in the *Revue des Deux Mondes* that "the comparative study of literature has put in circulation a myriad of new ideas" (cited in Pichois and Rousseau 1967: 18; l'étude comparée des littératures a mis en circulation une foule d'idées nouvelles). If from the 1840s on, then, comparative literature has become an accepted enterprise, at least in France, this is not to say that this new way of looking at literature also was honored with official chairs at French universities. For sure, a number of courses in comparative literature were instituted, mostly under the tutelage of chairs in foreign literatures, but no independent chairs. The first such chairs were created in Italy and in Switzerland. The very first chair seems to have been created in Naples, although accounts differ to its regard. According to Jost (1974: 12) a chair in comparative literature was created in Naples in 1861 for the Italian scholar and politician Francesco de Sanctis (1817–1883) who, however, only took up his professorship in 1871. For Pichois and Rousseau (1967: 19), de Sanctis already became professor in comparative literature at Naples in 1863 upon the creation of a chair there. In Switzerland a chair in "littérature moderne comparée" was created in Geneva in 1865. France followed in 1890 with the appointment of Joseph Texte to a newly created chair in comparative literature at the University of Lyons.

Beyond France: Hugo Meltzl and Max Koch

In the second half of the nineteenth century comparative literature spread to the rest of Europe, and beyond. The Hungarian periodical *Tudománytár*, founded in 1834, regularly reported on various European literatures (Berczik 1972). However, not everything that appeared in its pages unhesitatingly was in support of a Goethean *Weltliteratur*. In 1836 the journal published an article by the German poet and critic Wolfgang Menzel (1798–1873), a staunch opponent of Goethe and Heinrich Heine. Menzel blamed Goethe for what he considered the sins of the early *Junges Deutschland* (Young Germany) movement: "world citizenship, Saint-Simonism (a form of utopian socialism named after the French writer and social critic Saint Simon [1760–1825], *TD*), anti-religious attitudes, immorality" (Berczik 1972: 161; Weltbürgertum, Saint-Simonismus, anti-religiöse Einstellung, Immoralität). In Berczik's words:

> the ill-guided young writers propagated a world literature in the sense of Goethe's which, if one is not careful, supplants national literature, Menzel says ... [and] ... in the final part of his essay he reproaches the *Junges Deutschland* writers that they proclaim the Republic of Literature, the "World Republic," and that "this is being prepared for by world literature."
>
> (Die irregeleiteten jungen Schriftsteller verkünden im Sinne Goethes die Weltliteratur, die – wenn man nicht gut aufpasst – das nationale Schrifttum verdrängen wird, – sagt Menzel ... [and] ... im Schlussteil seines Aufsatzes wirft er den Dichtern des "Jungen Deutschland" vor, dass sie die Republik der Literatur, die "Weltrepublik" proklamieren, und "diese wird durch die Weltliteratur vorbereitet.")
>
> (Berczik 1972: 161)

More importantly, the first ever comparative literature journal properly so named was founded in 1877 in present-day Cluj (officially Cluj-Napoca) in Romania, but which at the time went by the names of Klausenburg in German and Kolozsvár in Hungarian, and which was the capital of the then province of Transylvania in the Austro-Hungarian Empire. Edited by Hugo Meltzl (1846–1908; also known as Hugo von Meltzl and Hugo Meltzl de Lomnitz) and Samuel Brassai (1800–1897) the journal first appeared under a multilingual title, which in all languages used basically said it to be a "journal of comparative literature." As of 1879 it changed its title to *Acta Comparationis Litterarum Universarum*, and it is under this title that it entered the history of comparative literature. Meltzl became the sole editor upon Brassai's retirement in 1883, and this until the journal's demise in 1888. Brassai belonged to the Hungarian-speaking population of Transylvania, Meltzl to the German-speaking minority long established there. In the countryside around Cluj Romanian was the dominant language. Brassai's and Meltzl's journal not only reflected the multilingualism of the region but actively promoted polyglottism as a standard for comparative literature. In the first of three parts of a programmatic article on the "Present Tasks of Comparative Literature" published in the first three issues of the journal, Meltzl declared that "a journal like ours, then, must be devoted at the same time to the art of translation and to the Goethean *Weltliteratur* (a term which German literary historians, particularly Gervinus, have thoroughly misunderstood)" (Meltzl 1973: 56). In the second part, fearing that his emphasis on translation in the first part of his statement had been misunderstood, he hastened to correct himself and to substitute the "principle of translation" with "*the principle of polyglottism*." Still, he declared, it should be obvious that,

> These polyglot efforts have nothing in common with any kind of universal fraternization ... the ideals of Comparative Literature have nothing to do with foggy, "cosmopolitanizing" theories; the high aim (not to say tendencies) of a journal like ours would be gravely misunderstood or intentionally misrepresented if anybody expected us to infringe upon the national uniqueness of a people. ... It is, on the contrary, the *purely national of all nations* that Comparative Literature means to cultivate lovingly ... Our secret motto is: nationality as individuality of a people should be regarded as sacred and inviolable.
> (Meltzl 1973: 59–60)

This leads Meltzl to mount a defense for small literatures, for the "spiritual life of 'literatureless peoples'," and thence also for "folk literature," even to the point of comparing the extinction of a people's literature to that of the people itself. Surely, he continues, this should be impossible "in a time when certain animal species such as the mountain goat and the European bison are protected against extinction by elaborate and strict laws" (Meltzl 1973: 60). Returning to the issue of "world literature," he claims it to be generally misunderstood in his day,

> for today every nation demands its own 'world literature' without quite knowing what is meant by it ... by now, every nation considers itself, for one good reason or another, superior to all nations, and this hypothesis, worked out into a complete theory of *suffisance*, is even the basis of much modern pedagogy which today practically everywhere strives to be "national."
> (Meltzl 1973: 60–61)

In the first part of his programmatic statement, he had already given as his opinion that, "as every unbiased man of letters knows, modern literary history, as generally practiced today, is nothing but an *ancilla historiae politicae*, or even an *ancilla nationis*" (Meltzl 1973: 56). Meltzl concludes the second part of his essay as follows:

> True "world literature," therefore, in our opinion, can only remain an unattainable ideal in the direction of which, nevertheless, all independent

literatures, i.e. all nations, should strive. They should use, however, only those means which we have called the two most important comparative principles, translation and polyglottism, never acts of violence or barbaric hypotheses which will be profitable for nobody but which unfortunately appear occasionally even in the great European journals.

(Meltzl 1973: 61)

The principle of polyglottism had implicitly already been flagged in the journal's first name, appearing as it did on its title page in eleven languages. In the third part of his programmatic statement, on "Decaglottism," Meltzl proposes ten working languages for the journal: German, English, French, Icelandic, Italian, Spanish, Portuguese, Swedish, Dutch, and Hungarian, next to Latin – no Romanian. In practice, most articles were in German and Hungarian. In its later years the *Acta* increasingly concentrated on one of the aspects that Meltzl highlighted as the province of what he considered "world literature" – that is to say, the folkloric – offering examples from around the world in the original with adjacent translations.

It should also be said that the *Acta*, notwithstanding its ambitions, and probably at least partially due to its relatively inauspicious site of publication, never had more than a few score subscribers and readers. These also formed the core of the Societas Comparationis Litterarum Universarum, labelled by Damrosch, in his entry on Meltzl in the *Routledge Companion to World Literature* (2012: 15, 2022a: 14), as "probably the world's first Comparative Literature Association." Damrosch (2012: 20), concludes that:

> It is only in recent years that comparatists have begun to recover the fully global perspective that Goethe anticipated and that Meltzl's journal truly began to embody. We can now return to the origins of comparative literature with new appreciation for the complexities of the pioneers' situations, nowhere better represented than in Meltzl's polyglot anti-cosmopolitanism. Little read in Meltzl's lifetime, the *Acta Comparationis Litterarum Universarum* makes fascinating reading today, and it can help us create a study of world literature that truly deserves the name.

Neohelicon, a Hungarian comparative literature journal founded in 1973 by the Hungarian Academy of Sciences with the particular purpose of supporting the publication of the International Comparative Literature Association's ongoing series of literary histories in European languages, took as its subtitle "Acta Comparationis Litterarum Universarum," thus laying explicit claim to Meltzl's legacy.

It is not only *Neohelicon* and the Hungarians though that claim Meltzl's legacy. In fact, if I have dwelt upon Meltzl in such detail it is because he has become somewhat of an iconic figure for comparatists, especially in the United States, since the beginning of the twenty-first century. Damrosch, but in his wake also Haun Saussy, have seized upon Meltzl to at least partially reground the genealogy of comparative literature in the direction of a globalized multilingual, or polyglottal, discipline. I will return to why this is so later in this chapter – suffice to say (at this point) that not everyone agrees with Damrosch's benign view of Meltzl, and even less with the twist given to it by Haun Saussy (Saussy 2006b) in his own contribution to the 2006 volume *Comparative Literature in an Age of Globalization* he compiled for the American Comparative Literature Association (Saussy 2006a).

Reasoning that "philological study that incorporates both German and Hungarian cannot plot its course on cognates or common ancestors, for Hungarian belongs to a separate language family entirely; the science will have to suspend its allegiance to genealogical reasoning and take its bearings from reports of contact or similarity," Saussy (2006b: 8) singles out Meltzl's inclusion of Hungarian as one of the working languages of the *Acta* as

> the first in a long series of gestures by which comparative literature questions the criteria for inclusion in the set of objects known as "literature," … and also the decisive swerve of an established academic discourse (the comparative philological method) toward a Goethean horizon in which world literature, coming from all directions, is whatever the world takes to be literature.
>
> (Saussy 2006b: 8)

Saussy is overlooking three things here. To begin with, Meltzl himself at the outset of the first part of his 1877 programmatic statement feels it necessary to insist that his new journal is not to be taken as a philological enterprise. Second, even if comparative philology, as Meltzl himself underlines, is indeed an "established academic discipline" in 1877, comparative literature, as Meltzl insists upon even more strongly, is not. And third, as David Marno highlights, Meltzl's "polyglot anti-cosmopolitanism," in Damrosch's characterization, is not, as Saussy implicitly takes it to mean because of its inclusion of Hungarian, "a sign of his refusal to be complicit with the general trend of nationalist-historicist sciences in the nineteenth century," (Marno 2008: 38). Rather, Marno argues, it is

> a position that has very transparent political motives: a last position accessible to someone who wants to advocate the literature of a country that had lost its war for national independence just two decades earlier, a country that around this time, in the aftermath of the 1867 compromise between Austria and Hungary, was becoming more powerful than it had been in more than 300 years.
>
> (Marno 2008: 40–41)

The fact is that not only did Meltzl not include Romanian as one of the working languages of his journal, he also excluded all other languages of all other minorities in the Austro-Hungarian Empire: Czech, Serbo-Croat,

Slovene, Slovak, as well as the language of that Empire's powerful neighbor (and neighbor particularly to Hungary) to the East, that is to say Russia. Meltzl's position on polyglottism, then, has at least as much to do with consolidating the position of his own country's language and literature in the contemporary political conditions as with his propagation of a Goethean *Weltliteratur*. In fact, in the second part of his 1877 programmatic statement Meltzl, when soft-pedaling on the importance of translation as announced in the first part, specifically in relation to Goethean world literature, had said that "the means should not be mistaken for the end ... Goethe was still able to conceive of his 'Weltliteratur' as basically, or even exclusively? (German) translation which for him was an end in itself" (Meltzl 1973: 58). Meltzl here seems to be implying that Goethe could afford his cosmopolitanism because even if he was comparing the position of German literature unfavorably with that of English and especially French literature, he was still writing from the comfort of a major language, and hence from a position of power. Meltzl's situation, when it comes not to his own native language, which was German, but to his national language, which was Hungarian (he gained some notoriety for holding his inaugural lecture as Professor of *Germanistik*, and against Gervinus's interpretation of Goethe's *Weltliteratur*, in Hungarian [Marno 2008: 40]), was exactly the opposite. He needs to defend polyglottism as a defense against the encroachment of German, yet he also needs to raise Hungarian above the status of the other minority languages in the Austro-Hungarian Empire, particularly Romanian. He does so by including Hungarian into his list of ten European literatures that according to him had achieved "classicism" (Schulz and Rhein 1973: 230). As Schulz and Rhein note, Meltzl never precisely defines what he means by the latter term. He does list the works with which he sees each of these literatures acceding to "classicism." For Hungarian literature this is with the nineteenth-century writers József Eötvös (1813–1871) and Sándor Petőfi (1823–1849). The latter was, next to a noted poet, also a revolutionary, who died most probably (his body was never recovered) in a battle for Hungarian independence. In his journal Meltzl repeatedly came back to the poetry of Petőfi, commenting upon it, translating it. Here again we can see Meltzl's dual interests in comparative literature as a discipline, a calling even, and a means of furthering patriotic concerns. It should be said, though, that Meltzl did pay critical attention to literature in Romanian and in languages other than his journal's ten working languages.

If for Damrosch and Saussy Meltzl is the good guy, and his journal the beacon shining bright at the beginning of the institutionalization of comparative literature, lighting the way for present-day and future comparatists and world literature scholars, the bad guy is Max Koch (1855–1931), professor at Marburg and later at Breslau (now Wrocław in Poland). In 1886 he founded the *Zeitschrift für vergleichende Litteraturgeschichte* (Journal of Comparative Literature), published in Berlin. Koch's journal published on almost the same things as Meltzl's, but did so exclusively in German, and from a German point of view. In fact, in his programmatic statement to his new journal Koch emphasized that "German literature and the advancement of its historical understanding will form the starting point and the center of gravity for the endeavors of the *Zeitschrift für vergleichende Litteraturgeschichte*" (Koch 1973: 77). Damrosch (2006a: 110) remarks that, "Koch's journal must have seemed to Meltzl to represent not merely a personal affront but also a real step backward in scholarly terms." Meltzl's journal was almost immediately overshadowed by its more powerful rival, and in 1888 it ceased publication. Notwithstanding Damrosch's rather negative judgment on Koch and his journal, one has to admit that Koch was probably simply more in tune with the way comparative literature in Europe was developing than Meltzl. Koch too drew upon the legacy of Goethe and his *Weltliteratur*, but unlike Meltzl, who rejected Goethe's penchant for world literature in German translation in favor of polyglottism, he welcomed it. In the opening statement to his journal he approvingly quoted Goethe's review of Carlyle's *German Romance* in *Über Kunst und Altertu*m VI, 2 that:

> True general tolerance will be achieved most surely when we leave untouched the special qualities of individuals and individual peoples but at the same time hold on to the conviction that the truly meritorious belongs to all mankind. For a long time now, the Germans have contributed to such a mediation and mutual acceptance. Those who know and study the German language find themselves in that marketplace where all nations offer their wares; by acting as interpreters, they enrich themselves.
> (Koch 1973: 75)

In the spirit of Goethe, then, Koch saw the use of German as the working language of his journal as actually promoting understanding among scholars of various nations because of its mediatory role. Indeed, while admiring Meltzl's principle of polyglottism, Damrosch admits that the actual number of articles published in languages other than German and Hungarian in Meltzl's journal, and especially in lesser-known languages such as Icelandic, and even Latin, was very small. We may even wonder whether such polyglottism may not have hampered the journal's accessibility rather than enhancing it. In any case, Koch's approach, with its turn to literary history – "but all consideration of world literature is, after all, comparative literary history" (Koch 1973: 76) – was certainly closer to that of the French "school" (Guillén 1993: 47, prefers to call it the "hour") of comparative literature then becoming dominant in Europe and even beyond, rooted in positivism, and turning away from for instance folklore. Meltzl had increasingly turned to folklore in the later issues of the *Acta*. Koch noticed that the interest in Germany in such studies had been waning for some time while in other European countries journals specializing in folklore had been founded. Still, he invited contributions on the subject to his *Zeitschrift*, perhaps to undercut Meltzl here too, as Damrosch (2006a: 110) suggests he also did in other ways.

Nevertheless, Damrosch too seems forced to admit that Koch was more alert to the times when he states that "more broadly, the great-power perspective became dominant in Comparative Literature for a full century thereafter" (Damrosch 2006a: 110). Moreover, as Schulz and Rhein (1973: 66) put it in their introduction to their reprint of Koch's opening statement to his journal, which kept appearing until 1910: "At a time when there was no other organ to propagate the aims and possibilities of the young discipline, Koch's two periodicals (next to the *Zeitschrift* he also edited nine volumes of *Studien zur vergleichenden Literaturgeschichte*, 1901–1909) fostered, kept alive and shaped comparative literature and bestowed upon it the academic respectability that it needed."

Comparative Literature: The French School

In his opening statement to the *Zeitschrift für vergleichende Litteraturgeschichte* Koch quoted Moritz Carrière (1817–1895), professor at the University of Munich, where he mainly lectured on aesthetics, on comparative literature as a "science" (Koch 1877; quoted in Schulz and Rhein 1973: 76; Carrière 1884). Certainly, this was in tune with the trend of the times, especially so in France which, although it was very late in recognizing the discipline with the institutionalization of dedicated university chairs, nevertheless during the second half of the nineteenth and the first half of the twentieth century continued as the undisputed center of comparative literature. As Guillén (1993: 35) stresses, summarizing René Wellek's survey of the history of comparative literature in the latter's *Discriminations* (1970), under the influence of the positivism of the French critic and literary historian Hippolyte Taine (1828–1893), who based himself on the philosophy of August Comte (1798–1857), one of the founders of the discipline of sociology and one of the earliest philosophers of science, two principles, or perhaps preoccupations, predominated in the approach to comparative literature imposing itself in France as of the 1850s: *factualism* and *scientism*. Scientism meant that phenomena in literature had to be explainable from ascertainable causes. This is where Taine's famous triad "race, milieu, moment" appears, explaining everything human by, or reducing to, the interplay between national character ("race" in the nineteenth century basically meant "nation" or "ethnicity," see for instance Robert Young 1995), the social environment, and historical time. In practice, this gave a strong boost to the study of national literatures as "naturally" emanating from, and giving voice to, a particular people's "national character" springing from precisely such interplay. The advent of Darwinian evolutionism would only strengthen this methodological tendency. Especially Ferdinand Brunetière (1849–1906), professor of French Language and Literature at the École Normale Supérieure in Paris and later also at the Sorbonne, took a Darwinian approach to literature, as demonstrated in his *L'évolution de la poésie lyrique en France* (1894; The Development of Lyrical Poetry in France). As Guillén (1993: 36) puts it,

The literature of a country thus became a biological variety, a subspecies of universal literature; and the task of the comparatist was to be the elucidation of the cross-fertilizations and other grafts that link these subspecies and give rise to their mutations, hybridization, and growth ... the integrity of the individual components of literature was not in doubt, owing to a firm belief in the uniqueness of the character of each people.

Under these conditions factualism then meant that such "elucidations" would have to happen on the basis of observable and demonstrable facts. In practice, this meant "comparing" works, authors, etc. from at least two different European literatures.

Brunetière and Fernand Baldensperger (1871–1958), together with Joseph Texte, who died very young in 1900, were the "face" of French comparatism around the turn of the twentieth century. In his opening address to the section on "histoire comparée des littératures" (comparative history of literatures) of a Historical Congress held in Paris in 1900, Brunetière readily admitted that "European literature is only a branch, or better yet a province, and maybe even a narrow province, in the almost infinite field of *Comparative Literature*" (Brunetière 1973: 159). At the same time, he also firmly stuck to "only one principle, which I hope you will understand as evident, and it is that the studies of comparative literature are related only to that which is comparable" and that "by a reasonable extension it follows that the productions of a great literature do not concern us except as we have seen the resultant consequences of this contact" (Brunetière 1973: 168). French school comparative literature, then, mainly concentrated on so-called "influence studies." Indicatively, Texte, who was a pupil of Brunetière's and followed the guidelines for the study of literature laid down by the latter in his *L'évolution de la poésie lyrique*, started off his career with a book on *J.J. Rousseau et les origines du cosmopolitisme littéraire* (1895; Jean-Jacques Rousseau and the Origins of Literary Cosmopolitanism). Baldensperger did the same with *Goethe en France* (1904; Goethe in France). The same Baldensperger, who first had taught at Nancy and Lyon, in 1910 became professor at the Sorbonne, and together with Paul Hazard (1878–1944), himself likewise professor at the Sorbonne as of 1919 and from 1925 on professor of comparative literature at the prestigious *Collège de France*, founded the *Revue de littérature comparée* (1921–).

Baldensperger held a visiting professorship at Columbia University (1917–19). In 1935 he became professor and chair of comparative literature at Harvard University, from which he moved to the University of California-Los Angeles in 1940 until his retirement in 1945. Hazard held a visiting professorship at Columbia University from 1932 to 1940. Thus, the influence of the French school of comparative literature stretched to the United States in the guise of its most prestigious universities – universities moreover that had been among the first to create chairs of comparative literature, Harvard in 1891 and Columbia in 1899. The handbooks on comparative literature that appeared in France in the first half of the twentieth century basically raised the ideas of Baldensperger and his followers to dogma. As late as 1951 Jean-Marie Carré, Baldensperger's successor at the Sorbonne, in his preface to his former pupil Marius-François Guyard's *La littérature comparée* (Comparative Literature), insisted that "comparative literature is not literary comparison," but that it is "a branch of literary history," and that it is "the study of international intellectual relations, of the actual connections that existed ... between the works, the inspirations, or even the lives of writers belonging to various literatures" (Carré 2009: 159). In a note, Carré repeats that, "the first general exposition (of the concept of Comparative Literature) was provided by our teacher Fernand Baldensperger in 1921" (in the first issue of the *Revue de littérature comparée*). He also refers to Paul van Tieghem's *La littérature comparée* (Comparative Literature) of 1931, which had been reprinted in 1946 (Carré 2009: 160), and which insists that "a clear and distinct idea of comparative literature supposes first of all a clear and distinct idea of literary history, of which it is a branch" (Van Tieghem 1931: 23; as quoted in English in Jost 1974: 25). And so it was, Guillén (1993: 37) somewhat ruefully notes, "that the idea of *Weltliteratur* was left far behind, its outlines blurred" in the French version of comparative literature dominant until World War II.

The Changing of The Guard

In his 1951 preface to Guyard's *La littérature comparée* Carré insisted that "comparative literature is not general literature," adding in a note that the latter is "a subject taught in the United States" (Carré 2009: 159–160). Perhaps Carré was thinking of the fact that already in 1901 Richard Moulton had been appointed professor of literary theory and interpretation and head of the department of general literature at the University of Chicago and that this same Moulton in 1911 had published *World Literature and Its Place in General Culture*. More likely, though, if we keep in mind that already Paul van Tieghem had defined "general literature" as being concerned with large syntheses, Carré was thinking of the trend, rapidly gaining ground in the USA after World War II, of teaching large "world literature" courses. In fact, ever since the middle of the nineteenth century the anglophone world had been elaborating a comparative literature of its own, more geared toward Carré's "general literature" than toward the meticulous study of "rapports de fait" (factual relationships) as had become increasingly the habit, and indeed the prescription, in the French tradition. As already mentioned in Chapter 1, what Schulz and Rhein (1973: 41) call "the first known formal presentation concerning the discipline of comparative literature in the United States" was an address on "Comparative Literature" given by Charles Chauncey Shackford at Cornell University in 1871. Shackford is interested in the laws that govern "universal literature," and thinks that

> the literary productions of all ages and peoples can be classed, can be brought into comparison and contrast, can be taken out of their isolation

as belonging to one nation, or one separate era, and be brought under divisions as the embodiment of the same aesthetic principles, the universal laws of mental, social, and moral development: the same in India and in England; in Hellas, with its laughing sea, and Germany, with its somber forests.

(Shackford 1973: 42)

"Literature," he declares, "can be studied not in the isolated works of different ages, but as the production of the same great laws, and the embodiment of the same universal principles in all times" (Shackford 1973: 46).

Hutcheson Macaulay Posnett

Ideas like Shackford's were taken up in a more systematic, some would say a more mechanical, way by Hutcheson Macaulay Posnett in his 1886 *Comparative Literature*. Posnett was Irish-born but taught at the University of Auckland in New Zealand at the time he wrote his book. By training he was a lawyer, and in 1890 he resigned from his university position and returned to Ireland where he practiced as a lawyer for the rest of his career. In a 1901 article – "The Science of Comparative Literature" – he claimed to have been the first to have elaborated "the method and principles" of the discipline (Posnett 1973: 186). As the title of the article illustrates, Posnett was a staunch believer in "science," and therefore it should not come as a surprise that for him

the fundamental principles of Comparative Literature, as I formulated and illustrated them fifteen years earlier [in *Comparative Literature*], are social evolution, individual evolution, and the influence of the environment on the social and individual life of man ... a scientific 'law' is only a brief summary of a vast number of observed and recorded facts.

(Posnett 1973: 188–189)

In *Comparative Literature*, when discussing "The Comparative Method and Literature," Posnett proclaimed that

the central point of these studies is the relation of the individual to the group. ... we therefore adopt ... the gradual expansion of social life, from clan to city, from city to nation, from both of these to cosmopolitan humanity, as the proper order of studies in comparative literature.

(Posnett 2009: 59)

"That cosmopolitan and world-wide spirit which is the servant of no one social group but the sympathetic friend of all," Posnett specified in 1901 with a reference to Goethe, "I studied in *Comparative Literature* under the name of 'world-literature,' and I illustrated its various characteristics by Hebrew, Greek, Latin, Indian, and Chinese examples" (Posnett 1973: 191). If Posnett can be accused, then, of having followed a narrowly positivist and social Darwinist road when elaborating his "principles and methods" of comparative literature, he certainly cannot be accused of limiting himself to Europe, even though he also seems to have thought that "the making of [the British] empire's literature ... going on before [his contemporary compatriot's] eyes" was a significant contribution to "that cosmopolitan and world-wide spirit which is the servant of no one social group but the sympathetic friend of all" (Posnett 1973: 191). Sounding a distinctly Goethean note, Posnett optimistically concluded that "now, when the science of Comparative Literature is a dream that has come true," it is a "study that is as certain to enlighten and expand the friendship of nations as to increase the knowledge and sympathies of individual men" (Posnett 1973: 206).

Posnett devoted a sizeable part of his book – pages 235–336 – to what he calls "world-literature." This is not the *Weltliteratur* of Goethe, though. Even though Goethe was an "admirer of world literature" (Posnett 1886: 42), for Posnett he still thought that "national literature is an outcome of national life, a spiritual bond of national unity, such as no amount of eclectic study or cosmopolitan science can supply" (Posnett 1886: 341). Nowhere does Posnett actually discuss Goethe's idea of *Weltliteratur*. Instead, his world literature is the third stage in a historically successive series composed of "clan literature," the literature of "the city commonwealth," "world-literature," and "national literature." World-literature for Posnett is literature produced in cultures held together by what he calls "religious" or "political" cosmopolitanism. Examples of the former are the Hebrew and Islamic cultures. Examples of the latter are the Greek, or perhaps better Hellenic, and Roman, or perhaps better Latin, cultures. "Between the world-religions of Israel and Islam and the world-cultures of Alexandria and Rome there are, no doubt, very wide differences," he admits,

> yet, though the former reach universality through social bonds of creed and the latter reach universality through the unsocial idea of personal culture, the outcome of both is to rise above old restrictions of place and time, and to render possible a literature which, whether based on Moses or Homer, may best be termed a "world-literature."
>
> (Posnett 1886: 236)

For Posnett, then, the determining characteristic of such a world-literature is its "severance of literature from defined social groups" or "the universalising of literature" (Posnett 1886: 236). Next to this "universal idea of humanity," further characteristics of Posnett's world-literature are "the critical study of language as the medium of sacred books or models of literary art" and "the rise of new aesthetic appreciations of physical nature and its relations to man" (Posnett 1886: 238). Next to the literatures already mentioned Posnett also sees Indian and Chinese literature as qualifying as world-literatures.

Though, as Schulz and Rhein (1973: 185) note, Posnett's *Comparative Literature* was initially greeted with some enthusiasm, especially in the United

States, it quickly came to be seen as overly mechanical and dated in its methodology because of what was perceived as its over-reliance on social Darwinism. Of late, though, as has happened with other early advocates of comparative literature, Posnett has been recast as a convenient forefather of more recent trends in the discipline. In 2004 Simon During, after having given a brief description of Posnett's methodology, concluded that:

> Posnett conceived of comparative literature as a social science which, along with the world-literature canon it addresses, forms a basis for the politics of cosmopolitan democratic individualism ... it does so not just because literature uniquely articulates those structures through which individuals recognize themselves as connected to and formed by an increasingly wide range of distant social formations, but because the comparative method enables recognition of social and cultural differences and, hence, encourages the dissemination of relativism as well as entry into a single world system.
> (During 2004: 314)

Here, During is obviously reclaiming Posnett for the more sociologically and systemically oriented form of comparative literature he also sees Pascale Casanova and Franco Moretti as advocating in their publications. I will return to the latter in Chapter 6. Beyond this, and even though there is no sign of his ever having read Posnett, some proposals put forward by Beecroft (2008, 2015), and to which I will also return in Chapter 6, show remarkable resemblances to Posnett's differentiation of literatures according to different forms of social organization.

Comparative Literature in The United States: The Early Years

In his editorial to the newly founded (and short-lived) *Journal of Comparative Literature* (1903), George Woodberry (1855–1930), who briefly occupied the chair of comparative literature at Columbia University before retiring early and devoting the rest of his life to traveling, lecturing, and writing, summarized the province of comparative literature as the study of sources, themes, forms, environments, and artistic parallels. In all these areas, he argued, a lot of work had already been done, especially under the influence of "German methods," but these concerned mostly the "externals of literature" (Woodberry 1973: 212). The question now became what was to be done with all this accumulated material? For Woodberry, the ultimate goal had to be the search for "the laws of the human soul" (Woodberry 1973: 213). He put forward that "to disclose the necessary forms, the vital moods of the beautiful soul is the far goal of our effort, – to help in this, in the bringing of those spiritual destinies in which human destiny is accomplished" (Woodberry 1973: 213–214). "With such thoughts in mind," Woodberry continued, "It may perhaps seem to some of us that the subject of international influences is not the main road of our travel." Instead, he advocated studying "the isolated phenomena of national literatures," feeling that "the approaching exploitation of the old literatures of the Orient" might be a fruitful field of investigation. In all this Woodberry is obviously holding a modest plea for the study of general literature, for the study of affinities, correspondences, parallels, and all those things that French orthodoxy disapproved of.

In 1894, Charles Mills Gayley (1858–1932), professor of English at the University of California, Berkeley, proposed the creation of a Society of Comparative Literature; in 1903 he published an article in *The Atlantic Monthly* in support of Woodberry's newly founded *Journal of Comparative Literature*. Gayley specifically interpreted Woodberry's editorial as "non-acceptance of a theory of evolution such as Brunetière's," and as a confirmation that "the study of international relations and influences is but one of the objects of Comparative Literature" (Gayley 1973: 101–102). In fact, Gayley saw anthropology as "the cradle of literary science" (Gayley 1973: 96) and finally called comparative literature "Literary Philology" (Gayley 1973: 103). All this did not prevent Baldensperger and other prominent European scholars from contributing to Woodberry's journal. Still, Carré's 1951 statement clearly shows the rift between the French and what since 1958 it has become customary to call the "American" schools of comparative literature.

The Crisis of Comparative Literature

The years from Woodberry's premature resignation from Columbia to World War II mostly were lean years for comparative literature in the United States. The subject had been rejuvenated somewhat by the arrival in the USA of a number of European scholars, mostly Jewish exiles from Nazi Germany, in the late 1930s and the 1940s. Prominent among these were Leo Spitzer, who arrived in the US in 1936, and Erich Auerbach, who came in 1948. But there was also René Wellek (1903–1995). Wellek was born in Vienna of Czech parents, Czechia being a part of the Austro-Hungarian Empire at the time. He was educated in Prague, where he moved among the Prague structuralists. In 1935 he took up a teaching post at University College London, and on the eve of World War II moved to the US, where in 1946 he founded the department of comparative literature at Yale University. In 1949 Wellek, with Austin Warren, published *Theory of Literature*, which for the next forty years was the most influential handbook for the study of literature in the United States. The book is widely seen as supporting New Criticism, while also showing the influence of European forms of structuralism. Wellek also wrote an eight-volume *History of Modern Criticism: 1750–1950*. Comparative literature in the US set much greater store by interpretation, or hermeneutics, and on emphasizing the humanitarian dimension of literature than did the French school. The rift between the long-dominant French school of comparative literature and what since has come to be known as the "American" school (Guillén again insists on using "hour" instead of "school" and the opposition of any supposedly "French" and "American" schools has been denounced as overly simplistic, but as shorthand the denominations can still serve in a general discussion such as in this volume) plainly erupted at the Second World Congress of the then recently formed International Comparative Literature Association in Chapel Hill, NC in 1958.

In a speech to the ICLA Congress at Chapel Hill, Wellek condemned the French school for its "obsolete methodology" which had laid on comparative literature "the dead hand of nineteenth-century factualism, scientism, and historical relativism," and instead advocated a more generous attitude toward what could be done under the label "Comparative Literature." Clearly echoing his own and Austin Warren's celebrated *Theory of Literature* (1949), Wellek argued for the study of the literary work of art's "literariness" (Wellek 2009: 169) and for a "holistic" conception that sees the work of art as a "diversified totality, as a structure of signs which, however, imply meanings and values" (Wellek 2009: 170). Once we do that, he contends,

> man, universal man, man anywhere and at any time, in all his variety, emerges and literary scholarship ceases to be an antiquarian pastime, a calculus of national credits and debts and even a mapping of networks of relationships ... literary scholarship becomes an act of the imagination, like art itself, and thus a preserver and creator of the highest values of mankind.
>
> (Wellek 2009: 171)

Wellek soon received support from H.H. Remak (1916–2009), professor of comparative literature at Indiana University, who, in the article with which he opened Newton P. Stallknecht and Horst Frenz's 1961 programmatic collection *Comparative Literature: Method and Perspective*, posited that comparative literature would best serve its purpose "by not only relating several literatures to each other but by relating literature to other fields of human knowledge and activity, especially artistic and ideological fields; that is, by extending the investigation of literature both geographically and generically" (Remak 1961: 10). For Remak comparative literature and the study of world literature dealt with largely the same issues, but comparative literature did so in a more restricted form as to space and time. World literature "deals ... predominantly with time- and world-honored literary productions of enduring quality ... or, les markedly, with authors of our own day who have enjoyed very intense applause abroad" (Remak 1961: 13). "Much of what we have been doing [in comparative literature]," he said, "is, in effect, comparative world literature" (Remak 1961: 12), the difference being that the former "is not bound to the same extent by criteria of quality and/or intensity" (Remak 1961: 13). Nor, he added, did the study of world literature necessarily involve the aspect of comparison, unlike comparative literature. Finally, he referred to the distinction made by Van Tieghem about "general literature" as dealing with large syntheses, but he saw the term as also covering "literary trends, problems and theories of 'general interest'" (Remak 1961: 15). Finally, he found none of these terms to be watertight, with overlap between them all, though he rather disliked "general literature" as too vague and preferred more precise indications for the various things it covered, such as for instance "literary theory" (Remak 1961: 19). In this, he joined Wellek, who at the end of his own "The Crisis of Comparative Literature" had also called for a "reorientation toward theory and criticism" (Wellek 2009: 170).

As we now know, Wellek's call for theory was followed with a vengeance in the 1960s to 1980s in the United States with the successive waves of structuralism, phenomenology, poststructuralism, reader reception studies, deconstruction, dialogism, and new historicism succeeding, and often tumbling over, one another, often sparked by the import of various European theories of French, German, or Central and East European origin. In one sense, this signaled the triumph of comparative literature. In another sense, it also brought about the demise of comparative literature, because "theory," unlike works of literature themselves, was not thought to suffer in translation, and could therefore readily be accessed in English. In practice, this meant that theory rapidly became the province also of English departments, with comparative literature, because of its exacting foreign language requirements, spurned as a "difficult" and untrendy subject.

In Europe, the newer insights found their way into what for a generation became the accepted handbook on comparative literature in France, Claude Pichois (1925–2004) and André-M. Rousseau's *La littérature comparée* (1967; Comparative Literature), and into Ulrich Weisstein's *Einführung in die vergleichende Literaturwissenschaft* (1968), translated as *Comparative Literature and Literary Theory* (1973) upon Weisstein's assuming the chair of comparative literature at Indiana University. Earlier, François Jost had published *Essais de littérature comparée* (1964), which became the basis for his very informative, fair, and even-handed *Comparative Literature* (1974), published while he was teaching at the University of Illinois. Pierre Brunel and Yves Chevrel edited a massive collection, *Précis de littérature comparée* (Outline of Comparative Literature), in 1989. Meanwhile, there grew up distinct practices of comparative literature in Europe again, struggling to reclaim a "scientific" basis for their endeavors. Such was the case with the reader reception theories of Hans Robert Jauss (1921–1997) and Wolfgang Iser (1926–2007), the empirical studies approach of S.J. Schmidt and Douwe Fokkema (1931–2011), the text linguistics, text grammar, discourse analysis and sociocritical discourse analysis approaches of János Petöfi (1931–2013), Teun A. van Dijk, and Marc Angenot, and the imagology of Hugo Dyserinck (1927–2020) and Joep Leerssen. Most of these efforts were largely to be situated in the field of "General" rather than "Comparative" literature, and in many continental universities the concomitant departments were consequently restyled as of "general and comparative literature" (Lernout 2006). All the while, there also flourished what Jost calls the "Russian school" of comparative literature, with Mikhail Bakhtin (1895–1975), Juri Lotman (1922–1993), but which we perhaps better call the Central and East European school, as it also legitimately includes Dionýsz Ďurišin (1929–1997), in Slovakia, and earlier not only the Moscow but also the Prague school of structuralism – suffice it to repeat here that as of the 1960s ideas and theories originating from Central and Eastern Europe found their way into Western literary theory, and that René Wellek himself served as an early bridge between a particularly Czech theory of literature, especially with regard to "literariness," and American literary theory and criticism.

René Etiemble

Serving as a bridge the other way, or at least being depicted that way in the foreword to the translation of his ground-breaking *Comparaison n'est pas raison: la crise de la littérature comparée* (1963), was the French comparatist René Etiemble (1909–2002). As can be gauged from its title, Etiemble's little booklet was a reaction to Wellek's "The Crisis in Comparative Literature," and Herbert Weisinger and Georges Joyaux consequently opted for the subtitle to Etiemble's original title for their 1966 English-language translation. "Etiemble's book," they said, "must ... be seen as the rainbow of academic peace raised after the storm of scholarly controversy," for

> French and American comparatists, as well as those of other lands, ought now to be able to agree that comparative literature is a series of methods of literary study held together by a common attitude of mind ... it seeks to establish the relations between literatures in as many different ways by as many different methods as can be devised; it limits neither the choice of subject nor the means by which it can be examined, and, indeed, it endeavors constantly to add to its store of objects of inquiry as well as to its arsenal of investigative techniques.
>
> (Etiemble 1966: ix)

In fact, Etiemble became most famous for a provocative speech he gave at the Fourth World Congress of the International Comparative Literature Association held in Fribourg, Switzerland, in 1964. Published in 1966 in the proceedings of that Conference edited by François Jost, Etiemble's "Faut-il réviser la notion de *Weltliteratur*?" was an impassioned plea for extending World Literature to really include all the world's literatures, and not just a few major European literatures.

In the preface to his *Essais de littérature (vraiment) générale* (1975; Essays in [Truly] General Literature), in which his 1964 ICLA speech was included, Etiemble gave an example of how Japanese literature rendered void all theories of literature based on European examples, and he concluded that "any literary theory built only on European phenomena will not fare any better from now on" (Etiemble 1975, 14; toute théorie littéraire qui s'élabore à partir des seuls phénomènes européens ne vaudra pas mieux désormais). To be honest, Albert Guérard, though in a much less provocative way, had already in 1940 lamented that in what commonly passed for the canon of world literature (his concrete example and point of departure had been a list drawn up by Sir John Lubbock in 1885 but he argued that things had not really improved since then) "the East is woefully under-represented" (Guérard 1940: 34). In other words, Guérard said, "the term *World Literature* is an obvious exaggeration," though it might be retained "as the voicing of a distant hope" (Guérard 1940: 34). In the meantime, he suggested, it would be more accurate to call the field "*Western* World Literature: a literature for Westerners, wherever they may be, and for Westernized Orientals" (Guérard 1940: 34).

Re-Thinking Comparative Literature in The United States

Etiemble was a polyglot, with an intimate knowledge of especially Arab and Chinese culture. When in the 1980s multiculturalism spread throughout the United States this ironically led to a yet increased anglophone monolingualism, and much the same thing happened with the parallel onset of postcolonialism, once again favoring English departments over those of comparative literature. World literature seemed to have shrunk to only what happened in English. In 1987, when comparative literature was at an absolute low in the United States, Sarah Lawall organized a National Endowment of the Humanities Summer Institute on World Literature, which resulted in the 1994 volume *Reading World Literature: Theory, History, Practice*. In her introduction Lawall insisted that the title of the volume should also be taken as "reading" the world, and that to this end the geographical, generic, and methodological reach of the essays was as wide as possible. She also stressed the specificity of the teaching, or "reading," of World Literature in the United States as a specifically American pedagogical practice. I will come back to this issue, and to Lawall, in Chapter 4.

A true comeback for world literature, though, and for comparative literature, in the United States only happened with 9/11 and its aftermath, waking Americans up to a wider and multilingual world. As I already mentioned, calls for a renewal of comparative literature often went hand in hand with the revisiting of earlier practitioners, often even the pioneers, of the discipline. In the previous chapter I showed how Edward Said in *Humanism and Democratic Criticism* (2003), returning in his final work to his own earliest inspiration at the beginning of his career, invoked the example of Auerbach, and how Emily Apter in the opening pages to her *The Translation Zone: A New Comparative Literature* (2006b) insisted that the debacle of the Iraq War is at least partially due to a lack of knowledge of languages and foreign cultures on the part of Americans, and how she too calls upon the examples of Auerbach and especially Spitzer in Istanbul in the 1930s. Gayatri Spivak in *Death of a Discipline* (2003) called for a renewal of comparative literature through an alliance with area studies.

The title of David Damrosch's *What is World Literature?* (2003) echoes the call for a "littérature engagée" launched by Jean-Paul Sartre (1905–1980) after World War II in *What is Literature?* (1947). For Damrosch (2003: 4) world literature encompasses "all literary works that circulate beyond their culture of origin, either in translation or in their original language." Furthermore, he sees it as "an elliptical refraction of national literatures," as "writing that gains in translation," and not as "a set canon of texts but a mode of reading: a form of detached engagement with the world beyond our own place and time" (Damrosch 2003: 282). In fact, he clarifies that

> world literature ... is a double refraction, one that can be described through the figure of the ellipse, with the source and host cultures providing the two foci that generate the elliptical space within which a work of literature lives as world literature, connected to both cultures, circumscribed by neither one.
>
> (Damrosch 2003: 283)

He recognizes that this poses the enormous problem of depth versus breadth of knowledge for the comparatist. How can one know enough about either point of the ellipse, or each of the two national cultures, that a work of world literature moves in? *A fortiori*, how can one know enough about all the different national literatures and cultures, or periods, in which works of world literature circulate?

One possible solution, Damrosch suggests, is to work collaboratively, and he points to the ongoing series of histories of literature in European languages produced under the auspices of the International Comparative Literature Association. Discussing a multi-volume project for a world history of literature then being coordinated in Sweden and since brought to fruition with the publication of the four volumes of *Literature: A World History* (2022) for which he himself served as one of the general editors, Damrosch in a 2008 article in *New Literary History* also points to the possibilities offered by new media such as the internet. Amy J. Elias, writing in the same issue of *New Literary History*, wonders what would happen "if the wisdom of crowds were combined with a community of experts in an interactive online format ... enacted by a gated wiki" (Elias 2008: 718). In fact, she suggests, "the database itself might be a new kind of literature or a new kind of historical notation" (Elias 2008: 720). The fullest possible solution to the problem of how to avoid amateurism for the individual "doing" World Literature, Damrosch suggests, is to learn more languages, and he laments that especially in North America a knowledge of foreign languages is not something that speaks for itself. Obviously, this is also where his sympathy for Meltzl and his "principle of polyglottism" finds its origins. Beyond this, though, and if we do not want to forcibly limit our reach to the number of languages we know, we will have to learn how to do with translations, but we should learn how to use them judiciously. Finally, one should understand that the task of the comparatist doing World Literature is not to provide the insider's or specialist's view on either one of the two foci contained in the ellipse in which the work of world literature moves; it is rather to bring out the strangeness of the work with regard to both these foci, thus offering a new and different perspective on the work, and in the process also dis-engaging the reader or student from his unconscious immersion in his own culture.

Franco Moretti in a 2000 article "Conjectures on World Literature" offered his solution to what he called the "problem" (Moretti 2004: 149) of World Literature: how to cope with the mass of information and reading that doing World Literature on the basis of first-hand and close reading of texts presupposes. "Distant reading" (Moretti 2004: 151) is to rely on the work done by specialists in national literatures, genres, authors, and individual works to then draw more general conclusions from this. This is another form of collaboration, suggested this time not so much by the example of the humanities as by that of the social sciences. Moretti consequently also proposes to translate these data into the visual imagery customary to the social sciences and suggested by his book *Graphs, Maps, Trees* (2005). Comparative literature, he feels, should study world literature via comparative morphology (as elaborated by primarily the biologist Ernst Mayr): "take a form, follow it from space to space, and study the reasons for its transformations" (Moretti 2005: 90). And of course, he adds,

> the multiplicity of spaces is the great challenge, and the curse, almost, of comparative literature: but it is also its peculiar strength, because it is only in such a wide, non-homogeneous geography that some fundamental principles of cultural history become manifest.
> (Moretti 2005: 90)

Moretti here almost joins Etiemble in his call for the simultaneous study of the most diverse literatures on earth, and like Etiemble he does so from a decidedly leftist inspiration, albeit that with Moretti this does not so much take the form of ethical engagement as dedication to a certain methodology of what he unabashedly calls his "Marxist formation" (Moretti 2005: 2) under the influence of the Italian philosopher Galvano della Volpe (1895–1968), who advocated a scientific Marxism.

Djelal Kadir in 2004 reacted to Moretti's position with

> comparative literature is neither a subject, nor an object, nor is it a problem ... comparative literature is a practice. ... it is what its practitioners do ... comparative literature takes on its significance by what is done in its name and by how those practices become ascertained, instituted, and managed.
> (Kadir 2004: 1)

Kadir calls for a radical re-thinking of comparative literature, and especially for what he sees as the discipline's possible complicity with hegemonic forms of power, and thus for the firm "worlding" of "world literature." The question then becomes, "who carries out its worlding and why?" (Kadir 2004: 2), because the result will always be the interested outcome of those in a position to assume the subject agency of the verb "to world" ... [and] ... the question for us as comparatists who are party to the resonant discourse on world literature, then, is what our own role might be in this worlding.

(Kadir 2004: 8)

Kadir powerfully revisited the issue in a 2006 article in which he called for a *negotiated comparative literature* that would "negotiate among cultural productions and discursive formations that arrogate to themselves the immunities of incomparability and the impunity of exceptionalism" (Kadir 2006: 133). Such a comparative literature also "would aim to negotiate the relationship between the reigning doxa of any given period and the discipline's apposite accommodation to that paradigm and its cultural *habitus* as *Realkultur*" (Kadir 2006: 135). In other words, such a comparative literature should constantly reflect on its own bases, and particularly on how at any given moment its own methods and pivotal concerns, such as for instance "world literature" right around the turn of the twenty-first century and even more specifically, at least in the USA, after 9/11, correlate to, or perhaps with, the, often unspoken, power assumptions of the cultures and societies in which they operate. Kadir powerfully returns to these issues in his *Memos from the Besieged City: Lifelines for Cultural Sustainability* (2011).

It seems as if by necessity, then, and not from idealism or choice, that Etiemble's 1960s call for including "the world" is at last being heeded. While postcolonialism and multiculturalism signaled the first intimations of such shifts, they largely stuck to intra-lingual "comparisons" between mother-country versus ex-colony literatures and therefore safely remained within the province of monolingualism – whether English or, later, also French – but did not challenge the "Western" linguistic order. Even if Western linguistic orthodoxy can be said to have come under threat from for instance the creolization theories of Edouard Glissant (1928–2011), a writer and theoretician who is not by coincidence from the Caribbean, which constituted the first focus of colonial and later postcolonial interest, this did not necessarily reach beyond national literature departments, or beyond national literature studies or interests. With the 9/11 events, the Afghan and Iraq wars, the capital crises of 2008 and 2011, the COVID-19 pandemic breaking out in 2020, and the economic and political power shift eastward to Asian nations with a different state and economic model rivalling those of the US, the need for other languages imposes itself again. This time, though, it is not European languages that matter but Asian ones. If there is a return, then, of comparative literature in the United States through a renewed interest in world literature this is certainly not the old form of the discipline. Comparative literature in the US now faces East and South rather than "back" toward Europe. In *Comparing the Literatures: Literary Studies in a Global Age* (2020) Damrosch captures the shifts involved. In a 2022 article charting the relationship between world literature and comparative literature Damrosch (2022b: 109) concludes that "always contingent, and often contested, the relations between comparative literature and world literature continue to evolve, increasingly to the mutual benefit of both." At the same time, Gerald Gillespie voiced concern about the direction in which he saw comparative literature moving in the United States. He saw two trends shaping up in the age of globalization. One was to look

> at the spread of influences and impacts from the 'West' upon other regions of the world, but not requiring deep knowledge of non-European cultures. Listening carefully to the complexity of non-Eurocentric expression as created by non-European people is not the prime interest.
> (Gillespie 2013: 364)

The other trend was "the push supposedly to reinvent world literature" and proposals to reorder comparative literature or replace it with "world literature." This second trend in his opinion was likely to "blunt the historical drive of the discipline of comparative literature to encourage a more effective kind of cultural reciprocity and exchange on the global level." And Gillespie in this respect referred to Dorothy Figueira's (2008, 2010) concern that

> the entrenched academic élite in the U.S. and even most of their imitators overseas who act as performative representatives in U.S.-American identity politics are a "Brahmin class" that reinvents ways, for example "world literature," to maintain control in contrast to a more generous and more demanding practice of comparative literature that explores and embraces the contributions of other cultures.
> (Gillespie 2013: 364)

In a spirited exchange of views with Damrosch, Saussy also voices concern with the direction in which world literature is taking comparative literature. He claims that comparative literature in the United States moves in either the direction of world literature or that of interdisciplinarity, and declares himself an advocate of the latter (Damrosch, Saussy, and Edmond 2016).

And Elsewhere

The volume (Tötösy and Mukherjee 2013) that comprises Gillespie's article has the ambition to explore the relationship(s) between comparative literature, world literature, and comparative cultural studies. It does so via a series of essays on theories of the three fields concerned in their interrelation, but it also does so by a set of essays discussing the practice of "comparative literature in world languages." In fact, the section's title is somewhat of a misnomer because next to Gillespie's essay on comparative literature in the US (and not in English, which would seem to have been the more logical choice given the section's heading), it comprises essays on comparative literature in Arabic, Chinese, French, German, Iberian Spanish and Portuguese, Italian,

Indian Languages, Latin American Studies, Russian, Central and Eastern Europe, and African literatures as world literatures. It also features essays demonstrating the "new work" in comparative literature, world literature, and comparative cultural studies the earlier sections of the volume seek to theorize or chronicle. What the volume in any case makes abundantly clear is that there is plenty of work in the three fields going on beyond the United States, and beyond Europe. As far as comparative literature is concerned this is of course not a new phenomenon. Latin American, Indian, Japanese, Korean, and African scholars have long been active in the discipline, both in their national contexts, including national comparative literature associations, and in that of the International Comparative Literature Association. This resulted, for instance, in Tania Franco Carvalhal's edited volume *Comparative Literature Worldwide: Issues and Methods* (1997), published under the auspices of the ICLA. Since the 1990s there has also sprung up a lively comparative literature community in China. As far as methodology is concerned, though, the scholars concerned almost uniformly took their cue from established practice in Europe and the US. This was also still overwhelmingly the case with the contributions by scholars from beyond Europe and the US published in the proceedings of the 1997 ICLA congress in Leiden (D'haen 2000). Only in the last three decades or so have things changed under the influence of postcolonialism, subaltern studies, dependency and decoloniality theory, and the propagation of new nationally oriented initiatives, as for instance in the People's Republic of China where a claim is made about a distinct "Chinese school" of comparative literature. These more recent developments are addressed in chapters to follow.

In Europe, Meanwhile …

What is often overlooked with all the talk about a "French" and an "American" school or hour, and more recently with all the attention going to Casanova's, Moretti's, and Damrosch's refashioning of comparative literature in relation to world literature, Galin Tihanov (2017) points out, is that in the first half of the twentieth century there also has been a lively debate about world literature in Central Europe that has largely passed under the radar in the rest of the world. Tihanov (2017: 469) gives the example of the Russian sinologist and japanologist Nikolai Konrad (1891–1970) who "essayed to understand the evolution of world literature by looking at how paradigmatic aesthetic formations travel around the globe, thus binding it together." Thus, Konrad saw the Renaissance in Europe as only one instance of the more general phenomenon of "a sociocultural renewal through reconnections with tradition." In his view, a movement we might call a Renaissance started in China in the eight century CE, thence travelled to Iran, and only then to Italy, so in an East-West direction. Realism in fiction he sees following the opposite direction: from Europe to the Middle East (albeit in the form of the short story rather than, as in Moretti's version, the novel) and then to East Asia. Another example is the Hungarian Mihály Babits (1883–1941) who, like

Posnett, and unlike Casanova and Moretti who see world literature as tied to European modernity and advancing globalization, saw world literature as an essentially pre-modern phenomenon brought to an end by the rise of Europe's nation states relentlessly promoting their national literatures. "Unabashedly Eurocentric, Babits's version of world literature is indicative of later attempts, notably by Ernst Robert Curtius, to reconstruct the unity of European culture by recasting it as a phenomenon of the past that holds lessons for the future" (Tihanov 2017: 471). For Antal Szerb (1901–1945), another Hungarian,

> the compass of world literature is severely circumscribed: it is the body of writing that has been relevant to Europe (Szerb briefly discusses American literature and the classical literatures of Islam, but not of China and Japan, although they too have had an impact on European literature at a later stage), and that has become truly canonical, that is, significant beyond a period or a single (national) culture.
> (Tihanov 2017: 471)

The work of these two Hungarians, according to Tihanov (2017: 471), "is an antidote – more radical in Babits, more qualified in Szerb – to the overwhelming current consensus, according to which world literature is conditioned by the rise of, and embedded in, globalization and transnationalism."

Tihanov also calls for a qualification of the concept of circulation popularized by Damrosch as a defining characteristic of what makes a work part of world literature or not. He recalls Ďurišin's concept of *zonality* according to which works circulate within specific geographical and cultural contexts in different periods, thus also introducing the issue of temporality. And (2017: 475) he points out that the debate on translation dividing proponents of world literature and of classic comparative literature has its roots in Russian Formalism, specifically in the work of Eikhenbaum, Tynianov, and especially Shlovsky. Tihanov (2017: 475) sees Damrosch as having "proceeded in the steps of the Formalists by foregrounding the legitimacy of working in and through translation" and having "confronted the tension between the singularity and multiplicity of language by concluding that studying literature in the languages of its socialization is more important than studying it in the language of its production, not least because this new priority restricts and undermines the previously sacrosanct monopoly of methodological nationalism in literary studies." Finally, he illustrates how works of literature themselves may question the issue of "world literature" via an analysis of Elias Canetti's novel *Die Blendung* (1930; Auto Da-Fé). Tihanov (2017: 478–479) concludes that

> Realizing that world literature functions as a historically shifting constellation of discourses that is chronotopically constructed, with social and ideological energies bubbling underneath and shaping this construct, is the first step towards denaturalizing it and opening up a space that would allow the possibility of questioning it.

In fact, in what Tihanov (2017: 469) calls the present "dominant Anglo-Saxon discourse of world literature" it is not only discourses on world literature in generally less well-known Central and East European languages such as Hungarian or Slovak, as with the work of Ďurišin, that are almost routinely neglected or that are being rediscovered only belatedly. The same thing goes for work in what undeniably was one of the major scholarly languages of the interbellum: German. Auerbach and Spitzer have made a remarkable comeback in recent American debates on world literature thanks to their being championed by Said, Apter, and others, but the work of their contemporary Curtius is much less well known, or at least less often referred to, although at the time when Auerbach's and Spitzer's fame reached a first zenith, in the late 1940s and throughout the 1950s, his work too, and especially his *Europäische Literatur und Lateinisches Mittelalter* (1948) made a great impression when it appeared in an English translation by Willard Trask as *European Literature and the Latin Middle Ages* in 1953. But there are others that have gone unnoticed. These days, Victor Klemperer (1881–1960) is best known for the diaries he kept throughout his life, and for his observations on the debasement of the German language under Nazism, on which he published a famous book in 1947: *LTI – Lingua Tertii Imperii: Notizbuch eines Philologen* (The Language of the Third Reich). The rest of Klemperer's scholarly output has been completely overlooked in English-language scholarship. During the Nazi years Klemperer, who as a scholar of Jewish descent lost his job as a university lecturer in Dresden, forcibly remained silent, but when after the war he was re-instated and eventually became a professor at the Humboldt University in Berlin in what was then the DDR or East Germany, he resumed publication. His *vor 33 / nach 45. Gesammelte Aufsätze* (1956; Before 33 / After 45: Collected Essays) contains an essay entitled "Weltliteratur und Europäische Literatur" (World Literature and European Literature) that had originally been published in 1929 in the German periodical *Logos*. In this essay Klemperer is concerned with preserving the pre-eminence of European literature and culture in a world that has changed dramatically with the First World War and its outcome – a war in which Klemperer himself had fought valiantly. He is equally keen on safeguarding a central place within European literature for German literature, along with French literature. To this end, he is not averse to harnessing Goethe's "world literature" as well as literary history. What makes this essay especially interesting is that it nicely illustrates why each statement on world literature needs to be understood in its own period and geopolitical context (D'haen 2021b).

At present, comparative literature scholars are once again rethinking Europe's place in the world, both in terms of the continent's ongoing process of unification and its diminished weight in the world. One result of European comparative literature scholars reconsidering their own, their national literature's, and their continent's repositioning in the world has been the creation of a European Society of Comparative Literature/Société européenne de littérature comparée with, as of 2021, its own *CompLit Journal of European*

Literature, Arts and Society. ESCL/SELC is in effect a European Comparative Literature Association created as counterpart not only to other "regional" associations such as the American Comparative Literature Association but also to the International Comparative Literature Association itself. Some of this undoubtedly has to do with the diminished weight of European scholars, even if only in sheer numbers, in the ICLA, an organ that until recently was in effect the almost exclusive hunting ground of Europeans and North Americans. Yet, it is not merely a matter of simply continuing to do in a European get-together what before was done in either national associations or the ICLA. Hinrich C. Seeba, in a 2003 article, rereads Ernst Robert Curtius as a post-World War II exponent of the return of world literature in the service of the unification of Europe. Seeing Curtius as the European counterpart to the "Americans" Wellek, Spitzer, and Auerbach, Seeba claims that:

> The comparative analysis of the themes, motifs and structures of this world literature became the norm for a transatlantic school of literary hermeneutics that regardless of its self-declared ideological disinterest did not only serve to emphasize the immanence of literature: "The Europeanisation of the historical picture," Curtius declares in the introductory chapter of his book, "is now a political requirement, and this not just for Germany." The aim was not only a new "world literature scholarship," but a new transnational world picture, that would make room in the European peace and unification process for the cultural tradition of the West threatened with extinction.
>
> (die vergleichende Analyse der Themen, Motive und Strukturen dieser Weltliteratur wurde zur Norm einer transatlantischen Schule der Werkinterpretation, die trotz ihres erklärten Ideologieverzichts nicht nur die literarische Immanenz im Auge hatte: "Europäisierung des Geschichtsbildes," so erklärt Curtius im einleitenden Kapitel seines Buchs, "ist heute politische Erfordernis, und nicht nur für Deutschland." Sie zielte nicht nur auf eine "Weltliteraturwissenschaft," sondern auf ein neues übernationales Weltbild, das die Kulturtradition des vom Untergang bedrohten Abendlandes in die europäischen Friedens-un Einigungsprozess einbringen sollte.)
>
> (Seeba 2003: 532)

If Seeba's analysis smacks perhaps a little of that "fortress Europe" mentality that the rest of the world, or at least parts of that world, have sometimes laid at the door of the European Union, Lucia Boldrini, who along with others has stood at the cradle of ESCL/SELC, almost concurrently with Seeba's article, in 2006 posited that the task of European comparatists is to engage with

> the necessary redefinition of a European comparative literature (a comparative literary re-thinking of what is Europe and what is European at the beginning of the twenty-first century): our role, the role of our discipline, at

the present moment, is to rethink Europe, its internal and external boundaries, how we have historically selected and defined them and how we do so today … to understand the boundaries we have created and those we have elided, the equivalences we have assumed; how we wish to open Europe up to what constitutes it and what is outside it, opening it to new forces that would be meaningless, today, to call 'other'; and to confront the otherness of the languages that we have traditionally considered to be ours.

(Boldrini 2006: 22)

Helena Buescu (2013) likewise is concerned about the relationship between comparative, European, and world literature.

I myself (2021a: 206) more recently put things somewhat more strongly:

for European literature and European comparative literature studies to matter in the world of the future they have to become "worldly" in the sense Edward Said (1984: 35) gave to that term: to be of the world, in the sense of being about the world in order to become a meaningful part of that world. In order to do so European literature will have to venture outside of its own borders, both those of its national literatures and those of Europe itself, and situate Europe in the world, a world that is no longer European-made but in which Europe plays a minor, perhaps even a subordinate role. To apprehend that situation and apply its lessons to both the future of what may be a European literature and to the interpretation of Europe's literary past is the task of the present, it is our task.

If in what Spivak called the "old comparative literature," the one for which she – I think rather gleefully – tolled the death knell in 2003, European literature equaled world literature, Europe's comparatists now are busy (re-)inventing their own "new" comparative literature, returning to their own "pioneers," re-"worlding," to use that term once again, their own discipline, their own literatures, and "European" literature. And there is nothing wrong with that, of course – after all, this merely repeats Goethe's own first thinking of *Weltliteratur* as a corollary to the changes *his* world was undergoing.

Conclusion

- World literature and comparative literature have developed concurrently, sometimes in intimate and sometimes in distant relationship with one another.
- Comparative literature for the first century of its existence has been mostly a European, and even primarily a French discipline, with especially as of the turn of the twentieth century an emphasis on actual comparisons between works, genres, authors, literatures; in this period world literature was considered a rather utopian horizon for comparative literature instead of a feasible proposition.

- After World War II the United States becomes dominant in comparative literature studies; this brings with it a shift of attention to broader issues having to do with what we now call theory of literature, and also to literatures from beyond Europe.
- Since the turn of the millennium the renewed and intense interest comparative literature in the United States has shown in world literature has propelled the discipline to the forefront of literary studies.
- At the same time scholars from other regions around the world have joined in the debate on comparative and world literature.
- In the meantime, comparative literature in Europe is re-thinking itself in function of Europe's changing role in the world.

4 World Literature as an American Pedagogical Construct

Overview

In the United States world literature has, since the beginning of the twentieth century, been taught at university level. The reasons for this are to be sought in the specific organization of US secondary and higher education. World literature courses were seen as furnishing new university students with some basic knowledge of their European cultural and literary heritage – knowledge it was found these students were lacking, at variance with their European counterparts. Especially in the first half of the century, such courses often took the form of "Great Books" courses. Although courses in world literature and in Great Books originated with comparative literature departments, they quickly, and for reasons connected with the pressure of numbers, migrated to English departments. All reading in world literature classes was in translation. World literature courses remained at an introductory level. They typically relied on massive anthologies, arranged along chronological or thematic lines, and often gathering numerous short works or excerpts from longer works. For all these reasons world literature classes eventually came to be looked down upon by comparative literature departments. This was especially the case after World War II. During the 1980s and the so-called "culture wars" in the United States, academic world literature courses came under heavy attack because of their historical bias toward European literature. This eventually led to major changes in the material included in world literature courses, and in the anthologies serving them. At the end of the twentieth century, and very explicitly after the turn of the millennium, world literature was reclaimed by comparative literature departments, but its teaching, both as to content and method, led to heated debate. The latter focused most explicitly on whether world literature courses inherently served to confirm and project American hegemony around the world, or whether they might serve to relativize it.

Higher Education in The United States

The one question to emerge clearly from Haun Saussy's 2004 American Comparative Literature Association Report published, along with a number

DOI: 10.4324/9781003366713-5

of reflections on and responses to it, as *Comparative Literature in an Age of Globalization* in 2006 was, according to the noted American comparatist and structuralist scholar Jonathan Culler, "how comparative literature should deal with 'world literature'" (Culler 2006: 90). He insisted that the question was not

> whether we should study all the literatures of the world, but about the stakes in the construction by comparative literature departments in the United States of "world literature," as displayed most concretely in world literature courses. (I suspect that this issue is addressed in quite different ways in other countries.)
>
> (Culler 2006: 90)

In fact, until relatively recently what Culler called an "issue" in the United States would not have been an issue at all in the rest of the world – as Sarah Lawall put it succinctly in 1988:

> Courses in world literature are a uniquely American institution. ... world literature exists elsewhere as a scholarly topic or as the subject of ambitious global histories, but it is not an academic institution ... only in the United States do we find a systematic attempt to encompass the "world" (however defined) in literature courses.
>
> (Lawall 1988: 53)

Why this is so has to do with the peculiar position of foreign language and literature teaching in United States academe.

In the previous chapter I mentioned that comparative literature in its orthodox definition and in Europe, or at least in Continental Europe, until well past the middle of the twentieth century largely remained the hunting ground of scholars who almost self-evidently possessed the multiple language skills necessary to its practice, and for whom European literature in its major languages was in practice equivalent to world literature. Not so in the anglophone world. In fact, although the first handbook of comparative literature was written by an Englishman, Hutcheson Macaulay Posnett's 1886 *Comparative Literature*, in England the interest in the discipline has always remained marginal at best. A. Owen Aldridge, in his 1986 *The Reemergence of World Literature*, reported that at the time of his writing there were only three comparative literature departments in all of England (Aldridge 1986: 41).

In the US, as in fact in most of Europe, the actual study and teaching of foreign – that is to say at the time mostly Western European – languages only became a matter of concern in the first half of the nineteenth century. When they did, though, scholars such as Henry Wadsworth Longfellow (1807–1882), Smith Professor of Modern Languages at Harvard, who qualified himself in a variety of European languages and literatures by several years of study abroad, can also be said to have been in practice, if not in theory or by name, comparative or world literature scholars. However, not every American college, or scholar, could afford such luxuries. Moreover, as the nineteenth century wore on and higher education became more generally institutionalized across an increasingly far-flung nation, which toward the end of the nineteenth century also adopted a pattern all of its own when it came to that higher education, there sprang up a peculiarly American division of labor between world literature and comparative literature.

Toward the end of the nineteenth century American higher education gradually adopted an organizational model that differentiated between research-oriented and more teaching-oriented institutions. The former eventually mostly came to call themselves universities while the latter often retained the appellation of a "college." Colleges typically offered, and often continue to offer, especially when they are so-called "liberal arts colleges," a general four-year undergraduate education roughly equivalent to what in Europe usually already (and at least partly) was offered at high school or secondary education level. The term "college" in Europe actually originally applied to institutes of "higher" learning for fifteen- to eighteen-year-olds, or in other words roughly equivalent to the age bracket today covered by "high school" in the USA. In Europe over the course of time some of these colleges grew into universities or university departments; others remained what are now "high schools" in America. To make matters even more confusing, in most Germanic countries, the linguistic equivalent to "high school" – that is to say, *Hochschule* (German), *Hogeschool* (Dutch) or *Höjskol* (Danish) – in the nineteenth century came to stand for what we now call universities. With the creation of Prussian-style research universities in the course of that same nineteenth century the term *Hochschule* etc. then became restricted to what in most Romance countries such as France, and also in England, came to be called *Ecoles Polytechniques* or Polytechnics – that is to say, institutes geared to more practical technical learning, whereas "University" (*Universität, Universiteit, Universitet*) became the proper term for research-oriented institutions.

When the United States also adopted the concept of the German-style research-oriented university at the end of the nineteenth century it did so with a difference. In (most of) Europe, students immediately entered a specialized course of studies leading to a marketable specialization, usually after four years of study. Beyond these four years they could do a doctorate or PhD, but very few actually did so. The US opted for a system whereby the first four years of college or university, as in the British system (even though there it often only involved a three-year course of studies), were given over to a broad course of study leading to a more general BA or BS. Specializations in medicine or law only became available as graduate studies, as did study leading to a doctorate in all other disciplines. These graduate degrees in the US comprised, and continue to comprise, a compulsory component of course work. In Europe specialization in one's discipline was considered complete after the first four years and only a dissertation was further required for a doctorate, no course work. In more recent years, things have gotten more complex in Europe, largely as a result of the so-called Bologna reform, named after the

Italian city in which a number of European ministers of education in 1999 signed a protocol aimed at harmonizing all of Europe's higher education along a three-year BA followed by a one- or two-year MA program.

Why is it necessary to go into such detail on higher education systems in the US and in Europe? Because the widely divergent fortunes of world literature in the US and in Europe are precisely due to this difference in higher education systems. In essence, the US had its BA and BS courses of study do what in Continental Europe (truly or supposedly; I will not get into that) already happened at the level of secondary education, especially at elite schools giving immediate access to university such as gymnasia in Germany, The Netherlands, or the Scandinavian countries, or the *lycées* and *athénées* of the Romance-language countries. The curriculum at such institutions always comprised a certain (and sometimes a fair) amount of foreign language training next to courses in the classics (Greek and Latin), philosophy, history, religious instruction, and the sciences.

In the US, especially away from the Eastern seaboard, such knowledge of languages was not so easy to commonly come by. This was due in part to the widely disparate levels of schooling in the US. It was also due to that country's more democratic (at the time we are speaking of here) attitude toward access to higher education which resulted in a less culturally homogeneous student body than in Europe. Undoubtedly, a working knowledge of foreign languages was for self-evident reasons also felt to be of less importance in the US. Even for the sons of the social and cultural elite, then, foreign languages as a rule were harder to come by in the US than in Europe, and they were not a natural part of one's upbringing, even if Latin and Greek were taught at high school level, and even if some knowledge of French and German, at least passively, may not have been exceptional within certain circles. We might conclude the latter from a brief article entitled "World Literature" that Thomas Wentworth Higginson (1823–1911), an American protestant minister, journalist, author, and fervent abolitionist, who fought for the Union in the Civil War but also advised Emily Dickinson on her poetry in an exchange of letters, in 1890 published in the general circulation periodical *The Century*.

Higginson quoted passages in German and French in the original. As Higginson strongly advocated foreign language teaching in the US, though, he may have been only putting his ideals in practice in this particular article. John Pizer (2006) points out that in the same year in which he published his article on "World Literature" Higginson had also published a biography of Margaret Fuller (1810–1850). Fuller was an American feminist and journalist mainly known for her *Woman in the Nineteenth Century* (1845). She was a member of the Transcendentalist circle around Ralph Waldo Emerson and eventually developed into one of the most influential nineteenth-century US literary critics. In 1839 she was the first to bring out a selection from Eckermann's conversations with Goethe in English translation. Pizer credits Fuller's early acquaintance with Goethe's ideas on world literature for her, at least in America at that time, unusually cosmopolitan outlook on literature.

Higginson, then, obviously took his cue from Fuller, and from Goethe, when he called for the teaching of world literature courses to impart, in Pizer's words, "to students those general values, ideas, and structures he finds at the root of all *belles lettres*" (Pizer 2006: 88). Higginson saw foreign language and literature courses at undergraduate level as a necessary first step in this direction.

However, the specific situation the USA found itself in at the turn of the twentieth century did not favor the realization of Higginson's ideals. The US between the middle of the nineteenth century and World War I went through an unprecedented wave of mass immigration. Most of these newcomers were of very different stock than the until then dominant British and West-Europeans. Their linguistic and cultural diversity only emphasized the role of English as a necessary agent of acculturation and cohesion in the country. But knowledge of the language was not enough. The need was also felt to actively promote, to quote Pizer again, "general values, ideas, and structures," yet not so much those of *belles lettres*, as Higginson had wished, but rather those that lay at the root of American culture as perceived by those who considered themselves its guardians. At the university level, this led to courses that introduced the students to "their" cultural heritage. This cultural heritage was thought to be embodied by a number of "Great Books" from the past. These ranged from philosophy over literature to the sciences. Given that these courses were seen as primarily introductory, and hence geared to incoming university students in their first or second year of studies (in American parlance: freshmen or sophomores), and given prevailing language conditions in the US, such courses were inevitably given in English, and with all reading material in English translation. What must have been one of the first, if not the very first, such courses were offered in 1901 at Berkeley (Graff 1987: 134). Still, it was only after World War I that Great Books courses became widespread in US higher education.

Richard Moulton

It is against this background that Richard Green Moulton in 1911 published *World Literature and Its Place in General Culture*, the first book-length publication on the subject in English. Moulton was an Englishman who had become first Professor of English and later, as of 1901, Professor of Literary Theory and Interpretation, and Head of the Department of General Literature at the University of Chicago. Before his removal to the USA, though, he had been active in university extension lecturing in England. In his book on world literature, he systematized what he had been doing for his working-class audience in England also for his US audience, thinking that what was needed in both cases was an introduction to the literatures of the world – read: Europe – as a shorthand for instilling in them a sense of their own nation's culture at the pinnacle of Western Civilization. In a sense this was complementary on the home front to what the British had been doing in India over the nineteenth century (Viswanathan 1989). There, following the historian and politician Thomas Babington Macaulay's advice in his 1835 *Minute on Indian Education*, English was introduced as the language of instruction as of the sixth year of schooling. Moreover, the teaching of British literature at both high school and university levels was to instill in the colonial subjects (or at least the more intelligent and more ambitious, but therefore also the potentially more dangerous ones) the right civic – read British – virtues and attitudes. For Macaulay this was entirely to the benefit of the Indians themselves, as the English language and English literature were more useful, and therefore more valuable, to them than their own languages and literatures. As Macaulay famously put it in his *Minute*,

> I am quite ready to take the Oriental learning at the valuation of the Orientalists themselves. I have never found one among them who could deny that a single shelf of a good European library was worth the whole native literature of India and Arabia.
>
> (Macaulay 2011)

In fact, British literature was taught as a university subject in India before it was taught in Britain itself, where Greek and Latin continued to dominate the humanities curriculum. As of the mid-nineteenth century British literature, through the kind of extension lecturing in which Moulton was involved, was also taught at so-called Working Men's Institutes in Britain itself, partially as a means to instill also in the rising working class the right virtues and attitudes, and this according to the ideas of Matthew Arnold, inspector of schools, poet, and social critic. After World War I, as a corollary to growing democratization, the study of English, and to a lesser extent of modern languages and literatures, gradually came to take the place of the classics for a growing student body increasingly recruited from (relatively) lower social levels in England. During and immediately after World War I the American (later English) modernist poet T.S. Eliot engaged in extension lecturing in London. The emphasis on Arnold's 1869 injunction in *Culture and Anarchy* to make "the best that has been thought and known current in the world everywhere" (Arnold 1978: 70) would eventually lead the English critic F.R. Leavis (1895–1978) to effectively cast a selection of four English-language writers (Jane Austen, George Eliot, Henry James, and Joseph Conrad; Leavis later added Charles Dickens) as something akin to "world literature" in his *The Great Tradition* (1948).

Moulton's book aimed at the same audience as the "Great Books" courses, and so he too had to rely on translations rather than on works in the original. Moreover, though Moulton bravely began the title of his book with "World Literature," its continuation "and Its Place in General Culture" indicates that what Moulton had in mind was in fact not too far removed from what "Great Books" courses had already started doing in the US by then. In his "Preface" he says that his book "presents a conception of World Literature, not in the sense of the sum total of particular literatures, but as a unity, the literary field seen in perspective from the point of view of the English-speaking peoples" (Moulton 1921: v). In the main body of his book he follows up on this with the statement that world literature will be "a different thing to the Englishman and the Japanese" (Moulton 1921: 7) and therefore, as an Englishman, he will "trace the Literary Pedigree of the English-speaking peoples" (Moulton 1921: 9). Or, as he puts it later on, "whatever of universal literature [by which he means all literature from all the world], coming from whatever source, has been appropriated by our English civilization, and made a part of our English culture, that is to us World Literature" (Moulton 1921: 297). Though Moulton's insistence that his choice of material is based on "intrinsic literary interest" (Moulton 1921: 8) or "intrinsic literary value" (Moulton 1921: 9) indicates that he wanted to set his enterprise apart from the Great Books courses in which the emphasis was on ideas rather, his claim that world literature is "nothing less than the Autobiography of Civilization" (Moulton 1921: 56) reveals that his "World Literature" too amounts to a form of "cultural heritage" for the use of "English-speaking peoples."

Building on Matthew Arnold's ideas about the Hellenic and Hebraic origins of European civilization as well as on then current theories about the linguistic and racial relationships of Europeans, and especially the English, to the rest of the world's peoples, Moulton divides the world's literatures into a number of categories dependent on their relevance to the literatures of the "English-speaking peoples" at the beginning of the twentieth century. In a general introduction Moulton first singles out the two "civilizations" that he saw as directly feeding into the culture of the English-speaking peoples via their Hebraic and Hellenic components: the "Semitic" and "Aryan" civilizations. Next, he lists as "extraneous" a number of civilizations, such as the Chinese and Japanese, that he deems not to have had any influence on English literary culture.

In the main part of his book Moulton first distinguishes a number of works that are so important that he dubs them "Literary Bibles" and to each of which he devotes a full chapter. The first of these, not surprisingly, is the Holy Bible itself, followed by "Classical Epic and Tragedy," "Shakespeare," "Dante and Milton: The Epics of Medieval Catholicism and Renaissance Protestantism," and "Versions of the Story of Faust" – the latter focusing on works by the Englishman Christopher Marlowe, The Spaniard Pedro Calderón de la Barca, and especially Goethe. One chapter deals with what Moulton calls "Collateral World Literature," by which he means works from the Semitic and Aryan civilizations that have contributed elements toward European, and particularly English, literature. Here Moulton discusses the Quran, the *Arabian Nights*, the Persian poet Omar Khayyam, James McPherson's (pseudo) Celtic *Ossian*, the Norse epic of Sigurd, and the Finnish *Kalevala*.

Next, Moulton has a chapter on "the comparative reading that instinctively draws together similarities and contrasts from different parts of the literary field" (Moulton 1921: 408). One such instance of comparative reading across time and space he adduces is that grouping together the *Bacchanals* of the ancient Greek playwright Euripides, *Ecclesiastes* from the Bible, Omar Khayyam's *Rubaiyat*, the second book of *The Fairie Queene* of the sixteenth-century English poet Edmund Spenser, and "The Vision of Sin" by the nineteenth-century English poet Alfred Tennyson on the grounds that they all deal with "moral chaos" (Moulton 1921: 374).

Then there is a chapter on "The Literature of Personality: Essays and Lyrics," and one on "Strategic Points in Literature," defined as "points in the literary field which are especially valuable for their bearing on the survey of the field of literature as a whole" (Moulton 1921: 408). Basically, he here includes a number of authors and works that he considers not quite important enough to figure into any one of his "Literary Bibles," but too important to pass over without mention: the ancient classical writers Plato, Lucretius, and Aristophanes, the medieval *The Romance of the Rose, Reynard the Fox*, and *Everyman*, Thomas Malory's *Morte d'Arthur* and Geoffrey Chaucer's *Canterbury Tales*, the medieval French *Chronicles* of Froissart, Miguel de Cervantes' *Don Quixote*; the Renaissance philosophers Desiderius Erasmus and Francis Bacon, the early Modern French writer François Rabelais, the seventeenth-century French playwrights Molière (Jean-Baptiste Poquelin) and Jean Baptiste Racine, the nineteenth-century historical novelists Walter Scott and Henryk Sienkiewicz, the nineteenth-century French writers Honoré de Balzac and Victor Hugo, and the nineteenth-century English romantics Byron and William Wordsworth.

In his next to last chapter Moulton draws a parallel between national literature and world literature in the sense that if national literature is, as "is generally recognized" (Moulton 1921: 429), a reflection of the national history of the country in question, so "World Literature is autobiography in the sense that it is the presentation of civilization in its best products, its most significant moments emphasized as they appear illuminated with the highest literary setting" (Moulton 1921: 437). Precisely because it is the "Autobiography of Civilization," *their* civilization, Moulton argues in his "Conclusion," world literature should be part of American students' general education, "not to be considered as an option that may be taken late, but as an essential in the foundation stage of education, part of the common body of knowledge which makes the election of optional studies intelligent" (Moulton 1921: 447).

Albert Guérard, in his 1940 *Preface to World Literature*, resurrects Moulton's "Literary Bibles." However, instead of making Goethe's *Faust* one of several works by various authors on the same figure, he opts for a generous selection from the principal works of Goethe as his Fifth Bible. Two more Bibles are meant to offset one another: that of *Romance*, from the medieval French writer Chrétien de Troyes to the American poet Edwin Arlington Robinson, and of *Ironic Nationalism*, from the *Romance of the Rose* and Chaucer over Cervantes to the twentieth-century English novelist Aldous Huxley's *Eyeless in Gaza*. Finally, there is what Guérard calls the *Bible of Social Pity*, from the early writings of Victor Hugo over Charles Dickens, the great Russians Fyodor Dostoevsky and Leo Tolstoy, and the French naturalist Emile Zola and his German counterpart Gerhart Hauptmann to the American John Steinbeck's *Grapes of Wrath*.

The Great Books

Moulton's recommendation to make world literature an integral part of the early stages of American university education found ready application, but his valiant effort to imbue such foundational courses with an almost exclusively literary content would have to wait a while yet. For the time being it was the more orthodox Great Books courses that carried the day, and not world literature courses. In the aftermath of World War I, the concern to introduce students to the Western heritage outweighed that of turning them into critical readers of that heritage. With large numbers of soldiers returning from Europe and being entitled to educational benefits, along with an increased ambition for upward mobility through advanced education on the part of the fast-growing middle class, American higher education became increasingly democratized. Most of these aspiring undergraduates had no foreign language skills or training whatsoever, nor did they have any training in the classics. John Erskine (1879–1951), Professor of English at Columbia University, during World War I had taught the equivalent of Moulton's extension lecture courses to US soldiers, and on his return to Columbia he proposed, and in 1920 got accepted, the introduction of a General Honors Course teaching the classics in English translation to all undergraduates. Eventually this developed into a two-course two-semester core curriculum. One course, called "Contemporary Civilization," concentrated on philosophical works. The other course became the famous "Humanities A" course, and concentrated on literary masterpieces. Comparable courses were instituted at the University of Chicago in 1931 and at Stanford in 1935, and from then on in countless US universities. As Herbert Lindenberger notes, these courses at least initially often went by the title of "Western Civilization" (Lindenberger 1990: s.l.).

Erskine's Great Books course (though he himself never called it by that name, nor did or does Columbia University), and others like it, were tailored to set students on a minimal common cultural footing firmly anchored in the Western tradition. Some of Columbia's most famous faculty members, such as for instance Lionel Trilling (1905–1975), for many years taught "Humanities A." It continues today under the title "Literature Humanities" and comprises perennial classics – that is to say, works that have never left its list of required reading – such as Homer's *The Iliad*, Aeschylus' *Oresteia*, Sophocles' *Oedipus the King*, Dante's *The Inferno*, and William Shakespeare's *King Lear*, while works by, for instance, Saint Augustine, Montaigne, and Virginia Woolf, as well as the Bible, have rotated on and off. The course continues as part of Columbia University's Core Curriculum, a mandatory set of courses for all undergraduates.

That the aims of "Lit Hum," as the course is commonly called, continue to reflect some of the ideas underlying the original Great Books courses appears from the description of the course on Columbia's website as "designed to enhance students' understanding of main lines of literary and philosophical development that have shaped western thought for nearly three millennia."

Lest we should think that in the third millennium things have not moved on from the early twentieth century, however, the next sentence hastens to add that "much more than a survey of great books, Lit Hum encourages students to become critical readers of the literary past we have inherited."[1] In the 2020s, "Lit Hum" continues unchanged as a Core Curriculum course at Columbia.[2]

That Lit Hum left a great impression on Columbia students can be gauged from David Denby's *Great Books: My Adventures with Homer, Rousseau, Woolf, and Other Indestructible Writers of the Western World* (1996). Denby re-attended the Lit Hum course at Columbia in 1991, thirty years after he had first attended it as a freshman. He had become enraged by how politicized the debate on literary canons had become during the so-called "culture wars" raging in the United States during the 1980s and 1990s. Therefore, he decided to go and ascertain for himself what this debate was all about in a course that centered, precisely and deliberately so, upon the Western canon.

World Literature Courses

Courses that went by the label "World Literature," and that more closely resembled what Moulton had in mind at least as far as their content was concerned, were pioneered in the late 1920s by Philo Buck, Professor of Comparative Literature at the University of Wisconsin. One difference between world literature and Great Books courses was that the former concentrated on works of the imagination or literature proper while the latter concentrated on the ideas contained in a number of works of varied provenance. A further difference, Pizer (2006: 101) contends, is that a Great Books course concentrates on just a few major and unabridged works while a world literature course typically is built around an anthology that comprises a multitude of shorter works and passages from longer works in an effort to achieve some representative historical and geographical coverage. Surely this is what we would deduce from the *Anthology of World Literature*, based on his class teachings, that Buck brought out in 1934 and that Lawall (Lawall 2004: 59–60) labels "the first single-volume academic anthology to attempt global scope." Buck, as Moulton advocated, focused on the European tradition, although he also included some Indian, Persian, and Arabic materials while, again like Moulton, excluding works from China and Japan on the grounds that their "vital influence upon the European tradition has been negligible or very recent" (Buck 1934: v). In later editions he did add some Chinese works. However, and at variance with Moulton's recommendations, Buck included no English-language works in his anthology.

As we have seen in the first chapter, Buck's not including English-language works in his *Anthology of World Literature* was not unprecedented. It was not unusual to see world literature as complementary to one's national literature, and Buck too may have been seeing his enterprise, and the course in world literature he gave and which his anthology served, as complementary to courses in English and American literature. What may also have played a role is the traditional "turf war" between university departments. This certainly came to the fore after World War II, when world literature courses rapidly became the province of English departments rather than, as with Buck and in the initial stages of their introduction, comparative literature departments. There are a number of reasons for this, but prime among these is the further round of democratization of American higher education brought about by World War II. Indicative in this regard may be the brief remark by the West Virginia educator and superintendent of schools Oliver Shurtleff who in 1947 was quoted as having said to the *West Virginia School Journal* that

> if I were to be asked to add a subject to the curriculum of high schools and colleges, I should add World Literature ... At this very time in the history of our world, this addition, it seems to me, would be quite pertinent.
> (Shurtleff 1947: 5)

Next to answering to a genuinely felt need to open more "windows on the world," to use David Damrosch's phrase (Damrosch 2003: 15), now that the US – because of World War II – had not only come out of the relative isolation into which it had withdrawn in the period between the two world wars but also actually found itself to be the dominant world power, the rapid popularization of world literature courses focusing on works of the imagination rather than on "ideas" as in Great Books courses was probably not unrelated to the parallel rise to dominance of the so-called "New Criticism" in the US. This critical and educational movement, primarily centered in English departments, focused on the intrinsic qualities of the literary work as artifact and structure rather than on the historical and biographical details of its creation. When in many places world literature courses became compulsory for undergraduates, the traditionally small comparative literature departments that before and immediately after World War II had started offering such courses simply could not cope with the rapidly swelling student numbers. Moreover, many comparative literature professors were reluctant to teach what they considered as degraded versions of what they really should be teaching. Indeed, while Higginson, Moulton, Erskine, and Buck were diligently plugging away at promoting Great Books and world literature courses in English translation and for undergraduates, "real" departments of comparative literature swore by courses in which literature was read in the original. In practice, this meant that they limited themselves to graduate teaching, as American students in general needed their undergraduate years to work up the necessary language skills to even be considered for enrolment in a comparative literature program or department. The combined result was that when the crunch came, world literature, being taught as it was in English and via translations into English, rapidly migrated to the biggest language department around, which invariably happened to be the English department anyway.

The New Critical paradigm, moreover, did away with – at least in theory and often in practice – any real need to have an intimate knowledge of a work's historical or linguistic background, or its author's biography. Given the supposedly low degree of specialization required to teach these courses, then, they often were assigned to junior faculty members. As these were almost invariably trained in English literature themselves, world literature courses rapidly came to be seen as at least partially a preparation for the study of English and even American literature, providing students with a minimal knowledge of Western literature as a prelude to their engagement with what really mattered (Brown 1953). In fact, Sarah Lawall, who served as general editor of the mid-1990s and early 2000s editions of the *Norton Anthology of World Literature*, said that when in the mid-1970 she first became involved with what was then still called the *Norton Anthology of World Masterpieces* she had never seen the anthology before, because "teaching French, Francophone, and comparative literature" she functioned in a "curricular framework that did not include world literature – the course was 'owned' by the English department" (Lawall 2004: 69).

The Crisis of World Literature

This state of affairs led to a major standoff between world literature and comparative literature at the end of the 1950s. At a conference on "The Teaching of World Literature" held at Philo Buck's University of Wisconsin in April 1959, Werner Friederich, Professor of Comparative Literature at the University of North Carolina in Chapel Hill, humorously but also scathingly rehearsed all that was wrong with world literature courses from the point of view of "legitimate" comparative literature departments. They promised more than they could deliver he maintained. In a famous diatribe he proclaimed that "sometimes, in flippant moments, I think we should call our programs NATO Literatures – yet even that would be extravagant, for we do not usually deal with more than one fourth of the 15 NATO-nations" (Friederich 1960: 14–15). They were taught in translation, laying them open to the accusation of amateurism. They used anthologies that because of the brevity and multiplicity of passages included confused the students. Finally, they were mostly taught by younger faculty members who were not really up to a job that would have been daunting even to experienced professors skilled in various foreign languages next to English (Friederich 1960: 14–18). In short, Friederich argued, such courses threatened the integrity of the discipline of comparative literature. Therefore, he advocated that world literature courses taught to freshmen and sophomores really be Great Books courses focusing on only a few major works or authors: "the true giants in literature – Aeschylus, Virgil, perhaps Petrarch, Molière, Schiller, Dostoevsky," and that they be used to illustrate "the basic meaning of Antiquity, Middle Ages, Renaissance, Classicism, Romanticism, Realism, Naturalism" (Friederich 1960: 17.) In another version of the same article/speech Friederich replaced Petrarch with Chaucer (Friederich 1970: 31). These courses should then be followed by "Foreign Literature in English Translation" courses covering a given foreign literature or a cluster of such literatures, and, given by specialists in the literatures concerned, they should be resolutely restricted to the undergraduate level.

Such a set of courses, Friedrich felt, would provide "a truly liberal education" for "a businessman, a physician, or a professor of English" (Friederich 1970: 35). If given well, Friederich hoped, such courses might even lead talented undergraduates to pursue graduate study in comparative literature proper, reading and studying literary works not in translation but in the original. At that graduate level, though, he also pleaded for extending the reach of comparative literature beyond its traditional European domain to embrace the cultures of Latin America, Asia, Africa, and Oceania. With its mixture of races and cultures, its history of migration, its geographical location, and its world leadership in matters military, economic, and political, Friederich concluded, the US was uniquely well placed to take the lead in matters cultural too, and part of such leadership would be a greater opening to the world beyond Europe and the US itself. Yet, just a few years earlier, in 1954, Friederich, along with David Henry Malone, had published an *Outline of Comparative Literature: from Dante Alighieri to Eugene O'Neill* that stayed well within the framework of the world literature courses he so critically scrutinized in 1959. Offering "a new panorama of Western literature" Friederich and Malone aimed to present "the constant flow of forms and ideas across national borders and the dissemination of cultural values among neighboring countries" as showing "the essential oneness of Western culture and the stultifying shortsightedness of political or literary nationalism" (Friederich and Malone 1954: Preface).

The Wisconsin conference where Friederich spoke followed closely after the ICLA conference at his own University of North Carolina in Chapel Hill where René Wellek had denounced "the French School" for "The Crisis in Comparative Literature." Friederich's rather triumphant statements with regard to the future of comparative literature in American academe reflected the already widely accepted belief, at least in the US, that "America had more than caught up with the leadership of France in the field of Comparative Literature" (Friederich 1960: 18). Given the strict separation between undergraduate and graduate teaching Friederich advocated, and given also that world literature courses largely remained under the wings of English literature departments, it took a while before the new wind that was felt to blow in US comparative literature departments also was felt in world literature teaching. Moreover, as sketched in the previous chapter, the turn to theory comparative literature departments took in the years after the Chapel Hill conference led them away from the concerns with the larger world as expressed by Friederich.

Ironically, it was a French scholar, René Etiemble, who most vocally took up these concerns (Etiemble 1966). Even more ironically given Wellek's denunciation of the French school of comparative literature, the theory US comparative literature departments turned to was largely French again. The first to arrive was phenomenological criticism as practiced by the so-called Geneva School (Lawall 1968). Main adherents in the US were the early J.

Hillis-Miller (1928–2021) along with the Belgian Georges Poulet (1902–1991), who taught at Johns Hopkins in the 1950s. Shortly thereafter Paul de Man (1919–1983; another Belgian) was instrumental in disseminating the thought of Jacques Derrida (1930–2004) in the US. In the 1970s de Man was one – many would say *the* – leader of the so-called Yale school of deconstructionism. As of the 1970s, English departments also entered the age of theory, with the fervor of various waves of structuralism, poststructuralism, deconstructionism, new historicism, multiculturalism, and postcolonialism rapidly succeeding each other. Most of this, though, primarily applied to graduate study and research. World literature meanwhile kept quietly bubbling along as an undergraduate course.

Anthologizing World Literature: The "Norton"

In fact, the proliferation of world literature courses in the US led to the creation, in the mid-1950s, of a working instrument tailored to the new conditions – that is to say, a major anthology that combined Buck's focus on foreign literature with Moulton and Guérard's inclusion of English-language literatures in their surveys. Norton's *World Masterpieces: Literature of Western Culture* appeared in 1956. In line with the by then well-established practice for world literature courses to be taught within an English department, the Norton's general editor was a specialist in English literature: Maynard Mack (1909–2001). Mack had a particular interest in Early Modern to Augustan literature, and strongly promoted New Criticism in the English department he led for many years at Yale University. The other editors were drawn from English again, as well as from classics, Italian, French, Slavic, and comparative literature. Many of them taught at Yale, among them René Wellek. Through its third edition, in 1973, the anthology went under the same title as the original edition. The fourth edition carried the title *The Norton Anthology of World Masterpieces: Literature from Western Culture*. The fifth and sixth editions, from 1985 and 1992 respectively, dropped the subtitle. An *Expanded Edition* appeared in 1995. In 2002 this expanded edition turned into *The Norton Anthology of World Literature*, Second Edition. In the meantime, there was also a seventh edition of *The Norton Anthology of World Masterpieces*, this time subtitled *The Western Tradition*.

The name changes the Norton underwent are of course not arbitrary or coincidental. Most immediately, they reflected the changes affecting the study of English and American literature as of the late eighties. This is the moment that multiculturalism, in American studies, and postcolonialism, in English studies, took over from "pure" theory as the leading paradigms. Predictably, this led to loud calls for a much-expanded canon (hence the 1995 Norton *Expanded Edition*) comprising generous selections of works by minority writers in the case of American literature, and by writers from the former British colonies for English literature. The ensuing so-called "Culture Wars" also led to the then current core curriculum undergraduate courses in Western literature being increasingly challenged as to their continuing relevance for a rapidly changing and increasingly diverse American student body, as well as for an equally rapidly changing world. Most famous in this respect became the struggle in 1988 over Stanford's Western Culture course, the then descendant – with a brief hiatus in the late 1960s and 1970s – of the 1935 Western Civilization course. Lindenberger (1990: s.l.) lists this course as comprising:

> Hebrew Bible, Genesis; Homer, major selections from *Iliad* or *Odyssey* or both; At least one Greek tragedy; Plato, *Republic*, major portions of Books I–VII; New Testament, selections including a gospel; Augustine, *Confessions*, I-IX; Dante, *Inferno*; More, *Utopia*; Machiavelli, *The Prince*; Luther, *Christian Liberty*; Galileo, *The Starry Messenger* and *The Assayer*; Voltaire, *Candide*; Marx and Engels, *The Communist Manifesto*; Darwin, selections; Freud, *Outline of Psychoanalysis* and *Civilization and Its Discontents*.

Inclusion of the *Aeneid*, selections from Thomas Aquinas, Hobbes's *Leviathan*, Goethe's *Faust* and *Werther*, and a nineteenth-century novel to be chosen by the instructor, were "strongly recommended." These works formed the common core to a number of tracks that allowed considerable variety in reading and contextualization. Still, after complaints from a number of minority groups on campus and after long debates in the University Senate, the Western Culture core course was replaced with a new one called "Cultures, Ideas, Values" that did not require a fixed set of common texts but the contents of which would be democratically decided upon from year to year by the faculty members teaching the course that particular year. It was stipulated, though, that each track around this core course must "include the study of works by women, minorities, and persons of color" and must study "at least one of the non-European cultures that have become components of our diverse American society" (Lindenberger 1990: s.l.). The changes to the Stanford program made the national headlines, and became a battleground between political and cultural conservatives, such as Allen Bloom and the then Secretary of State for Education William Bennett, and more generally left-wing progressives. One party lamented that Stanford was selling out "American" culture by debasing and diluting its cultural heritage. The other party upheld that the "old" canon had been restrictively and unjustifiably male, white, and Eurocentric.

While earlier editions of the Norton anthology had also already responded to claims, for example from feminist quarters, for wider representation, it is clear that the changes in the name and contents of the Norton anthology as of the fourth edition were increasingly determined by the claims of multiculturalism and postcolonialism. The *Expanded Edition* of 1995 basically added an equal number of pages of non-Western texts to the earlier exclusively Western edition. The Norton until the *Expanded Edition* indeed was (almost) exclusively Western. That is also why from the late 1980s and early 1990s on it came under attack by proponents of change. It was also the most successful anthology of its kind until then, to the point even of seeming to define the field in its "old" dispensation, and that is undoubtedly why it also became the foil against which all newcomers in what was suddenly perceived as a different market reacted. As Sarah Lawall, who had joined the Norton editorial team as of the 1979 fourth edition, and who became the general editor with the 1999 seventh edition, felt obliged to remark in 2004, when at least three major competitors had appeared on the market:

> many critics (especially those connected with new anthologies) seem to believe that the world literature anthology began in 1956 with the first edition of *The Norton Anthology of World Masterpieces* and that the future consists solely in reacting to the presumed origin.
> (Lawall 2004: 63)

Not only was there a well-established and flourishing tradition of earlier world literature anthologies, including Buck's mentioned earlier, she argued, but by the middle of the twentieth century there had also sprung up a "consistent set of beliefs and practices that would shape – and continue to shape – anthologies of 'world literature'" (Lawall 2004: 62). These included an almost exclusive concern for a literary work's cultural status but "little or no concern for analysis or pedagogy," an orientation toward "the generic-American-English-speaking student," an "educational mission to give this generic student a perspective on human evolution from barbarism to civilization, with special emphasis on Western tradition as the foundation of twentieth-century America," and an unspoken understanding that "the writers are male and, for the most part, European" (Lawall 2004: 62).

The 1956 Norton *World Masterpieces: Literature of Western Culture*, Lawall insisted, broke with these assumptions in the following ways:

> The encouragement of critical thinking and literary analysis instead of prescribed outlines of cultural history; a focus on imaginative literature instead of the transmission of Great Books; a preference for complete works instead of myriad extracts; and – aimed specifically at classroom teaching – an unprecedented amount of information about the texts: analyses of works, textual annotations, and individual bibliographies.
> (Lawall 2004: 63–64)

In fact, because it went so blatantly against then current practice it proved very difficult to find a publisher for what eventually became "the Norton." Prentice-Hall and Harcourt Brace, two of the biggest players in the American textbook market, turned the project down after initially having declared an interest in it. Finally, the anthology was taken on board by W.W. Norton and Co., a smaller publisher willing to take a risk. In other words, Lawall stressed, the Norton anthology was innovative in its day, and continued to be so, for instance including already in its 1985 edition a section "Contemporary

Explorations" that made room for non-Western voices. Not by coincidence she claimed some merit for the introduction of this particular innovation herself. Although not with so many words again, it is evident that she claimed the same kind of merit for the transformation of the *Expanded Edition*, the last to appear under the general editorship of Maynard Mack, and which she called unwieldy for a number of reasons, into the dual *Norton Anthology of World Masterpieces: The Western Tradition* and *Norton Anthology of World Literature* from the moment she took over as general editor in the late 1990s. Undoubtedly, although again she never explicitly alluded to it as such, Lawall, who was herself Professor of Comparative Literature at the University of Massachusetts, Amherst, also saw herself assuming the general editorship leading to the modernization of the Norton as reclaiming the territory of world literature from the English departments where for the longest time it had lingered. For all these reasons she was obviously not very happy with what she called

> a tendency to mystify 'the Norton' that is ultimately not very useful when examining theoretical or practical issues of anthology making or the persistent shaping power of certain historical and analytical habits; moreover, such mystification obscures the way that many of these habits persevere – if in more sophisticated form – today.
> (Lawall 2004: 63)

The Norton's Competitors

No doubt, one of the critics connected with a more recent anthology that Lawall had in mind is David Damrosch. Damrosch served as contributing editor to the 1994 *HarperCollins World Reader* under the general editorship of Mary Ann Caws and Christopher Prendergast. He also served as consultant on the Mesoamerican additions to the Norton *Expanded Edition* of 1995. Most importantly, he served as general editor himself for the six-volume *Longman Anthology of World Literature* published in 2004 (second edition 2008–2009). In a 2000 article, reprinted in Di Leo 2004, Damrosch had severely criticized both the Norton *Expanded Edition* and the *HarperCollins World Reader*. The *HarperCollins World Reader*, he found, "proceeds essentially by exploding the 'old world,' making room for a vivid gallery of snapshots of the 'whole world,' yet the result is fragmentary, inconsistent, a disorienting series of abrupt leaps from one brief selection to another" (Damrosch 2004: 41). The Norton *Expanded Edition* he found lacking in integration between the "old" and "whole" world parts. Drawing a line from some early twentieth-century anthologists to the HarperCollins and Norton anthologies he claimed world literature to have oscillated between extremes of assimilation and discontinuity: "either the earlier and distant works we read are really *just like us*, or they are unutterably foreign, curiosities whose foreignness finally tells us nothing and can only reinforce our sense of separate identity" (Damrosch 2004: 44). Instead of acquiescing in having to choose between what he calls "a self-centered construction of the world" and "a highly decentered one," Damrosch proposes "an *elliptical* approach" in which contemporary America will

> logically be one focus of the ellipse for the contemporary American reader, but the literature of other times and eras always presents us with another focus as well, and we read in the field of force generated between these two foci.
>
> (Damrosch 2004: 44)

The ideas he presented in this article, and which he had already defended in earlier publications, likewise provided the groundwork for his 2003 *What is World Literature?*

Whereas the *Norton Anthology of World Literature*, like its other Norton predecessors, is strictly chronological in organization, both the *Bedford Anthology of World Literature*, edited by Paul Davis, Gary Harrison, David M. Johnson, and John F. Crawford (2003), and the *Longman Anthology of World Literature*, while still adhering to chronology for their overall organizing principle, also introduce thematic units that cut across chronology. In the Longman anthology, for instance, a number of selections feature "resonances." The ancient Greek Homer's *Odyssey* is thus followed by the early twentieth-century Austrian-Czech-Jewish Franz Kafka's story "The Silence of the Sirens," the mid-twentieth-century Greek poet George Seferis's poem "Upon a Foreign Verse," and selections from Derek Walcott's late twentieth-century Caribbean epic *Omeros*. All of these, of course, refer to (events in) the *Odyssey*. In this particular case the three works resonating with the "original" are all themselves works of the imagination, from the same period (the twentieth century), and although written in three different languages (German, Greek, English, though the latter with the input of French Caribbean "créole"), they also come from what we could roughly define as "the West," although again of course this could be contested with regard to Wallcott and his *Omeros*, which is an icon of postcolonialism and as such can be seen as dissenting from the Western tradition. In other instances, though, the resonances can be critical reactions to an original, can come from different periods, and from both West and "non-West." This is the case with (a passage from) Kuntaka's "The Life-force of Literary Beauty," Goethe's "On *Shakuntala*," and (a passage from) Rabindranath Tagore's "Shakuntala: Its Inner Meaning," all of them relating to the original play *Shakuntala* by the classical Sanskrit writer Kalidasa. Next to these "resonances" the Longman also features "perspectives," units that gather material on a specific topic. An example is the "perspective" on "Tyranny and Democracy" with texts by the ancient Greeks Solon, Thucydides, and Plato. Both the Norton and the Longman carefully list already in the table of contents in which language a text was originally written, and they list the translator. Both anthologies also take care to let chronology decide on sequence, with in many cases sections on non-Western literatures preceding those on Western literatures. Thus, all possible care seems to be taken to offer as even-handed a survey of "world literature" as possible.

Yet Lawall, writing in 2004, after the publication of her own *Norton Anthology of World Literature* in 2002, and obviously feeling that Damrosch's critique of 2000 was no longer warranted, implicitly took both the *Bedford Anthology of World Literature* and Damrosch's *Longman Anthology of World Literature* to task for basically reverting to an approach that she had just been at pains to demonstrate that the original 1956 Norton had transcended – that is to say, a focus on cultural rather than literary issues, and dispersal over a wide range of shorter extracts rather than concentration on fewer complete works. While praising the newer anthologies for their "viable approaches to cultural complexity" and for including "a wide range of valuable material," Lawall also found that by doing so they "shift attention to a higher, combinatory level while minimizing the time spent on rereading individual texts" (Lawall 2004: 83). Instead, she argued, the Norton continued to follow "a work-centered approach using a wide variety of texts and with the study of aesthetic structures as a way to elucidate the intersecting paths of meaning … that situate a text" (Lawall 2004: 85). Indeed, she even somewhat defiantly suggested that the *Norton Anthology of World Literature* deliberately courted unpopularity because of its consistently aesthetic approach to literature in an age when "'aesthetic' … has a bad press" (Lawall 2004: 85).

Since 2012 the *Norton Anthology of World Literature* has been under the general editorship of Martin Puchner, Professor of English and Comparative Literature at Harvard University. The new edition presented itself as "the Third Edition," thus stressing the continuity with the earlier editions under Lawall, but also insisted (Puchner 2012: xxv) that it "represents a thoroughgoing, top-to-bottom revision of the anthology." The fourth edition appeared in 2018. It is organized along chronological lines and with thematic clusters. The first of the six volumes, A, starts off with a section on "Ancient Mediterranean and Near Eastern Literatures" which itself opens with a cluster on "Creation and the Cosmos" containing "A Cannibal Spell for King Unis" (Egyptian), "The Great Hymn to the Aten" (Egyptian), "The Babylonian Creation Epic" (Akkadian), passages from Hesiod's *Theogony* and *Works and Days* (ancient Greek), "Early Greek Philosophy: Thales, Heraclitus, Empedocles, Anaxagoras" (ancient Greek), and passages from *On the Nature of Things* by Lucretius (Roman, Latin). The section then continues with works from ancient Egyptian literature, *The Epic of Gilgamesh*, passages from the Hebrew Bible, ancient Greek literature with passages from Homer's *The Iliad*, Aesop, Sappho, a large cluster on Athenian drama, Plato's *Symposium*, a cluster on "Travel and Conquest," works from Latin by Catullus, passages from Virgil's *Aeneid,* from Ovid's *Metamorphoses*, and a cluster on "Speech, Writing, Poetry." Then follow sections on "India's Ancient Epics and Tales" and on "Early Chinese Literature and Thought." The ambition to avoid

Eurocentrism shows in Volume B, which in its opening section on "Circling the Mediterranean: Europe and the Islamic World" gathers works translated from ancient Greek, Latin, Persian, Arabic, Old English, Anglo-Norman, Ge'ez (ancient Ethiopian), Old French, Occitan-Provençal, Old German, Castilian, Hebrew, Italian, Flemish, Italian, English, and Welsh. This section is then followed by sections on "India's Classical Age," "Medieval Chinese Literature," and "Japan's Classical Age." At the time of writing, the Norton, which announces itself on the Norton website as "the most trusted anthology of world literature," is going into its fifth edition, with yet more revisions and new translations,

> such as Emily Wilson's *Iliad* and Kimi Traube's *Don Quixote*, an entirely new feature called Translation Lab, and newly refreshed clusters throughout on themes such as storytelling and travel ensure that diverse foundational texts will speak to today's readers in new ways. What's more, the complete anthology is now available in ebook format.[3]

Worlding World Literature

One thing that is clear from Culler's statement cited at the beginning of this chapter, and from world literature anthologies published since 2000, is that the initiative has passed again from English departments to departments of comparative literature. With the exception of the Bedford anthology, the four editors of which were all professors (sometimes emeriti) at the University of New Mexico, both the general editors and a significant number, if not the majority, of the subsidiary editors of the Norton and the Longman hail from comparative literature departments. Ideally, this should facilitate opening up world literature to the world beyond that covered by English-language literature. Here, however, the importance of Culler's remark that what is presently at stake is how comparative literature departments in the US construct "world literature" in their world literature courses comes to the fore. In a number of articles on comparative and world literature Djelal Kadir has referred to this as "worlding" (Kadir 2004, 2006, 2011). What he means is that the comparatist talking of world literature should be aware of "where she is coming from" so as to avoid unconsciously reproducing the hegemonic unbalances of power in the world that she professes to correct by furthering the cause of "world" literature over any form of national literature. For Kadir the "compelling question" is "who carries out [world literature's, TD] worlding and why," and "the inevitable issue is the locus where the fixed foot of the compass that describes the globalizing circumscription is placed" (Kadir 2004: 2).

This, then, is where we have to utter some reservations as to all recent American anthologies of world literature, and where we have to concur with Lawall at least partly as to the continuation, albeit it in a more sophisticated form, as she put it, of habits that date back at least to the middle of the twentieth century. Let me hasten to add that it would seem very difficult to change these habits anyway, which only goes to show to what an extent they are part and parcel of the teaching of world literature in the United States. To begin with, even though as I have just mentioned the Norton and the Longman have a cast of editors that is largely drawn from comparative literature, by far the majority of these – there are very few exceptions indeed – is American or at least teaches at an American university. Although some of its editors originate from beyond North America – Puchner and Wiebke Denecke are German, Emily Wilson is British, Vinay Dharwadker is Indian – this is the case even with the most recent editions of the *Norton Anthology of World Literature*. Perhaps one will object that this is only normal as the US seems to be the only country – at least until recently – where world literature courses are being taught. It is hard to see, though, how the relatively homogeneous provenance of these teams of editors would not influence their choices and, perhaps more importantly still, their stance toward these choices. Inevitably, there emerges an American view on world literature. Second, there is no denying that the HarperCollins, Bedford, and Longman anthologies are geared toward what Lawall called the generic American student. In line with changing demography and expectations of political correctness, of course, that generic American student is now no longer seen as predominantly white and male, but rather as inherently multicultural, with perhaps even a bias in favor of the former minorities as far as representation of non-Western works is concerned, but also with regard to works from the Western tradition. Still, the emphasis remains on the American-English-speaking student in that all material is presented in English translation and, at least if we are to believe Lawall's evaluations of the Bedford and the Longman anthologies as earlier summarized, is selected and arranged so as to provide that student with a comprehensive idea of his or her "cultural heritage," however much expanded that heritage may be as compared to the previously exclusive emphasis on the Western cultural heritage. For all these reasons all these anthologies – and I would include the Norton now – always remain skewed with regard to the rest of the world, as Gayatri Spivak implies in her 2003 *Death of a Discipline*, when she expresses her suspicion of contemporary world literature anthologies in English translation. She implies that such anthologies, while aiming initially at the US academic market but in practice pre-empting that of the entire world, linguistically, by (re)presenting and hence reducing all the world's literatures to "in English" literature, and culturally, by "U.S.-style world literature becoming the staple of Comparative Literature in the global South," project the world as "American" to Americans and "America" as the world to non-Americans (Spivak 2003: 39). Notwithstanding the best of intentions, then, American proponents of world literature always risk turning the practice of what they are doing against their avowed aims, thus perhaps unconsciously and almost against the grain upholding a cultural hegemony they consciously profess to be combating.

Two considerations here impose themselves. The first has to do with translation. This has always been a contentious issue in world literature, and I will return to it in a later chapter. Suffice it here to say that translation has very much become a focus of attention in literary studies, and specifically in comparative literature, over the last fifteen years. There are two solutions to the threat of a basically self-confirming "world projection" inherent in the presentation of the literatures of the world exclusively in English (American) translation. The first, as was the proposal already of Friederich, is to study all materials in the original. This is obviously not a viable possibility given the multiplicity of languages involved and the nature of American undergraduate education. The second and more feasible option is to adopt what to Goethe was the highest form of translation – that is to say, a translation that preserves the strangeness, the foreignness of the original and thus, literally, brings home to the reader, in this case the student, that she is stepping into "another" world. This is a world that can be rendered comprehensible but that can never be completely apprehended, that cannot, so to speak, be "domesticated" to the point where the student starts to feel familiar with it. In other words, it is a world that can never be her "own."

This brings me to the second consideration. Even with the best of anthologies available, a course in world literature can only cover a limited part of the wealth of material offered in any anthology. What gets taught, then, and how it is taught in final instance depends upon the individual teacher, or at best (or sometimes worst) a team of teachers. Earlier I mentioned that Damrosch proposes the figure of the ellipse as an appropriate metaphor for what he sees as an ideal approach for world literature. The constant shifting between the two foci in the ellipse – that of the reader's time and place and that of the text's – leads to what Damrosch calls a "detached engagement" on the part of the reader with "worlds beyond [her] own place and time" (Damrosch 2004: 281). This detached engagement is pretty close to the kind of estranged reading brought about by the form of translation briefly proposed in my previous paragraph; in fact, such detached engagement can be greatly helped by this form of translation. As mentioned, though, in the final instance it will be the task of the teacher to make sure that the two foci of a Damroschian ellipse are kept "in focus" in order to bring out the desired detached engagement on the part of the student. This is also what Kadir sees as the task of "worlding" a text, but it is only part of that task. The further part consists in making the student aware of the simultaneous act of appropriation and distancing she is engaged in, and of its implications for the relationship between her place and time and that of the text, a relationship that, as we saw just a few paragraphs ago, is almost always one of power.

In essence, what Kadir calls for is a meta-stance with regard to the very process of "doing" world literature. Another such call comes from John Pizer (2006). Pizer emphasizes the similarities between the world Goethe found himself in, in an age after the break-up of the Napoleonic empire that for a moment had threatened to bring all of Europe under its sway, but also an age that saw the quickening of commerce and of communications, and the world we have found ourselves in after the fall of the Berlin Wall in 1989 and the quickening of globalization. Therefore, he advocates including as inalienable part of a world literature course a reflection on the very history of what he calls the "Goethean" paradigm so as to make the students see the rationale of their enterprise – rather than worlding a particular reading, then, Pizer is here worlding the very course "world literature" itself. Such a move seems even more imperative after the massive changes – some might say the disruptions – the world, including the Western world and with it the United States, has undergone since Pizer's writing: the financial crises of 2008 and 2011, the rise of authoritarian and populist regimes around the world, the COVID-19 pandemic, climate change, and rising tensions in trade relations between major industrial and financial blocks along with military build-ups around the world, with even a major war raging in Europe in the 2020s.

Conclusion

- Because of the specific structure of higher education in the United States, and because of the relative lack of knowledge of foreign languages there, world literature courses in translation in one guise or another came to be part of the university curriculum in the USA from early on.
- Over the course of the twentieth century there developed a tension between the proponents of "Great Books" courses, which concentrated on the ideas contained in the works read and also included non-literary works, and those of world literature courses, which focused on literary works and on aesthetic issues.
- For most of the twentieth century world literature courses were the province of English departments; only recently have comparative literature departments taken over, leading to decisive shifts in the content and methodology of such courses.
- World literature courses in American academe rely heavily upon anthologies in English translation; the nature, form, and arrangement of these anthologies has been, and continues to be, the subject of heated debate.
- World literature has become an issue in the current debate on the position of the United States in a fast-changing world.

Notes

1 http://www.college.columbia.edu/core/lithum; accessed 11 October 2010.
2 http://www.college.columbia.edu./core/lithum; accessed 30 August 2023.
3 https://wwnorton.com/books/9781324063049; accessed 30 August 2023.

5 World Literature in European Academe

Overview

In Europe, in spite of its being the cradle of *Weltliteratur*, world literature as such until recently was only seldom taught. As of the beginning of the twenty-first century, though, spurred by the renewed interest in the subject in the United States, but also by changes in the academic landscape such as the reforms imposed by the Bologna declaration of 1999 and economizations leading to retrenchment in the humanities, and especially in modern language and literature departments, world literature has gained a firmer footing in European academe. This is the case all over Europe, but in the present chapter I focus on three countries from Europe's so-called semi-periphery: Spain, Portugal, and Denmark.

In Germany, the renewed interest in world literature shows from the rising number of publications on the subject, both articles and books (Schrimpf 1968; Steinmetz 1988; Schmeling 1995; Schmeling, Schmitz-Emans, and Walstra 2000; Koch 2002; Sturm-Trigonakis 2007; Ezli, Kimmich, and Werberger 2009; Lamping 2010, 2015; Löffler 2013; Moser and Simonis 2014; Ette 2016a, 2016b, 2016c, 2021). The same thing goes for France (Pradeau and Samoyault 2005; Valentin 2007; Landrin 2010; David 2011, 2018; Dantzig 2019; Freudiger 2019; Marx 2020; Sakai and Sawada 2021; Moura 2023). And so too in Italy, where many of the works of Moretti better known in English also, and usually first, appeared in Italian – but he is not the only one (Gnisci, Sinopoli, and Moll 2010; Coletti 2011).

Europe's Semi-Periphery

Lawall gave a 2009 article on anthologies of world literature the title "The West and the Rest." This is indeed the opposition that in more recent work on world literature has received most attention and to which the more recent editions of the Norton and Longman anthologies of world literature have sought to provide an answer. However laudable and necessary these initiatives might be, they leave another problem unsolved, and even unmentioned. This is the problem of what I will call "the Rest of the West." Earlier I referred to

DOI: 10.4324/9781003366713-6

Friederich in 1959 blasting then current programs or courses of comparative literature taught in American universities (often only in the more elite ones) as in reality teaching only one quarter of the then NATO languages. Friederich's untaught "other" quarters at the time covered much of the rest of the Romance- and Germanic-language West. Likewise untaught remained the literatures of all other European nations not members of NATO, foremost all Slavic literatures, with the exception of Russian literature which has been part of world literature as taught in the US from the very beginning. Practically speaking, all these are what are variously referred to as Europe's "minor," "small," or "smaller" literatures, ranging from the various Scandinavian languages over Dutch and Portuguese, this notwithstanding the number of Portuguese speakers in the world these days rivalling or surpassing the German-speakers, to all Central, East, and South-East European languages, as well as modern Greek, not to speak of "minority" languages within larger national constellations boasting a "majority" language – think of Basque in Spain, Frisian in the Netherlands, Reto-Romance or Rhaetian in Switzerland, but also Welsh, Irish, and Scottish Gaelic, Letzeburgs (in Luxemburg), Sami in Norway, Sweden, and Finland, or what of late has come to be referred to as "ultra-minor" languages, such as the language of the Faroe Islands, a set of islands in the North Sea belonging to Denmark but with a semi-autonomous statute, or the various Inuit languages spoken in also semi-autonomous Greenland, likewise a constituent part of the Kingdom of Denmark. The issue of such ultra-minor literatures is addressed in an issue of the *Journal of World Literature* (2017 2.2). The scant attention paid to the literatures in these languages also shows in the American world anthologies discussed in the previous chapter (D'haen 2013, 2014, 2017a).

In a 1997 special issue of *symploké* dedicated to "refiguring Europe," Anna Klobucka, drawing upon Immanuel Wallerstein's economics-based world-systems theory (although in his later writings Wallerstein has also pronounced on cultural matters), and invoking Goethe's frequent metaphorical use of the market to speak about the "value" of a particular literature, posited that

> the almost uniform characterization of the biased perspective of traditional comparative literary studies as "Eurocentric" generally fails to take into account the fact that literatures and cultures of the European periphery have only on token occasions been considered as rightful contributors to the common 'European' cultural identity.
> (Klobucka 1997: 128)

The same thing is even more true for world literature, and recent theorizing about the latter offers little consolation to Europe's so-called "minor" literatures, in effect the literatures of Europe's semi-periphery. It should be noted that semi-periphery, at least in the cultural or literary context, not necessarily applies to geographically or economically ex-centric countries but may just as well pertain to the culture of countries that in all other respects would seem to be quite "central," such as for instance the Netherlands or Belgium (Spoiden 1997).

The theories of both Casanova and Moretti, in their "irradiation" or "diffusionist" perspective centered upon Paris, or Paris and London, cast Europe's minor literatures as purely re-active in relation to the "center" or "centers" of Europe. Moreover, as noted earlier, American academe has to a large extent replaced the earlier French and German dominance in comparative literature and literary theory, even though often re-working initially European, and again particularly French and German, ideas, concepts, and theories. The renewed interest in world literature in the US has led to an ever-greater attention to non-European literatures, and hence to the progressive inclusion of ever more non-European texts in American anthologies of world literature, in practice the *only* such anthologies until very recently. If anything, this has led to an ever-growing marginalization, or perhaps we should say "peripheralization," of Europe's minor literatures. In recent US re-castings of world literature, it is the world's other "major" literatures – Chinese, Japanese, Arabic, Indian – that have moved from peripherality or semi-peripherality to co-centrality with the "old" European, or latterly perhaps rather Euro-American, "core." From this perspective Europe's minor literatures plummet to the status of truly "peripheral" literatures (D'haen 2016).

The literatures Friederich in his 1959 statement referred to as one fourth of the literatures in the then fifteen NATO member states that received any actual sustained attention in American programs or courses in world literature were, next to English, French, German, Spanish, and Italian, and discussion on world literature was almost exclusively restricted to German, French, and US comparative literature circles. This is not to say that elsewhere in Europe no work was being done on world literature, but this usually shadowed what was being done in French and German academe. Only seldom did it filter into the more general or "global" discussion, and then usually only when done in a "major" European language or translated therein. This situation has basically persisted to this day, with US academe, and the English language, increasingly supplanting their German and French counterparts. Work on world literature done outside the main European centers and the US usually has only been recognized as such retrospectively and certainly at least partially as a result of the renewed interest in world literature in the US from the end of the twentieth century onward. In what follows I concentrate on three examples from Europe's so-called "semi-periphery" – Scandinavia, Spain, and Portugal – to gauge the impact of the renewal of interest in world literature beyond the core area of "comparative literature talking about world literature." Undoubtedly other examples from other European literatures could be cited. It just happens that the three cases I do deal with in more detail are the ones I know best. Beyond this, though, I think they are also symptomatic of a trend manifesting throughout Europe. In most cases this will involve both a return to "native" precursors to claim an "alter-native" approach to world literature and an unspoken, but I think nonetheless implied resistance to a world literature fashioned by anglophone hegemony. In later chapters I turn to the world beyond "the West."

Scandinavia

In Scandinavia, and particularly in Denmark, the renewed interest in world literature has led to a revival of the work of the Danish critic and literary historian Georg Brandes (1842–1927). Influenced by the positivism of the French historian Hippolyte Taine, under whom he studied in Paris in 1866–1867, by the critical practice of the equally French critic Sainte-Beuve, and by German philosophy, especially that of Georg Wilhelm Friedrich Hegel (1770–1831), Brandes between 1872 and 1890 wrote a ground-breaking series of volumes on European literature from 1800 to 1848 under the general title of *Hovedstrømninger*, translated as *Main Currents in Nineteenth-Century Literature*. Sainte-Beuve had shown the way toward a criticism that went beyond mere description and evaluation, situating works and authors in their various contexts, and comparing them with other works and authors. Brandes likewise advocated comparison as a fruitful entry into the world of European literature in the introduction to his first *Main Currents* volume. Comprised of *Emigrant Literature* [Emigrantlitteraturen] (1872), *The Romantic School in Germany* [Den romantiske Skole i Tyskland] (1873), *The Reaction in France* [Reaktionen i Frankrig] (1874), *Naturalism in England* [Den engelske Naturalisme] (1875, where "naturalism" refers to nature poetry and not to the later literary movement that now goes by that same name), *The Romantic School in France* [Den romantiske Skole i Frankrig] (1882), and *Young Germany* [Det unge Tyskland] (1890), *Main Currents* switches from France to Germany to France to England, and then back to France and finally back to Germany, describing the literature of the period under investigation as a Hegelian process of action and reaction between revolution and restoration, progressivism and conservatism, the struggle for freedom and the wish for containment, in literature as in politics.

In his entry on Georg Brandes in the *Routledge Companion to World Literature* (D'haen, Damrosch, and Kadir 2012, 2022), Svend Erik Larsen highlights how the work of Brandes provoked diametrically opposed reactions in different parts of the world. In France, where his work has hardly been translated, at variance with Germany and the English-speaking countries where almost everything he ever wrote was diligently translated during his own lifetime, Brandes was vehemently opposed by Fernand Brunetière and later, in an obituary in 1927, derided by the equally eminent comparatist Ferdinand Baldensperger for "the superficiality of [his work's] knowledge and the lack of substance of its edifice" (Baldensperger 1927: 143; quoted in Larsen 2012: 24, 2022: 21). In China, however, Brandes's cause was taken up by the famous novelist and critic Lu Xun (1881–1936), by many considered the most important Chinese writer of the first half of the twentieth century. Lu Xun, on the left of the political spectrum, praised Brandes for his progressivism. In his own country and in Germany, where he lived part of his life, Brandes's reputation fluctuated. In the middle of the twentieth century his work fell into oblivion, but more recently he, like

Meltzl, has been reclaimed as an alternative "founding father" of comparative literature in a world perspective. The grounds for this are to be sought in his critical practice in *Main Currents*, but also in a brief essay on "World Literature" ("Verdenslitteratur" in Danish, but actually first published as "Weltliteratur" in the German journal *Das litterarische Echo*) that he wrote in 1899, and which is currently being reprinted in all kinds of collective volumes on world literature and on the "new" comparative literature, such as the 2009 *Princeton Sourcebook in Comparative Literature* and the 2012 *Routledge Reader in World Literature*.

The reason for the revival of interest in Brandes is, according to Larsen (2012: 26–28, 2022: 23–26), that Brandes, in four distinct ways, can be seen as anticipating what currently occupies the "new" comparatists. He is interested in the diffraction (perhaps we should say the "refraction") of local cultures: "World literature of the future will appear the more appealing, the stronger it represents the national particularity, and the more diversified it is, but only when it also has a general human dimension as art and science" (*Samlede Skrifter* 12: 28; quoted in Larsen 2012: 26, 2022: 24). He is a proponent of a globalized cultural approach. He favored transnational themes in his dealings with literature: "Brandes would have been sympathetic to the resurfacing contemporary debate on cosmopolitanism and also to central global themes of literature: risk society, migration, trauma and forgiveness, international justice or genocide" (Larsen 2012: 28, 2022: 25). Finally, he paid great attention to issues of translation, especially with regard to the imbalances of power involved. Brandes specifically took up the latter point in his 1899 essay on world literature. Though he starts off his essay by saying that, although he is aware that the term "Weltliteratur" has been coined by Goethe (erroneously, as we have seen in Chapter 1, but taken for granted at the time), he does not remember exactly what it refers to, and therefore he will start from his own assumptions on the matter. He notices that next to some writers who have become household names in world literature – Shakespeare for instance – there are others, such as Shakespeare's contemporary Christopher Marlowe, who although not necessarily less great have remained only nationally or locally famous. He then stresses the importance of translation in gaining an author or a work access to world literature, especially so in the modern period, that is to say since the rise of the vernaculars as literary languages, and he stipulates that "in no other language do translations play so great a role as in German" (Brandes 2009: 63), thus echoing, consciously or not, Goethe.

"It is incontestable," Brandes argues, "that writers of different countries and languages occupy enormously different positions where their chances of obtaining worldwide fame, or even a moderate degree of recognition, are concerned" (Brandes 2009: 63). French writers are luckiest when it comes to their chances of becoming known to the world, next come English and German writers, and then Italian and Spanish. Russians, even though few people know the language, are so many that they too have a fair chance of becoming world famous.

But whoever writes in Finnish, Hungarian, Swedish, Danish, Dutch, Greek or the like is obviously poorly placed in the universal struggle for fame ... in this competition he lacks the major weapon, a language – which is, for a writer, almost everything.

(Brandes 2009: 63)

With the clause that "when a writer has succeeded in France, he is known throughout the world" (Brandes 2009: 63), Brandes, at least as far as the nineteenth-century situation is concerned, anticipates Pascale Casanova's (1999 and 2004) definition of Paris as the Greenwich Meridian of the literary world.

Translation, because of its "inescapable incompleteness" (Brandes 2009: 63), Brandes feels, cannot compensate for writing in a minor language, and this is why lesser writers writing in a world language easily gain far greater recognition than do far greater writers in less-known languages. But sometimes it is also simply a matter of chance, he argues, taking as his example the Danish writers Hans Christian Andersen and Søren Kierkegaard. The former, Brandes says, achieved world fame, the latter is "unknown in Europe" (Brandes 2009: 65). Yet, Brandes notes, "among us [Danes] Andersen is thought of as one among many, nothing more" while Kierkegaard is "the greatest religious thinker of the Scandinavian North" (Brandes 2009: 65). Nor does it help to write deliberately for fame and fortune, and with an eye to becoming a world author, in the process by-passing one's own roots and environment. Brandes concludes:

When Goethe coined the term "world literature," humanism and cosmopolitanism were still ideas that everyone held in honor. In the last years of the nineteenth century, an ever stronger and more jealous national sentiment has caused these ideas to recede almost everywhere. Today literature is becoming more and more national. But I do not believe that nationality and cosmopolitanism are incompatible. The world literature of the future will be all the more interesting, the more strongly its national stamp is pronounced and the more distinctive it is, even if, as art, it also has its international side; for that which is written directly for the world will hardly appear as a work of art.

(Brandes 2009: 66)

In 1872 Brandes, who had started teaching *Belles Lettres* at the University in Copenhagen in 1871, unsuccessfully applied for the professorship in Aesthetics at his university. This may seem to have been a strange move for somebody primarily interested in literature (actually, Brandes was interested in many things besides literature; he was for instance also involved in the founding of *Politiken*, still today one of Denmark's leading newspapers), but it was actually very logical in the Scandinavian situation. In Denmark, Sweden, and Norway, literature during the nineteenth century was taught as part of the wider discipline of "aesthetics," comprising all the arts, along the lines laid out by Kant in his *Critique of Judgment*. In Sweden, in 1906, a new discipline called "litteraturhistoria med poetik" (literary history and criticism) was created, and this in the 1970s was renamed "litteraturvetenskap" (literary "science" or scholarship). Swedish literature forms part, in fact the larger part, of this discipline, while foreign languages and literatures form subjects of their own. "World literature," then, is an integral part of the courses offered by "litteraturvetenskap," along with Swedish literature and what elsewhere might well be called "theory of literature." As Anders Pettersson puts it:

> There are no separate chairs in Swedish literature in Sweden, so all study of Swedish literature is incorporated into *litteraturvetenskap*, where it plays a very dominant role ... when presenting my academic subject in English-speaking contexts, I call it "Swedish and Comparative Literature."
> (Pettersson 2008: 464)

In Denmark and Norway foreign languages and literatures are subjects in their own right, as is "Nordisk litteraturhistorie" or "Scandinavian literature," comprising Danish, Norwegian, Swedish, and Icelandic, with different emphases depending on the particular country. Next to this, Danish universities used to have an "Institut for Aestetiske Fag," which at Aarhus translated as "Department of Aesthetic Studies," with various sections, one of them being the "Afdeling for Litteraturhistorie,"[1] which, on the English-language webpage, was not given a translation, but in the English-language course catalogue corresponded to "Comparative Literature."[2] It is also as "Comparative Literature" scholars that members of the Faculty of Arts teaching "litteraturhistorie" announced themselves to their colleagues abroad. Under the heading "World Literature" the Aarhus University website in 2010 stated that "the degree program in comparative literature focuses on European literature, but you also have the opportunity to discover Russian or South-East Asian literature, for example."[3] The Department of Aesthetic Studies also listed a "Center for Verdenslitteraere Studier," or "Center for the Study of World Literature."[4] In the meantime there have been a number of reorganizations at Aarhus University, and what in English is called a department of "Comparative Literature and Rhetoric" is now part of a "School of Communication and Culture."[5] In Danish it is called "Literaturhistorie og Retorik."[6] In 2022 there is no longer any mention of a Center for the Study of World Literature at Aarhus University. Instead, world literature is listed as one of the core activities of the comparative literature program, with the scholars involved participating in an active network across all literature studies programs at the University as well as in an expanding international network. And there is still an obligatory MA course/module on world literature in the comparative literature program. The Center for the Study of World Literature also served as institutional reference for five small introductory books in Danish (Thomsen 2008b; Ringgaard and Thomsen 2010; Andersen 2011; Jørgensen and Baggesgaard 2015; Baggesgaard 2016) published with

Aarhus University Press in a series called *Verdenslitteratur* (World Literature). While one might have wondered, then, whether this terminological and organizational turmoil augured the demise of world literature studies at Aarhus University barely a decade after its institutionalization, it turns out that world literature in the meantime has simply been accepted as an inevitable part of a comparative literature education. The same question imposes itself when we find that while in 2010 the Copenhagen PhD School in the Humanities was – rather ironically given his failure to win the chair in Aesthetics – still called the Georg Brandes School this label has disappeared from the University website in 2022 where there now is only mention of the PhD School at the Faculty of Humanities. In the University of Copenhagen study guide website prospective students of the bachelor program *litteraturvidenskab* (roughly: comparative literature) are told that they will "dykker ned i verdenslitteraturen" (delve into world literature).[7]

Although the way it is embedded in Scandinavia's academic structures, then, is very different, and apparently rather wavering, the interest in world literature in Scandinavia in some ways parallels that in the US, in that it is very much pedagogically oriented. What predominates is a concern to expose beginning university students to a variety of works from different provenance. In fact, the Scandinavians take things even a stage further than the Americans in that over the last two decades they introduced world literature into high school teaching. In Sweden a mixed committee of academics and high school teachers has drawn up a list, a canon one could say, of world literature for use in high schools. The emphasis is on contemporary rather than historical works of literature, and on fair geographical and gender representation. The choice for contemporary works rather than works of historical importance is grounded in the (supposed) interest of the students and in the desire to make the chosen works relevant to their lifeworld. It is also to a large extent governed by what is available in Swedish translation, thus once more showing up the intimate relationship, at least on the pedagogical level, between canonicity, or perhaps in this case better canonicability, and translation. The relative preponderance of works originally written in English, whether it be works of historical importance originating in Britain or the US, or contemporary so-called post-colonial works, is also to be explained from this conundrum: even though English is undoubtedly the foreign language most widely disseminated in Sweden, as in all Scandinavia (and the world, we might add), it also is the language from which most is translated into Swedish, thus offering a much wider range of choice of works than any other literature in any other language.

In Denmark there appeared in 2009 a literary history for high school students called *litteraturDK*. Written by the then chair of comparative literature (*litteraturhistorie*) at Aarhus University, Svend Erik Larsen, in collaboration with three colleagues, academics and high school teachers, *litteraturDK* aims to study "local literature in a global perspective." *litteraturDK* starts from the premise that Denmark's being subject to an increasing process of globalization has implications for how literature is taught. Danish high school students live a "globalized reality as it is experienced in Denmark" and literature "belongs to a larger media landscape defined also by other languages than Danish and other media than verbal language" (Larsen 2010: 16). This reality

> promotes an encounter between several cultures and it therefore inevitably contains a strong historical dimension, which more often than not is excluded from the close-reading strategies pursued in the teaching of literature or reduced to factual comments of varying relevance.
> (Larsen 2010: 16)

Literature, then, needs to be re-conceptualized from a "world literature" perspective geared to local Danish conditions. Consequently, in *litteraturDK*

> every chapter offers a different viewpoint on how literature during a thousand years has suggested answers to questions about what it means to face the conditions of human existence living in Denmark as a country within moving boundaries and with a changing but always crucial interaction with the larger world.
> (Larsen 2010: 24)

Moreover, *litteraturDK*

> is not a literary history of *Danish* literature but a history of *literature in Denmark*, that is about the texts which have been read, used, imitated, remediated, arrived along labyrinthine routes, transformed completely once they arrived and thereby constituted examples of the permanent presence of the greater world inside the local confinement.
> (Larsen 2010: 25)

Even if not a full-blown history of world literature, then, *litteraturDK* does bring into play insights and strategies gleaned from recent discussions on world literature as well as from older such reflections by Goethe and Brandes, and translates them into a workable paradigm for a specific twenty-first century locale. At the same time, and even if only for its own local audience, teaching Danish literature in such a setting also lifts it from its otherwise restrictive national environment and recasts it as part of world literature, thus providing at least some solace for Brandes's lament about the relative invisibility of literatures from smaller nations and in less known languages. Of course, the real remedy to the imbalance of power that Brandes noted regarding a writer's chances of gaining worldwide fame would lie in similar literary histories, for high school and/or university teaching, to also be created and published in major languages and countries, and preferably in English, and soon perhaps also in Chinese, or other emerging world languages.

The work Larsen and colleagues have undertaken on the level of high school anthologies and literary histories is paralleled on the research level by a study such as Mads Rosendahl Thomsen's *Mapping World Literature: International Canonization and Transnational Literature* (Thomsen 2008a). While recognizing the merits of the works of Damrosch (2003), Casanova (1999 and 2004) and Moretti (2000 and 2005), Thomsen also offers some intriguing counter-proposals of his own, such as looking at world literature from what he calls "shifting focal points" (Thomsen 2008a: 33–60), under which he subsumes "centers, temporary sub-centers, old and emerging world literatures, international canonization without the support of a major national literature, and temporal shifts in the historical horizon" (Thomsen 2008a: 54). Examples he offers are, as far as centers are concerned, Athens, Alexandria, Rome, Paris, London, and New York, as temporary sub-centers Russia, with the Russian novel, in the period 1860–1880, Scandinavia, with the theatre and the novel, in the decade 1890–1900, the US in the 1920s and the Latin America of the "boom" in 1960–1980, the emergence of American literature in the 1920s versus the established major literatures of Europe in the 1920s, Borges as a "lonely canonical," and Modernism as moving from being "new" to being the "new antiquity" for post-post-modernism. I have put forward a similar proposal with respect to Brussels as "shadow"-rival to Paris in the second half of the nineteenth century (D'haen 2017b; see also Min 2013). Whatever one may think of some or all of these proposals, they show a definite desire to go beyond the old center-periphery constructions and to re-map the world of world literature along more, and more varied axes, than those hitherto prevailing and prejudicing a true evaluation of literatures beyond the pale of "traditional" world literature which Thomsen still sees as very much tied to the paradigm of comparative literature as it has been operative for the past one hundred-plus years, and as tied to national literatures as its constituent parts. Instead, when it comes to the present map of world literature, Thomsen proposes to start from what he calls "constellations of works," that is to say: "very different texts [that] share features that make them stand out on the literary canopy" (Thomsen 2008a: 4). Some such constellations he investigates in the second half of his book are migrant writers and holocaust writers. Again, one may differ as to the applicability of such criteria, and even as to the novelty of what Thomsen here proposes, as his "constellations," after all, sound very much like thematic groupings. For his metaphorical model Thomsen invokes stellar constellations as humanly imposed patterns upon heavenly bodies otherwise disparate in space. Although he nowhere mentions this, Thomsen presumably also has in mind Walter Benjamin's "constellations" yoking together past and present, thus lending even greater historical and theoretical weight to his construction (Benjamin 1982). In 2018 Thomsen, together with Dan Ringgaard, published a volume on Danish literature in the Bloomsbury "X as World Literature series" (Ringgaard and Thomsen 2018).

Spain

Just a few paragraphs ago I referred to Chinese as a – perhaps even *the* – language of the future. In Europe too, though, and next to English and

French as long-standing languages with global or near global reach (even though in changing relations of hegemony over the past few centuries), we find languages and cultures that, once powerful yet later considered "peripheral," have latterly re-surfaced as emergent world languages by dint of the former colonial empires in which they were disseminated. Along with Earl Fitz (2002) I am thinking here particularly of Spain and Portugal. Especially the latter, because of its smaller size, its geographically more ex-centric position, and its "eclipsed" history since at least the eighteenth century, would squarely seem to fit into Europe's "semi-periphery." In any of the going re-theorizations of world literature that I have just mentioned, the old home countries concerned – Spain and Portugal themselves, and their literatures – would seem destined to play only a minor role. Pride of place would go to literatures in Spanish and Portuguese produced in the former colonies: Spanish America and Brazil, and in the longer run also lusophone Angola and Mozambique. In this respect the situation of Spain and Portugal is significantly different from that of, for instance, England, and particularly France.

England, because of its relatively small number of English speakers as compared to many of its former colonies, partially in the singular but certainly in the aggregate, risks being eclipsed, and is already partially at least eclipsed, by literature in English produced outside of the British Isles, first in the United States, later in the so-called "settler colonies" (Canada, Australia, and partially South Africa), and latterly also in India and perhaps in the future likewise sub-Saharan Africa. For the time being, though, and because of the status of English, in whatever variant, as the undisputed world language of commerce and diplomacy, England continues to be an important linguistic, cultural, and literary center. France, meanwhile, easily remains the largest French-speaking country in the world, at least for the moment, although of course in the longer run it might well be equaled or surpassed by some "francophone" African countries. Perhaps most importantly, though, both France and England are indisputably part of the European cultural "core." Indeed, for Moretti, and at least as far as the period since 1800 is concerned, they are "the" core. For Casanova, of course, the matter is even simpler: Paris is the core.

Spain, and even less so Portugal, cannot lay claim to the same centrality in Europe. Moreover, both Spain and Portugal by now have been dwarfed by their former colonies when it comes to number of speakers. At the same time, while London and Paris continue to function as major clearinghouses and publishing centers for English and French language literature, in Spanish and Portuguese rival centers have arisen with Mexico City, Buenos Aires, and São Paulo, even though Barcelona still plays a major role in Spanish-language literature publishing and the same thing goes for Lisbon for lusophone Africa. There is a tension, then, between the role to which Spanish and Portuguese literature risk being reduced in the "new" world literature paradigm, and their networked position because of historical conditions. The acute awareness of these tensions is leading to initiatives aimed at raising the visibility of Spanish and Portuguese literature in world literature terms. I will here concentrate on two such initiatives: one, more modest, from Spain; the other, quite ambitious, from Portugal. In both cases, these initiatives also build on longer-standing native traditions of comparative literature and literary history writing and anthologizing.

In Spain, an ancestor to be recovered is the Spanish and, after his flight from Spain because of the Civil War in 1936–1939, Argentinian writer and critic Guillermo de Torre (1900–1971). Not long after the conclusion of World War II, in 1949, de Torre pondered on "Goethe y la literatura universal" (Goethe and world literature). Goethe, while unleashing a most important idea on the world, had not been very precise in its definition, de Torre found. When having to choose between two definitions offered in Shipley's then well-known and widely used *Dictionary of World Literature*, namely that of all literature in the world and the totality of those works that have gained recognition beyond their national borders, de Torre opts for the second possibility, or for what he labels, using quotation marks, "literatura mundial" (de Torre 1956: 282). However, he immediately objects – and here he starts sounding like Brandes in his 1899 article on world literature – if we then take translation, a necessary instrument for cross-border dissemination, as our yardstick, we notice that many coincidental factors intervene, such as a given country's socio-economic importance driving its cultural irradiation, the popularity of certain genres, or other aleatory facts. Some works are even written especially for a world market, he claims. Any such works he calls, denigratingly, "cosmopolitan" rather than "world" literature. Still, we should also not fall over into only applauding what is rooted in local or national conditions. The proper instance to really stake out world literature, then, de Torre asserts, is comparative literature. As an example, he invokes *A Short History of Comparative Literature from the Earliest Times to the Present Day* (1906, 1904 in French, 1905 in Spanish) of Frédéric Loliée. Loliée in his conclusion sees all literatures "blend in harmonious unity" (Loliée 1906: 314) and "united in an all-embracing unity" (Loliée 1906: 358); in fact, he confidently propounds, "we are approaching unity" (Loliée 1906: 374). De Torre finds such a trust in the coming of a *Weltliteratur* not overly utopian in the early years of the twentieth century, before the World Wars. Since then, however, he contends, things have changed dramatically. Still, he also thinks, it is inevitable that from the recent disasters of World War II a federal Europe will emerge, a "Superestado" (superstate) which alone can guarantee a lasting peace. Why, he asks, should we not then conceive in such a world "the effective realization of a world literature, on a par with the national literatures, and in which would figure representative entries from the latter, but more equitably so, and chosen less capriciously, than at present?" (de Torre 1956: 289; la realización efectiva de una *literatura universal*, coexistente con las demás literaturas nacionales, y en cuyo dominio entrarían representaciones de estas últimas, pera más equitativas y menos caprichosamente elegidas que las actuales?).

One attempt at such a more equitable representation is carried out at the University of Santiago de Compostela, in Spain, where César Domínguez, who regularly addresses world literature in courses such as "Global comparative literature" and "East/West comparative poetics," also offers a course on "literatura y arte en el mundo antiguo y medieval" (literature and art in the classical and medieval world) in which he discusses, along with the usual suspects from Greek and Latin antiquity as well as the usual medieval romances, knights' tales, and lyrical poetry from Romance, Germanic, and Celtic languages, also the Mesopotamian *Epic of Gilgamesh* (in an English translation), a "selección de poemas, hispanoárabes, trovadorescos provenzales y chinos" (a selection of Spanish-Arab, troubadour, and Chinese poetry), a selection from the Japanese Murasaki Shikibu's *Genji Monogatari* (The Tale of Genji), and a selection from *The Travels of Ibn Battuta* in a translation from the Arabic. As general anthology and background, he uses the first volume of Martín de Riquer and José María Valverde's *Historia de la literatura universal* (History of World Literature) mentioned in Chapter 1, and Jordi Llovet's *Lecciones de literatura universal: siglos XII a XX* (Readings in World Literature: Twelfth to Twentieth Centuries). With the Spanish-Arab poems and the *Travels of Ibn Battuta*, Domínguez includes a number of items that at least potentially stress the relationship of Spain to the world of Islam, and especially to the Arab world, in line with recent Spanish ambitions, also in the diplomatic and economic spheres, to bank on its medieval "three cultures" (Christian, Islamic, Jewish) past in order to claim the role of mediator between Europe and the Arab world. In the attention he gives to literatures beyond what is usually thought of as "Europe," and particularly to the Arab world, Domínguez is also picking up on the work of a scholar whom he himself (Domínguez 2013) has rightly claimed as perhaps the earliest precursor of world literature studies: Juan Andrés (1740–1817). Andrés was a Spanish Jesuit who, after the expulsion of the Jesuits from Spain in 1767, spent most of his life in Italy, where he published, in Italian, a seven-volume world history of literature, *Dell'origine, progressi e stato attuale d'ogni letteratura* (1782–1799; On the Origin, Progress and Present State of All Literature), followed by a nine-volume revised and expanded edition (1808–1817). The ten-volume Spanish edition (1784–1806), in a translation by Andrés's brother Carlos, was used as a textbook at the Real Colegio de San Isidro in Madrid, where a chair in literary history was established in 1785, and at the University of Valencia, making these "the first European institutions where world literature was taught" (Domínguez 2013: 2). The first volume of Andrés's work also appeared in French in 1805, in a translation by J.E. Ortolani, as *Histoire générale des sciences et de la littérature depuis les temps antérieurs à l'histoire grecque jusqu'à nos jours*.

In reading *The Tale of Genji* next to European medieval romances, and Chinese poems next to medieval Spanish-Arab and Provençal poetry, Domínguez is also picking up on what another Spanish comparative literature ancestor, namely Claudio Guillén (1924–2007), has dubbed the B and C models of supranationality. The B model applies "when phenomena or processes that are *genetically independent*, or belong to different civilizations, are collected and brought together for study" on the grounds of "*common sociohistorical conditions*" (Guillén 1993: 70). The C model applies when "some *genetically independent* phenomena make up supranational entities in accordance with principles and purposes derived from the *theory of literature*" (Guillén 1993: 70). The A model implies direct contact or chronological linearity, and in the cases Domínguez here treats this is out of the question. For models B and C Guillén specifically refers to East/West examples, thus showing Domínguez the lead. For model B, though, he also specifically points to work in comparative literature done in East and Central Europe by V.M. Zhirmunsky (1881–1971) and Dionýsz Ďurišin (Guillén 1993: 82). Here too we can see how diffusionist models of literary history – in this case when it comes to theory rather than creative literature – can easily miss what is really going on "on the ground," so to speak, because of their superior level of aggregation. Ďurišin, while hardly acknowledged in the Euro-American "core" of comparative literature, has been extensively translated, and his theories taken up, in Spain, and especially at the department of comparative literature at Santiago de Compostela, by Dario Villanueva, Fernando Cabo, and César Domínguez himself (Domínguez 2012a, 2022a). In Italy the work of Ďurišin has also had indubitable impact, even if only because of the 2000 book he co-edited with the Italian comparatist Armando Gnisci on the literary Mediterranean.

Domínguez is at least partially applying the "regionalist" principles of Dionýsz Ďurišin as they apply to the Mediterranean space of which Spain has been so integral a part for most of its history when he sees the neglect into which the work of Andrés fell after the first third of the nineteenth century, when there were various re-editions of *Dell'origine*, as a symptom of a "geopolitical division North/South of knowledge" (Domínguez 2013: 1) that in discussions of world literature translates into an opposition Goethe/Andrés. Roberto Dainotto in *Europe (in Theory)* (2007) traces how Europe's South, also in literature, as of sometime in the seventeenth century came to be regarded by the then dominant North of Europe as the continent's internal "Other." This internal division of Europe was at least in part caused by the turn toward the North Atlantic in the seventeenth and eighteenth centuries allowing a number of north-western European states to economically draw ahead of the rest of Europe. The expectation of continued success when following the same road at the same time led to a downgrading of nations that followed a different path, also in literary historiography. Of course, this process internal to Europe very much resembles all Europe's looking down upon the rest of the world as of roughly the same period via the process Said defined as "Orientalism." The result, in any case, was that Goethe became the reference for all subsequent work on world literature, rather than Andrés – in all fairness it should also be said that Andrés never used the term "world literature" but rather spoke of "ogni letteratura" or "all literature." Of late, however, and not least thanks to Dainotto and Domínguez, Andrés has received renewed attention in a world literature context – Waïl Hassan made his work the focus of attention in his 2021 American Comparative Literature Association presidential address.

Portugal

In Portugal, as in many other European countries, there have long existed book series especially designed to disseminate what we would now call "world literature," whether in the form of single translated volumes or anthologies. The Lisbon publisher Portugália Editora from 1942 until the 1970s ran a series called "Antologías Universais." But there is also a series of five volumes published between 1966 and 1997 by the poet Herberto Helder of what he called "Poemas mudados para Português por Herberto Helder" (Poems changed into Portuguese by Herberto Helder). Helena Buescu and João Ferreira Duarte (2007: 175) describe these five volumes as follows:

> The 1966 volume (*O Bebedor nocturno* [The Night Drinkard]) collects materials from Ancient Egypt, the Old Testament, Maya and Nahuatl lore, Ireland, Scotland, Finland, Japan, Indochina, Indonesia, Greece and Madagascar, together with Zen poems, Arab and Al-Andaluz poems, "Eskimo" and Tartar poems, Haikus and "Red-Skin poems." *As Magías* (1987), in turn, offers poems from the Belgian poet Henri Michaux, D.H. Lawrence, Robert Duncan, Blaise Cendrars and Stephen Crane, among others, lined up with native materials from Central Asia, Equatorial Africa, Sudan, Gabon, British Columbia, India, Panama, Australia, Colombia, Ancient Greece, Mexico and Mongolia. As to the 1997 trilogy, *Ouolof* collects texts from Mayan and Amazonian sources, as well as poetry by Zbigniew Herbert, Jean Cocteau, Emilio Villa, Marina Tsvetaieva and Malcom Lowry. *Poemas ameríndios* starts out with a long poem by Ernesto Cardenal [he himself working with several sources of 16th Century Nahuatl texts, as well as the Florentine Codex] and goes on to gather texts culled from Aztec and Quichua cultures, as well as texts from an array of native North and South American sources. Finally, *Doze nós numa corda* seems to shift away from the logic governing the previous volumes by privileging Western sources: Antonin Artaud, Carlos Edmundo de Ory, Henri Michaux (whose poetry takes up almost two thirds of the book) and a short poem by Hermann Hesse which closes the collection.

While this is perhaps the most salient example of a series of volumes covering a, in this case highly personal, selection of "world poetry," there are also other, more systematic Portuguese anthologies, edited by, among others, Jorge de Sena, Vasco Graça-Moura, Diogo Pires Aurélio, Nina e Filipe Guerra, and Pedro Tamen.

The examples just mentioned predate the re-emergence of thinking about world literature at the turn of the twenty-first century. In 2002, though, Earl Fitz, clearly influenced by the renewed interest in world literature, suggested that

While English departments may regard globalization as a threat to their long-standing hegemony within the Academy, for Luso-Africanists and Luso-Brazilianists it represents an *abertura* (opening) of tremendous potential, an opportunity to bring our literature to the attention of the rest of the world.

(Fitz 2002: 442)

A major effort in this vein was realized at the University of Lisbon's Centro de Estudos Comparatistas (CEC), where Helena Buescu, who founded the Centro around the turn of the century, together with a worldwide team of collaborators put together a six-volume anthology of what, taking her cue from the 2007 French publication on "littérature-monde," she calls "literatura-mundo in Portuguese." In a 2010 working paper setting out the premises upon which the then still to be composed anthology would be based, she starts from the premise that this "literatura-mundo" comprises both works written in Portuguese and translated into Portuguese, and that it should lead to an integrated vision of the relationships obtaining between both of these (2010 working document of the CEC). Invoking the original ideas of Goethe, as expressed by himself and as taken up by later proponents of world literature, particularly Guérard, Etiemble, and Damrosch, Buescu posits that

> this anthology is, then a way of upholding a conversational vision of literature, a legitimate complement to other visions, equally legitimate in terms of their own specializations, but incapable of covering the entire field of what literature can do (and always does): a concept of literary conversation that not only points to the transnational and trans-historical nature of the phenomena it comprises, but that also projects an awareness of literature that is potentially planetary and, to speak the truth, humanist.
> (esta antología é pois uma forma de defender uma visão conversacional da literatura, legítima forma de complementar outras visões, igualmente legítimas em termos de especialização, mas não capazes de cobrir todo o campo do que a literatura pode fazer (e sempre fez): uma concepção de conversa literária que não só indica o carácter transnacional e trans-histórico dos fenómenos que abriga, mas ainda projecta uma consciência potencialmente planetária e, em boa verdade, humanista da literatura.)
> (2010 working document of CEC)

The first volumes of the anthology would contain

> [a] closely reasoned collection of texts from the various literatures in Portuguese, opening up the possibility of reading each of these literatures starting from various intersections, thus to contribute to their mutual (re) cognition ... such a perspective undoubtedly contributes to enrich each of the individual national literatures concerned ... but it contributes, above all, to their mutual illumination through a comparativist perspective that allows

for the recognition of the global dimension shared by the literatures written in Portuguese.

(Um conjunto muito significativo de textos escritos nas várias literaturas de língua portuguesa, oferecendo a possibilidade de ler cada uma das literaturas a partir de cruzamentos vários, bem como de construir o seu (re)conhecimento mútuo, ... uma tal perspectiva contribui sem dúvida para o enriquecimento de cada uma das literaturas nacionais individualmente consideradas. ... mas contribui, sobretudo, para a sua iluminação mútua, através de uma perspectiva comparatista que permita reconhecer a dimensão mundial para que apontam as literaturas escritas em português.)

(2010 working document of CEC)

[The other volumes] would gather a closely reasoned collection of world literature texts, holding out the possibility of reading them on the basis of translations made, with few exceptions, especially for this volume. Its publication will therefore permit and promote cross-cultural reading and understanding. Such a perspective contributes toward elaborating a comparativist approach that allows for the recognition of a global dimension to which the translations into Portuguese of texts from an enormous diversity of genres, ages, languages and historical-cultural periods would contribute.

(Pretende reunir ... um conjunto muito significativo de textos escritos nas várias literaturas de âmbito mundial, oferecendo a possibilidade de os ler a partir de traduções feitas, com poucas excepções, especialmente para este volume. A sua publicação permitirá assim construir cruzamentos vários, bem como abrir a uma leitura e o conhecimento mútuos. Uma tal perspectiva contribui para a complexificação de uma perspectiva comparatista que permita reconhecer a dimensão mundial para que apontam as traduções para português de textos pertencentes a uma enorme diversidade de géneros, épocas, línguas e períodos histórico-culturais.)

(2010 working document of CEC)

The anthology *Literatura-Mundo Comparada: Perspectivas em Português* published in the meantime (Buescu 2018–2020), then, implicitly re-affirms the centrality of Portugal, and of Portuguese literature, for literatures in Portuguese, for world literature in Portuguese, and for literature in Portuguese as world literature. It relocates the country and its literature parallel to what the Portuguese writer and Nobel Prize winner José Saramago does with the Iberian peninsula in his novel *The Stone Raft*. As Klobucka puts it:

The island that used to be the Iberian Peninsula does not, after all, go on floating aimlessly around the Atlantic: it becomes (perhaps provisionally) anchored and reterritorialized in a sort of de-centered central position, "in the middle of the Atlantic, between Africa and South America," reflecting contemporary Iberia's, and particularly Portugal's, desire to capitalize on its historically irreversible colonial experience by assuming a major [sic] mediating function in the global community of nations.

(Klobucka 1997: 132)

Paradoxically, such an anthology also emphasizes the semi-peripherality of Portugal vis-à-vis Europe by converting its ex-centricity into a new centrality, not with regard to Europe but to the world, a world of "its own," so to speak. As my discussion of Domínguez's course relative to Spain's positioning vis-à-vis the Arab world has intimated, and as the colonial heritage of Spain warrants also with respect to Latin America, and in fact increasingly also to North America with its rapidly growing Hispanic population, a similar claim could easily be made for Spain and Spanish literature. Buescu summarized her views on lusophone literature in a world literature context in two articles, one (2021) she authored alone, and the other (2022) co-authored with her former PhD student Simão Valente.

Lisbon's Centro de Estudos Comparatistas also participated in the "University and School together for a European Literary Canon" project, funded by the European Union and coordinated by the University La Sapienza in Rome. This resulted in a series of volumes or CDs, each including 15 common chapters plus a chapter on a writer from the national canon, in Portuguese (Buescu, Ribeiro, and Silva 2012), Italian (Antonelli et al. 2012), Spanish (Arbor Aldea 2012), Romanian (Fotache and Papadima 2012). A German equivalent apparently never materialized although at the University of Kiel there is a website dedicated to the German part of the project.[8] There is, however, an article in German, by one of the participants from the University of Kiel, that summarizes the project (Gómez-Montero 2013). As the project aimed at providing teaching materials for high schools around Europe it echoes the Danish case described earlier. A project such as this is part of a recent turn toward conceiving of Europe's various national literatures no longer necessarily as separate entities, but as constituent parts of a larger European entity in a global context and next to other such larger entities, whether geographically or culturally delimited or defined. This trend also surfaces in the four-volume *Literature: A World History* (Damrosch and Lindberg-Wada 2022). An example of a volume that treats European literature as one integrated whole and not as a set of juxtaposed national literatures is *European Literary History: An Introduction* (Levie and De Pourcq 2018).

In Italy, Armando Gnisci and Franca Sinopoli for a long time have been pleading for extending the study of literature beyond narrow national boundaries, and for re-situating Italian literature within the wider contexts of European literature, of the Mediterranean (Ďurišin and Gnisci 2000), and of the wider world (Sinopoli 2022).

What transpires from these cases, then, is that in the early decades of the third millennium the "world" of world literature looks different from different locations. As we saw, this was already the case with earlier histories and anthologies of world literature, usually depending upon the national point of

122 *World Literature in European Academe*

departure of the author or authors. It was certainly also the case with the research carried out in the former Soviet Institutes of World Literature in Moscow, and in Ďurišin's Institute for World Literature in Brno. In the Yugoslavia of Josip Broz Tito, from the 1960s to the 1980s, the creation of the Non-Aligned Movement (of which Tito was one of the leaders) led to yet a wholly different "alignment" of the world's literatures as researched and taught in Yugoslavia's Institute of World Literature (Bahun 2012, 2022). At present, however, we see wholly new alignments appearing.

Conclusion

- In the history of world literature, "minor" or "smaller" European literatures have been routinely semi-peripheralized.
- With the shift of attention in the United States to other parts of the world than Europe, and hence also to other "major" literatures, those minor European literatures have become peripheral.
- In a number of European reactions to this state of affairs we can recognize attempts to re-calibrate such minor literatures within the newly emerging world literature paradigm – quite often this involves the recovery of native precursors.
- In Europe approaches to teaching world literature have only really gained momentum over the last two decades and have developed along different lines in different countries but they show interesting variations upon the American model.

Notes

1. http://litteraturhistorie.au.dk/; accessed 28 November 2010.
2. http://mit.au.dk/coursecatalogue/index.cfm?elemid=37465&topid=37465&elemid=40508&topid=40508&sem=F2011&udd=&art=&hom=; accessed 28 November 2010.
3. http://studieinfo.au.dk/bachelor_introduction_en.cfm?fag=1231; accessed 28 November 2010.
4. http://cvs.au.dk/; accessed 28 November 2010.
5. https://cc.au.dk/en/about-the-school/departments; accessed 07 April 2023.
6. https://cc.au.dk/om-instituttet/afdelinger; accessed 07 April 2022.
7. https://studier.ku.dk/bachelor/litteraturvidenskab/; accessed 09 April 2023.
8. https://www.uni-kiel.de/elica/index.htm; accessed 10 April 2023.

6 World Literature as System

Overview

Goethe often spoke of world literature in metaphorical terms related to the domain of trade and of the exchange of goods. So did Marx and Engels when, in their 1848 *Communist Manifesto*, they mentioned world literature. In their wake there have sprung up several systemic approaches to literature, and to world literature, stressing not the intrinsic literary value of such or such a work, author, or genre, but examining the circulation of literary works, genres, and authors within a transnational and even a global context. Two recent such approaches are those of Pascale Casanova, interpreting all of world literature as centered upon Paris as of the end of the Renaissance, and of Franco Moretti, tracing the emergence, growth, and spread of the novel as a world literature genre. Both approaches have run into severe criticism, but the amount of debate they have engendered, and its heat, are in themselves proof of the centrality of world literature to contemporary literary studies. Other scholars have proposed less globally ambitious schemes, focusing on regional circuits in a global context: Dionýsz Ďurišin, Karen Thornber, Alexander Beecroft.

The "Free Trade" of Literature

Eckermann records that on Sunday 15 July 1827 Goethe, in the context of a conversation on Thomas Carlyle's *Life of Schiller* remarked that,

> It really is a very good thing that with this close intercourse between Frenchmen, Englishmen and Germans we have a chance of correcting each other's errors … this is the great advantage that world literature affords, one which will in time become more and more obvious.
>
> (Strich 1949: 249)

The English "intercourse" here stands for the German "Verkehr," which, as Jonathan Arac reminds us, translates in "a standard dictionary" as "*traffic, transportation, communication, commerce, intercourse* in its sexual as well as other senses, and *communion*" (Arac 2004: 96). We might add to that the term

DOI: 10.4324/9781003366713-7

"circulation." Elsewhere, Arac quotes a passage from Goethe's 1830 preface to the German translation of Carlyle's biography of Schiller to make the point that,

> Goethe argued that world literature arose because the Napoleonic Wars had forced all the combatant nations into "aware[ness] of much that was foreign," producing "intellectual needs that were previously unknown" [and that] to assuage these needs required "free intellectual trade relations (*freien geistigen Handelsverkehr*)."
>
> (Arac 2008: 755)

Many commentators have pointed out the almost seamless analogy Goethe here establishes between the circulation of ideas and that of goods. In fact, of course, ideas also traded as goods, that is to say in the form of "material" books and periodicals. While Goethe was imaginatively moving from the free exchange of intellectual goods to the trade in actual material goods in his use of analogy, with Karl Marx (1818–1883) and Friedrich Engels (1820–1895) the vector goes the other way in their *Communist Manifesto* (1848).

The relevant passage, which I quoted in full in Chapter 1, has often been explained, especially after the Russian Revolution of 1917 and by Soviet literary critics, as Marx and Engels investing "world literature" with a utopian dimension, as the future realization in the realm of culture of the erasure of boundaries they also conceived of as the ultimate goal of a classless society. In reality, Peter Gossens contends, the use of the term in the *Communist Manifesto* of 1848 signals the end of the idea of *Weltliteratur* as "utopian model for society" (Gossens 2010: 15; geschellschaftsutopisches Modell). For a number of younger writers, the concept of *Weltliteratur* had, between Goethe's death and the socially driven revolutions of 1848 that shook all of Europe, and partially based on a utopian reading of Goethe's *Wilhelm Meisters Wanderjahre*, been enlarged from the literary to the social realm, especially in the orbit of early social-democratic thought. With the failed revolutions of 1848, however, such utopianism had lost all credibility. Hence, Gossens argues, the passage in which Marx refers to world literature:

> in one sense situates itself in the context of a national understanding of culture that sees in the accumulation of [national] literatures a model for world literature and hence has left behind the era in which peoples were united as one people. On the other side the thought of world literature for Marx is not revolutionary in the socialist sense, but as a strategy fueled by the bourgeoisie that, along with the free trade that Marx criticizes at the same time, in the final analysis serves imperialist and colonialist ends in the sense of a "free development of capital."
>
> (zu einen steht sie argumentativ in der Nachfolge eines nationalisierten Kulturverständnisses, das in der Addition der "Literaturen" ein Modell von Weltliteratur entdeckt und damit den Völker verbindenden Gestus der Frühzeit hinter sich gelassen hat. Ausserdem, und das ist die andere

Seite der Medaille, ist der Gedanke der Weltliteratur für Marx nicht revolutionär im Sinne des Sozialismus, sondern eine von der Bourgeoisie angestossene Strategie, die, wie der zur gleichen Zeit von Marx bekritisierte Freihandel, letzlich imperialistische und kolonialistische Ziele im Sinne einer "freie[n] Entwicklung des Kapitals" ... verfolgt.)

(Gossens 2010: 16)

To bring out the full import of Marx and Engels's remarks, the passage that immediately follows upon that which I earlier referred to should also be quoted:

The bourgeoisie, by the rapid improvement of all instruments of production, by the immensely facilitated means of communication, draws all, even the most barbarian, nations into civilisation. The cheap prices of commodities are the heavy artillery with which it batters down all Chinese walls, with which it forces the barbarians' intensely obstinate hatred of foreigners to capitulate. It compels all nations, on pain of extinction, to adopt the bourgeois mode of production; it compels them to introduce what it calls civilisation into their midst, i.e., to become bourgeois themselves. In one word, it creates a world after its own image.

(Marx and Engels 2010: 16)

In Chapter 1 we saw that Goethe himself was not completely at ease with the implications of the already ongoing commercialization of literature in his time, and especially in the twentieth century philosophers, theoreticians, and critics of a more generally progressive or left-leaning bent have tended to follow him in this. The Hungarian Geörgy Lukács (1885–1971), the German Theodor Adorno (1903–1969), and the American Fredric Jameson (1934–) have all expressed their deep suspicion, or sometimes their outright condemnation, of what they saw as the "popular," that is to say the commercially driven in culture in general and in literature in particular. The irony, of course, is that they often found the popular to be quite a different thing. For Lukács, after his early *The Theory of the Novel* (1974 [1916]) and his turn to Marxism, only instances of true realism qualified as valid literature in a pre-Marxist or communist society. They did so because they depicted their characters as in a dialectical, and hence critical, relation to their world (Lukács 1983 [1937], 2001 [1938]). This kind of realism Lukács recognized in the works of Sir Walter Scott, Honoré de Balzac, Maxim Gorky, and Thomas Mann. In contrast, works written for entertainment could only pretend to be realist, because their characters were implicitly in alignment with the dominant tenets of their society. Modernist works of any kind disqualified themselves in Lukács' eyes because they followed the market logic of capitalism in responding to fast-changing fashions as embodied in the -isms succeeding one another in European literature since the middle of the nineteenth century. Adorno, heavily influenced by Lukács, criticized the culture industry for its "commodity fetishism" and hence its complicity with an alienating power structure (Adorno and Horkheimer 1988 [1944], 1969 [1951], 2003 [1966]).

The leading neo-Marxist American critic and literary theoretician Fredric Jameson, himself heavily influenced by Adorno, directs his critique specifically against postmodernism and instead defends the continuing oppositional relevance of the avant-garde along modernist lines (Jameson 1984, 1991). With this stance Jameson is close to the German philosopher Jürgen Habermas (1929–), who upheld a similar position in his "Modernity, an Incomplete Project" (Habermas 1992 [1980]), and the equally German writer and philosopher Walter Benjamin who in his "Six Theses on History" (1982 [1940]) had argued the necessity to continuously re-think history from an oppositional perspective, oppositional that is to dominant power. In all this, of course, Lukács, Adorno, Jameson, and Benjamin subscribe to the role of the politically committed intellectual as a rootless and alienated individual, in the Marxist sense, in his (bourgeois or industrial capitalist) society. Benjamin and Adorno, along with Max Horkheimer (1895–1973), were leading figures of the so-called Frankfurt School at the Institute for Social Research of the University of Frankfurt in Germany. Habermas still is. Because they were inspired by Marxist thought but wanted to apply this in a critical spirit and not subject to the doctrinaire interpretations of orthodox communism as it had come to power in the Soviet Union and later in most of Eastern and Central Europe after World War II, they are usually referred to as neo-Marxists or Western Marxists. Their work has been very influential for the development of more recent cultural studies approaches.

While a graduate student at Yale University in the mid-1950s, Jameson studied under Auerbach, who in his essay "Philology and *Weltliteratur*" of 1952 had voiced suspicions similar to those of Adorno and Horkheimer with regard to "a standardized world" with as ultimate possible consequence "a single literary culture, only a few literary languages and perhaps even a single literary language," as "herewith the notion of *Weltliteratur* would be ... at once realized and destroyed" (Auerbach 2009 [1952]: 127). However, as he saw such a homogenization of world literature as not immediately imminent, Auerbach gives over most room to discussing the need to find a point of departure, what he called an *Ansatzpunkt*, from which to synthesize the overwhelming wealth of material world literature lays out before the researcher or literary historian. Damrosch (2003) and Apter (2006a), and from other perspectives altogether Wai-Chee Dimock (2006a, 2006b) and Djelal Kadir (2011) have taken Auerbach's lesson to heart. Damrosch (2003) finds his *Ansatzpunkt* in his elliptical or triangulated reading of the past and the distant, or the present and the near. Apter (2006a, 2013) finds it in translation. Dimock (2006b) finds it in American literature as world literature. Kadir (2011) finds it in looking for literary, philosophical, and academic exiles and wanderers making up a loose network of precursors to the eventual discipline of comparative literature. Both Apter (2006a) and Kadir (2011) make Auerbach himself into an *Ansatzpunkt* when they cast him as the subject of one of their chapters. For all four, however different they otherwise might be, the method pursued is basically philological in that it consists of a close study of the texts analyzed. In a very loose sense, we could also say that notwithstanding all their differences all four of them stay close to a typically American paradigm, hallowed since the New Criticism, of close reading.

Systemic World Literature

The answers some other would-be historians of world literature have come up with are very different. Whereas the approaches to world literature discussed in the previous paragraphs and chapters mostly argued from an ideational base implicitly assuming the value of "high" literature and of the literary works they dealt with, in the *Communist Manifesto* Marx and Engels are arguing literature from a materialist point of view – that is to say, as operating in and under market conditions. In other words, what is in question here is not the aesthetic value of one work over another, but rather which works "circulate" better in terms of that other possible translation of "Verkehr" we alluded to earlier. In the second half of the twentieth century, particularly, there have emerged a number of approaches – most of them influenced in one way or another by Marxist principles – that concentrate on the circulation of literature rather than on making distinctions in terms of literary value. In the words of the Belgian comparatist José Lambert (1987) these are "systemic" approaches in that they study literature as system and not as isolated instance. In other words, with them the question is not which work is to be more highly rated, but which work *has been* more highly rated, or more widely disseminated, at which moment in time and where and why.

Three such approaches are the cultural semiotics of Yuri Lotman (1922–1993), of the university of Tartu in Estonia, the theory of interliterary processes of Dionýsz Ďurišin (1929–1997), and the polysystem theory of Itamar Even-Zohar (1939–). Of these three only Ďurišin ever explicitly worked on world literature himself, presenting the synthesis of his thoughts on the subject in his 1992 book *Čo je svetová literatúra?* (What Is World Literature?). Because of his untimely death, just before the renewed interest in world literature in the United States and Western Europe, as well as for the specific reasons discussed by Domínguez (2012a, 2022a), Ďurišin's theories have remained almost unknown in the West, and particularly so in the United States (Swiggers 1982; Bassel and Gomel 1991). As such they have played no role in the current debate on world literature, at least not on the level at which the leading interlocutors in that debate operate. In Italy and in Spain, though, Ďurišin has had some influence (Domínguez 2012a, 2022a). An example of how Ďurišin's ideas can be applied is to be found in a book he co-edited with Armando Gnisci (1946–2019) in 2000, *Il Mediterranea: una rete inter-letteraria* (The Mediterranean: an Inter-Literary Network). A thorough discussion of Ďurišin in the context of Czech and Slovak world literature studies, as of the entire tradition of these studies, is Zelenka (2022).

Tihanov (2019) does the same for the Russian Formalists. Even-Zohar's influence has been most marked in translation studies, and I will deal with him in the relevant chapter. Lotman, like Ďurišin, died before the revival of interest in world literature. However, his "cause," so to speak, has been picked up by Ilya Kliger (2010) in reaction to more recent systemic theories. Likewise in reaction to these same theories, Alexander Beecroft (2008, 2015) has developed an approach to world literature based on the social systems theory of the German sociologist Niklas Luhmann (1927–1998). The theories in question, formulated by Pascale Casanova and Franco Moretti, respectively, can in fact be said to have galvanized, rejuvenated, and re-oriented the discussion on world literature at the turn of the third millennium.

Pascale Casanova and *The World Republic of Letters*

Casanova, in her *République mondiale des lettres* (1999), published in English translation as *The World Republic of Letters* in 2004, starts from the theories of the French sociologist Pierre Bourdieu (1930–2002). As her *Ansatzpunkt* Casanova refers to Fernand Braudel's injunction in his *Civilisation matérielle, économie et capitalisme* (1979; Civilization and Capitalism) to describe the world "from a certain vantage point" (Casanova 2004: 4). Casanova observes "world literary space as a history and a geography" (Casanova 2004: 4). The structures of this worldwide literary space, she claims, have been consistently obscured by two generally accepted customs. The first is to look upon the writing of literature as an act of pure creation. The second is to look at literature within the framework of national literatures. Both of these could be termed as being part of the literary "habitus" with the term used by Bourdieu for a mindset that has become interiorized to the point of seeming "natural" to those that operate in what Bourdieu again called a certain "field," in this particular case the field of literature. Whereas Bourdieu mainly restricted his analyses to the national sphere, Casanova argues that literature does not, or does not exclusively, play itself out within the confines of a national literature; nor is it an act of pure creation. In fact, she reminds us, several writers, and not the least among them, have themselves hinted at this truth, but the "field" – and here we can think of the realm of literature itself but even more of the academic field concerned with the study of literature – has consistently, out of habitus, ignored this.

As instances upholding her views, she cites the passage from Goethe quoted earlier in this chapter. She finds further support with Paul Valéry (1871–1945), an early twentieth-century French poet, critic, and philosopher, and an important European public intellectual in the years between the two world wars. Valéry talked of civilization as "a form of capital whose increase may continue for centuries" and of culture as "a form of capital" (Casanova 2004: 9–10). And she approvingly cites Antoine Berman (1942–1991) that the emergence of a *Weltliteratur* runs parallel with that of a *Weltmarkt* (Casanova 2004: 14; Berman 1984: 90). Just as for Marx the world and its history formed a battleground for power between the classes, so with the literary world for Casanova: "Its history is one of incessant struggle and competition over the very nature of literature itself – an endless succession of literary manifestos, movements, assaults, and revolutions ... these rivalries are what have created world literature" (Casanova 2004: 12). And just as on the Stock Exchange the value of shares and bonds rises and falls, so she says, approvingly citing Valéry (1960 [1939]) again, on "the bourse of literary values" (Casanova 2004: 12).

On Casanova's literary stock exchange literary works, and the national literatures to which they belong, are valued according to their cultural or symbolic capital, to use another term from Bourdieu's sociological arsenal. The older and the more universally recognized a work is, and the more "classics" a specific literature numbers, the higher their stock. Other assets of what Casanova calls the "literary patrimony," or "capital," of a culture or country are a well-developed literary establishment made up of publishers, translators, critics, literary journals, bookstores, libraries, universities, and academies providing the necessary "volume of trade" and bestowing literary "credit" upon the works circulating in the culture or country in question. A major asset is the language a writer or a literature uses. Some languages rank higher than others because of their seniority, their historical importance, the number of speakers, and their literary capital accumulated over the ages. The latter also explains why the languages with the greater number of speakers do not necessarily note highest on the literary stock exchange. The more literary capital accrues to a specific language the higher that language's "index or measure of literary authority" (Casanova 2004: 20):

> Such an index would incorporate a number of factors: the age, the "nobility," and the number of literary texts written in a given language, the number of universally recognized works, the number of translations, and so on. It therefore becomes necessary to distinguish between languages that are associated with "high" culture – languages having a high degree of literary value – and those that are spoken by a great many people. The former are languages that are read not only by those who speak them, but also by readers who think that authors who write in these languages or who are translated into them are worth reading. They amount to a kind of license, a permit of circulation certifying an author's membership in a literary circle.

First on a European scale and more recently on a world scale, Casanova sees literatures and writers battling for pre-eminence. Before the thirteenth century in Europe there is no rivalry on the European literary scene, at least not between separate literatures, as there is only one literary system using only one language: Latin. There is, of course, Greek being used in the Byzantine empire, but literary contacts between that empire and the rest of Europe always remained very limited. And equally self-evidently, within the non-

Byzantine part of Europe and within the one literary system prevalent there, authors may still vie with one another for greater recognition. It is only with the emergence of literatures in the vernacular, though, that we see an opposition shaping up between the dominant system and a rival one. This first happens in Italy, with Dante (1265–1321), Petrarch (1304–1374), and Boccaccio (1313–1375) challenging the hegemony of Latin by creating, "inventing" so to speak, a powerful vernacular literature. This is not to say that Latin immediately disappears as a literary language nor, and even less so, as the language of authority, in religion and in science. In the religious sphere Latin preserved its dominance until the sixteenth century, and then only lost it to the vernacular where Protestantism eventually gained the upper hand, while remaining dominant until the middle of the twentieth century where Catholicism continued to reign. In science Latin remained dominant until the seventeenth century, and only gradually gave way to the vernaculars after that. It is from the challenge to Latin as the language of science in Joachim Du Bellay's *Deffence et illustration de la langue francoyse* (Defense and Illustration of the French Language) of 1549 that Casanova dates the establishment of France, and more particularly Paris, as the center of the literary world. Even if Italian predates French as a vernacular literary language, it is in France that there first arises a truly "national" literature in the vernacular, and centered upon a single major center, Paris. Whereas French, and a French literary system, spring up in rivalry with Latin and the Latin-dominated European-wide system, henceforth other "national" systems in Europe will emerge in imitation of, and in rivalry with, French and the French system. Implicitly, therefore, French literature continues to function as the fixed point from which, and against which, all other literatures measure themselves; that is also why Casanova metaphorically calls Paris "the Greenwich meridian of literature" (Casanova 2004: 87).

Parallel to this Casanova sees "literature," and this very much along the lines developed by Bourdieu about the various professional and other fields he distinguishes as operating in modernity and modern society, as assuming the character of an autonomous domain, irrespective of nation or state. It is the existence of a semi-independent so-called "Republic of Letters" in the sixteenth to eighteenth centuries, loosely uniting writers and thinkers across Europe, who moreover often kept in contact by means of "letters," first using Latin and later French as their means of communication, that inspired Casanova for the title of her book. Paris, then, becomes and remains the literary center of this autonomous domain, functioning as the great clearinghouse for works, writers and literatures that aspire to recognition beyond the purely national or local level. Casanova sees this system as continuing to function until at least the 1960s, and even beyond. It does so by serving as the point where foreign works are being translated, reviewed, praised (or damned), and from there on disseminated into the wider world. In essence, Casanova is here claiming for Paris, and for the French language and the French literary system, what Goethe had suggested might be the role of

German as privileged mediator for first Europe's and later the world's literatures. Even Goethe, though, had recognized the pre-eminence of Paris in matters of culture and literature, or its greater "literary capital," which also equals "authority," in Casanova's term.

Criticism of Casanova

Many objections and questions can be raised with regard to Casanova's views in general, and to her resolute and absolute focus on Paris as *the* center of the world literary system in particular. One of the earliest, most closely reasoned and forceful attacks came from Christopher Prendergast, who objects that much of what Casanova is doing is grounded in metaphors and anecdotes rather than in "a more theoretically robust explanation" (Prendergast 2004a: 8). Although he expresses admiration for Casanova's drawing upon a wide-ranging set of examples to illustrate her theory, he also questions her choice of examples, arguing that the hypotheses from which she starts necessarily "skew the picture, such that the inclusions and omissions, as well as the distribution of emphasis in the discussions, constantly return us in one way or another to the shores of the *Vieux Continent*" (Prendergast 2004a: 9). Moreover, Prendergast contends, Casanova's prioritizing of the categories of "nation" and "literature" to mount her construction of world literature as an international competition leads her to completely misinterpret, in the case of "nation," some of her prime examples, among whom Kafka, Joyce, and Beckett, and in the case of "literature," the realities of how texts, and indeed oral materials, function in societies other than the (West-)European. Casanova's exclusive concentration on the struggle between nations, according to Prendergast, also leads her to grossly misread developments that may be internal to national literatures as steered or provoked by inter-national competition. Objections to Casanova's approach were also voiced by Debjani Ganguly (2008).

Helena Buescu (2012) argues that Casanova completely by-passes the historical notion of the Republic of Letters. The latter, she reminds us, was also, and indeed primarily so, concerned with "letters" in a much broader sense than Casanova's narrow concentration upon "literature" in the sense of "belles-lettres." Moreover, Buescu adduces, the historical Republic of Letters antedates the rise of national literatures, so for Casanova to ground her theory about the development of a "World Republic of Letters" in what she conceives as the struggle between national literatures is an anachronism. Like Prendergast, Buescu too questions Casanova's brushing aside of the Italian precedence in the use of the vernacular for both literary and other purposes, and her not mentioning any other European vernaculars if not as pre-dating then at least as paralleling the emergence of French as a national literary language. She points out, for instance, that the use of Portuguese antedates by several centuries that of French for some of the purposes Casanova sees the latter as fulfilling as of the sixteenth century, and that Spanish and Portuguese grammarians of the late fifteenth and early sixteenth centuries were already concerned with the role of European vernaculars in colonial settings.

Mads Rosendahl Thomsen has proposed the existence of "shifting focal points" for an international canon as a corrective to Casanova's exclusive concentration upon Paris (Thomsen 2008a: 33). Although his concept of such "focal points" does not quite correspond to what Casanova means when she talks of Paris as the ultimate authority-holding and recognition-conveying center of world literature until the 1960s, we could pick up on Thomsen's suggestion by, as he does, pointing to the at least temporary emergence of rival centers to Paris. As Casanova herself intimates, this is certainly the case with London and New York as of the 1960s, parallel to the loss of prestige and usage of French as *the*, and over the last few decades indeed even as *an* international language of trade, diplomacy, and culture. But we could argue that similar shifts occurred for instance around the turn of the twentieth century with the rise of Berlin and Vienna as potential alternatives for Paris as the literary centers of Europe, and that it is only political vicissitudes that have cut short that rise. Berlin, indeed, might actually be re-emerging as such in the twenty-first century, if not on a world scale then at least on a European one, with both Paris and Berlin having to cede first place on the world scale to English-language centers. But we could also argue that Weimar, or perhaps rather Goethe himself, at the time of his writing about world literature occupied a similarly central position within "European, in other words, World Literature" (Strich 1949: 351). After all, Goethe for "all the world," that is to say Europe at the time, himself stood as the ultimate arbiter of literature in the first third of the nineteenth century.

Criticism of Casanova on a more fundamental level perhaps is expressed by Jerome McGann, who asks:

> What if we decide that the center/periphery map has been drawn Under Western Eyes only and that it gives poor service in a truly globalized world? What if – going further still – we were to propose, to theorize, that in such a world, this myth [of literature as an aesthetically autonomous system] resembles less a map than a kind of equilibrium device, a cultural gyroscope for maintaining cultural status quo? It seems to me, looking from my marginal American position, that such thoughts are now common among non-Euro-Americans.
>
> (McGann 2008: 651–652)

David Damrosch scathingly sums up much of the early criticism of Casanova when in a footnote in his own 2003 *What is World Literature?* he condemns *La République mondiale des lettres* for its "implicit triumphalism" and suggests that it might have been better titled "*La République parisienne des lettres*" (the Parisian republic of letters) because it is "an unsatisfactory account of world literature in general" yet "actually a good account of the operation of world literature within the modern French context" (Damrosch 2003: 27).

Still, on the same page that he indicts Casanova, Damrosch himself admits that "for any given observer, even a genuinely global perspective means a perspective from somewhere, and global patterns of the circulation of world literature take shape in their local manifestation" (Damrosch 2003: 27). Therefore, he asserts, he himself in his book will be concentrating "particularly (though not exclusively) on world literature as it has been construed over the past century in a specific cultural space, that of the formerly provincial and now metropolitan United States" (Damrosch 2003: 27–28). By referring to the USA as "metropolitan" Damrosch perhaps has in mind the distinction that Prendergast also invokes in his critique of Casanova, and which he borrows from Anne Querrien (1986). Prendergast sums up Querrien's views as follows:

> The capital is a political and cultural "centre," with the power and the authority to dominate a wider "territory," to keep in place a "social hierarchy" and to "subjugate a population ... to a common heritage." A metropolis on the other hand "is not a centre and has no centre," it "has no identity to preserve," it "begins with the slightest desire to exchange," is "made up of networks," puts "an incongruous mix of beings into circulation" and is the place where migrants find their socially predetermined destination.
>
> (Prendergast 2004a: 20)

For Prendergast, twentieth-century Paris is both capital and metropolis, serving different and even partially antithetical functions, one for the nation, the other for "the world." This also suggests the possibility of two different literary systems co-existing in one singular place and of the national system, instead of serving as the arbiter for the world, re-aligning itself along "world" lines generated elsewhere rather than the other way around. Perhaps we can even speculate that this is what has been happening over the last two decades or so with French literature, as Casanova suggests, becoming more "postcolonial." The publication in 2007 of the manifest "Pour une littérature-monde" in Paris but arguing for a world literature in French not rooted in "l'hexagone" (the hexagon, shorthand for continental France) would then go to support this view.

Be all this as it may, we may wonder whether Damrosch's own 2003 book does not reveal at least a residual American bias, even if packaged much more subtly than Casanova's French equivalent. Damrosch, in his triangulated readings, from the epic of Gilgamesh and pre-Columbian Mexican incantations to the "Zairean" (now again: Congolese) Mwbil Ngal's novel *Giambatista Viko*, and from ancient Egyptian poems over Mechtild von Magdeburg, Franz Kafka, and P.G. Wodehouse to Rigoberta Menchú and Milorad Pavič's *Dictionary of the Khazars*, demonstrates how the cultures of the globe can be made intelligible and accessible to his American readers. These readers are, in the first instance, American undergraduate students, and, to a lesser extent, graduate students of comparative literature. Consequently, Damrosch's main concern, in line with the typical American approach to world literature as I discuss elsewhere in this book, is essentially didactic or pedagogic. It therefore follows the more generally American didactic preference for detailed readings of singular texts usually associated with the New Criticism. In contrast, Casanova's book, as Louis Menand put it in a joint review of *The World Republic of Letters* and James English's *The Economy of Prestige* (2005), is "simply [an] effort ... to understand literature sociologically" (Menand 2005). The same point is taken up by Frances Ferguson in one of the most spirited defenses of Casanova. Against Damrosch's and Prendergast's complaints that Casanova misses the subtleties of such and such an author (Kafka is Prendergast's example), Ferguson objects that Casanova writes as a sociologist of literature and can therefore dispense with close reading. Contrary to what Casanova has often been charged with, Ferguson argues, she does not write from a personal, because a chauvinistically French and Parisian, stance. "We should not mistake her argument about the centrality of Paris in the world republic of letters for an expression of personal partiality cloaking itself in the language of system," Ferguson reprimands Damrosch and Prendergast (Ferguson 2008: 665). "Casanova's discussion," Ferguson maintains, "is methodologically unified, in that she identifies the way inequality operates in the literary field and can thus provide a fresh sense of how the linguistic materials of literature function in the unequal distribution of literary capital" (Ferguson 2008: 669). It is certainly not a coincidence that it is two critics and academics of a decidedly "leftist" or neo-Marxist bent, Perry Anderson in *The London Review of Books* and Terry Eagleton in *The New Statesman*, who wrote some of the most positive reviews of Casanova's book upon its appearance in English in 2004.

Damrosch simply finds himself in the opposite corner to Casanova's systemically informed investigation of the mechanics of (admittedly, a particular crosscut of) world literature. And while his approach, at first sight, might be more "open" than Casanova's, his own admittance that any take on world literature is always going to be a perspective from somewhere basically repeats Moulton's similar assertion in the very first book on world literature. Obviously, Damrosch's perspective is more circumspectly phrased and is less directly and unabashedly unilateral than Moulton's. Waïl Hassan has argued that

> the pedagogical application of the concept of "world literature" in the United States since [the] Second World War has developed in step with the political, economic, and strategic remapping of global relations, sometimes in subtle ways that tend to mask its affiliations with power.
> (Hassan 2000: 38)

However, he also notes, "there are ... other non-hegemonic conceptions of difference that self-consciously historicize their understanding of world cultures and literatures while maintaining 'critical vigilance' (to use Gayatri Chakravorty Spivak's term) toward their own affiliations with power" (Hassan 2000: 40). While Damrosch is clearly engaging in such self-conscious historicization, one still cannot fail to wonder whether Damrosch's perspective is not just as intimately related to a particular mapping or re-mapping of global relations as is Casanova's. The bottom line then seems to be that Damrosch and Casanova are simply "writing" different "world literatures."

Gisèle Sapiro and Delia Ungureanu edited a 2020 issue on Casanova for the *Journal of World Literature* which in expanded form also appeared as a book in 2022 – contributions by among others Damrosch, Thomsen, Samoyault, and Tsu.

Franco Moretti and Conjectures on World Literature

In a statement that has become famous, and also much reviled, Franco Moretti in 2000 declared that, given the multiplicity of the world's languages and the overwhelming number of texts written in those languages, "world literature is not an object, it's a *problem*" (Moretti 2004: 149). He proposed to solve this problem by what he calls "distant reading" (2004: 151). This basically involves not the close reading of literary texts themselves but what literary historians have said about them, and especially about the regularities found in larger aggregations of texts. These regularities are then interpreted with a combination of methods drawn from the social and the biological sciences. More specifically, Moretti combines evolution theory and world systems theory as developed by the American social and economic historian Immanuel Wallerstein (1930–2019) in *The Modern World System* (1974–2011). Wallerstein sees the entire world starting to function as one overall economic system of exchange with the voyages of discovery, and particularly with the discovery of the Americas. World systems theory posits the unity of the world's economic system (and in its wake, or concomitant with it, also other systems such as the military and political ones) as of the sixteenth century, with a core (Western Europe), a semi-periphery (the rest of Europe), and a periphery (the rest of the world) in a relationship of exchange. These exchanges can be charted according to volume, intensity, kind of products, and so on. The same thing can be done for literature, both in the form of actual material goods, such as the trade in books, or in translations, and in that of the ideas and forms embodied in those books: genres, styles, motifs, etc. Moretti published the results of a research program carried out along such lines in his *Atlas of the European Novel, 1800–1900* (1998). Having been inspired from the very beginning of his studies at the University of Rome under Galvano Della Volpe (1895–1968) by the latter's scientific Marxism, the study of literature according to world systems theory principles made Moretti realize the basic inequality at work in the world literary system.

Although couched in different terms, and elaborated according to a different methodology, then, Moretti's starting position at least is very close to Casanova's. His study of the European novel between 1800 and 1900, for instance, led him to discern a system with Paris and (to a slightly lesser degree) London at the core, a number of countries immediately surrounding France along with Scandinavia as a semi-periphery, and most of Central and Eastern Europe as the periphery. Moretti quotes Itamar Even-Zohar, applying polysystem theory rather than world-systems theory, as having reached largely similar conclusions about the power relationships obtaining between core and more peripheral literatures (Moretti 2009a: 402). "The study of world literature is – inevitably," Moretti says, "a struggle for symbolic hegemony across the world" (Moretti 2004: 158).

In his 1998 book and his 2000 article, Moretti distinguishes between the model of the tree, which he takes to stand for "the passage from unity to diversity," and that of the wave, which he sees as "uniformity engulfing an initial diversity" (Moretti 2004: 160). The tree he associates with national literatures developing and distinguishing themselves from one another over time; the wave he links to market forces radiating out from a core. For the study of what he calls the "comparative morphology (the systematic study of how forms vary in space and time)" (Moretti 2004: 158) of world literature, Moretti deploys graphs, maps, and trees in a combination of evolution and world-systems analysis (Moretti 2005). He had already used evolution theory in one of his early books, *Modern Epic* (1996), while world-systems analysis, as we just saw, largely inspired his 1998 book on the European novel. Now he combines the two into one model for world literature, although active in different historical times. Evolution, leading to divergence, or the tree-metaphor, pertained before (roughly, and as Moretti himself says, oversimplifying things) the eighteenth century. World-systems analysis, or convergence, modelled along the maps and graphs metaphors, applies from the eighteenth century onwards. When elements emanating from the core and diffusing themselves into the periphery meet with local forms, the resulting combination can – and does – lead to new original forms. Moretti's example is the diffusion of the novel in the nineteenth and twentieth centuries.

Radiating out from a core in Western Europe centered on Paris and London, the novel, when it reaches semi- and full peripheries, retains the plotlines exported from the center but adopts indigenous characters and styles. The result, as Moretti puts it, is "a hybrid form," but one that, rather than amalgamation, produces "dissonance, disagreement, at times a lack of integration between what happens in the plot, and how the style evaluates the story, and presents it to the reader" (Moretti 2009a: 406). In other words, what we have is "form as struggle," a struggle "between the story that comes from the core, and the viewpoint that 'receives' it in the periphery," and the fact that the two are not "seamlessly fused is not just an aesthetic given ... but the crystallization of an underlying *political* tension" (Moretti 2009a: 406). Finally, he sums up the situation with regard to world literature, and particularly with regard to the fact that apparently "we still do not know what [it] is," as follows; perhaps, he says, this is because

> we keep collapsing under a single term two distinct world literatures: one that precedes the eighteenth century – and one that follows it. The "first" *Weltliteratur*, a mosaic of separate, "local" cultures; it is characterized by strong internal diversity; it produces new forms mostly by divergence; and

is best explained by (some version of) evolutionary theory. The "second" *Weltliteratur* (which I would prefer to call world literary system) is unified by the international literary market; it shows a growing, and at times stunning amount of sameness; its main mechanism of change is convergence; and is best explained by (some version of) world-systems analysis.

(Moretti 2009a: 407)

The "intellectual challenge posed by *Weltliteratur* in the twenty-first century," then, Moretti concludes, is to learn "to study *the past as past* ... and *the present as present*" (Moretti 2009a: 407).

Against Moretti

If anything, Moretti's views on world literature have occasioned even more reactions than have Casanova's, and even more piqued reactions from American comparatists. The large amount of attention Moretti's initial articles on world literature generated undoubtedly also has to do with the fact that they started appearing already in 2000, whereas Casanova's book, although in its original French version predating Moretti's very first article on the subject, remained untranslated until 2004, and only then really started being noticed beyond France. Jonathan Arac, in 2002, admitted that Moretti's 2000 "Conjectures on World Literature" made him uneasy because it so patently went against what in American academe had been the rule for at least some decades, namely the actual reading and analysis of specific texts. This is an issue that has continued to rankle in American academe, as the "Preface" to a 2009 *SubStance* issue on close reading reveals. Beyond this, however, Arac also has more fundamental questions about some of Moretti's claims. One of these has to do with Moretti's positioning of France and England, or Paris and London, at the core of a world system of literature, and his description of the meeting between what emanates from the core and what it finds in the periphery as resulting in a "compromise." I described the mechanism earlier. Arac points out that Henry Fielding's *Joseph Andrews* (1742) "defines itself as a 'comic epic in prose, *written after the manner of Cervantes*'," and that consequently "Moretti's modern core itself has arisen by adaptation from what, by a later date, had become the periphery" (Arac 2002: 38).

Moreover, Arac contends, in the model that Moretti adopts, Wallerstein's world-systems analysis, "the relation between core and periphery is synchronic – only its relation to the periphery allows the core to be core, and the two together define the system at a given point in time" (Arac 2002: 38). With Moretti,

> the centre's relation to the core operates by "influence" ... that is, the centre is earlier than the core: what in Wallerstein is spatial becomes, in Moretti, temporal; and the result comes closer than Moretti might wish to the old priorities of Western comparatism.
>
> (Arac 2002: 38)

Finally, Arac notes, Moretti's "distant reading" seems to eliminate the necessity for the scholar or student of world literature to know any but one dominant language, that is to say English, as it does not require any direct contact with literary texts themselves, but only with "second-hand" literary history, criticism, and theory, most or all of which may be available in English. The danger, Arac implies, is that this may reduce the actual material, even second hand, used to draw up Morettian large scale analyses of world literature to material written in English, thus in practice restricting "the world" of world literature to what is written about it in what is arguably the dominant or even hegemonic world language of what is equally arguably the world's hegemon, a phenomenon he dubbed "Anglo-globalism." Debjani Ganguly (2023) counters such "anglo-gobal" apocalypticism.

In a later article, on William Dean Howells and the languages of American fiction, Arac tempered his "suspicions" about Moretti's "distant reading." Arguing that "philological criticism is not just the same as close reading," he pointed to the examples of Mikhail Bakhtin and Edward Said as evidence that

> philological care for language and the work of language in human life may operate in the study of discourse practices and patterns that cross the bounds of individual works, even as those patterns are discerned and delineated through scrupulous attention to particular textual moments.
> (Arac 2007: 1)

"Yet," he pursued, "sometimes even this may be too close," so "despite my suspicions of Franco Moretti's 'distant' reading, my essay pursues a case where distance seems the right path" (Arac 2007: 1).

Critical noises similar to Arac's initial "suspicions" were made by Emily Apter, who finished off Moretti with the remark that his approach "favors narrative over linguistic engagement, and this, I would surmise, is ultimately the dangling participle of Moretti's revamped *Weltliteratur*" (Apter 2003: 256). A more whole-scale condemnation came from Gayatri Spivak, who, with reference to Arac's 2002 article, dismissed Moretti and Moretti-like endeavors because the world-systems theorists they relied upon she found to be "useless for literary study – that must depend on texture – because they equate economic with cultural systems" (Spivak 2003: 108). Spivak also objected to Moretti's ambition to treat those scholars in the periphery who did pay attention to the "texture" of literary works, in this case the novel, as "native informants" (Spivak 2003: 108).

A different kind of doubt was raised by Efraín Kristal (2002) regarding Spanish American literature, in which, he argued, not the novel but poetry and the essay were the dominant genres until the middle of the twentieth century, and unless or until Moretti's analyses can account for this it can hardly be called a "world system of literature." Francesca Orsini (2002) voiced pretty much the same objections with regard to the Indian subcontinent. Wai Chee Dimock chimed in with the by then familiar objections to Moretti's "distant reading" when she cautioned "against what strikes me as his over-commitment to general laws, to global postulates operating at some remove from the phenomenal world of particular texts" (Dimock 2006a: 90). Nirvana Tanoukhi (2008) questioned the applicability, and the lingering Eurocentric aspects, of Moretti's theories with respect to the African postcolonial novel. Earlier we saw that Frances Ferguson abounds with praise for Casanova. She is considerably more reserved about Moretti. Most importantly, the difference to her seems to reside in that Casanova attempts to elaborate a complete theory of world literature while Moretti stops at a partial one, thereby truncating the reach of his explanatory models. As Ferguson puts it:

> Moretti's desire to use graphs, maps, and trees to make the history of the novel more perspicuous points to the novel's loneliness and vulnerability even in its triumph. For the story of the survival of the novel is also very much the story of the disappearance of other narrative forms – the disappearance of painting and sculpture that could tell the story of Narcissus and Echo or the stories of Jonah and Noah, the movement of drama into the margins of public life, and the death-by-preservation of oral narratives that exist as their own fossil remains within the pages of books. Any study of the evolutionary history of any representational form, in other words, needs to incorporate into itself an account of its own nature – the things it is made of.
>
> (Ferguson 2008: 677)

Moretti himself answered his critics in 2003 with "More Conjectures." Systematically countering their objections, he concluded that,

> the way we imagine comparative literature is a mirror of how we see the world. ... "Conjectures" tried to do so against the background of the unprecedented possibility that the entire world may be subject to a single centre of power – and a centre which has long exerted an equally unprecedented symbolic hegemony.
>
> (Moretti 2003: 81)

In the work he has done since then Moretti has equally systematically elaborated on his earlier proposals (Moretti 2005, 2009a, 2009b, 2010).

In 2010 Moretti, together with Matthew Jockers, founded the Stanford Literary Lab, modelled on collaborative practices familiar from the exact and applied sciences. The establishment of the Lab consolidated Moretti's turn toward the digital humanities already signaled in a 2009 article (Moretti 2009b) in *Critical Inquiry* in which he presented the results of an exercise in "quantitative stylistics," essentially a statistical analysis of the titles of seven thousand British novels published between 1740 and 1850. He extended his research to "quantitative analysis of plot" in the *New Left Review* article

"Network Theory, Plot Analysis" (2011). These two articles, along with his earlier essays on world literature, were collected in *Distant Reading* in 2013. The same year appeared "'Operationalizing' or, the Function of Measurement in Literary Theory," in the opening paragraph of which he identified what he called "the new field of computational criticism" with what "has come to be called ... the digital humanities" (Moretti 2013b: 103). Moretti retired from Stanford in 2016 but the Lab carries on. Several articles resulting from research at the Lab were collected in *Canon/Archive: Studies in Quantitative Formalism* (Moretti 2017). In 1922 Moretti gauged the possibilities and pitfalls of the digital humanities in *Falsche Bewegung: Die digitale Wende in den Literatur- und Kulturwissenschaften*, collecting a number of his essays in German translation. A 2023 issue of the *Journal of Cultural Analytics* (Fischer et al. 2023) discusses the state of the art in various ways in which world literature can be studied by digital means.

Other World Literature Systems

Reactions to Casanova and Moretti's proposals have also come from proponents of the other systemic theories I mentioned at the outset of this chapter. They tend to stress that what Casanova and Moretti are doing can also be done, and done better, by other systemic theories. A good example is a 2010 article by Ilya Kliger, in which he argues that Yuri Lotman's cultural semiotics operates "with categories – such as boundary, translation, centre, periphery – that turn out to be crucial for some major recent attempts to formulate a methodology for the study of literature as a world system" (Kliger 2010: 259). One advantage of confronting a Lotmanian approach with those of Casanova and Moretti, according to Kliger, would be that it offers a "geopolitically different perspective," different from that of Western scholars who until now have dominated the conversation on the subject, and that we might thus gain "something like a second-world, or (semi-)peripheral, view of world literature to complement the view from the 'centre'" (Kliger 2010: 259). This would help us see that in Lotman's terms ideas and theories about world literature are also "geopolitically, or 'semiospherically' conditioned" (Kliger 2010: 259). Specifically, Kliger sees the Western conceptualizations of world literature as conditioned by the culture industry, and by a will to see, as Arac also noted, the relation between center and (semi-)periphery not only, and perhaps not even primarily, as spatial but rather as temporal. This implies the primacy of the center, in this case the West, and more specifically Moretti's Paris and London or Casanova's Paris, over the periphery, and also that whatever is "original" is always seen as originating from the center, with the periphery passively and incompletely absorbing what radiates from the center. "A less linear temporality, as well as a more tangled geography," Kliger concludes, "underlies the center-periphery relations as Lotman conceives of them in his late essays on the semiotics of culture" (Kliger 2010: 263). Specifically, Kliger claims,

Lotman's theories leave more room for innovation from the periphery, or in the exchange between the center and the periphery, and they construe that relation on a more even basis. The center-periphery relation in Lotman is a "*functional* one," Kliger argues, "between centripetal and centrifugal forces of signification, the former producing totalizing narratives and universal models and norms while the latter generates incongruities, accidents, chance encounters and semiotic lacunae" (Kliger 2010: 266).

Alexander Beecroft has critiqued both Casanova and Moretti on the grounds that their theories are unable to overcome the chronological limitations they have set themselves, and which with Casanova do not go farther back than the sixteenth, and with Moretti, at least as far as his work on the novel is concerned, the eighteenth century. Instead, Beecroft proposes a six-mode model of literature across all time inspired upon the systems theory of the German sociologist and pioneer of systems theory Niklas Luhmann (1927–1998). In Luhmann's view all human society is ruled by communication between individuals but also between groups of different compositions and levels of intricacy, hierarchy, and organization. All these function within a total system of communication. Some of his many publications are *Soziale Systeme: Gundriß einer allgemeinen Theorie* (1984; Social Systems) and *Ökologische Kommunikation* (1989; Ecological Communication). It is especially the latter volume that Beecroft references. Each of his six modes is linked to a specific form of social organization stretching from the simplest to the most complex, and to that organization's relationship to its environment. His theory, Beecroft claims,

> will recognize the multiple centres and systems of cultural power in operation across human history, and in addition will affirm that profound theoretical insights can and must come from the study of diverse literatures, rather than from the study of a core tradition or from the work of a dedicated class of theoreticians exempted from the cultural labour of textual analysis. ... in sum, it will be a theory of "world literature" rather than "world-literature", focused on the production of verbal art and its relationship to its environment as a genuinely universal phenomenon in human culture.
>
> (Beecroft 2008: 91)

The six modes that Beecroft distinguishes are:

> The *epichoric* is a mode of literary production in which literature is produced within the confines of a local community.

> The *panchoric* refers to literary texts and systems of circulation operating across a range of epichoric communities, united to some degree in language and culture, but generally fragmented politically.

> The circulation of literature within a *cosmopolitan* literary system is distinct from that encountered in a panchoric system, partly because cosmopolitan literary languages can be used by groups speaking a variety of mother tongues and partly because cosmopolitan literatures tend to represent themselves as agents of an ideology of universal rule, whether or not that ideology is seen as practiced or practicable [Beecroft cites Sanskrit, Greek, Persian, and Latin as examples]. Where a panchoric literary language allows literature to circulate among a set of political entities sharing a native language (but likely not a political regime), a cosmopolitan literary language creates a cross-cultural system, in which speakers of many languages share a common literary idiom.
>
> Texts circulating in the *vernacular* but not yet in a *national* context, when the history of a given literature, and its contemporary practices, are mapped onto the history and contemporary status of a particular political state.
>
> *global* literature. This category, still more conjectural than real, consists of literatures whose linguistic reach transcends national, even continental, borders. In some senses, a global literature resembles a cosmopolitan literature, except that (at least for the moment) global literatures continue to represent themselves as systems of national literatures to an extent that cosmopolitan literatures do not. They are in that sense inter-national rather than extra-national.
>
> (Beecroft 2008: 92–98)

At various points Beecroft sees the theories of Casanova and Moretti intersecting with his own categories, but his approach, he argues, is not hampered by the same chronological or generic limitations. He proposes

> rather than a division of labour in which national-literature specialists produce raw data for processing by world-literature scholars ... a sharing of labour by which, say, specialists in Persian literature find useful theoretical and practical insights in the work of Sinologists, or Anglo-Saxonists in the work of specialists of Old Kannada.
>
> (Beecroft 2008: 100)

Such an approach, he believes, holds out

> the possibility of world literature, unhyphenated, as a coherent field of study; taking as its object not a world-literary system which maps roughly onto Wallerstein's world system, but rather, and simply, the literature – the verbal artistic production – of the world.
>
> (Beecroft 2008: 100)

In 2015 Beecroft reworked and elaborated the proposals from his 2008 article into the book-length *An Ecology of World Literature: From Antiquity to the Present Day*. In the introduction to this book, Beecroft (2015: 2) explains that in the early 2000s he read the seminal texts of Casanova, Moretti, and Damrosch, but while thinking them valuable he also thought that they fell short of providing a model for extending the reach of the two literatures he was working on at the time, ancient Greek and classical Chinese, beyond their immediate linguistic "core" area. "All three," he says,

> provided what seemed to me very valuable insights into how literature circulates across the large spaces of our contemporary world, but the discussions of Moretti and Casanova focused almost exclusively on the literature emerging from the modern West and from the non-West's reaction to Western modernity, and it was difficult to use their theories to understand the ways that texts that were pre-modern or non-Western (or both) were circulated and understood.

Damrosch, Beecroft continues, "does have a great deal to say about such texts but avowedly and deliberately from the perspective of how the modern West understands and makes use of them." So, he was

> left searching for a theoretical model that could make sense of things like the relationship between political fragmentation and cultural unity I had found in early Greece and China and that would be useful for constructing an undergraduate course not taking as its premise the value we, as modern readers, add to the texts we read.

The solution Beecroft found with Sheldon Pollock's concept of "the Sanskrit cosmopolis" as elaborated in the latter's *The Language of the Gods: Sanskrit, Culture, and Power in Premodern India* (2006). This led him (Beecroft 2015: 3) to the recognition that the different models for "understanding how literature circulates" are "different concrete answers, emerging in specific contexts, to the same set of problems about the interaction between literatures and their environments." Finally, in a more concise formulation of the definitions he already gave in his 2008 article, Beecroft says he arrived at "a scheme of six patterns for this interaction: the epichoric (or local), panchoric (a generic term I derived from Panhellenic), cosmopolitan, vernacular (drawing both from Pollock), national (where I was inspired to an extent by Casanova), and global." Though he nowhere mentions Posnett (1886, 1973 [1901], 2009 [1886]), and even though Posnett defined the spheres in which he saw his world literature functioning as determined rather by politics, religion, or what he called "culture," it is clear that Beecroft's systematization of the relationship literatures bear to their environments runs at least somewhat parallel to Posnett's.

Conclusion

- From the very beginning word literature has been conceived of as a system of exchange of ideas, motifs, structures, and genres, as well as of the material carriers of all these things.
- Marxist and neo-Marxist critics have tended to prefer realist or modernist strategies as appropriate for a world literature in the service of the worldwide spread of socialism.
- Around the turn of the millennium two systemic approaches, by Casanova and Moretti respectively, have attempted to explain the world circulation of literature by positing Paris, in the case of Casanova, and Paris along with London, in the case of Moretti, as the center or centers of a world literary system.
- Casanova and Moretti have been severely criticized but more often than not they are faulted not for doing what they themselves claim they set out to do, but for not doing what their colleagues think they should have done.
- Most recently, attempts are being made to also construct world literature approaches based on other systemic theories of literature.

7 World Literature and Translation

Overview

Goethe himself was a prodigious translator, and he considered translation a necessary instrument for the spread of world literature. In fact, he thought that the German language and German literature had a great task ahead of them in serving as mediators, through translation, for world literature. Most commentators on world literature after Goethe have likewise recognized the importance of translation. For the early twentieth-century German writer and philosopher Walter Benjamin, translation was even the most important means for a work of literature to survive its own period and gain a meaningful afterlife. In the final quarter of the twentieth century a number of scholars, building on the polysystem theory of Itamar Even-Zohar, have elaborated an approach to translation that makes the latter, instead of a handmaiden to "real" literature, the engine of change in literature. Toward the end of the century there have even been calls that translation studies would replace comparative literature as the central discipline in the transnational study of literature.

The Indispensable Instrument

"The indispensable instrument" is what Albert Guérard calls translation in his 1940 *Preface to World Literature*. Indeed, the question of translation forms an inevitable part of any discussion on world literature. As long as world literature in practice was restricted to the traditional and inevitable comparatist trinity of French-English-German, with perhaps Italian and Spanish thrown in for good measure, along with the classical languages that until roughly the 1960s would have been considered an inalienable part of the high school education of anyone (at least in Europe) aspiring (or rich enough) to pursue university studies, and on top of that some "minor" language (usually the comparatist's mother tongue when he or, less frequently she, originated from one of Europe's smaller or less powerful countries), insistence on reading in the original could be said to have been a reasonable, even if already fairly demanding, requirement. Beyond this, though, and certainly in the

DOI: 10.4324/9781003366713-8

American situation as sketched in an earlier chapter, translation is inevitable, even if perhaps regrettable. Certainly Posnett (1886), writing at the dawn of the systematic study of comparative literature, at least in English, feels that translation, even if a necessary choice, is always also a poor one, especially when it comes to poetry. He pointedly quotes Shelley, from the *Defence of Poetry*, on

> the vanity of translation; it were as wise to cast a violet into a crucible that you might discover the formal principle of its colour and odour, as seek to transfuse from one language into another the creation of a poet.
> (Posnett 1886: 47–48)

Moulton, on the contrary, is much more sanguine on the subject. "It is obvious," he says, "that the study of literature as a whole is impossible without a free use of translations" (Moulton 1921: 3). For many, he admits, reading literature in translation is only a "makeshift" and smacks of "secondhand scholarship" (Moulton 1921: 3). Yet, he points out, many creative writers, and some of the greatest among them, men such as John Dryden and Alexander Pope, were prodigious translators. For sure, he admits, literature in translation suffers a loss, but think also of what one gains:

> one who accepts the use of translations where necessary secures all factors of literature except language, and a considerable part even of that ... one who refuses translations by that fact cuts himself off from the major part of the literary field.
> (Moulton 1921: 4)

And he approvingly quotes the nineteenth-century American writer-philosopher Ralph Waldo Emerson to the effect that the latter "rarely read any Greek, Latin, German, Italian – sometimes not a French book – in the original which [he could] procure in a good [English] version" (Moulton 1921: 4).

With the democratization of higher education in the USA as of World War I, and in Europe as of World War II, the almost complete erosion of the classics in high school education in Europe and the Americas, the multiculturalization, postcolonization and globalization of literary studies, and the concomitant call for an ever greater multiplicity of languages and their literatures to gain access to "world literature" in the anthologizing and educational sense, any requirement, or even expectation, of reading all in the original is obviously illusory. Equally obviously, even prior to 1960 the language combination theoretically expected of an "orthodox" comparatist would have been beyond the reach of most actual practitioners of the discipline, and far beyond the reach of most "ordinary" readers of world literature. The latter is why as of the beginning of the twentieth century there have appeared, at least in most or many European languages, popular anthologies in translation either of world literature in the broadest sense or of specific genres, usually poetry, or book series specifically, or at least partly, dedicated to such translations.

In English one could think of the Penguin Classics, with a translation of Homer's *Odyssey* as inaugural volume in 1945, and later the Penguin Twentieth-Century Modern Classics series. Both these series also contain works originally in English. Like all other Penguins, the Classics and Modern Classics series were first published by Allen Lane, but since the 1970s have formed part of the Pearson Longman Company. In the United States the Modern Library of (originally) Boni and Liveright started publishing what was then modern European literature in English translations in 1917. In Portugal Portugália Editora in Lisbon published a series "Antologías Universais" from 1942 until the 1970s. In Copenhagen Hasselbachs Kulturbibliotek has been publishing both classics and more modern works of world literature in Danish translation since before World War II. Albert Bonniers Forlag, in Stockholm, brings out its Klassiker series with both Swedish and foreign works in Swedish translation. In the Netherlands the publishing house De Wereldbibliotheek makes good its name, "The World's Library," by publishing both Dutch and foreign works of world literature in Dutch translation. At the beginning of the twentieth century there also sprang up a series of world literature in translation in China, under the guidance of the man who became China's most celebrated writer of the twentieth century, Lu Xun, and his brother Zhou Zuoren.

The grandfather of all these enterprises is the *Universal-Bibliothek* or "library of world literature," which, since 1867, has been published by Reclam Verlag, originally in Leipzig and since 1945 in Stuttgart. This series publishes works in German next to works in other languages and bi-lingual works. On the occasion of the sixtieth anniversary of their *Universal-Bibliothek* in 1927 Reclam commissioned an essay from the then best-selling Swiss-German author Herman Hesse (1877–1962). Hesse is primarily known for his novels *Siddhartha* (1922), *Steppenwolf* (1927), *Narziß und Goldmund* (Narcissus and Goldmund, 1930), and *Das Glasperlenspiel* (The Glass Bead Game, also known as Magister Ludi, 1943). Most of his works explore a character's inner journey toward auto-cognition and fulfilment. Hesse's novels were very popular between the two world wars – he won the Nobel Prize in 1946 – and again in the 1960s and 1970s, during the so-called flower-power years. In 1929 Hesse's essay appeared in the *Universal-Bibliothek* in a slightly expanded version as a little booklet under the title *Eine Bibliothek der Weltliteratur*. For Hesse, collecting a good library containing the basic works of world literature is an essential part of *Bildung*, the German ideal of a well-rounded education, and akin to making sure that your body is in excellent shape, the so-called *Körperkultur* eagerly practiced in the Weimar Republic Germany of the 1920s and early 1930s. While allowing for personal preferences which will make each person's selection at least slightly different from anyone else's, when it comes to drawing up his own list Hesse includes most of what we would still regard as classics today, although obviously some of his choices are steered by either period or national considerations. However, he stipulates, many of the works he lists would be unavailable to most of his readers if it were not for translation. Fortunately, he says "we Germans have the good luck to possess an extraordinarily rich treasure of good translations from foreign and dead languages" (Hesse 2008: 5; wir Deutsche [haben] das Glück über einen ausserordentlichen reichen Schatz an guten Übersetzungen aus fremden und toten Sprachen zu verfügen). Regardless, Hesse feels that much is still lacking on this score, and moreover each translation, however good, is only an approximation (Annäherung) of the original (Hesse 2008: 11). As language changes over time, finally, new translations of older works become necessary, and he points to the Bible, which he feels is no longer immediately accessible in Martin Luther's sixteenth-century translation.

Walter Benjamin and Translation

Hesse wrote his Reclam essay not long after the publication of one of the most famous texts in translation studies, Walter Benjamin's 1923 "The Task of the Translator," an introduction to a translation of the *Tableaux parisiens* of Baudelaire. Benjamin (1892–1940) was a German-Jewish author, philosopher, historian, and social critic. A prolific writer, Benjamin published major essays on Baudelaire and Paris in the nineteenth century, translating parts of Baudelaire's *Les Fleurs du mal* (*Flowers of Evil*). He also wrote on Goethe and Proust, and on many other writers, as well as on social and cultural issues. His most famous essay next to "The Task of the Translator" is "The Work of Art in the Age of Mechanical Reproduction" (1936). Fleeing Nazi Germany Benjamin established himself in Paris in 1933. Upon the German invasion of France, he fled to Spain, but fearing extradition to Germany he committed suicide. Benjamin's work gained wide popularity in American academic circles in the 1960s and 1970s, especially through the intervention of Hannah Arendt, herself a refugee from Nazi Germany and by then an influential philosopher and political scientist in the USA.

Hesse's text, although in much simpler language, in many ways reverberates with Benjamin's. For Benjamin too, "while a poet's words endure in his own language, even the greatest translation is destined to become part of the growth of its own language and eventually to be absorbed by its renewal" (Benjamin 2000: 18). In other words, whereas the original endures as is, even though its meaning may change as the language changes, a translation because of this very same fact, but also because its own language changes too, always is overtaken by time and, as is Hesse's argument with regard to Luther's Bible translation, needs re-doing in time. Benjamin's essay also contains the important insight that the afterlife of a work lies in translation, while at the same time the translation only becomes relevant because of the work's afterlife. If we translate this into world literature terms, we can take this to mean that a work stops being "world literature" when it is no longer *being* translated or, in Damrosch's term, but in fact this is also the term used by for instance Guillén (1993: 40), when it no longer "circulates" beyond its language and culture of origin.

Finally, Benjamin also discusses the difference between good and bad translations. He first makes a detour to discuss the various degrees of "translatability" of an original. Contrary to common expectation, for Benjamin it is those texts that are to the highest degree purely informative that are the most untranslatable. Such texts, he argues, are completely hidden in translation because the only thing that matters is their content, and this can be perfectly rendered in translation. Consequently, they read in translation as if they were originals and all sense of their foreignness is lost to the reader. As such they also pose no challenge to the translator. On the contrary, "the higher the level of a work, the more does it remain translatable even if its meaning is touched upon only fleetingly" (Benjamin 2000: 23). "Content," then, is not what matters. "The task of the translator," for Benjamin, "consists in finding that intended effect [Intention] upon the language into which he is translating which produces in it the echo of the original" (Benjamin 2000: 19–20). It should be remembered that Benjamin always writes with "the true language" of Holy Writ in mind, in which there is no gap between language and truth, as there is no mediation of meaning: revelation simply is what it is. In such a case, Benjamin writes,

> Translations are called for only because of the plurality of languages ... just as, in the original, language and revelation are one without any tension, so the translation must be one with the original in the form of the interlinear version ... the interlinear version of the Scriptures is the prototype or ideal of all translation.
> (Benjamin 2000: 23)

Although overlaid here with both messianic and Heideggerian overtones, Benjamin's ideas on translation also echo Goethe's. In fact, Benjamin hails Goethe's Notes to the *West-östlicher Diwan*, along with some observations by Rudof Pannwitz in the latter's *Die Krisis der europäischen Kultur* (1917; The Crisis of European Culture), as "the best comment on the theory of translation that has been published in Germany" (Benjamin 2000: 22).

Goethe himself translated from many languages, including a number he himself was not directly conversant with, but which he worked through mediation of other translations or translators, a practice later also taken up by for instance Ezra Pound in his translations from the Chinese. Birus (2000) stresses that the extensive knowledge of, and intercourse with, foreign literatures that Goethe's concept of *Weltliteratur* presupposes likewise presupposes extensive translational activity. Though he thinks that Berczik (1963: 288) exaggerates when the latter claims that, for Goethe, "world literature ... is nourished foremost by translations; more, it is almost identical to the art of translation" (Birus 2000: 5), Birus still approvingly quotes Goethe himself, in his review of Carlyle's *German Romance*, as stating that, "Whatever one may say about the shortcomings of translation, it nonetheless remains one of the most important and most worthy activities in the business of this world" (Birus 2000: 5). In this sense, Birus concludes,

> Goethe regards the process of development of world literature as profoundly bound up with the medium of literary translation, over and above our striving for the widest possible direct knowledge of the various literatures, and over and above the lively interaction among *Literatoren* (that is poets, critics, university teachers, etc.).
>
> (Birus 2000: 5)

In the "Note on *Uebersetzung*" (translation) Goethe appended to the *West-östlicher Diwan*, he outlined the three "Arten" or kinds of translation he discerned. The first kind is that which "acquaints us with the foreign according to our own lights, a simple prose translation is most suitable here" (Goethe 1819: 526; macht uns in unserm eigenen Sinne mit dem Auslande bekannt; eine schlicht-prosaische ist hiezu die beste). Translation here is a purely "functional" exercise; the only thing that matters is the content of the original without bothering about style, versification or other matters. The second stage or "Epoche" is "where one is concerned with entering into the foreign situation, but really only with the intent of appropriating to oneself the foreign and to refashion it according to one's own lights" (Goethe 1819: 527; wo man sich in die Zustände des Auslandes zwar zu versetzen, aber eigentlich nur fremden Sinn sich anzueignen und mit eignem [*sic*] Sinne wieder darzustellen bemüht ist). Here the translator "naturalizes" the original within his own literary target system. Finally, there is the third stage:

> A translation that aims to identify itself with the original finally approaches the condition of an interlinear version and much furthers understanding of the original, it leads us back to the original text, stronger, it forces us back to that text, and thus finally the circle is closed in which the foreign and the native, the known and the unknown move closely together.
>
> (Eine Uebersetzung die sich mit dem Original zu identificiren [*sic*] strebt nähert sich zuletzt der Interlinear-Version und erleichtert höchlich den Verständniss des Originals, hiedurch werden wir an der Grundtext hinangeführt, ja getrieben, und so ist denn zuletzt der ganze Zirkel abgeschlossen, in welchem sich die Annäherung des Fremden und Einheimischen, des Bekanntenn und Unbekannten bewegt.)
>
> (Goethe 1819: 532)

This third kind of translation, then, does not strive to naturalize the original in the target language but instead aims to preserve the former's strangeness, its foreignness. This is also what Pannwitz, in the book Benjamin refers to, expresses when he says that

> the basic error of the translator is that he preserves the state in which his own language happens to be instead of allowing his language to be powerfully affected by the foreign tongue ... he must expand and deepen his language by means of the foreign language.
>
> (Benjamin 2000: 22)

The Rise of Translation Studies

It is not surprising that Homi Bhabha seizes upon Benjamin's essay, and precisely also upon the latter's citation of Pannwitz, in his own essay "How newness enters the world: Postmodern space, postcolonial times, and the trials of cultural translation" (Bhabha 1994c). It is precisely in the making foreign one's own language in the act of translation that the possibility of newness enters the world for the postcolonial, migrant, diasporic, or other minority author: by making the present not the transitional moment between the inevitability of a future issuing from a teleological past but rather a moment where time halts and re-direction is possible. Cultural translation, in other words, becomes the site for Bhabhian in-betweenness, hybridity, and third space.

In truth, what Bhabha was militantly, almost oracularly, certainly spectacularly, putting forward as a revolutionary program for postcolonial cultural translation was not different from what practicing writers had been aware of at least since Cervantes in the early seventeenth century passed off his *Don Quijote* as translated from the Arabic. Almost concurrently with Bhabha's writing on translation, moreover, the then emergent discipline of translation studies had been describing Bhabha's translational "newness" as commonly practiced in most actual literary translation. The term "translation studies" was coined by James S. Holmes in 1972 (Holmes 2000) in an article that constituted one of the first systematic attempts to map the rapidly growing proliferation of approaches, research, and theories having to do with "translation" in the widest sense of the word. Susan Bassnett, in 1980, consolidated much of these trends in her still widely used and several times updated primer *Translation Studies*. Specifically with regard to literature, what Bassnett, and with her the so-called Tel Aviv-Leuven-Amsterdam school of translation studies picked up on was literary polysystem theory as elaborated by Itamar Even-Zohar in a number of articles in the early and mid-1970s, largely while he was on a research stay in the Low Countries, and in close conversation with James S. Holmes and a number of scholars at the universities of Amsterdam, Antwerp, and Leuven. At the same time Even-Zohar also closely collaborated with his colleagues Benjamin Hrushovski and Gideon Toury at the Porter Institute for Poetics and Semiotics of Tel Aviv University in a tradition inspired by various schools of structuralism. Starting from structuralist premises Even-Zohar as of the 1970s came to see society, and culture, as multi-layered, with sub-systems operating within a larger system. This led to his polysystem theory in which systems dynamically interrelate with one another, thus leading to continuous transformation.

As far as their interest in translation was concerned, Even-Zohar and Toury worked both in what Holmes had termed descriptive translation studies. Even-Zohar was particularly concerned with the function of translated literature within his more comprehensive view of all literature as an interlocking "polysystem" composed of central and peripheral sub-systems (such as genres, but also such as translated literature versus literature in the original) battling it out for supremacy. Toury concentrated rather on establishing the norms that ruled actual translations. For a description of these norms he drew upon, and refined, the terminology of "shifts" between original and translation that for instance the linguist J.C. Catford had also developed in an influential 1965 book. In earlier approaches such shifts, on both the micro (words, sentences, nuances) and macro (the structure of the text as a whole, including its arrangement in chapters or other forms of ordering, prefaces, notes, and other so-called paratextual features) levels, would have been evaluated in terms of "equivalence" – or not – between original and translation, or between "source" and "target" text. Some such shifts might be deemed inevitable because of insuperable differences between source and target language or culture, others were simply deemed "failures" on the part of the translator, whose highest "norm" was always supposed to be the greatest possible fidelity to the original. In all fairness it should also be said that much of the earlier terminology, and the emphasis on "equivalence," derived from research and theorization primarily pertinent to non-literary translation, and in the context of the translator-training institutes that as of the 1950s had started to appear all over Europe.

Now, however, scholars working on literary translations adopted this very same terminology, coupled with the insights of Even-Zohar and Toury, not to "find fault" with the work of literary translators, but to study what shifts they made as part of the process, or the strategy, of adapting the translated work to the receiving culture. The title of a collection of essays edited by Theo Hermans in 1985 is a fair indication of this shift of emphasis: *The Manipulation of Literature: Studies in Literary Translation*. Probably the best-known early exponent of this approach was André Lefevere, who eventually came to see translation as only one form of what he called the "refraction" of literature, next to for instance criticism and historiography. In one of his best-known articles, "Mother Courage's Cucumbers: Text, System and Refraction in a Theory of Literature" (2000 [1982]), Lefevere showed how what at first sight are blatant distortions in the American translations of the German playwright Bertolt Brecht's play *Mutter Courage und ihre Kinder* (Mother Courage and Her Children) are in fact changes effected because of constraints upon what was acceptable to an American public, possible because of political conditions, and presentable according to an American "horizon of expectations," at the moment of production of these translations.

According to Lefevere, a translation always represents "a compromise between two systems," the originating and the receiving one (Lefevere 2000: 237). "The degree of compromise in a refraction," Lefevere adds, "will depend on the reputation of the writer being translated within the system from which the translation is made," while "the degree to which the foreign writer is accepted into a native system will, on the other hand, be determined by the need that native system has of him in a certain phase of its evolution" (Lefevere 2000: 237). Lefevere is here expressing on the level of an individual author what Even-Zohar had put in more general terms when he said that "through the foreign works, features (both principles and elements) are introduced into the home literature which did not exist there before," and that

> the very principles of selecting the works to be translated are determined by the situation governing the (home) polysystem: the texts are chosen according to their compatibility with the new approaches and the supposedly innovatory role they may play within the target literature.
> (Even-Zohar 2000: 193)

According to Even-Zohar there are three situations in which a literature may be particularly receptive to such "import" via translation: "when a literature is 'young,' in the process of being established," "when a literature is either 'peripheral' (within a large group of correlated literatures) or 'weak,' or both," and "when there are turning points, crises, or literary vacuums in a literature" (Even-Zohar 2000: 194).

Translation, Postcolonialism, and Feminism

Susan Bassnett (1993) emphasizes the enabling role of translation for post-colonialism and feminism. For the former she draws a parallel with the work of the Brazilian *antropófagos*, specifically that of Haroldo de Campos (1929–2003), who started the concrete poetry movement in Brazil in the 1950s, and his brother Augusto de Campos (1931–). After the poet Oswald de Andrade's 1928 *Manifesto Antropófago*, the brothers developed a theory and a practice of translation in which Brazilian authors would appropriate, devour, or cannibalize, European ancestors and models to digest them and transform them into something entirely Brazilian. For the latter Bassnett invokes the work of a number of Canadian feminist translation studies scholars. What both these Brazilians and Canadians have in common, she argues, is "the aim of celebrating the role of the translator, of making the translator visible in an act of transgression that seeks to reconstruct the old patriarchal/European hierarchies" (Bassnett 1993: 157). In fact, both groups can also be seen as answering to some of Even-Zohar's different kinds of situations in which translations can, and usually do, play an important role in a particular literary system. The case of the Brazilians is that of a still relatively young literature that until the 1920s, notwithstanding such exceptions as the late nineteenth-century novelist Machado de Assis, had always felt itself at the same time also as "peripheral" to the literatures of Europe. *Antropofagismo* allows the Brazilians to both import from European literature what they can use and at the same time, at least metaphorically, transcend the stage of imitation or dependence by reversing the customary role between source and target literature, casting the latter now as the active, possessive partner in the transaction rather than the passive, receptive one. Haroldo de Campos (1981: 180, 208–209) himself coined the neologisms *transcriação, transluminação, transfusão*, and *transluciferação* for his creative attitude to translation/adaptation, and which with

Edwin Gentzler (2017: 7) become "transcreation," "transtextualization," "transparaization," "transillumination," and "transluciferation."

Bassnett makes a point of how such metaphors were also used for the traditional roles between the sexes, and how feminist translation theory therefore also implies a subversion or reversal not only of these same metaphors but also of real gender relationships in society. That such feminist translation studies should have arisen in Canada, and primarily in French-speaking Canada, has therefore everything to do with the likewise relatively "young" status of Canadian literature, and certainly Canadian literary theory in general at the time, and the even younger status of French-Canadian literature, which found itself doubly peripheral as a "minor" literature in what was itself a "peripheral" culture. At the same time the influence of women writers, with Margaret Atwood, Margaret Laurence, Alice Munro, Mavis Gallant, and Carol Shields on the English-language side, and Anne Hébert and Nicole Brossard on the French-language side, all with a markedly feminist inclination, was particularly strong in Canadian literature. Especially a group around Nicole Brossard has been instrumental in elaborating a feminist translation studies approach.

In both the Brazilian and the Canadian case, then, as Bassnett quotes Lefevere (1992),

> translation is not just "a window opened on another world," or some such pious platitude ... rather, translation is a channel opened, often not without a certain reluctance, through which foreign influences can penetrate the native culture, challenge it and even contribute to subverting it.
> (Bassnett 1993: 159)

This is very different from Damrosch's view in *What is World Literature?*, where he describes "world literature," at least in one of its manifestations, and as enabled by translation, as exactly such a "window" (Damrosch 2003: 15). As Bassnett puts it:

> Writing does not happen in a vacuum, it happens in a context and the process of translating texts from one cultural system into another is not a neutral, innocent, transparent activity ... translation is instead a highly charged, transgressive activity, and the politics of translation and translating deserve much greater attention than has been paid in the past.
> (Bassnett 1993: 160–161)

World Literature and Translation

For world literature, the point that Bassnett and Lefevere, drawing out the implications of Even-Zohar's polysystem theory, can be seen to be making is that one and the same "world literature author" may fulfil completely different functions in different literary systems. For instance, in Dutch nineteenth-

and twentieth-century literature Byron, Yeats, and T.S. Eliot have played very different roles from those they played in a number of other contexts, and from those that now usually make for their inclusion in world literature anthologies, especially in the United States. Byron was quite frequently translated into Dutch during the period 1825–1845, but it was a narrow selection from his works, mostly the so-called "oriental tales," some lyrical pieces, and isolated passages from the longer poems. Byron as the poet of romantic nationalism and revolt never found favor with his Dutch translators or with the Dutch public. This was mostly because the Belgian revolt of 1830 against the Dutch (what is now Belgium having been incorporated into a Kingdom of the United Netherlands in 1815 by the Congress of Vienna) made the Dutch particularly unreceptive to revolutionary feelings of nationalism, at least on what they considered their own soil. Moreover, the majority of Byron's translators were students, or young men, while working on their translations. They almost all went on to become Protestant ministers and staunch upholders of a Dutch variant of petit-bourgeois or *Biedermeier* culture. Not surprisingly, they all came to repudiate Byron as altogether too frivolous and morally dangerous. The versatilities of Byron's poetry left no impression upon Dutch poetry except in the form of a parody that turns Byron's *Don Juan* inside out to preach good morals to upstanding young men. In short, Byron served as a negative catalyst for the Dutch literary system of the mid-nineteenth century, and both the selection of what was translated from him and the contemporary discourse pertaining to it show this (D'haen 1990, 2005).

Translations of W.B. Yeats were mainly the work of one man, the Dutch poet Adrian Roland Holst, who repeatedly returned to translating Yeats over the course of a very long poetic career spanning the 1910s to the 1970s. Again, though, the Yeats of Roland Holst is not the modernist Yeats we know from our contemporary anthologies or literary histories; nor is he the postcolonial Yeats of Edward Said in *Empire and Culture* (1993). Because of the selection Roland Holst makes from Yeats, and because of the interpretation he puts upon his own work and life, and upon Yeats, the latter emerges as almost exclusively the poet of the Celtic Twilight. Within the Dutch literary system, however, Roland Holst needed the example of a foreign authority to escape the overbearing influence of Herman Gorter, a leading Dutch poet around the turn of the century, and a close friend of Roland Holst's family. Although once considered one of Holland's major poets, Roland Holst now has largely faded, as his poetics are considered old-fashioned and dated even by the standards with which we now measure the early twentieth century. In fact, whereas Yeats continues to sound fresh in English, Roland Holst in his Yeats translations, and indeed in a great part of his own production, sounds predictably and artificially "poetical" and stale (D'haen 1991, 2006).

In contrast, the Dutch poet mainly responsible for translating T.S. Eliot, Martinus Nijhoff, has increasingly emerged as the real leading poet of that same early twentieth century, mostly because of two long poems that rather resemble Eliot's *The Love Song of J. Alfred Prufrock* and *The Waste Land*, although these are precisely the poems by Eliot that Nijhoff never tackled. Instead, Nijhoff translated various shorter poems by Eliot and, probably toward the end of his life, some plays. Therefore, the Eliot we have in Dutch translation is once again a very selective and partial one, though his own poetic practice shows that Nijhoff was very well acquainted also with the rest of Eliot's *oeuvre*. Whereas Roland Holst and Nijhoff both resorted to translation to fashion their own poetics, Roland Holst, like the Dutch Byron translators of the nineteenth century, did not finally bring "newness" to the Dutch literary system. Nijhoff did, and the generation of poets following him looked back to him and not to Roland Holst. At least, that is how things look now. Of course, there is nothing to prevent future poets eventually going back to Roland Holst and developing a wholly new poetics from him and from his translations of Yeats. The irony in all this is that Nijhoff probably himself seized upon Eliot as his example to evade the overbearing influence of Roland Holst, who, slightly older than Nijhoff, certainly looked formidable at Nijhoff's debut, and in fact throughout most of the latter's career (D'haen 2009).

In all this, the fact remains that, as Lefevere says, "the refraction … is the original to the great majority of people who are only tangentially exposed to literature" (Lefevere 2000: 246). In other words, to the Dutch reader Roland Holst's Yeats *is* Yeats, and so with Byron, and with T.S. Eliot. In truth, this is a tenuous point, as in fact there would be few Dutch readers of Yeats, Byron, or Eliot in translation that would not also be sufficiently conversant with English to at least be able to get a fairly good idea of the original. The matter would be very different, of course, for the translations from the Chinese, specifically Li-Po or Li Bai, by another early twentieth-century Dutch poet, J.J. Slauerhoff, mostly by way of Arthur Waley (D'haen 2023b). Likewise, in other cultural contexts, such as for instance that of the United States, translation might be the only access to any or almost any foreign literature. Still, the fate of Byron and Yeats in Dutch translation may explain why these two poets have never had much of an "afterlife" in the Netherlands, and therefore do not loom very large in a hypothetical Netherlands-generated "canon of world literature."

A different case of afterlife occurs in the numerous postcolonial rewritings of European classics, all of them forms of the kind of cultural translation that Bhabha also explores in the article referred to above, and as example of which he uses Wallcott's *Omeros* rewriting Homer. Well-known other cases are Jean Rhys in *Wide Sargasso Sea* re-writing Charlotte Brontë's *Jane Eyre*, Maryse Condé in *La migration des coeurs* doing the same with Emily Brontë's *Wuthering Heights*, and J.M. Coetzee grounding *Foe* in Daniel Defoe's *Robinson Crusoe*. Shakespeare's *The Tempest* and Joseph Conrad's *Heart of Darkness* have been the subject of numerous rewritings from both a feminist and a postcolonial point of view (Nakai 2000; Zabus 2002; Farn 2005). Arguably, to many contemporary readers Bertha Mason is not the crazy murderess from *Jane Eyre* but the duped French-créole Antoinette from *Wide Sargasso Sea*.

In all these cases we could see similarities with the *antropofagismo* of the Brazilians discussed before: the "original" work disappears after having been consumed by its "afterlife." Or, for the reader that does go back to the "original," the latter has been utterly changed by its "translation." If, as Bassnett argues, "the new notion of translation confer[s] new life on the source text" (Bassnett 1993: 152), this is not to be taken as a simple continuation of the latter's former life but rather as an "updated" version, giving it new meanings, tying it to new locales, different times. We could compare this to Jorge Luis Borges's story "Pierre Menard, autor del Quijote" (Pierre Menard, author of the Quixote), in which the early twentieth-century French polyglot Pierre Menard is said to have literally written Cervantes's *Don Quixote* all over again starting from a painstaking reconstruction of Cervantes's times, situation, and language. The result is a *Quixote* that is entirely identical to that of Cervantes yet completely different – in fact a profound interpretation of and reflection on Cervantes's masterwork for Menard's, and our, time.

Translation Studies and the "New" Comparative Literature

In 1993, Susan Bassnett concluded her *Comparative Literature: A Critical Introduction* with a chapter entitled "Towards Translation Studies," in which she gave a very upbeat and militant prognosis as to the future of translation studies. Until then translation studies had been considered a branch, and for the longest time a minor branch, of comparative literature. However, she posited, "cross-cultural work in women's studies, in post-colonial theory, in cultural studies has changed the face of literary studies generally," and given the importance of translation in all of these, "we should look upon translation studies as the principal discipline from now on, with comparative literature as a valued but subsidiary subject area" (Bassnett 1993: 161). Since the time of Bassnett's writing, the study of translation certainly has gained in importance, but instead of becoming a major discipline of its own, its evident success, like that of "theory" with comparative literature in the 1970s and 1980s, rather seems to have led to its dissipation into all kinds of adjacent disciplines. At present it undoubtedly is one of the major foci of interest in the most recent comparative literature update paradigm of world literature studies, thus sharing the fate of the discipline Bassnett once thought it would replace.

In fact, the re-emergence of world literature as of the early years of the twenty-first century has spawned fresh reflections on the role of translation. In a 1992 article entitled "The Politics of Translation," Spivak had already, albeit in the context of a reflection on Third World feminism and not on world literature, argued that

> in the act of wholesale translation into English there can be a betrayal of the democratic ideal into the law of the strongest ... this happens when all the literature of the Third World gets translated into a sort of with-it

> translatese, so that the literature by a woman in Palestine begins to resemble, in the feel of its prose, something by a man in Taiwan.
>
> (Spivak 2000a: 400)

Her reproach here very much resembles that she earlier made of Foucault and Deleuze when in "Can the Subaltern Speak?" she accused these French philosophers of mistaking the Western working-class man as representative for all the oppressed in the world, and of their own discourse as empowered to speak for all discourses on oppression. In *A Critique of Postcolonial Reason* (1999) Spivak extends her remarks to literature. Branding the recent interest in world literature in the United States as "the arrogance of the cartographic reading of world lit. in translation as the task of Comparative Literature" (Spivak 2003: 73), she vehemently opposes "U.S.-style world literature becoming the staple of Comparative Literature in the global South" (Spivak 2003: 39). Instead, and this in both her 1992 article and her 2003 book, she advocates learning and teaching local languages and gaining an intimate knowledge of the local cultures. When translation is necessary, it should "make visible the import of the translator's choice" (Spivak 2003: 18). She propounds a "new Comparative Literature" where a "joining of forces between Comparative Literature and Area studies" (Spivak 2003: 20) would "persistently and repeatedly undermine and undo the definitive tendency of the dominant to appropriate the emergent" (Spivak 2003: 100). This can only be done by close textual analysis, looking for what Spivak calls signs of "planetarity" (Spivak 2003: 81) by-passing the necessarily hegemonously localized geographies of "globalization" and "world literature" in any of its present, and particularly its most recent US comparative literature, avatars. Spivak's impassioned plea seems triggered by the same fear that led Erich Auerbach, in his "Philology and World Literature" of 1952, to lament that

> man will have to accustom himself to existence in a standardized world, to a single literary culture, only a few literary languages and perhaps even a single literary language ... and herewith the notion of *Weltliteratur* would now be at once realized and destroyed.
>
> (Auerbach 2009: 127)

Obviously taking up Spivak's call for a "new Comparative Literature," and drawing on the writings of Jacques Derrida, Edward Said, and Leo Spitzer, Emily Apter boldly proposes to re-ground the discipline in "the problem of translation" (Apter 2006b: 251). "A new comparative literature," she professes, "would acknowledge [the] jockeying for power and respect in the field of language" and hence "seeks to be the name of language worlds characterized by linguistic multiplicity and phantom inter-nations" (Apter 2003: 244–245). In a 2008 article Apter seems to be at the same time echoing and questioning Spivak's concerns about the hegemonic dangers of English for new postnational paradigms (such as world literature) when she feels that

Postnationalism can lead to blindness toward the economic and national power struggles that literary politics often front for, while potentially minimizing the conflict among the interests of monocultural states and multilingual communities (as in current U.S. policy that uses an agenda of cultural homogeneity to patrol "immigrant" languages and to curtail bilingual education) ... though planetary inclusion may be the goal of new lexicons in contemporary comparative literature, they often paradoxically reinforce dependency on a national/ethnic nominalism that gives rise to new exclusions.

(Apter 2008: 581)

After a brief discussion of new names given to postnationalism in literature – world literature, cosmopolitanism, planetary, etc. – Apter then turns to possible solutions for handling such transnational constellations as offered by translation studies, and particularly by investigations of "untranslatability" figuring in two collaborative undertakings: the *Vocabulaire européen des philosophies: Dictionnaire des intraduisibles* (Vocabulary of European Philosophy: A Dictionary of Untranslatables) under the general editorship of Barbara Cassin, and *The Novel*, the five-volume Italian version of which appeared in 2001–2003, and the two-volume condensed version of which in English dates from 2006, both with Franco Moretti as general editor.

I will not go into Apter's discussion of Cassin's project here but will concentrate instead on that of Moretti's. Apter, like many other commentators of Moretti's, is particularly intrigued by Moretti's conjecture, in his 2000 article, that the spread of the European novel retains the plotlines exported from the center but adopts indigenous characters and voice. Almost echoing Bhabha on how "newness" enters the world, Apter, putting things in translation terms, wonders whether "new genres [are] made by virtue of translation failure?" and whether "the lack of a common ground of comparison [is] a spur to literary evolution?" (Apter 2008: 293). "Is a genre's travel the measure of its aliveness," she asks, and "its drift the gauge of force required to break open the bounds of a closed world-system?" (Apter 2008: 293). Taking up while at the same time countering Spivak's 2003 call for a combination of language learning and area studies to resist the hegemonic cartographies projected by a world-literature-in-translation studies US-style, Apter marshals translation for a "translational humanities responsive to fluctuations in geopolitics, and which intersects with but is not confined to national language frontiers" (Apter 2008: 297). Offering Cassin's vocabulary of European philosophy and Moretti's study of the novel as examples, Apter posits the collective authorship both these projects imply as, "like multiple language learning and off-site academic immersion," "one of the more viable ways of experiencing 'in-translation' or '*un*translatability' as explosive conceptual practices capable of limning new cartographies of the present" (Apter 2008: 297). In 2014 Apter, along with Jacques Lezra and Michael Wood brought an English edition of Cassin's *Vocabulaire* as *Dictionary of Untranslatables: A Philosophical Lexicon*.

In 2013 Apter elaborated the ideas she first aired in her 2008 article into a full-length book with the title *Against World Literature: On the Politics of Untranslatability*. This recalls Susan Sontag's 1964 essay "Against Interpretation," subsequently the lead-off essay in a book with the same title (1966). Sontag turned against then reigning hermeneutic regimes of interpreting literary texts to make them accessible and comprehensible. She thought such methods flattened and betrayed the impact a more sensuous approach to the text awakens in the reader. Apter sees the approach of a world literature rooted in translation as likewise by-passing what really matters in a text, that is to say the authenticity of the original language. Already in 2001 Apter, echoing Auerbach (1969 [1952]), had warned of a "translationally translatable monoculture" (2001: 3). Apter's views have been influential, but they have also been severely criticized (Damrosch 2014, Theo Hermans and Helen Gibson in Large et al. 2018: 38–39 and 138 respectively). The fiercest critique has been delivered by Venuti (2019). Byron Taylor (2022) makes a plea to recover Apter's "untranslatability" as an instrument to bring about a "rebirth" of theory in the fields of comparative literature and translation studies.

In the final chapter of his *The Birth and Death of Literary Theory* Galin Tihanov (2019) sees contemporary debates on world literature pitting the proponents of translation, in particular Damrosch, versus the opponents, in particular Apter, as a rehearsal, although without referencing them, of those animating Russian Formalism, with Roman Jakobson insisting on studying literary works in the original – hence his focus on poetry – and Bakhtin and particularly Shlovsky favoring translation – hence their focus on prose. Citing passages from Shlovsky's *A Sentimental Journey: Memoirs, 1917–1922*, in which the latter criticizes Gorky's world literature project, Tihanov reminds us that the Russian Formalists were very much interested in world literature, although their contributions to the debate have gone largely unnoticed in Western academe, as is the case with their Czech and Slovak counterparts (Zelenka 2022).

Lawrence Venuti, in his piece on "World Literature and Translation" for the *Routledge Companion to World Literature*, amplifies upon Lefevere's earlier remark that for most readers the translated version is the only one they know of a particular work not written in their own native language by advancing that "for most readers, translated texts constitute world literature" (Venuti 2012: 191, 2022: 139). Summarizing a lot of recent discussions on the role of translation in literary studies, and referring among others to Casanova (1999, 2004) and Moretti (2000), Venuti concludes that, "To understand the impact of translation in the creation of world literature, we need to examine the canons developed by translation patterns within the receiving situation as well as the interpretations that translations inscribe in the source texts" and that "to be productive, to yield the most incisive findings, this sort of examination must combine distant and close reading of translations to explore the relations between canons and interpretations" (Venuti 2012: 191, 2022: 138–139). Venuti (2008) is well-known for arguing that translators and translations do not receive enough attention when it comes to the study of literature. Gauti Kristmannsson (2014) is of the same opinion when it comes to translation studies and world literature.

Ann Steiner nuances Venuti's remark on translation patterns in the sense that she sees translation as part of what she terms "the economy of literature," along with "sale systems, publishing traditions … government support, [and] taxes" (Steiner 2012: 316, 2022: 259). These mechanisms, along with other factors such as the hegemonic or peripheral position a certain culture or language occupies in the world order of things, explain the uneven flows of translation between languages, cultures, and literatures. Certain cultures, such as for instance the American, translate very little themselves from foreign literatures while their own literature is widely and massively translated into other languages. Other cultures, such as most West-European ones, translate almost exhaustively from English, but not necessarily on any comparable scale between each other's literatures. Moreover, the works actually translated differ widely as to their status, with, next to a number of perennial classics such as the Bible, or Shakespeare, a preponderance of works in popular genres. The latter typically have a short life span, both in the original and in translation. Yet the translation patterns they are subject to, and the mechanisms these patterns are themselves subject to, certainly also deserve attention in the context of world literature studies. Of course, the Danish critic Georg Brandes in his 1899 article "World Literature" had already argued as much.

This raises the question to what extent translation does provide access to world literature for works from minor or smaller literatures such as that of the present-day Netherlands and Flanders, the northern Dutch-speaking part of Belgium. Some extensive work on Dutch-language literature in translation has been done by Johan Heilbron, a Dutch literary historian who has worked with Gisèle Sapiro, probably the best-known theoretician and historian of translation in France today. Like many of her contemporaries, including Pascale Casanova, Sapiro works within a largely Bourdieuian theoretical framework. In 2008 Heilbron contributed a chapter on "the evolution of the cultural exchanges between France and the Netherlands in the era of English as a hegemonic language" (L'évolution des échanges culturels entre la France et les Pays-Bas à l'hégémonie de l'anglais) to *Translatio: Le marché de la traduction en France à l'heure de la mondialisation* (Translation: the translation market in France in the era of globalization), a volume edited by Gisèle Sapiro. Relying on both the *Index translationum* as well as other, also Dutch national, data, Heilbron arrives at the conclusion that

> traditionally the number of translations from Dutch into other languages has been extremely small. Notwithstanding the fact that the United Provinces were a major power in pre-modern Europe and that the Netherlands has a number of important international publishers, Dutch authors have been rarely translated and they have not had any real international recognition.

(traditionellement, le nombre des traductions du néerlandais vers d'autres langues est extrêmement faible. En dépit de la position de force des Provinces-Unies dans l'Europe pré-moderne et la forte présence d'éditeurs internationaux, les écrivains néerlandais ont été très rarement traduits et n'ont pas eu de véritable reconnaissance littéraire internationale.)
(Heilbron 2008: 322)

In fact, Heilbron here is only summarizing with respect to the French situation, backed up with hard figures, what he had already said in greater detail and more generally in a Dutch-language article of 1995, and an English-language one of 1999. In the latter article, "Towards a Sociology of Translation: Book Translations as a Cultural World System," and loosely adopting Immanuel Wallerstein's well-known world systems theory but carefully distinguishing his own sociologically- and culturally-oriented approach from Wallerstein's economic historiographic one, Heilbron divides the global field of translations into central, semi-central or semi-peripheral, and peripheral languages and literatures on the basis of the number of book translations made from them, the so-called ex-translations. For the period roughly equivalent with the late 1970s and early 1980s Heilbron found that four languages and their literatures could be deemed central: English, French, German, and Russian, with each of them yielding more than 10 percent of translations worldwide. In fact, English could be said to occupy a hyper-central position, accounting for more than 40 percent.

As Heilbron (2008) notes, it is not that Dutch-language works were not being translated at all. In the sixteenth and seventeenth centuries, when the United Provinces (the earlier version of the present-day Netherlands) were a leading power in Europe, some Dutch-language authors had some renown. Still, none ever entered the ranks of world literature. In the eighteenth and nineteenth centuries, very little was translated from Dutch. The situation started to improve in the twentieth century, with the number of translations steadily rising to stabilize at some 500 to 600 titles per year from the 1960s to the time of Heilbron's 1999 article. Notwithstanding these rising numbers, no Dutch-language writer had succeeded in gaining, or continuing to enjoy (the nineteenth-century Flemish Hendrik Conscience and the Dutch turn-of-the-twentieth-century Louis Couperus enjoyed considerable international fame in their day), international recognition as a major literary figure. Even the one Dutch-language writer that regularly at least gets a nod internationally, and whose novel *Max Havelaar* has been translated a few times in most major and a respectable number of smaller languages, the nineteenth-century novelist Multatuli (penname of Eduard Douwes Dekker), has never made it into the list of "world authors." Heilbron (2008) also gives a number of reasons for this lack of translational and world literature success, and most of them come down to what in terms outlined by Pierre Bourdieu (1992), Pascale Casanova (1999, 2004), and John Guillory (1993) can be subsumed under the label "cultural" or "literary capital." According to Jack McMartin (2019a, 2019b,

2019c, 2020, 2021), McMartin and Paola Gentile (2020), and Frank Albers (2019), the situation may be slowly improving when it comes to the translation of (some) contemporary Dutch-language authors, but it remains an uphill battle (D'haen 2023a). That the same thing goes even for much "bigger" literatures is one of the arguments Venuti (2012, 2022) develops in his contribution to the *Routledge Companion to World Literature.*

Stefan Helgesson (2018d) provides ammunition for Venuti's argument when he discusses the uneven relations obtaining between literatures when it comes to translation. In the first part of his chapter Helgesson heavily leans on Heilbron (1999) and Heilbron and Sapiro (2007) for general data on frequencies of translation as source and target languages between especially English and Portuguese. Not surprisingly, English emerges as the dominant partner. To illustrate his point Helgesson contrasts the translation frequency of J.M. Coetzee's work with that of the little-known Mozambican José Craveirinha (1922–2003). Interestingly, though, Helgesson also demonstrates how the work of Craveirinha, regardless of his hardly ever having been translated, circulates in a number of world literary contexts because of Portuguese being an imperial language. The same thing transpires from Buescu's (2018–2020) multi-volume anthology for other lusophone authors.

An interesting twist to most critics' assertion that translation into a major language makes for access to world literature is given by Albert Braz (2016) via a discussion of the Canadian Erin Mouré's (also known as Erín Moure and Eirin Moure) *Sheep's Vigil by a Fervent Person: A Transelation of Alberto Caeiro/Fernando Pessoa's O Guardador de Rebanhos* (2001). As the use of "transelation" instead of "translation" in the title to Mouré's exercise indicates, hers is not a straightforward translation. In fact, although Braz finds that Mouré in many instances has translated Pessoa's text rather faithfully, he also finds that in many other instances she diverges radically from the original, creatively re-fashioning Pessoa/Caeiro to fit her own personality. Echoing my discussion of the difficulties small literatures face when it comes to entering the world literature lists, Braz (2016: 587) asserts that "among the European bodies of writing often ignored in international discussions of 'Western' letters is of course Portuguese literature, the tradition from which Pessoa and Caeiro hail." Hence, he argues (2016: 577), "a defining characteristic of peripheral literatures is their dependence on translation to enter world literature." This is the service Mouré ostensibly aims to render for Pessoa's text. "However," Braz objects (2016: 577), "in order for translated texts to circulate beyond the cultures in which they are produced, they must survive the act of being rendered into other languages" and "this is something that does not always occur in creative translations, which usually aim to re-imagine the source text rather than to reproduce it." "Thus," he concludes, "if the translation differs significantly from the source text, such as Erin Mouré's *Sheep's Vigil by a Fervent Person: A Transelation of Alberto Caeiro/Fernando Pessoa's O Guardador de Rebanhos*, it is not self-evident that the original will be able to enter the world literary system." With this, Braz also qualifies the claims of scholars such as Bassnett (2006) and Henitiuk (2012), and ultimately of Damrosch (2003) and other proponents of world literature, that translation preserves the core of the original. "The notion that a text's origins necessarily survive its translation into another language and culture is precisely what Mouré's treatment of Caeiro/Pessoa should lead us to question" and ultimately "it should lead us to ponder what is the collective identity of the translated texts that circulate in world literature" (Braz 2016: 588).

Mouré in the work of hers that Braz discusses adopts exactly the opposite stance of what Venuti terms the invisible translator: she foregrounds herself. Instead of allowing the alterity of the foreign text and the culture it originates from to shine forth she domesticates them. As such, she prevents "newness" (to use a term Bhabha [1994c] uses in a different context) from coming into the "world" of the target language. Braz here invokes the insights of Stephen Henighan (2008, 2012) who contends that English-language writers are lulled into complacency by the "widespread misconception that globalization means that the whole world speaks English" (2008: 137; quoted in Braz 2016: 586). "English-language fiction has stalled," he claims, because of

> the decline of translation. Alert readers of Spanish, French, German, Italian, Portuguese and other languages participate in an international aesthetic debate; readers and writers of English condemned to silence by insular fantasies of global relevance, are missing out on the next wave of literature.
> (Henighan 2008: 138–139; quoted in Braz 2016: 586)

By domesticating Pessoa in her "transelation," Mouré passes up on the possibility of enriching English-language literature via the kinds of translation both Goethe and Benjamin advocated.

Building upon Goethe, Walter Benjamin, Spivak (2000b), and Pizer (2006), Shaobo Xie (2020) turns Apter (2013) on how untranslatability precludes the possibility of world literature on its head. Xie (2020: 160) derives four key points from Goethe's and Benjamin's positions on translation:

> a) Taking untranslatable foreignness of other nations for granted or leaving them untouched is the prerequisite for meeting or understanding those nations; b) Divesting those nations of their idiosyncrasies or foreignness means taking away their ontological substance; c) Both Goethe's concept of world literature and Benjamin's translation theory are "Other"-oriented, respecting the peculiar and untranslatable foreignness of each source language so as to expand, deepen and enrich the target language; d) For both of them translation and untranslatability are two constitutive sides of any project of building connections between different peoples in the domain of literature and culture.

"Untranslatability," Xie argues (2020: 158) "offers the productive space in which a new text emerges by way of translation" and he (2020: 162) concludes that "as such, untranslatability is not, as Apter and other contemporary scholars insist, a foe to world literature, but a friend; not that which makes world literature an untenable concept, but that which urges us to reconceptualize it" and "untranslatability, one can argue, is not an obstacle to world literature, and is in no way incompatible with it." Again, this echoes Bhabha's ideas on how newness enters the world, but also Haroldo de Campos's *antropofagismo* and Jorge Luis Borges's 1951 lecture on the Argentine writer and tradition. That tradition, Borges says, is "the whole of Western culture" and Argentine writers "have a right to this tradition, a greater right than that which the inhabitants of one Western nation or another may have" – "we can take on all the European subjects, take them on without superstition and with an irreverence that can have, and already has had, fortunate consequences" (Borges 2000: 426). On the same track, Campos, according to Thayse Leal Lima (2017: 461), cultivated "an idea of world literature as a dialogic relationship between texts, in which both the receiving and the exporting traditions participate in processes of mutual influences and transformations," and

> more than a mode of reading and circulation (Damrosch 2003), it could be said that these relationships conform to a mode of re-creation. Significantly, in Campos's theory, translation arises as the primary tool for the constant literary mediation and reinvention that forges world literatures.

In Campos's view, "a translation holds a degree of separation from the original, and enjoys a literary status of its own" (Lima 2017: 462). Lima (2017: 462) underlines that

> this proposition carried a significant political subtext. In affirming the aesthetic potential of translation, Campos was also asserting the power of peripheral literatures in appropriating and transforming established traditions. Thus, translation here works a form of resistance to the hierarchical and asymmetric shape of world literary relations.

Lima (2017: 462) argues that Campos's theory is "part of the longstanding debate about Latin America's peripheral status within the international literary arena." In fact, Latin America's peripheral status in the world literature arena runs parallel to its concomitant status in matters geopolitical.

Conclusion

- The study of world literature has always recognized the importance of translation.
- The systematic study of translations as influencing the national as well as transnational development of literature has really only come into its own in the latter half of the twentieth century.

- An author or a literary work may occupy quite different positions in different literatures as a result of translation.
- Some influential contemporary critics warn of the potentially unwittingly homogenizing consequences of feeding students world literature in translation, thereby dulling the real differences between languages, literatures, and cultures, and in practice reducing all literature to literature in the language of translation; rather than introducing students to a world beyond their own culture this naturalizes the world for them as their own.
- Translation studies has become an inalienable part of comparative literature, and of present-day world literature studies.

8 World Literature, (Post)Modernism, (Post)Colonialism, Littérature-Monde, Decoloniality

Overview

In the early 1990s the well-known postcolonial critic Homi Bhabha proposed that postcolonial literature might be the new world literature. For him the literature of the displaced, the exiled, the uprooted, the marginalized, more accurately reflected the state of the present-day world than the postmodern literature produced by so-called mainstream literatures in the West. In reality, the division between postcolonialism and postmodernism is not so clear-cut. In fact, many contemporary writers may be seen to fit both categories. We might even see postmodernism and postcolonialism as twin facets of the process of globalization under which both movements were and in certain respects are still playing out. Lucien Goldmann, in *Le Dieu caché* (1955) and *Pour une sociologie du roman* (1964), argued that writers, and artists in general, anticipate by one generation or approximately twenty-five to thirty years upon what eventually becomes a dominant worldview in the society from which they originate. If we go along with Goldmann's argument we can see postmodernism as expressing, at the very moment the West, and especially its leading power the United States, seemed to be more hegemonic than ever, that same West's internalized underlying sense of its impending undoing, or perhaps more precisely of the undoing of those hitherto dominant in the West, by the rise of multiculturalism on the domestic level and of postcolonialism abroad. Moreover, most of the writers that fit Bhabha's postcolonial category wrote in English, the language of the world's foremost former colonizer and the United States. This raises the question whether the postcolonial as commonly conceived of in present-day literary studies, rather than an alternative to "Western" literature, is not simply one more projection of that same Western hegemony in matters linguistic, literary, theoretical as well as practical. If such issues have increasingly come to the fore in anglophone literary criticism, they have until recently been much less debated in other languages, or they have taken another turn in those languages. In French-language literature there has been a much-noted manifesto in a leading Parisian daily, followed by a collective volume and the debate ensuing. In Spanish- and Portuguese-language theory and criticism issuing from Latin America the discussion has centered on decoloniality.

DOI: 10.4324/9781003366713-9

Postcolonial Literature as World Literature

Together with Edward Said and Gayatri Spivak, Homi Bhabha is considered one of the most influential founding theoreticians of postcolonialism. He has introduced and popularized notions such as "mimicry" and "hybridity." Most of his early essays have been collected in *The Location of Culture* (1994). In his eponymous introduction to this volume Bhabha cites Goethe's remarks in the latter's introduction to Thomas Carlyle's *Life of Schiller* (1830) that through the Napoleonic Wars nations had become aware of "much that was foreign" and conscious of "spiritual needs hitherto unknown" (Strich 1949: 351; Bhabha cites another, older translation, viz. that by Joel Spingarn [1921], which gives the same passages as "many foreign ideas and ways" and "previously unrecognized spiritual and intellectual needs," Bhabha 1994a: 11). Goethe goes on to say that this has led to "a sense of relationship as neighbors" (Strich 1949: 251; Spingarn as quoted by Bhabha: "the feeling of neighborly relations," Bhabha 1994a: 11). Bhabha, however, wrenches this in another direction by posing the question what would happen if such "needs" as Goethe refers to would "emerge from the imposition of 'foreign' ideas, cultural representations, and structures of power" (Bhabha 1994a: 12). With a reference to Goethe as an "Orientalist who read Shakuntala at seventeen years of age" (Bhabha 1994a: 11), and who in his autobiography referred to the Hindu monkey god Hanuman as "unformed and overformed," Bhabha (1994a: 12) suggests that world literature might be based not on the recognition of what is common in all literatures, as has often been the interpretation put upon Goethe's *Weltliteratur*, but rather rooted in "historical trauma" (Bhabha 1994a: 12). As Bhabha puts it: "The study of world literature might be the study of the way in which cultures recognize themselves through their projections of 'otherness'" (Bhabha 1994a: 12). Hence, he proposes,

> where, once, the transmission of national traditions was the major theme of world literature, perhaps we can now suggest that transnational histories of migrants, the colonized, or political refugees – these border and frontier conditions – may be the terrains of world literature.
> (Bhabha 1994a: 12)

Bhabha's suggestion that the literature of migrants, and by extension that of postcolonialism, might be the new world literature, has been taken up again and again in the 1990s and in the early years of the twenty-first century. In her position paper on the 1993 Bernheimer report on "Comparative Literature in the age of Multiculturalism," Emily Apter (1995) directly refers to Bhabha's introduction to *The Location of Culture*, quoting the sentences immediately preceding those I just cited. Reading the history of post-World War II American comparative literature as a succession of, and a dialogue among, exilic voices, and primarily those of Wellek, Spitzer and Auerbach, Said, Spivak, and Bhahba, Apter is of the opinion that translating the discursive maneuvers of unhappy consciousness characteristic of postwar criticism into a politicized, multicultural critical idiom, postcolonialism is in many respects truer to the foundational disposition of comparative literature than are more traditional tendencies and approaches ... with its interrogation of cultural subjectivity and attention to the tenuous bonds between identity and national language, postcolonialism quite naturally inherits the mantle of comparative literature's historical legacy.

(Apter 1995: 86)

The Bernheimer report itself, and especially the reactions to it, Apter reads as "crude generational/cultural warfare over Eurocentrism" and "a contest for the title of who lays claim to the exilic aura of comparative literature's distinguished past" (Apter 1995: 94). Echoing Bhabha's reference to "border and frontier conditions," Apter recasts the debate as a "border war, an academic version of the legal battles and political disputes over the status of 'undocumented workers,' 'illegal aliens,' and 'permanent residents'," and concludes that "postcolonialism will claim its place whether Continental comparatism likes it or not" (Apter 1995: 94–96). What is important, and even "imperative," she argues, is "to continue reinventing world literature with a concern not to warehouse theoretical culture," because, and again echoing Bhabha's statement above, she feels that this "'dissensual' confusion of First and Third World critical perspectives" gives cohesion to the field of comparative literature and that moreover "the exilic melancholy of theory is profoundly in sync with the narrative movement of comparative literature and comparative culture" (Apter 1995: 94). Mads Rosendahl Thomsen seems to follow up on Apter's suggestion when he proposes that

it is hard to overlook the fact that the most significant thinker related to the post-colonial discourse, Edward W. Said, was at the same time a strong proponent of world literature ... he translated Auerbach on world literature, and kept returning to the idea of it ... was this the paradigm for which he really hoped, rather than the establishment and fortification of a dichotomy between centre and periphery?

(Thomsen 2008a: 25)

Although Apter frames her remarks as if postcolonialism at the time of her writing still had to do battle to conquer its place under the comparative literature sun, by the mid-1990s such was surely no longer the case in English departments in the USA and the UK. In the mid-1980s, when post-colonialism indeed was still struggling to gain a firm footing, Fredric Jameson had anticipated things to come. As Vilashini Cooppan reminds us, Jameson's "Third-World Literature in the Era of Multinational Capitalism," published in 1986, quickly became "notorious for its claim that all third-world texts are necessarily national allegories," but is "largely forgotten for what it has to say about *Weltliteratur*" (Cooppan 2004: 17). Indeed, Jameson had almost presciently started off his article with "in these last years of the century, the old question of a properly world literature reasserts itself" before going on to say that "today the reinvention of cultural studies in the United States demands the reinvention, in a new situation, of what Goethe long ago theorized as 'world literature'," and to then assert that "any conception of world literature necessarily demands some specific engagement with the question of third-world literature" (Jameson 2000: 318). Jameson's specific suggestion that all third-world literatures are necessarily allegorical quickly drew heavy critical fire, and under postcolonialism proper became almost completely discredited. Still, Jameson's insistence on linking the literary works produced in what was then, before the fall of the Berlin Wall and the implosion of the "second" world of the communist nations, still called the Third World to economic, and in their wake social and political, conditions pertaining in the nations concerned as well as to their position in the wider scheme of world economics, especially as ruled by late capitalism, did find some ready echoes, though most often elaborated along lines very different from those pursued by Jameson himself.

Amitava Kumar, in his introduction to a 2003 volume called *World Bank Literature*, quotes Jameson on the need for "the reinvention, in a new situation, of what Goethe long ago theorized as 'world literature'," and then wonders whether "World Bank Literature" could be "a new name for postcolonial studies?" (Kumar 2003: xx). Kumar argues that expositions about world literature routinely by-pass the economic issues at the back, or at the heart, of the texts in question, and equally routinely select texts on the basis of so-called universal values. Instead, he argues, what we should do is pay attention to how literature comprises and reveals local or national economic realities of dominance, suppression, oppression, and exploitation in a global context, or in the context of globalization:

> The focus on the World Bank, as an agent and a metaphor, helps us concretize the "wider context" of global capitalism. As we witnessed during the protests on the streets of Seattle or Washington, D.C., Davos, or Quebec City, the opposition to the World Bank, the IMF, and the WTO is both widespread and collective. On that basis alone, the analytic shift from the liberal-diversity model of "World Literature" to the radical paradigm of "World Bank Literature" signals a resolve not only to recognize and contest the dominance of Bretton Woods institutions but also to rigorously oppose those regimes of knowledge that would keep literature and culture sealed from the issues of economics and activism.
> (Kumar 2003: xix–xx)

As examples Kumar cites Arundhati Roy's *The God of Small Things*, Pankaj Mishra's *The Romantics*, Amit Chaudhuri's *A New World*, and Jhumpa Lahiri's *Interpreter of Maladies*, all of which show how economic globalization affects the lives of Indians, whether in India itself or when moving to the

US. All of these would also squarely fit the postcolonial mold, and in Chaudhuri's and Lahiri's cases also the multicultural one. If, in 1995, Apter then still found it necessary to defend the inclusion of postcolonialism as a legitimate discourse in comparative literature thinking about world literature, in 2003 Kumar apparently already sees the need to dissolve the term in favor of a more fitting one to better respond to the conditions of globalization.

Cooppan argues that for Jameson, in his 1986 essay, "even as nationalism, 'that old thing,' is more or less sublimated in America into the placeless form of global postmodernism, 'a certain nationalism is fundamental in the third world'" (Cooppan 2004: 17). For Bhabha, on the contrary, "the currency of critical comparativism, or aesthetic judgment, is no longer the sovereignty of the national culture" conceived as Benedict Anderson's "imagined community" (Bhabha 1994a: 6). Rather, Bhabha envisages new "modes of cultural identification and political affect that form around issues of sexuality, race, feminism, the lifeworld of refugees or migrants, or the deathly social destiny of AIDS" (Bhabha 1994a: 6). In this new "geopolitical space," Bhabha argues, "the Western metropolis must confront its postcolonial history, told by its influx of postwar migrants and refugees, as an indigenous or native narrative *internal to its national identity*" (Bhabha 1994a: 6). Where Jameson and Bhabha meet, I think, is in the dialectic between postmodernism and postcolonialism that both their arguments imply. For Jameson postmodernism is a mode expressive of America's inner reality, which he sees as

> epistemologically crippling, and reduc[ing] its subjects to the illusions of a host of fragmented subjectivities, to the poverty of the individual experience of isolated monads, to dying individual bodies without collective pasts or futures bereft of any possibility of grasping the social totality.
> (Jameson 2000: 336)

In third-world culture, on the contrary, he maintains, "the telling of the individual story and the individual experience cannot but ultimately involve the whole laborious telling of the experience of the collectivity itself" (Jameson 2000: 336).

Postcolonialism and Postmodernism

For Bhabha, the popular use of the "post" in "postmodernity, postcoloniality, postfeminism" only makes sense "if [the latter] transform the present into an expanded and ex-centric site of experience and empowerment" (Bhabha 1994a: 4). Concretely, he proposes, "if the interest in postmodernism is limited to a celebration of the fragmentation of the 'grand narratives' of post-enlightenment rationalism then, for all its intellectual excitement, it remains a profoundly parochial exercise" (Bhabha 1994a: 4). "The wider significance of the postmodern condition," he continues, lies in the awareness that the epistemological "limits" of those ethnocentric ideas are also the enunciative boundaries of a range of other dissonant, even dissident histories and voices – women, the colonized, minority groups, the bearers of policed sexualities ... for the demography of the new internationalism is the history of postcolonial migration, the narratives of cultural and political diaspora, the major social displacements of peasant and aboriginal communities, the poetics of exile, the grim prose of political and economic refugees.

(Bhabha 1994a: 4–5)

Postmodernism and postcolonialism thus meet in Bhabha's new "geopolitical space, as a local or transnational reality" (Bhabha 1994a: 6).

In fact, while most proponents of postcolonialism usually see it as offering an alternative road to a world literature that transcends the traditional limitations imposed upon it by Western thinking, my contention would be that what I will call its tangled relationship to postmodernism risks enclosing it yet again within those very same limitations. For Bhabha, postcoloniality is "a salutary reminder of the persistent 'neo-colonial' relations within the 'new' world order and the multinational division of labor," while at the same time bearing witness to what he calls cultures constituted "otherwise than modernity" (Bhabha 1994a: 6). Such "cultures of postcolonial *contra-modernity*," he contends, "may be contingent to modernity, discontinuous or in connection with it, resistant to its oppressive, assimilationist technologies" (Bhabha 1994a: 6). At the same time, he maintains, "they also deploy the cultural hybridity of their borderline conditions to 'translate', and therefore re-inscribe, the social imaginary of both metropolis and modernity" (Bhabha 1994a: 6). Elsewhere (D'haen 1994), I have proposed the term "counter-postmodernism" to indicate the same relationship between metropolis, postcolonialism, and modernity, or, more precisely perhaps, to indicate how postmodernism and postcolonialism, the latter together with its twin multiculturalism, "shadow" postmodernism within the more general framework of modernity. Aijaz Ahmad I think intimated very much the same thing when in 1992, still using the earlier term "third-world literature," he proposed that: "There now appears to be, in the work of the metropolitan critical avant-garde, an increasing tie between postmodernism and the counter-canon of 'Third World Literature'" (Ahmad 1992: 125).

Hans Bertens (1991), contextualizing the debate on postmodernism around 1990, distinguishes an "avant-garde," a "poststructuralist," and an "aesthetic" postmodernism, and links these various postmodernisms both to different historical stages in the use of the term, roughly speaking the 1960s, 1970s, and 1980s, and to different stances, inspired by opposing socio-political convictions, toward contemporary literature and culture in general. These stances, moreover, are perceptually defined. In other words, they depend upon how one *reads* a particular work rather than upon any "objective" quality of the work itself. An avant-garde reading, primarily associated with Ihab

Hassan (1982 [1971], 1975, 1980, and 1987) and Douwe Fokkema (1984 and 1986), foregrounds the work's technical features distinguishing it from works in a previous mode, and specifically from modernism. It sees postmodernism as an artistic current, characterized in its literary manifestations, and particularly in fiction, by a common set of techniques, conventions, and themes. A poststructuralist reading, associated with Brian McHale (1987 and 1992) and Linda Hutcheon (1984, 1985, 1988, and 1989), focuses on the de-centering of the (bourgeois) subject, the deferment of meaning, and the problematical status of the text. What Bertens calls an "aesthetic" reading fits the period approach of Jameson (1984 and 1991) and his neo-conservative humanist counterparts, and stresses the artificiality, the emptiness, the lack of depth, the purely formal interests of the postmodern work. This reading sees postmodern works as directly translating late capitalism's commodifying influence into an "aesthetic" experience, reduplicating as it were the very personality (or non-personality) make-up multinational late capitalism demands: functional man, broken up in disparate units, without any essence to him, man as malleable putty, what Gerhard Hoffmann (1982) has called "situational" man. In this sense, too, aesthetic postmodernism (both in its neo-Marxist and its [neo-]conservative reading) sees postmodern works, functionally speaking, as the continuation of earlier forms of mass-culture. Particularly in its neo-Marxist version, such a reading blames postmodernism for having sold out to the culture-industry of late capitalist consumer society, thus also taking up Theodor Adorno's, and the Frankfurt School's, more general point with regard to mass culture after World War II (Adorno 1991a [1944] and 1991b [1967]). Since 1984, the date of publication of Jameson's influential article "Postmodernism, or the Cultural Logic of Late Capitalism," and especially as of 1991, the date of appearance of the book with (almost) the same title, Jameson's view has largely monopolized discussions of postmodernism, at least in the United States. It is this view that we also see articulated in Jameson's 1986 article on third-world literatures.

What a counter-reading of postmodernism seizes upon is the latter's universalizing claim regardless of its being grafted upon an aesthetic avant-garde practice that was also highly specific in its conditions and circumstances, that is to say located in the United States (Huyssen 1986). After all, this is where late, multinational, consumer capitalism first flowered, and where the central categories of modernity leading to such late capitalism were worked out and applied most categorically. The United States, after all, is the most "true West." Kumkum Sangari (1990: 242–243) neatly summarizes the point:

> Postmodern skepticism is the complex product of a historical conjuncture as both symptom and critique of the contemporary economic and social formation of the West. But postmodernism does have a tendency to universalize its epistemological preoccupations – a tendency that appears even in the work of critics of radical political persuasion. ... the world contracts into the West; a Eurocentric perspective ... is brought to bear

upon "Third World" cultural products; a "specialized" skepticism is carried everywhere as cultural paraphernalia and epistemological apparatus, as a way of seeing; and the postmodern problematic becomes *the* frame through which the cultural products of the rest of the world are seen. ... Such skepticism does not take into account either the fact that the postmodern preoccupation with the crisis of meaning is not everyone's crisis (even in the West) or that there are different modes of de-essentialization which are socially and politically grounded and mediated by separate perspectives, goals, and strategies for change in other countries.

The fact remains that some of the best-known postcolonial authors, Salman Rushdie probably being the prime example, based on their literary techniques can be categorized just as easily as postmodern. Adam and Tiffin, for example, note that, "there is a good deal of formal and tropological overlap between 'primary' texts variously categorised as 'post-modern' or 'post-colonial'" (Adam and Tiffin 1991: vii). But, they also note,

> If there is overlap between the two discourses in terms of "primary" texts ... there is considerably less in the "secondary" category. ... it is thus in the selection and reading of such "primary" texts, and in the contexts of discussion in which they are placed, that significant divergences between post-colonialism and post-modernism are most often isolated.
> (Adam and Tiffin 1991: vii)

Stephen Slemon (1991: 4) makes the same point when he remarks that Hutcheon's (1988) analysis of intertextual parody as a constitutive principle of postmodernism resembles the post-colonial practice of "rewriting the canonical 'master texts' of Europe," but with the difference that

> whereas a postmodernist criticism would want to argue that literary practices such as these expose the constructedness of *all* textuality, ... an *interested* post-colonial critical practice would want to allow for the positive production of oppositional truth-claims in these texts.
> (Slemon 1991: 5)

Hutcheon herself concurs when she says that

> the post-colonial, like the feminist, is a dismantling but also constructive political enterprise insofar as it implies a theory of agency and social change that the post-modern deconstructive impulse lacks ... while both "posts" *use* irony, the post-colonial cannot *stop* at irony ...
> (Hutcheon 1991: 183)

Counter-postmodernism can thus be seen as yet another reading of "postmodernism," complementary while at the same time oppositional to those enumerated before. Instead of submitting to the demise of the subject as posited by these other readings, and if we follow Simon Gikandi when he posits that "entry into the European terrain of the modern has often demanded that the colonized peoples be denied their subjectivity, language, and history" (Gikandi 1992: 2), a counter-postmodern reading as proposed here "writes" the subjectivity, history, and language of those hitherto suppressed by the discourse of modernity as applied by Western bourgeois society. As such, it makes this discourse accessible to those traditionally excluded or repressed by Western modernity. Ironically, by thus marking the end of modernity as the exclusive instrument of hegemonic Western man, and the advent of modernity for the hitherto repressed, counter-postmodernism may well be the only truly "*post*-modern" reading of postmodernism in that it posits the transcendence of "orthodox" Western or metropolitan modernity, and the attainment of an-"Other" modernity. As such, counter-postmodernism also adds an emancipatory "counter-ethics" to those of poststructuralist and aesthetic postmodernism, breaking the free-play impasse of the one, and productively challenging the other. Counter-postmodernism thus posits a postmodernism practiced by subaltern, post-colonial, or multicultural writers to recover the "history, language, and subjectivity" of the West's "Others." In the way counter-postmodernism seizes upon the Western hegemonic and colonial discourse of modernity, and of that discourse's reading of "postmodernism," it is not just the postmodernism of the West's "Others," but also the "Other" to postmodernism as we are accustomed to think of it. As the "Other" to Euro-American postmodernism, then, counter-postmodernism feeds "difference" back into the center. In fact, it is only in this return that postmodernism recognizes itself as not just Bhabha's "celebration of the fragmentation of the 'grand narratives' of postenlightenment rationalism" (Bhabha 1994a: 4) but as an articulation of the particular condition of the West (or in first instance the United States) *in relation* to the rest of "the world." As Bhabha puts it in "The Postcolonial and the Postmodern: The Question of Agency":

> We see how modernity and postmodernity are themselves constituted from the marginal perspective of cultural difference ... they encounter themselves contingently at the point at which the internal difference of their own society is reiterated in terms of the difference of the other, the alterity of the postcolonial site.
>
> (Bhabha 1994b: 196)

Postcolonialism as Western Projection

Bertens, although using a totally different vocabulary, predicates a similar return of a difference that already was, albeit only belatedly realized as such, when, drawing upon Ernesto Laclau and Chantal Mouffe's "radical democracy" from their *Hegemony and Socialist Strategy: Towards a Radical Democratic Politics*

(1987), he sees postcolonialism and multiculturalism as part of "a new round in the realization of the potential of Enlightenment vision" (Bertens 1994: 244). In this "current round of democratization," he argues, "an older Enlightenment dispensation is giving way to a new one in a process in which the Enlightenment is – belatedly – forced by its own momentum to confront the problem of the Other" (Bertens 1994: 245). Contrary to Jameson's views, Bertens argues that "one can see postmodernism, then, as Enlightenment principles finally coming home to roost, while, paradoxically, that home is simultaneously being subjected to a thorough deconstruction" (Bertens 1994: 245). Proponents of multiculturalism and postcolonialism will hardly feel like quarrelling with the emancipatory prospects sketched here for their respective constituencies. At the same time, they may well fear this latest avatar of postmodern thinking to be yet another sly maneuver on the part of the West via theory to preserve its "imperious" (Sangari 1990: 243) grasp on an ever more refractory literary production worldwide. The room here made for multiculturalism and postcolonialism under the umbrella of "postmodernism" invites the risk of being construed as yet another attempt on the part of the West to appropriate to itself "some of the more forward-looking products" of "marginal" cultures (Tiffin 1991: viii), meaning not only some of the more highly regarded literary works from these cultures but likewise the very theory underlying multiculturalism and post-colonialism. Specifically, as the editors of *Past the Last Post* state in their introduction, it may function as "a way of depriving the formerly colonised of 'voice', of, specifically, any theoretical authority, and [of] locking post-colonial texts which it does appropriate firmly within the European episteme" (Adam and Tiffin 1991: viii). Similar suspicions with regard to postcolonialism, along different lines of analysis, have been uttered almost from its very emergence, by Kwame Anthony Appiah (1991), Ella Shohat (1992), Vijay Mishra and Bob Hodge (1991), and Arif Dirlik (1994).

A world literature under the aegis of postmodernism and/or post-colonialism, then, at least in some interpretations projects a world that remains relentlessly "Western," whether in extending the postmodernism of the West, and perhaps even of only one nation of the West, to comprise all of the world, as happens for instance in Bertens and Fokkema's *International Postmodernism* (1997), or in countering such postmodernism with a post-colonialism that for its definition is finally dependent upon what it subverts. In fact, postcolonialism, even if only because of its "post"-status, but also for the reasons just adduced, might well be regarded as another instance of what the American-Chinese critic Rey Chow has called a "post-Europe and ..." construction, where whatever "new" theory or approach that defines itself through difference from European or American theory remains fatally beholden to the primacy of the latter (Chow 2004). Gikandi goes so far as to consider postcolonial theory, the subject of which he sees as "global culture linked with postmodernism" (Gikandi 2001: 638), as the product of knowledge production about the nations newly independent from Britain by Third World intellectuals migrating themselves into the academic institutions of the First World, there to function as what Gikandi calls "émigré native informants" (Gikandi 2001: 646). What links them, according to Gikandi, is the submerged point of departure for their construction of a postcolonial literature in English as world literature in the attitude toward literature propagated (some would say preached) in England by F.R. Leavis from the 1930s through the 1960s, but disseminated throughout the British colonies and former colonies in secondary and university teaching, and which effectively posited Englishness and English literature as central to a particular worldview (Gikandi 2001: 649–650). The German literary historian Horst Steinmetz had, in 1988, already suggested that instead of interpreting world literature as either comprising all of the world's literatures in all their manifestations or as designating a canon of masterpieces, where both these interpretations basically applied to the past, we should heed Goethe's own hints that he saw world literature as a contemporary and future phenomenon. Specifically, Steinmetz says, we should see world literature as referring to the period stretching from Goethe's own lifetime to our own, and which he sees characterized by an ever-growing convergence between the lives led by people all over the world. The latter is caused by the same phenomena that Goethe too invoked when he saw a world literature coming into being: improved means of communication, faster circulation of cultural goods, mass media. The historical context of literature since Goethe's epoch, Steinmetz claims, is no longer national but global. Even what he sees as a return to the regional in these postmodern times is merely a locally differentiated manifestation of a global phenomenon. We might deduce that under these circumstances the postcolonial is merely one such form of "glocalization."

Even if one grants postcolonialism the power to truly represent the diversity of the peoples of the world beyond the West, there still remains the danger of reverse occlusion:

> The political and disciplinary collisions between the Eurocentric premises of traditional comparative approaches to literary and cultural study and the inherently and necessarily anti-Eurocentric stance of postcolonial politics and theory appear to have colluded towards a subtle yet unmistakable reinforcement of a monolithic and monologic "European" identity, in which the ideal notion of "Europe as Subject" [Spivak 1988: 271], devoid of historical and geopolitical determinants of its own, is mirrored by the oppositional construct of Europe as Object, a staunchly self-identical metropolitan Other to the richly fragmented (post)colonial Self.
> (Klobucka 1997: 126)

For "Europe," of course, we can here equally well read "the West."

It is precisely such dangers that Gayatri Spivak seems to warn of in the revised version of her famous 1988 article "Can the Subaltern Speak?" in the "History" chapter from *A Critique of Postcolonial Reason* (1999). In the original version of her article Spivak upbraids Michel Foucault and Gilles Deleuze in an interview these two French philosophers gave in 1977 when discussing the plight of the oppressed and agreeing that "reality" happens on the factory floor, in prison, at the police station, where "concrete experience happens," for not seeming to be "aware that the intellectual within socialized capital, brandishing concrete experience, can help consolidate the international division of labor" (Spivak 1988: 275). In the 1999 version she slightly elaborates on this by saying that Foucault and Deleuze, by exclusively concentrating on the experience of the Western "masses" help to "consolidate the international division of labor by making one model of 'concrete experience' *the* model" (Spivak 1999, 255–256). She then extrapolates this to literary studies when she continues that "we are witnessing this in our discipline daily as we see the postcolonial migrant become the norm, thus occluding the native once again" (Spivak 1999: 256). It is hard not to read this addition as a direct comment, a critique even, of Bhabha's position in *The Location of Culture*.

Waïl S. Hassan makes the same point more directly and more topically when he remarks, in terms that seem a direct echo of Bhabha's, that "[the] emergent canon of postcolonial-literature-as-world-literature ... inscribes 'writing back,' diaspora, migrancy, border-crossings, in-betweenness, and hybridity as the defining features of the 'postcolonial condition'" (Hassan 2002: 60). While such issues are important, he continues, "they are extremely limited when we remember that the vast majority of African and Asian populations are not diasporic, migrants, or bilingual, and may, indeed, have never even traveled beyond the borders of their native countries" (Hassan 2002: 60). And Neil Lazarus pointedly observes that,

> Even if, in the contemporary world system the subjects whom Bhabha addresses under the labels of exile, migration, and diaspora, are vastly more numerous than at any time previously, they cannot reasonably be said to be paradigmatic or constitutive of "postcoloniality" as such.
> (Lazarus 1999: 136–137)

Bhabha (1994a) in the early 1990s seemed to make room for if not a merger between postcolonialism and world literature then at least some form of collaboration. Very quickly, though, scholars of postcolonialism sought to disengage themselves from the rising tide of world literature unleashed by the groundbreaking publications of Casanova (1999, 2004), Moretti (2000), and Damrosch (2003). Robert Young (2012: 213) remarks that although world literature and postcolonialism "share a fundamental perspective on literary studies that at first sight ought to put them in dialogue with each other; both seek to move the study of literature beyond the confines of the classic boundaries of European literature," there nevertheless "has been little direct exchange between these two separately demarcated domains of literary study." "The reason," he proffers, "must lie in the fact that their respective positions with relation to literature remain largely incompatible and disjunctive" (Young 2012: 213). While "in general, concepts of world literature offer themselves as disinterested," ruled by "questions of judgment and taste," and (at least until recently) "remained predominantly European in emphasis" (Young 2012: 214), "the basis of postcolonial literature has never been, in the first instance, aesthetic criteria, but rather, the effect that it seeks to achieve – it is a literature written against something, namely conditions that obtain in the everyday world" (Young 2012: 216). For Peter Hitchcock (2009: 5) world literature's "assumed neutrality" functions as an excuse for Western cosmopolitan readers to evade their own responsibility for what is wrong with the world. The argument here largely echoes the charge that postcolonialism, when it itself was the up-and-coming paradigm, brought to bear upon its postmodern predecessor, namely that the latter, emphasizing aesthetic criteria, is a-political because disinterested, while the former is oppositionally committed (Slemon 1991: 5; Hutcheon 1991: 183). That critics committed to postcolonialism saw the rise of world literature as a potential threat to their own discipline shows from Elleke Boehmer (2014). Contrary to Young (2012: 213) finding the relation between world literature and postcolonialism "disjunctive," she finds that "in institutional and pedagogic terms the growth of interest in world literary perspectives does appear to be producing some convergence of the field" (Boehmer 2014: 299). However, she also fears that the "acceleration in the shift from postcolonial to world within the academic mainstream" may entail "a gradual marginalization" or even "trivialization" of the postcolonial (Boehmer 2014: 300). World literary studies, focusing on issues of translation and dissemination, risks bypassing the "often ethically difficult and historically specific questions" postcolonial studies raises. Still, she feels that postcolonial criticism as an "always already 'worlded' mode of critical reading and commentary" could usefully join "pedagogic and critical forces with world literary perspectives and studies" (Boehmer 2014: 302). Indeed, she opined,

> a conjunction of world literary and postcolonial studies need not necessarily involve the co-optation of the one by the other; of the seemingly more peripheral by the increasingly more hegemonic field [and] in a globalizing world it is at least conceivable that, if world literary studies were to join forces with the postcolonial, this could produce a more radical and expansive conception of the world than previously existed in the former domain, and, as a corollary, a constructive interrogation of its still-definitive Eurocentric paradigms.
> (Boehmer 2014: 307)

Young (2012: 218) stressed the ethical dimension of postcolonial studies as what distinguished it from world literature studies: "if world literature is universal, postcolonial literature, though partial, achieves a certain universality through its relation to the ethical." Hitchcock (2012: 22) discusses the ethics of any world literature concept. In the second half of the 2010s Young's and Boehmer's suggestions were picked up by several scholars of Asian origin but often teaching in the United States: Pheng Cheah, Debjani Ganguly, B.

Venkat Mani, Aamir Mufti, and Baidik Bhattacharya. They decisively wrench the world literature debate toward the "worlding" option raised by Said (1983) and Kadir (2004). In "The World, The Text, and the Critic" (1984), Said, building upon Martin Heidegger's "On the Origin of the Work of Art" (1935), evoked how a "world" arises from each actualization of a text in the act of reading it. For Said it is the critic that in his interpretation of a text guides the reader to "world" the text in a particular way, and thus to see the world also in a particular way.

In *What Is a World? On Postcolonial Literature as World Literature* (2016) Pheng Cheah elaborates ideas he had aired earlier via articles in *New Literary History* (Cheah 2009, 2014). He proposes a "normative conception of world literature," as part of the title to his 2014 article reads. By thus positing an inherently future-directed approach Cheah by-passes the geographical emphasis of world literature studies current at the time and returns (though he never mentions him) to what Steinmetz (1988) deemed Goethe's original intention with his *Weltliteratur*. Cheah ascribes to postcolonial literature as world literature the "power or efficacy to change the world according to a normative ethicopolitical horizon" (Cheah 2016: 6). We could see Cheah as inflecting Damrosch's definition of world literature as a way of reading in a pointedly postcolonial direction. He uses Michelle Cliff's Clare Savage novels, set in Jamaica, Amitav Ghosh's *The Hungry Tide*, set in Bangladesh, and Nuruddin Farah's *Gifts*, set in Somalia, as examples to argue that postcolonial literature resists the West's worlding of the rest of the world by refusing to go along with the uni-temporality of globalization as Western imposition. Specifically, Cheah argues,

> these novels are examples of literature that seeks to have a worldly causality in contemporary globalization ... the source of literature's worldly force is the heterotemporality of precolonial oral traditions that have survived the violence of slavery, folk practices, subaltern rituals and practices of survival, religious ethics, and even the geological time of the landscape.
>
> (Cheah 2016: 13)

The postcolonial novels he discusses, Cheah maintains, "employ formal means to revive non-Western temporalities in the present that can aid in worlding the world otherwise." Put differently, "they generate alternative cartographies that enable a postcolonial people or a collective group to foster relations of solidarity and build a shared world in which self-determination is achieved" (Cheah 2016: 17). While ostensibly answering to Boehmer's appeal for a "more radical and expansive conception of the world" Cheah in fact narrows it to one specific domain. Instead of, as Boehmer (2014: 307) saw it, world literature being the "seemingly more hegemonic field" and postcolonialism the "seemingly more peripheral," with Cheah the relations are reversed. With the same move, Cheah turns world literature studies from a descriptive discipline as practiced by Casanova, Moretti, Damrosch, and their followers, into a prescriptive one under the aegis of the postcolonial. His world literature is world-making and the world it should make is a postcolonial one.

In *Postcolonial Poetics – 21st-Century Readings,* Boehmer (2018) gives a particular twist to Cheah's (2016) world-making argument. In her 2014 article she had suggested that "with its antecedents in comparatism a 'world literature' approach offers substantial critical tools to deal with questions of form, or what Said called the aesthetic integrity of a text." (Boehmer 2014: 303). In her introductory chapter to *Postcolonial Poetics*, she argues that postcolonialism has for too long neglected questions of aesthetics, leading to its marginalization in critical terms. The rise of world literature could at least in part be explained as a move to re-introduce these concerns into the field of literary studies. Echoing earlier oppositions between postmodernism and postcolonialism, but now with reference to world literature, Boehmer explicitly opposes an interested postcolonial reading to a disinterested world literature reading, and a committed reader transformed by his postcolonial reading practice to a non-committal world literature reader. In an attempt to wrest the initiative from world literary studies, Boehmer (2018: 15) emphasizes the world-shaping qualities of postcolonial literature via what she calls a transformative postcolonial reading practice. Against "world literature's assumptions of a general interchangeability across cultural divides" she posits that "a transformative postcolonial reading practice may lie in soliciting the reader's attention in specific ways, and in their consequent internationalization of the text's communicative shapes and structures" (Boehmer 2018: 14).

Debjani Ganguly (2016) argues much along the same lines as Cheah as to the world-making possibilities of world literature. At variance with the other uses the term has passed through from Goethe on, she argues that since 1989, a date which for various reasons she considers crucial, "the radical spatio-temporal shifts generated by the information age produce the global novel that helps imagine the new chronotope 'world'" (Ganguly 2016: 2). To support her argument Ganguly draws upon theoreticians from Heidegger and Derrida to Said and Arendt, but when it comes to actual analyses her post-1989 "world novels" (Ganguly 2016: 38) are exclusively anglophone: Salman Rushdie's *Shalimar the Clown*, David Mitchell's *Ghostwritten*, Don DeLillo's *Falling Man*, Michael Ondaatje's *Anil's Ghost*, Art Spiegelman's *In the Shadow of No Towers* and *Maus*, and Janet Turner Hospital's *Orpheus Lost*. It should be noted here that Ganguly's corpus, including works from the UK, the US, Sri Lanka/Canada, India/UK/US, Australia/Canada/US, is not exclusively post-colonial. Of course, it also depends on what one subsumes under the rubric of the postcolonial. Do works from the so-called settler colonies qualify? Including from what once was Great Britain's first colony and also the first to become post-colonial by declaring independence – the US? Is the UK itself perhaps now also post-colonial if not quite postcolonial in the sense we usually attribute to the unhyphenated variant? Paul Giles (2022: 389) gives an interesting twist to the question of anglophone world literature when, noting that in discussions of world literature the ubiquity of "global English" is often chafed at, he points out that the diversity of the Englishes used around the world, and what they give expression to, is now such that "global English" "should be seen as an inherently heterogeneous term" and not, quoting Arac (2002: 44), "a monolingual master scheme."

If Cheah (2016) aims to remold world literature as future-directed postcolonialism, Aamir Mufti in *Forget English! Orientalisms and World Literatures* (2016) brings a postcolonial genealogical perspective to bear upon it. World literature, he argues, both arises from and contributes to the unification of the world under a bourgeois regime of market economics imposing itself worldwide through European and foremost British imperialism. The dominant attitude of Europe to the rest of the world he defines, following Said (1979), as Orientalism. In particular, he sees the philological work of William Jones on Sanskrit and Indo-European languages at the end of the eighteenth century and the interest it sparked in classical Indian literature, combined with Herder's casting a literature in the vernacular as the determinant of a people's identity, as laying the foundations for the emergence of the idea of national (in Europe) or indigenous (beyond Europe) literatures. The resulting differentiation process called into being the simultaneous appearance of the disciplines of the study of national literatures as separate entities, comparative literature dealing with a combination of such entities, and world literature as the composite of these entities. Without denying that languages other than English, and primarily French, may have played a role in this process, for Mufti it is English, fueled by first the global spread of the British Empire and more recently the hegemony of the United States, that has served as a catalyst, even if only by its inevitable mediating role as the sole remaining lingua franca for translation – of primary works of literature as of literary scholarship – to weld the world's literatures into one world literature. Joe Cleary (2021) likewise links world literature, specifically under modernism, to English-language "empires," whether British or American. Siraj Ahmed (2018) sees philology, in the guise it took as of the end of the eighteenth century, as instrumental in enabling nineteenth-century imperialism and its present-day aftermath.

B. Venkat Mani (2017) returns us to the country and the language that gave birth to the term and concept of "world literature," or, more precisely, *Weltliteratur*. Elaborating on the concept of "bibliomigrancy" he introduced in 2012, Mani details how world literature is coded and recoded by practices of book circulation, categorization, and translation, and what the role of libraries is in this. While primarily focused on the German-language area, what he finds is easily translatable to other language areas. And like Mufti (2016), Mani too traces the origins of our present-day practices in all this to the beginnings of modern philology in eighteenth- and nineteenth-century orientalism. Elsewhere (Mani 2021: 823) he asks what is "the role of the state in the business of national and world literatures?" with the aim "to articulate the relationship between literary catalogues and their creation of readerships, especially when the said relationship is mediated by the state." He focuses upon the Indian case.

Ato Quayson (2021) turns the "postcolonial and diasporic lens" on world literature, taking the reader through how postcolonial studies, Deleuze and Guattari's minor literature theories, and diasporic studies have affected world literature studies. Bavya Tiwari and David Damrosch curated two special issues of the *Journal of World Literature* (4.3 [2019] and 5.3 [2020]) on "World Literature and Postcolonial Studies." A selection under the same title appeared in book form in 2023.

Baidik Bhattacharya in *Postcolonial Writing in the Era of World Literature: Texts, Territories, Globalizations*, a volume that appeared in the same year as Boehmer's *Postcolonial Poetics*, turns the tables between postcolonial and world literature studies. "Postcoloniality is … the prehistory of [the] present celebration of world literature," Bhattacharya claims (2018: 1). For him (2018: 2), "the nineteenth-century ideal of world literature has been exhausted through the global reach of Anglophone postcolonial literature, and, as a consequence, the world literature paradigm is dead." In fact, he claims (2018: 2), "authors like Naipaul, Coetzee, or Rushdie offer the most persuasive and empirical embodiment of the Goethean *Weltliteratur*." Cheah had already normatively claimed world literature for postcolonial literature, Baidik now also claims descriptive world literature studies – there is no world literature but anglophone postcolonial literature! Bhattacharya's claim may seem extreme, but in fact he is simply carrying to its logical conclusion what is implicit also in Cheah's (2016) and Boehmer's (2018) volumes. All three engage almost exclusively with English-language writers and works to make their point. Earlier I listed Cheah's selection. Boehmer draws mainly upon Ben Okri, Chinua Achebe, Fred D'Aguiar, NourbeSe Philip, Chimamanda Ngozi Adichie, Nadifa Mohamed, Tayeb Salih, and a selection of South African authors. In 2012 Young (2012: 220) insisted that "while aesthetic value is not a major focus for postcolonial literature, the questions of language and of translation are central even if they operate unacknowledged beneath the surface." In fact, Young (2012: 220) argues, "language anxiety is fundamental to postcolonial writing" and "is articulated directly with respect to the decision as to which language the writer should choose to write in." Ngugi wa Thiong'o at a given moment opted for Gikuyu instead of English, a foreign imperial language he deemed unfit to give expression to his Kenyan reality. Achebe on the contrary chose to write in English, but an English locally inflected by its Nigerian context, in effect creolizing it. No one will contest that both wa Thiong'o and Achebe are major authors. Nobody will deny that they have a place in world literature. Yet if we follow Bhattacharya's reasoning to its logical conclusion, wa Thiong'o should be excluded. And with him all other post-World War II writers using any language other than English and, moreover, not bona fide postcolonial. In Bhattacharya's "world literature" the "world" thus is reduced to what fits a narrowly defined segment of anglophone literature only. In his 2022 survey article on the relationship between postcolonialism and world literature Bhattacharya once more exclusively focuses on anglophone publications. In fact, the role of the English language in discussions of world literature is a constant interest for Bhattacharya. In an earlier article, "On Comparatism in the Colony," he remarks on what he sees as "the strategic erasure of [the] colonial history [of comparative literature] in recent discussions of world literature" (Bhattacharya 2016: 709), and specifically in what he mentions as the founding texts of the most recent development in the discipline: those of Casanova (1999, 2004), Moretti (2000), and Damrosch (2003). He traces this history to the philological work of William Jones and the *Linguistic Survey of India* (1894–1928), curated by George Abraham Grierson. Marshalling what eventually became the grid of Indo-European languages with Jones and of India's languages with Grierson, Bhattacharya argues, was only possible via the mediating role of English reducing temporal (Jones) or spatial (Grierson) differentiations to comparable units. "In both Moretti and Damrosch," according to Bhattacharya (2016: 710), "comparatism is premised on the conjecture that once translated into English, texts from different locations and historical epochs become comparable instantaneously; it is the sheer weight of English as a world language that overrides any contextual difference." Thus, "The entrepreneurial thrust of recent critical scholarship does not entertain any distinction between the colonial mission of governing native populations and the reorganization of contemporary cultural heterogeneity as long as they are useful in straitjacketing everything through English" (Bhattacharya 2016: 711). And thus, paradoxically given Bhattacharya's implicit critique, echoing Spivak (2003) and others, of this historical process, comparative literature, along with its scion world literature, is claimed as an anglophone province.

World Literature and "Anglophony"

As postcolonialism, in theory as well as in the primary literature it focuses upon, at least until recently has mostly been confined to the anglophone realm it even further prejudices the world literature it potentially comprises in favor of what Arac (2002) and Spivak (2003) already saw as a hegemonic construct. Nicholas Brown, reflecting on "anglophone literature" in the context of Goethe's commercial metaphors for speaking about *Weltliteratur* and on how Marx and Engels use similar metaphors in the *Communist Manifesto*, comments that

> as plainly as we can see the legacy of the Goethean conception in contemporary multicultural discourse, it is just as clear that the Marxian narrative, where particular cultural forms colonize territory along with economic ones, represents the truth of Goethe's metaphor.
>
> (Brown 2001: 831)

Waïl Hassan finds that, "One of the ironies of postcolonial studies is that colonial discourse analysis began with several theorists who studied colonialism in the Arab world: Albert Memmi (in Tunisia), Frantz Fanon (in Algeria), Edward Said (in the Levant)," but that "the sophisticated theoretical apparatus" built on their work rarely takes into account Arabic literature (Hassan 2002: 45). In fact, he notes, postcolonialism confines its attention to literatures written in former colonies or by authors emanating from former colonies and in the language of the ex-colonizer, in practice English and French (and even the latter only very recently, see for instance Moura 1999, Bessière and Moura 1999 and 2001). Therefore, he continues,

> postcolonial studies profess to make the balance of global power relations central to its inquiry, yet seems [sic] to inscribe neocolonial hegemony by privileging the languages (and consequently the canons) of the major colonial powers, Britain and France ... even the substantial colonial and postcolonial writing in other European languages such as Dutch, German, Italian, Portuguese, and Spanish, is no less excluded from post-colonial debates than texts written in the languages of the colonies: Arabic, Bengali, Hindi, and Urdu, not to mention the oral literatures of Africa, Native Americans, and Australia's Aborigines, which pose a serious challenge to postcolonial theories based on contemporary notions of textuality.
> (Hassan 2002: 46)

Some of the questions Hassan raises are addressed in the two issues of the *Journal of World Literature* (4.1 and 4.2) Francesca Orsini and Laetitia Zecchini (2019) edited, especially with respect to Indian and African perspectives. Orsini (2019) specifically discusses debates on world literature in English, Hindi, and Urdu in India in the interbellum, and (2023) on multilingual literature(s) in India. Why the other literatures Hassan mentions have largely been disregarded in postcolonial debates undoubtedly has to do precisely with this debate being conducted almost exclusively in English while the discussion with respect to the literatures in question happens in other languages, and sometimes with a different terminology. This is certainly the case with Latin American literatures – I return to this further on in this chapter. As to the literature of Native Americans and Australia's Aborigines, Canada's First Nations, or New Zealand's Maori, it seems to me these have been "internalized" under the rubric of multiculturalism rather than the postcolonial.

From the perspectives of Hassan and Gikandi someone like Salman Rushdie, who is often considered, at one and the same time, the quintessential postcolonial novelist and an exemplary postmodernist, might well be regarded as a prime example of Spivak's (1988) subaltern who cannot "speak," however linguistically inventive and eloquent their novels for the rest may be. "Subaltern Studies" refers to an organized collective of Indian historians around the journal *Subaltern Studies*, and to the approach they have elaborated for dealing with the history of decolonized and postcolonial societies, and especially that of India. Inspired by the theories of the Italian Marxist Antonio Gramsci, who coined the term "subaltern" to refer to groups or individuals that find themselves in a position of inferiority, they analyze history from the standpoint of those discriminated against because of race, cast, gender, language, or religion.

Historians and sociologists associated with subaltern studies are Ranajit Guha, Gyan Prakash, Dipesh Chakrabarty, and Partha Chatterjee.

"No novel that I know of articulates more powerfully the theme of postcolonial migrancy in a mutable postmodern world than Salman Rushdie's *The Satanic Verses*," according to Gillian Gane (2002: 18). Interpreting India, and Indian migrants in the world, to the West in the hegemonic language of the West, Rushdie can be seen as what Spivak in her *Critique of Postcolonial Reason* has called a "Native Informant" (Spivak 1999: ix). Rushdie would then be a member of that intermediate class that Spivak, in the language of Ranajit Guha, the founding editor of *Subaltern Studies*, defines as the social layer that under colonialism would have stood between the "elite," that is to say "'dominant foreign groups,' and 'dominant indigenous groups at the all-India and at the regional and local levels' representing the elite" and "the social groups and elements included in the terms 'people' and 'subaltern classes'" (Spivak 1999: 271; quoting Guha 1982). Such an intermediate group then represents "*the demographic difference between the total Indian population and all those whom we have described as the 'elite'*" (Spivak 1999: 271; quoting Guha 1982).

> At the regional and local levels [these intermediate groups] ... if belonging to social strata hierarchically inferior to those of the dominant all-Indian groups acted in the interests of the latter and not in conformity to interests corresponding truly to their own social being.
> (Spivak 1999: 272; quoting Guha 1982)

If we translate this as pertaining to postcolonial postmodern writers, they can be seen as "subalterns" that cannot truly speak either but only ventriloquate in the language of "the master." In fact, Gikandi (2001) includes Rushdie in his group of "émigré native informants."

In *Death of a Discipline* (2003) Spivak enlarged on her suspicions about the use of English as the necessary lingua franca for the study of world literature through anthologies. In this she had a perhaps unexpected ally in Marjorie Perloff, who in the 1995 Bernheimer volume lamented that, "because the United States is currently the only superpower in the world, it gets to call the shots when it comes to a lingua franca," and that "such essentializing of English ... perpetuates the old notion of centers and margins which the new comparative literature model is supposedly countering" (Perloff 1995: 178). The "new" comparative literature that Perloff (1995) invoked was that of multiculturalism and postcolonialism. In 2003 Spivak also called for a "new" comparative literature, but hers is one of globalization and planetarity. Ritu Birla suggests that with *Death of a Discipline* Spivak moved beyond "problems of historical representation," and hence of postcolonialism in its "historical" stage we might add, to "the history and politics of globalization" and thereby from "the mechanics of othering to the possibilities of alterity" (Birla 2010: 97). Drawing upon ideas and a vocabulary inspired by the French philosopher Emmanuel Levinas (1906–1995), *Death of a Discipline*, Birla posits, has posed *the planet* as a name for an alterity that we inhabit, a way of being in the world that requires the imagination of what we cannot know, the universe, from a perspective that cannot produce mastery through mirroring.

(Birla 2010: 97)

Instead of "world," which as we have seen always implies someone's world, or "globe," which is tainted with the economic power imbalances of globalization, "planet" infers a view from outside, in which all is equal in its alterity, that is to say in that which we cannot, that we must not, fully apprehend of the other, but that we must nevertheless respect precisely in its difference. To respond to the other, though, we have to try and bridge the difference. This is where the imagination, and hence literature, is our only helpmate. World literature under this aegis, then, becomes not a way of "mastering" the world, but of respectfully experiencing it in, and as, difference. Wai Chee Dimock, in *Through Other Continents: American Literature Across Deep Time* (2006b) and in the volume she edited with Lawrence Buell, *Shades of the Planet: American Literature as World Literature* (2007), has taken up Spivak's call for a planetary approach, although it seems to me that she has done so only partially with an eye to the alterity that Spivak calls for, and rather in the sense of "englobing" the world through, and in, American literature. More recently, planetarity has been taken up not as what covers the entire planet geographically or in terms of humanity but as what concerns the very health of the planet itself – I return to this in a later chapter.

Littérature-Monde

Long before Spivak, another comparative literature scholar, René Etiemble, had launched his *Ouverture(s) sur un comparatisme planétaire* (1988; Openings[s] towards a Planetary Comparatism), although with him the term "planetary" carries a different load than with Spivak. In this volume Etiemble republished the 1977 revised version of his 1963 *Comparaison n'est pas raison* (The Crisis in Comparative Literature, 1966), along with a number of texts in various ways reflecting upon that 1963 original. As in almost all his work, this volume too was a plea for a comparatism truly encompassing "the world," and not just a tiny Eurocentric part of it. For French comparative literature, let us recall, it was French literature that had always remained the yardstick of the discipline. French literature remained the ideal against which were measured the "other" literatures in French, or of the so-called "francophonie," a term that always implied a second best next to the "real" thing – that is to say, French literature from France, the "hexagone," itself. This attitude was frontally attacked with the publication of "Pour une littérature-monde en français" (for a world literature in French) in the Parisian daily *Le Monde* of 16 March 2007. This manifesto bore the signature of forty-four authors, the best-known among them being the Moroccan Tahar Ben Jelloun, the

Guadeloupeans Maryse Condé and Gisèle Pineau, the Martinican Edouard Glissant, the Canadians Jacques Godbout and Nancy Huston, the Haitian-Canadian Dany Laferrière, the Lebanese Amin Maalouf, Erik Orsenna, Didier Daeninckx, Jean Rouaud, and the future Nobel Prize winner (2008) J. M.G. Le Clézio. Particularly noted was the participation of Edouard Glissant (1928–2011) who, next to a series of highly regarded novels, and various collections of poetry, all set in the Caribbean, also wrote several influential theoretical essays on the relationship of Caribbean, and particularly French-Caribbean or Antillean literature, to French and European literature. Key works are *Discours antillais* (1981; Caribbean Discourse) and *Traité du Tout-Monde* (1997). Glissant was the chief inspiration for the writers of *Créolité*, a group comprising Patrick Chamoiseau, Jean Bernabé, and Raphaël Confiant. In 1989 they published a pamphlet entitled *Eloge de la créolité/In Praise of Creoleness*, advocating the use of a hybrid language feeding upon the native creolized French of the Caribbean islands for their literature.

Noting that in autumn 2006 five of the seven major French literary prizes had gone to foreign-born authors, the manifesto proclaimed that this was a historical moment that signaled a Copernican revolution because it "reveal[ed] what the literary milieu already knew without admitting it: the center, from which supposedly radiated a franco-French literature, is no longer the center" (Toward 2009: 54). The result, the manifesto claims, is "the end of 'francophone' literature – and the birth of a world literature in French" (Toward 2009: 54). At the same time, it also means the return of "the world, the subject, meaning, history, the 'referent'" in French literature, and the overcoming of the stale pre-occupation with self-reflexivity that, for the longest time – in fact, ever since the nouveau roman – had plagued French literature (Toward 2009: 54). In Britain writers from the former Empire had been taking in the major literary prizes as of the 1980s, creating a new fiction from their plural identities. In France, meanwhile, foreign-born authors were still expected to "blend in" and become "French" to the core. Now, however, all was different: "the emergence of a consciously affirmed, transnational world-literature in the French language, open to the world, signs the death-certificate of so-called francophone literature ... no one speaks or writes 'francophone'" (Toward 2009: 56). In fact, the manifesto claims, "in a strict sense the 'francophone' concept presents itself as the last avatar of colonialism" (Toward 2009: 56). Instead, there will now be a "world-literature" or "littérature-monde" in French, and this in the sense of spanning the world because of the French language being spread around the world, and in the "worldly" sense of referring to the world, beyond "the age of suspicion" (a reference to Nathalie Sarraute's 1956 *L'ère du soupçon*, or *The Age of Suspicion*, the programmatic statement of the French *nouveau roman*) in a "vast polyphonic ensemble, without concern for any battle for or against the pre-eminence of one language over the other or any sort of 'cultural imperialism' whatsoever," and "with the center placed on an equal plane with other centers" and "language freed from its exclusive pact with the nation" (Toward 2009: 56).

The *Le Monde* manifesto immediately drew heavy critical fire, from the general secretary of the Organisation Internationale de la Francophonie (International Organization of Francophone Countries) and former President of Senegal, Abdou Diouf, and from Nicolas Sarkozy, in the daily *Le Figaro*, almost on the eve of the presidential elections that he would go on to win, but also from Amadou Lamine Sall and Lylian Kesteloot (Forsdick 2010a: 125–126). Diouf obviously did battle for his own organization. Sarkozy lamented what he called the "Americanization" of "la francophonie," with several well-known writers in French, such as Condé and Glissant, living and teaching in the United States. Lamine Sall and Kesteloot, the latter an early anthologizer and historian of Francophone African and Caribbean literatures, pointed out that the celebration of the 2006 literary prize winners as signaling the sudden emergence of foreign-born authors writing in French blatantly disregarded earlier such generations active since the immediate post-World War II period. While this critique was certainly justified, and while there was undoubtedly, as Lamine Sall and Kesteloot implied, an element of self-marketing involved on the part of the signatories to the manifesto, it should also be said that there is a significant difference between the writers of the generation Lamine Sall and Kesteloot referred to and those of the manifesto. The former were generally speaking anti-colonial and supportive of the newly independent nations they originated from. The latter rather fit the postcolonial mold of anglophone transnational lineage. Forsdick notes that

> Lamine Sall and Kesteloot concluded by critiquing the text's defence of a post-national, apolitical cultural utopianism that makes no attempt to grasp the consistently politicized postcolonial context of the Francosphere, a space in which the nation state, rightly or wrongly, may be seen as more important than ever.
>
> (Forsdick 2010a: 126)

Other critics took the Manifesto and its authors to task for imitating too closely English or Anglo-American models, particularly those of postcolonial and world literature studies, and for what Forsdick calls "the oxymoronic contradictions of a phenomenon that claims a global reach but persists with a monolingual definition" implied in the "en français" of the manifesto's title (Forsdick 2010a: 127). It is perhaps to forestall further such criticism that the 2007 volume collecting twenty-seven texts by signatories of the manifesto, *Pour une littérature-monde*, edited by Michel Le Bris, himself also a signatory of the *Le Monde* manifesto, and Jean Rouaud, quietly dropped the "en français." The volume's programmatic title article, to which Le Bris signed his name, remains a more elaborate version of the original manifesto though. Nowhere does Le Bris use the term "postcolonial," but it is clear that the English-language writers he mentions – Kazuo Ishiguro, Salman Rushdie, Michael Ondaatje, Ben Okri, Hanif Kureishi, and Zadie Smith – fall under the rubric of what we would call the postcolonial or the multicultural. This leads Dominique Combe to venture that the Manifesto is "above all, based on an apparent inferiority complex with respect to the postcolonial anglophone novel" (Combe 2010: 231). Combe also links the Manifesto, in its title, but also in its views, such as for instance on the creolization of the French language by "littérature-monde" authors, to the work of Glissant, especially to the latter's novel *Tout-Monde* (1993) and his *Traité du Tout-Monde* (1997), and to the French-Antillean "créolistes" Chamoiseau, Confiant, and Bernabé, although Chamoiseau and Confiant, "even though regularly featuring in *Le Monde*, keep ... surprisingly silent" (Combe 2010: 239; pourtant habitués des colonnes du *Monde*, restent ... étonnamment silencieux).

In a companion piece to his article on the *littérature-monde* manifesto Forsdick elaborates on the role of Glissant within French-language literature and thought, defending the Martinican author from the barbed criticism of Chris Bongie (2008), itself to a large part based on Peter Hallward's 1998 reading of Glissant, that the author as of the late 1990s had shifted from his former oppositional stance, as instanced in *Le discours antillais* (1981; Caribbean Discourse), to an accommodationist one, with his signing of the *littérature-monde* manifesto being an instance of the latter. Instead, Forsdick maintains, "Glissant has continued to be instrumental in allowing the emergence, in the French-speaking world, of debates that we might recognize as *postcolonial*, but with which the French equivalent of that label has only been associated since 2005" (Forsdick 2010b: 128; as my references to Moura 1999, Bessière and Moura 1999 and 2001 indicate, Forsdick is rather cavalier here in his dating of the debate in French). In a changing world in which both France and its former colonies of the "francophonie" as well as its DOM-ROMs (*départements* and *régions d'outre-mer* – overseas departments and regions) need to rethink their relations, Forsdick argues, Glissant "has attempted to elaborate, as opposed to simply import, the conceptual and lexical apparatus by which such a situation may be analyzed" (Forsdick 2010b: 134). Mary Gallagher, in fact, suggests that one could go further and, instead of seeking the salvation of French-language literature in imitating anglophone notions of postcolonialism, as does the manifesto, "ask whether the political and cultural orthodoxy of postcolonialism is not, in fact, a dominant global discourse against which francophone poetics sounds a singular or a refractory note, if not quite a dissident blow" (Gallagher 2010: 24). This in fact is what she sees Glissant's writings on poetics, on the relations between European and American literature, and on world literature, as doing. The manifesto, on the contrary, "shrinks the conceptual scale and content of the *world*, a term that comes to mean at worst 'anywhere but France' and at best 'anywhere else preferably with postcolonial cachet'" (Gallagher 2010: 32). The manifesto, she argues,

> demonstrates none of that complex sense of the world that informs all of Edouard Glissant's writing on the Tout-monde ... for the complexity of Glissant's notion largely derives from his effort to conceive of the world

as a nonreductive totality, as a(n imperfectly interconnected) whole, a whole that can no longer be thought about exclusively in terms of the postcolonial plot.

(Gallagher 2010: 32)

Of course, the fact remains that Glissant himself put his name to the manifesto ...

If the manifesto, when compared to the subtlety of Glissant's ideas, can indeed only be called naïve, the same thing goes when one compares it to work on postcolonialism in English, while at the same time it avoids none of the pitfalls the latter also faces when fashioning itself as the pivot of a "world literature." Moreover, for all the admiration they express for English-language postcolonial developments, the drafters of the manifesto do not seem too much *au courant* with what had been going on there precisely regarding French-language literature. Only a year before the publication of "pour une littérature-monde" Emily Apter had suggested that

> francophonie might ... no longer simply designate the transnational relations between metropolitan France and its former colonies, but linguistic contact zones all over the world in which French, or some kind of French, is one of many languages in play.
>
> (Apter 2006a: 55)

And even if one can understand that Le Bris and Rouaud may not have been aware of an article that had appeared only recently in a collective volume that did not immediately concern them, it is perhaps a little stranger that they also do not seem to have been aware of a book, in English it is true, that pretty much, though with far greater sophistication, outlined the kind of program they drew up in their manifesto: Charles Forsdick and David Murphy's 2003 *Francophone Postcolonialism*.

Forsdick (2010a) notes that the manifesto, apart from the early and mostly negative reactions just briefly sketched, drew little further attention in France itself. Outside France, however, it was taken up in academic circles and continues to be discussed. An interesting twist is that one of the signatories to the 2007 manifesto since then has gained particular notoriety: Le Clézio won the 2008 Nobel prize for literature. It is well-known that the Swedish Academy keeps an ear to the ground for what is happening in literary Paris. "From the 1940s onwards, the Academy came to accept a set of literary ideals that have their roots in French modernism," the former Permanent Secretary of the Swedish Academy declared (Engdahl 2008: 207). Perhaps Le Clézio's appearance in "pour une littérature-monde" contributed at least somewhat, then, to his canonization as a "world author"?

In 2010 there also appeared a collective volume, edited by Christie McDonald and Susan Rubin Suleiman, under the title *French Global: A New Approach to Literary History*, in which a host of well-known literary scholars, among whom for instance F. Abiola Irele, Emily Apter, Tom Conley, Verena Andermatt Conley, Christopher L. Miller, and Gisèle Sapiro, next to the volume editors themselves, look at the relationship of French literature to the world outside of the hexagone. In a survey article, Françoise Lionnet (2012, 2022), who also features in *French Global*, discusses "World literature, *francophonie*, and Creole cosmopolitics."

Decoloniality

The term postcolonial, as discussed above, was originally restricted to English-language literature, and more recently also came to be used for French-language literature. To a lesser extent this is also the case for Dutch-language literature. The term is much less frequently used in hispanophone and lusophone scholarship where terms such as decoloniality and decolonization are much more current, especially so in and with respect to Latin America. This does not mean that these latter terms have no purchase in English, albeit in social studies, history, and political science rather than in literary studies (Shepard 2006). The same goes for Dutch usage (Emmer 2022). Stuart Ward (2016) mentions its use as "a novel term" by the British colonial administrator Lord Hailey in 1946 and 1947. Sabelo J. Ndlovu-Gatshen (2015) has proposed "Decoloniality as the Future of Africa." In literature, Ngugi wa Thiong'o titled his groundbreaking 1986 book on the politics of language in African literatures *Decolonising the Mind*. Chinweizu (1980, 1987) used the term. Maurice Labelle (2020) labels Said's early engagement with the writings of Fanon and the Palestinian struggle his "decolonial beginnings."

Latin American advocates of decoloniality in general admit that there are resemblances to postcolonialism yet make a sharp distinction between the two approaches. Rather than on Said, Spivak, and Bhabha, the main theoreticians of postcolonialism, Walter Mignolo (1988, 1995, 2000, 2007a, 2007b, 2011, 2021) and Nelson Maldonado-Torres (2006, 2007, 2011) build, next to on Frantz Fanon (1952, 1961), on the liberation theologian Enrique Dussel, and especially on Anibal Quijano (1991, 1999, 2000a, 2000b, 2007). Quijano (1991) defined the concept of "coloniality" as distinct from "colonialism." Whereas the latter indicates actual relations of possession and administration between colonial powers and their colonies, the former signals the lasting unequal relations between the former colonial metropolises, and by extension the European-North American complex, and the formerly colonized world. Decolonialists consider the conquest of the Americas as foundational for Europe's colonial worldview, which they see as continuing down to the present, and which they find embodied in Western science and scholarship emanating from Western institutions, including those of higher learning. Mignolo (2007a, 2007b), who has been running the modernity/coloniality/decoloniality program at Duke University since 1998 (Escobar 2007), sees postmodernist and postcolonial critiques of modernity as emerging from within the Eurocentric modernist project itself. Decolonialists aim to "delink" from Western knowledge by appealing to the lived experience of ordinary people, mostly indigenous, outside of Europe, and their cosmovision. Rather than the universal, they seek out the local. This is aptly illustrated in the almost programmatic title of one of Mignolo's best-known books: *Local Histories/Global Designs* (2000). A vituperous critique of decoloniality especially as practiced by Mignolo is Neil Larsen (2022).

The earliest Latin American literary phenomenon to be widely noticed and studied also beyond the region itself already signals a form of decolonization. Magical or magic realism did not, as is often thought, originate in Latin America. Jean Weisgerber (1987) has demonstrated how the emergence of the term in German in 1925, with the publication of Franz Roh's *Nach-Expressionismus. Magischer Realismus*, and its subsequent evolution in Europe, specifically in German-Austrian, Italian, Dutch-Flemish, and French literature and criticism, indicated a desire to represent the universal "idea," almost in a Platonic sense, beyond reality, and via an excess of logic or rationalism, as it were turning rationalism against the shortcomings of the rational representation of reality (D'haen 1995, 1997, 2020). As such, it emerged from the same atmosphere as Surrealism. The Cuban author Alejo Carpentier frequented the circles of the Surrealists in Paris during the interbellum. Their works first alerted him to the possibilities of the supernatural in fiction. Yet, in the preface to *El reino de este mundo* (1949), which amplified and under the title "De lo real maravilloso americano," found its way into the volume of essays *Tientos y diferencias*, and which is usually taken to have launched the Latin American variant of magic realism, Carpentier (1967) takes great pains to distinguish his use of the supernatural from that of the Surrealists. In fact, he says, he is using the same techniques the Surrealists are using, but while with the Surrealists in their European context these amount to mere "tricks of prestidigitation" (Carpentier 1967: 115), the mechanical combination of heterogeneous elements to evoke the frisson of the fantastic, with him they reflect the different reality of Latin America: what is "fantastic" in Europe is only "natural" in the Latin American context. Carpentier seizes upon Latin America's history as ultimate proof for his narrative gambit: "But what is the history of America if not a chronicle of the marvelously real?" (Carpentier 1967: 120; ¿Pero qué es la historia de América toda sino uno crónica de lo real maravilloso?). With Surrealism, and with European magic realism, language is used to constitute another reality beyond Western commonsense reality – a reality that is *not* there in the Western view: it is and remains truly *sur*-real. With Carpentier's magic realism language is used to constitute an alternative reality to Western reality, but it is a reality that is *really* there, though the means used to describe it – the language, vocabulary and syntax of Western reason – fail to fully apprehend it. The Eurocentric variant uses the unreal to constitute an alternative reality that remains alternative, and that is ultimately the creation of Western rationalism, albeit of its crisis – Western language turned against itself. Carpentier's magic realism reveals the existence of an-*Other* reality beyond Western reality. As Western language fails to fit this *Other* reality, it can only be described in the language of Western "un-reason," that is to say magic (Carpentier 1967). Of course, the Eurocentric attitude is symptomatic of Western culture's universalizing ambition, extending its own sense of what is "real" to the entire world, and which, caught in the prison-house of its own paradigmatic thinking, can conceive of any alternative only as "beyond reality." Carpentier's attitude, on the contrary, results from his, or his country's or society's partial exclusion from Western culture. For him, "reality" as defined *tout court* in the discursive formations of the West is not universal but needs to be explicitly qualified as "Western." With one blow, there opens up the possibility of a critique of Western culture and its discursive formations from the outside. At the same time, we could see Latin American magic realism as an early case of what we now call glocalization. On magic realism as a world literary genre, and on Latin American literature in relation to world literature more in general, see Mariano Siskind (2012, 2014, 2022), Figlerowicz and Mertehikian (2023), Hoyos (2016), and Coutinho (2018).

I mentioned that decolonialists ground their theories and analyses in the local rather than the universal or the global. The same goes for postcolonialism. In this regard both decoloniality and postcolonialism have a quarrel with cosmopolitanism, a worldview often associated with world literature as a deracinated concept. Not surprisingly, the rise of interest in world literature since the 1990s has been paralleled by a similar increase in the interest in cosmopolitanism (Brennan 1997 and 2018; Nussbaum 1997 and 2019; Cheah and Robbins 1998; Robbins 1999; Dharwadker 2001; Vertovec and Cohen 2002; Appiah 2006; Beck 2006; Walkowitz 2006; Delanty and Inglis 2011; Robbins and Horta 2017; Helgesson et al. 2018). In fact, the opposition between the global and the local, the universal and the particular, the cosmopolitan and the rooted, has been part and parcel of the discussion of world literature since the very beginning. Goethe was Europe's foremost cosmopolitan in his day and with his thoughts on world literature he obviously reached beyond the local, but at the same time his investment in German-language literature and his belief in the pivotal role that German literature was to play in world literature can be seen as an *avant-la lettre* decolonialization of his own culture and literature from the dominance, not to say the near-hegemony of French language and literature in eighteenth-century Europe. Brandes (1899) even thought that to be universal an author had to be rooted in his local culture. César Domínguez (2012b, 2022b) summarizes the debate on world literature and cosmopolitanism. Interesting from a decolonial perspective is that he starts from how differently Jonathan Culler (2007) and Benedict Anderson (1998) interpret Mario Vargas Llosa's novel *El hablador* (1987; The Storyteller 1989). Anderson sees it as a nationalist hispanophone Peruvian tale. Culler sees it as directed to a cosmopolitan readership – an early case of Walkowitz's (2015) "born translated" novels. Both, Domínguez remarks, overlook Latin American theory, in this case Ángel Rama's (2008 [1982], 2012) concept of transcultural narrators, which he sees as exemplified in Vargas Llosa's novel. Rama developed his theory of narrative transculturation from the anthropological concept of cultural transculturation elaborated by the Cuban Fernando Ortiz (1881–1969). Whereas European anthropologists conceived of native cultures as giving way to colonization and modernization, a process they termed acculturation, Ortiz (2002 [1940], 1995) argued that both the native and the invading culture were transformed and eventually resulted in a hybrid, a process for which he used the term transculturation. In fact, Ortiz's concept, and Rama's application of it to the literary field, can be seen as themselves transculturations of the European "original," just as magic realism Latin American style can be seen as a transculturation of European magic realism. In both cases the existing linguistic term and the concept it covered did not correspond to Latin American reality and therefore what was needed was a new term covering an-Other concept: the untranslatablity of the European mode or concept provokes, as Haroldo de Campos called it, a Latin American *transcreação* or transcreation (Lima 2017).

In Chapter 5 I quoted Earl Fitz (2002) that especially Brazilian literature might fruitfully be studied in the increasingly important field of inter-American, or hemispheric American, Studies. "Freighted with the kind of suspicion and rancor, however, that stem from centuries of economic exploitation, political intervention, and both cultural hegemony and cultural disdain, [this] remains an issue that has long divided many Brazilian (and Spanish American) intellectuals," Fitz says, and he points to the "anthropologist, novelist, and intellectual Darcy Ribeiro" arguing

> that the proper destiny of Latin Americans is to join together in "common opposition to the same antagonist, which is Anglo-Saxon America, in order to bring together, as is happening in the European Community, the Latin American Nation dreamed of by Bolivar"(Ribeiro 2000: 321–322).
>
> (Fitz 2002: 443)

Joshua Lund explicitly posits that "in Ribeiro's view from the margin, Europe's centrality is relativized (decentered) within a global context" and Lund sees Ribeiro, along with Cuban historian Fernando Ortiz and the Brazilian critic Antonio Candido (1918–2017), putting a peripheral position and vision to "the sometimes polemical task of carving out their own centers from which to enunciate" (Lund 2001: 72). Ribeiro, Ortiz, and Candido are carrying out this task by turning the theories and instruments of hegemonic Eurocentrism against themselves, Lund argues, quoting Mignolo (1988: 50) to the effect that "Ribeiro – as much as Ortiz or Candido – is identifiable as 'someone who was trained as [a Western academic]' … and at the same time was part of the 'other'" (Lund 2001: 73). Efraín Kristal (2002) does something similar when he opposes Franco Moretti's diffusionist and Eurocentrist view of world literature and instead casts Spanish America as center. What we see emerging here is a world literature emphasizing what has increasingly come to be called "the global South," and that is rooted in resistance to Northern hegemonies – political, economic, linguistic, and literary.

Whereas since 2010 or so postcolonialism has come to pay increasing attention to world literature studies, such has not been the case with decoloniality. In fact, the neglect has gone both ways: if world literature has included discussion of Latin American works of literature, this has been much less the case with Latin American decoloniality theory, and decoloniality has paid even more scant attention to world literature. And yet, the work of some Latin American critics at times moves close to issues also addressed in world literature studies. Roberto Schwarz (1970, 1992, 2001), for example, discusses issues of peripherality with respect to Brazilian culture and literature. Schwarz was influenced by Candido (1965, 1975, 1993), with whom he studied and whose colleague he was at the University of São Paulo, and with whom he shares a strongly sociological bent. The same can be said of a third Brazilian critic, Luiz Costa Lima (1980, 2003, 2009). Two world literature scholars that aim to bridge the gap with Latin American literature are Hassan (2018, 2019) and Helgesson (2018a, 2022a). Both focus on the possibilities of South-South comparisons (Hassan 2017) involving Latin American, mostly Brazilian, literature and, respectively, Arabic literature and African literatures in European languages. Helgesson (2018b) discusses Candido in the context of recent discussions of world literature, and he has done the same (2017) with Ngugi wa Thiong'o, and (2014) with the lusophone Mozambican Mia Couto and the francophone Algerian Assia Djebar. Kerry Bystrom and Joseph R. Slaughter in 2018 edited a volume on "the global South Atlantic" discussing relations between African and Latin American literature from a world literature perspective. Andrea Bachner (2021) focuses on comparison between Latin America and China. In 2017 Marta Puxan-Oliva and Annalisa Mirizio edited a special issue of the *Journal of World Literature* (2.1) devoted to "Rethinking World Literature Studies in Latin American and Spanish Contexts."

Earlier in this chapter I quoted Bhabha as arguing that in what he called the new "geopolitical space" of the end of the twentieth century "the Western metropolis must confront its postcolonial history, told by its influx of postwar migrants and refugees, as an indigenous or native narrative internal to its national identity" (Bhabha 1994a: 6). Europe's metropolises not only faced the influx of migrants and refugees from former colonies but likewise from what in German were called *Gastarbeiter*, or labor migrants, originating from countries around the Mediterranean, primarily Turkey, Morocco, and Algeria. These labor migrants started coming to Western Europe from the 1960s onwards – they had been preceded by intra-European labor migrants, again mostly from Mediterranean countries such as Italy, Spain, and Portugal, heading for the West European coal mines. Later, as of the 1990s but especially in the 2000s, there followed an influx of refugees from Africa, the Middle East, and Asia, fleeing wars and economic disasters. In literature, the "internalization" of these migrants happened via works of multiculturalism, often using a vocabulary borrowed from postcolonialism. Susan Stanford Friedman (2018) and Sandra Vlasta (2022) address this "migration literature."

Conclusion

- Postcolonialism has been proposed as the new world literature.
- Postcolonialism and postmodernism, supposedly each other's opposites as expressions of, respectively, resistance and accommodation to the Western world, in fact have a tangled relationship.
- Postcolonialism can be seen as a projection of, rather than resistance to, Western thought.
- Postcolonial world literature has in practice largely meant English-language postcolonial literature.
- In the French-language context the postcolonial debate turns around "la francophonie."
- In Latin America the debate that in English passes for postcolonialism rather happens under the aegis of decoloniality.
- In Europe interest in migration literature, developing out of multicultural and postcolonial studies, has sharply increased over the past two decades.

9 Asian, African, and Oceanian Perspectives on World Literature

Overview

In Chapter 4 I cited Werner Friederich ironically referring to what in the late 1950s passed for "world literature" as NATO literature, and that this was already an overstatement as usually only about one fourth of the literatures in the then fifteen NATO countries received any actual sustained attention. The literatures in question were French, English, German, Spanish, and Italian, and discussion on world literature was almost exclusively restricted to German, French, and US comparative literature circles. This is not to say that there was no work being undertaken on world literature elsewhere, particularly in Europe, but this usually shadowed what was being done, primarily, in the major European French and German academic centers, filtered only rarely into the more general or "global" discussion, and the latter usually only when done straightaway in a "major" European language or translated therein. This situation has basically persisted to this day, with US academe, and the English language, increasingly supplanting German and French preponderance. As discussed in a previous chapter, scholars from Europe's so-called "semi-periphery" over the last few decades have entered the debate. Since the revival of interest in world literature around the turn of the twenty-first century, work on other regions and in other than European languages has also proliferated. In what follows I turn to work done in or about Asia to gauge the impact of the renewal of interest in world literature beyond the core area of "comparative literature talking about world literature." In many cases this will involve both a return to "native" precursors to claim an "alter-native" approach to world literature and an unspoken, but I think nonetheless implied resistance to a world literature fashioned by Euro-American and particularly anglophone hegemony. Especially Chinese and Indian scholars, many of the latter working in the US either permanently or during part of their career, have been active in the field. But others have also joined the chorus, even if their work hitherto has been less voluminous or noted.

DOI: 10.4324/9781003366713-10

Global South and Chinese World Literature

In 1986 A. Owen Aldridge in *The Reemergence of World Literature: A Study of Asia and the West* reminded his readers at the outset that "in the mind of many Third World critics, the concentration [in comparative literature studies] on European values and texts represents a survival or reflection of a colonialist mentality" (Aldridge 1986: 10). "Even when Eastern masterpieces have been recognized as such," he continues,

> they have often been treated as precursors of later European works, not as models or cultural achievements in their own right ... it is now time for the classics of the East to be viewed as the foundations of independent traditions and made available to Western students.
>
> (Aldridge 1986: 10)

However, Aldridge also admits that no satisfactory methodology for the study of literature East-West has yet been devised. Practice in the West is usually to simply add a couple of Eastern masterpieces to the traditionally Western canon of world literature. The custom in the East has been to unleash Western theory upon Eastern literatures. And yet, he notes, there is the promising beginning of the emergence of comparative literature departments especially in Japan, and along what he terms the "Taiwan-Hong Kong Axis," and in the participation of scholars from these departments in international conferences such as those of the International Comparative Literature Association, as well as increasing attention from Western scholars for Asian literatures. Aldridge dedicated his book to René Etiemble, the French scholar who already in the 1960s had called for a widening of comparative literature practice, and for discussions on world literature, to take in all of the world, and particularly such major literary traditions as the Arabic, the Indian, the Japanese, and the Chinese. In fact, he had even suggested that the future of comparative literature and world literature might well lie with Chinese (Etiemble 1966: 27–30).

John Deeney (1981 and 1990) and Aldridge (1986) maintained that comparative literature, and the interest in world literature, emerged only late in the Chinese context, basically as of the 1970s and 1980s, and they mostly refer to examples from Taiwan and Hong Kong. Since Deeney's and Aldridge's days, things have changed. In their overview of the history of comparative literature in China in the twentieth century Zhou Xiaoyi and Q.S. Tong (2009 [2000]) chronicle a thriving academic practice of comparative literature before the 1940s and again as of the 1970s, even crediting the discipline, after its reintroduction into mainland China in the late 1970s, with having been one of the most liberal areas of study in contemporary China. At the same time, though, they also point out that the enthusiastic responses to the call for a "Chinese School of Comparative Literature" launched by Deeney in 1986, a school which he saw destined to take the lead in a "Third World" comparative literature context, have fed into "a politics of recognition that aims to establish Chinese comparative literature as an equal partner on the international stage of comparative literature" (Zhou and Tong 2009: 352). As such, Zhou and Tong argue, "Chinese comparative literature as a critical practice may thus be considered a product of China's pursuit of modernity in the twentieth century" (Zhou and Tong 2009: 353). Such a pursuit also implies the tacit primacy, if not the superiority, of the West, as it comprises, according to Zhou and Tong, the "total acceptance of Enlightenment values and practices" (Zhou and Tong 2009: 353). The deconstruction of Eurocentrism as of the 1990s, they further argue, has discredited these values, and hence also the binary premises upon which comparative literature rests. Therefore, they suggest, instead of "comparative literature," with its ingrained imbalance between the West and the Rest, the term "cross-cultural studies," implying equality between all cultures concerned, might be more appropriate all around, in the East as well as the West (Zhou and Tong 2009: 354). For much the same reasons Anders Pettersson proposes the term "transcultural literary history" (Pettersson 2008).

As elsewhere, the more recent renewal of interest in world literature has also in China, that is to say mainland China, led to the reclamation of "forgotten" or "submerged" precursors. Indeed, whereas the revival of comparative literature in mainland China, after the caesura in Chinese intellectual life occasioned by Maoism and the Cultural Revolution, and after the liberalization of the late 1970s, mainly under the guidance of Peking University's Yue Daiyun, took its bearings primarily from American academe, more recent research insists on "native" ancestors pre-dating 1949. Longxi Zhang (2012a, 2022b) makes a case for Qian Zhongshu (1910–1998) and particularly the latter's 1948 book of criticism in classical Chinese *Tan yi lu* or *Discourses on the Art of Literature*. The book refers to, and quotes, not only Chinese but also Western writers, often in the original. For Zhang, Qian Zongshu

> effectively lays down the foundation of East-West comparative studies buttressed by a traditional philosophical argument ... demonstrating that in assimilating ideas from the West, Chinese scholars follow an intellectual genealogy of their own, rather than just act upon a desire to emulate the West.
>
> (Zhang 2012a: 82, 2022b: 47)

Jing Tsu recovers even earlier ancestors. Tsu (2010, 2012, 2022a) points out that the term "world literature" (*shijie de wenxue*) was introduced in China as early as 1898, when Chen Jitong, a mandarin and Chinese military attaché in Europe, used it in a conversation – appropriately so given Goethean antecedents! – with another Chinese writer, Zeng Pu. Chen Jitong, according to Tsu, was "motivated by a felt indignation, rather than humility, over the lack of proper recognition of Chinese literature by western readers" (Tsu 2012: 165, 2022a: 126) Given Europe's centrality in matters cultural and literary, however, "entry into its literary platform was key to forging a more even nexus of cultural exchange" (Tsu 2012: 165, 2022a: 126). When Chen Jitong first used "world literature" in Chinese the Chinese Empire was still a reality, albeit very much weakened under the onslaught of Western and Japanese economic, political, and military pressures. In the early years of the twentieth century, it became increasingly apparent that the days of the Chinese Empire were numbered. It was against this background that Lu Xun (1881–1936), who would subsequently become the greatest Chinese writer of the first half of the century, and his brother Zhou Zuoren (1885–1967), in 1909 put together *Yuwai xiaoshuo ji* (A Collection of Fiction from Abroad). Tsu labels this collection "a formally expressed literary concern with the experiences of the perishing nations and ethnicities … devoted to the struggles of oppressed races and nations" (Tsu 2012: 166, 2022a: 127). Instead of Chen's "nostalgic, if genuine, wish to regain the cultural grandeur befitting erstwhile empires" (Tsu 2012: 165, 2022a: 126), with Lu Xun we find a socially progressive vision that links those excluded by both the traditional centers of power in China itself and the hegemonic powers of Western colonialism. As Tsu puts it, the Lu Xun/Zhou Zuoren collection "helped to shift the literary focus of cultural hegemony to the interstices of emergent, minor, oppressed, injured, and sub-global narratives" (Tsu 2012: 166, 2022a: 127) As such, she contends,

> a new conceptual grammar for world literature gained ground, differentiating the national and world literary space along lines of conflict rather focusing on a common literary humanity … if Goethe had imagined *Weltliteratur* to emerge from a world community with little in common, Lu Xun responded with a borderless literature of oppression without global triumph.
> (Tsu 2012: 166, 2022a: 127)

Zheng Zhenduo between 1924 and 1927 wrote *Wenxue dagang* (The Outline of Literature) which Tsu characterizes as "the first important, systematic attempt at a world literary history in China" (Tsu 2010: 299). However, to say that Zheng Zhenduo "wrote" his *Outline of Literature* is misstating the case. In fact, as Tsu demonstrates, Zheng Zhenduo compiled his work largely on the basis of John Drinkwater's *The Outline of Literature* (1923), with additional material taken from John Albert Macy's *The Story of the World's Literature* (1925), mostly simply translating the originals. To this Zheng added a number of chapters on Chinese literature. The principle of the universality of humanity upon which he inspired himself he had gleaned from Caleb Thomas Winchester's *Some Principles of Literary Criticism* (1899), and Richard Green Moulton's *World Literature and Its Place in General Culture* (1921 [1911]) and *The Modern Study of Literature* (1915). To frame anthologies or studies of world literature along overall human categories rather than along historical, national, or generic lines was not unusual in the first half of the twentieth century: Arthur E. Christy and Henry H. Wells emphatically titled their 1947 volume *World Literature: An Anthology of Human Experience*. Tsu also points out that Macy's book was translated no less than five times between 1935 and 1992, and that at least four other histories of world literature appeared in Chinese between 1932 and 1937. About Zheng Zhenduo's *Outline of Literature*, however, she comments that the

> idea of world literature allows for national interests to overlap and cross bounds but keeps the fundamental concern with power intact ... world literature ... is neither an exception to nor innocent of the modality of power that is created in any context of prestige.
>
> (Tsu 2010: 309)

In fact, she claims, while it was "convenient for Zheng to make a passionate case for relinquishing national interests ... it was precisely his preoccupation with such a nation-bound identity that motivated him to turn to the world as the desired forum for China's literary participation" (Tsu 2010: 309).

Pre-occupations similar to those of Zheng Zhenduo also seem to undergird at least some of the more recent Chinese forays into world literature. China's increasingly projecting itself as a major, perhaps in future *the*, world power, leads to a re-thinking of world literature in line with China's commercial and political ambitions. In first instance this makes for a desire for a greater participation of Chinese literature in world literature. Second, it makes for a recasting of what in the wake of Lu Xun and Zhou Zuoren's 1909 collection of translated fiction became all the rage in the 1920s and 1930s in China, that is to say the championing of the "weak and small races/nations" (Tsu 2010: 299), into the present Chinese enthusiasm for the "global South" that it seeks to lead.

The implications of some of these views clearly appear from the evolution of Wang Ning, a comparatist that as of the early 1990s has been one of the most prolific, and I would say almost "seismographic," interpreters of the relation of Chinese literary scholarship to Western theory and practice. In his scholarly trajectory as embodied in his English-language publications, we can discern an evolution from translating, interpreting, and adapting Western models for use with reference to Chinese literature and literary studies, to advancing the claims of native-grown Chinese works, traditions, methods, and approaches to be treated on a par with Western ones. Wang debuted in the early 1990s with articles on Chinese postmodernism and on how Western concepts of comparative literature could be applied to Chinese literature (Wang 1993a, 1993b, 1996a, 1996b). At the same time, he (1997) already expressed a desire to "decolonize" the study of that literature. Nevertheless, in the early 2000s, Wang (2005) still emphasizes how Chinese critical discourse remains largely tributary to Western and particularly American influences. In fact, he starts off his 2005 article by drawing a parallel with what happened in the early twentieth century when, he says,

> During the May 4 period, almost all the Western cultural trends and critical theories flooded into China through translation, mostly from

English and occasionally from Japanese and Russian, exercising a strong influence on Chinese literary creation and critical interpretation. Many Chinese writers, such as Lu Xun, Guo Moruo, and Cao Yu, and literary theorists would rather recognize being inspired by Western literature and theories than by their Chinese precursors.

(2005: 649)

Likewise, he finds that (2005: 650), after a period in which Western influence was largely dormant, from the Communist take-over of 1949 to the end of the Cultural Revolution, since 1978 "more and more foreign, especially Western, cultural trends and literary theories have been coming into China through translation, directly influencing the critical and creative construction of contemporary Chinese literary and theoretical discourse." Gradually, though, Wang starts to adopt a much more critical position vis-à-vis Western theory.

In a 2010 article Wang reflects on the size of the Chinese population, its wide and increasing spread to all corners of the earth, China's rising economic power, how the Chinese language is therefore bound to gain a greater purchase on the world, and what the implications are for Chinese literary historiography. Unabashedly, he compares Chinese to English in its wide dissemination, but also in how this implies a certain measure of hybridization. "Quite a few scholars are greatly worried about this phenomenon," he notes, but to him,

> if it really achieved the effect of being inclusive and hybridized like English, Chinese would become the second major world language next to English, for it could play the unique role that English cannot play, and in more aspects, it could function as a major world language in an interactive and complementary way to English.
>
> (Wang 2010a: 167)

He compares the hundreds of *Kongzi xueyuan* (Confucius Institutes) the Chinese government has been setting up worldwide over the last decades to the British Council institutes that until a short while ago spread Britain's language, culture, and influence abroad. With the "rise of 'Chinese fever' in the world," he asks, "what shall [Chinese] literary scholars ... do to remap world literature?" (Wang 2010a: 170). Just as English literature has been transformed from "a national literature to a sort of world literature since English literature is more and more 'postnational'," so too "Chinese literature: also from a national literature to a sort of transnational and postnational literature" (Wang 2010a: 172).

Invoking "the pioneering Neo-Confucianist ... Tu Wei-ming's concept of 'Cultural China'," Wang maintains that

> we can for the time being define Chinese literature in two senses: one is the literature produced in greater China: mainland China, Hong Kong,

Macao and Taiwan in Chinese which is the people's national language or mother tongue; and the other is the literature produced overseas in Chinese which is the writers' mother tongue although not necessarily their national language.

(Wang 2010a: 173)

Invoking Spivak's (2003) insistence on area studies as the proper domain for a renewed comparative literature along with the popularization of Chinese via the Confucius institutes, Wang (2010a: 173) is of the opinion that International Chinese literature studies will become, "like its counterpart of international English literature, a sub-discipline in the broader context of comparative literature and world literature." Literature in Chinese, then, as a world literature, similar to literatures in English or anglophone, in French or francophone, in Portuguese or lusophone literatures. Only bigger. Although Wang is careful to invoke the fate of English and literature(s) in English as an example, it is clear that he is seeing the new Chinese literary historiography also, and perhaps in first instance, as rival to this example.

In another 2010 article Wang posits "that the globalization of material, cultural, and intellectual production, accompanied by the dissolution of Eurocentrism and 'West-centrism' and by the rise of Eastern culture and literature, has assisted at world literature's birth from the ashes of comparative literature" (Wang 2010b: 2). World literature, Wang argues, implies translation, and translation in Chinese literary history has mostly served foreign literatures to colonize Chinese literature and culture. In the present context, however, cultural globalization "will help promote Chinese culture and literature worldwide" (Wang 2010b: 13). Indeed, as of the end of the first decade of the twenty-first century, Wang assumes an increasingly self-confident Chinese stance and calls for an authentically Chinese approach in literary studies, including comparative and world literature studies. As such he picks up on the long-standing claim that there is, or there be, a distinctive Chinese School of Comparative Literature, a claim forcefully put forward also by Wang's contemporary and colleague Shunqing Cao, for instance in the latter's 2013 *The Variation Theory of Comparative Literature*, his earlier (1988) *Chinese and Western Comparative Poetics* (in Chinese) where he interpreted Western critical concepts from a Chinese perspective, and his 2012 four-volume edited collection *A History of Chinese and Foreign Literary Theory* (in Chinese). In a review of the latter work Wang (2013: 3) argues that its strength

> lies in that it for the first time put Chinese literary theory in a broad context of world literary theory highlighting its different characteristics and unique position. It also demonstrates that to write a comprehensive history of world literary theory should not overlook the literary theory and criticism in those non-Western countries, especially China, where there is its own autonomous body of literary theory with *The Literary Mind and the Carving of Dragons* (by Xie Liu) as its landmark.

Wang leaves no doubt that he underwrites and shares Cao's ambition for a home-grown Chinese comparative literature.

Wang's growing assertiveness on behalf of Chinese literature and literary studies again transpires from his 2015 article "On the Construction of World Poetics," which starts off with the reminder that Goethe's earliest thoughts on world literature were triggered by his reading of a Chinese novel in translation. Chinese literary theory, Wang insists, also influenced Western constructs of comparative poetics. Mainstream scholarship has largely ignored this debt. However, "now that world literature is becoming an aesthetic reality, the 'post-theoretic era' has arrived in literary theory," and

> its advent enables the previously marginalized theoretical discourses to come to the forefront in a break from a unified West-centric orthodoxy, and enables scholars from small ethnic communities or non-Western groups to engage in dialogues with their Western and international counterparts on a level playing field.
> (Wang 2015:187)

For Chinese scholars of comparative and world literature the goal is no longer to use Western theories but rather "to construct our own theories so that we can make our unique voice heard in the clamour of different theoretical discourses in today's globalized context" and as "Chinese literature occupies a growing place in the domain of world literature and the country's world importance continues to increase, there will be a corresponding rise in the international position of Chinese literary theory" (Wang 2015: 195).

As Wang (2006: 163) reminds us elsewhere, the Chinese Ministry of Education in 1998 integrated comparative literature and world literature into one discipline for graduate study. Perhaps Wang's vision of world literature is the realization of what Rey Chow in 2004 envisaged as a "new" form of East/West comparison, in which Asian literatures would be freed from what she calls the "post-European and ... " complex in which the implicit awareness of "the European" as the original term of comparison always haunts the term after the "and," thus allowing in its stead for "other possibilities of supplementarity, other semiotic conjunctions mediated by different temporal dynamics, ... as yet unrealized comparative perspectives, the potential range and contents of which we have only just begun to imagine" (Chow 2004: 307).

More moderate and subtle is the very erudite approach of Longxi Zhang. Zhang was educated at Peking University and Harvard, and for many years taught in the US before moving to Hong Kong where until his retirement in 2023 he occupied the chair of Comparative Literature and Translation. He made his name with well-received books on East-West comparison in which he advocated ways of cross-cultural understanding (Zhang 1992, 1999, 2005). More recently he has addressed the same topic in the framework of world literature. In *From Comparison to World Literature* (2015) he starts out by noting that comparative literature and world literature for most of their history have been decidedly Eurocentric. However, he says (2015: 2), "Perhaps the time is now for world literature finally to engage literatures of the entire world rather than just one particular dominant region, and to give us a truly global view of human creativity in the various forms of literary manifestations." He is particularly concerned with China, a country that "is often thought to be the opposite of Europe, inhabiting an improbable space of a Foucaultian *heterotopia*, with its non-phonetic scripts representing the irreducible writing of a Derridean *différance*, symbolizing the ultimate non-European Other." Zhang (2015: 3) sees it as his task "to examine such claims to cultural incommensurability and fundamental differences between China and the West, and to argue not only for the possibility, but also the necessity of cross-cultural understanding against all odds, despite all the differences." Whereas works from the Western canon are likely to be known also outside the West because of the historic dominance of the West in most matters, including in the field of culture,

> for works from non-Western traditions, world literature now provides an excellent opportunity to move beyond their local, national environment to a much larger context in which they can be understood and appreciated by readers they never anticipated to reach, readers with very different background, cultural values, reading habits, and expectations.
> (Zhang 2015: 9)

In a 2021 article Zhang broadened his interest from China to East Asia, to what of late has increasingly come to be called the "sinosphere." This term covers various meanings. Joshua Fogel (2009) is specifically concerned with Sino-Japanese relations when he uses the term. Thornber (2009) focuses on interrelations between Japanese, Chinese, Taiwanese, and Korean literatures around the turn of the twentieth century but prefers the term "contact nebulae" (modelled on Mary Louise Pratt's [1991] "contact zones"). Damrosch (2016) and Sowon Park (2016, 2018) speak of a "scriptworld" for cultures using versions or derivations of the Chinese script. Leaning mostly on Fogel, Zhang stipulates that for him the sinosphere is "a temporally and spatially evolving concept in history" (Zhang 2021: 283) that was "connected through ideas and a written language" (Zhang 2021: 284). Crucial in this was the role of literature, with important texts by Chinese authors circulating throughout East Asia in the original, making the sinosphere "a shared literary space beyond borders of the different countries and their linguistic and cultural differences" (Zhang 2021: 285). The original sinosphere and its scriptworld came to an end around the turn of the twentieth century because of Western colonial powers taking advantage of a weakened Qing Empire, the rise of Japan after the Meiji Restoration, and the rise of nationalisms in East Asian and South-East Asian countries. Yet, Zhang argues,

> as narrow-minded nationalism and its imaginary of ethnic or racial purity have led to horrific violence and war in the twentieth century, it becomes

edifying to revisit history with a global and comparative lens, one that is also attentive to transformative possibilities in the future.

(Zhang 2021: 289)

This is where world literature comes in as what Tihanov (2019) terms a "regime of relevance": in the geopolitical context developing since the opening of China under Deng Xiaoping in 1979, the fall of the Berlin wall in 1989, the attacks on the Twin Towers in New York in 2001, and the various economic and political crises accompanying and following these events, world literature emerges as the more relevant approach, more relevant in any case than nation-bound approaches. This applies in particular to East Asia. Zhang questions though whether the idea of the sinosphere does not simply replace one "centrism" with another: Sinocentrism for Eurocentrism? Historically speaking, he argues, "China" did not refer to a particular state or ethnicity but was a purely cultural concept "not bounded by racial consanguinity or geographical provenance" which "made it possible for different individuals or groups to claim to be Chinese, i.e. civilized, even if they are not from 'China' as such" (Zhang 2021: 291). Zhang concludes that in the study of comparative and world literature today "there must be a paradigmatic change from the national to the regional or even global, from a heavy concentration on the modern to a more expansive horizon that includes the historical past and the premodern" and that "in such a broad context beyond narrow-minded nationalism … we may rethink East Asia and the idea of the sinosphere and Chinese scriptworld as potentially meaningful in offering some insights into the idea of an alternative paradigm" (Zhang 2021: 293). Hwa Yol Jung (2015) pays tribute to Zhang's role in bringing comparative literature and world literature to bear upon cross-cultural studies. In 2023 Zhang published both a book-length plea to extend the canon of world literature in which Chinese literature functions as a focal point for discussing all issues usually raised with respect to the field: Goethe, translation, circulation, cosmopolitanism (Zhang 2023a). In the same year Zhang (2023b) also published a history of Chinese literature based on his contributions to *Literature: A World History* (Damrosch and Lindberg-Wada 2022).

Next to the "sinosphere" there has also emerged, modelled upon already existing concepts such as "francophone," "lusophone," and "anglophone," the concept of the "sinophone." Yucong Hao (2017) says the term was coined by Shu-mei Shih in 2004. In fact, it was already coined in 1988 by Ruth Keen and used by Coulombe and Roberts in 2001. In "The Concept of the Sinophone" Shih (2011: 710) says that sinophone studies is "conceived as the study of Sinitic- language cultures on the margins of geopolitical nation-states and their hegemonic productions" and that it "locates its objects of attention at the conjuncture of China's internal colonialism and Sinophone communities everywhere immigrants from China have settled." Sinophone studies

> disrupts the chain of equivalence established, since the rise of nation-states, among language, culture, ethnicity, and nationality and explores

the protean, kaleidoscopic, creative, and overlapping margins of China and Chineseness, America and Americanness, Malaysia and Malaysianness, Taiwan and Taiwanness, and so on, by a consideration of specific, local Sinophone texts, cultures, and practices produced in and from these margins.
(Shih 2011: 710)

Sinophone studies for Shih implies "a trenchant critique of China-centrism" but "equally involves a critique of Eurocentrism and other centrisms, such as Malay-centrism in Malaysia. It is, in short, always a multidirectional critique" (Shih 2011: 710–711). The sinophone for her finally

> encompasses Sinitic-language communities and their expressions (cultural, political, social, etc.) on the margins of nations and nationalness in the internal colonies and other minority communities in China as well as outside it, with the exception of settler colonies where the Sinophone is the dominant vis- à- vis their indigenous populations.
> (Shih 2011: 716)

In other words, it excludes works written by the majority Han in China and wherever they make up the majority population.

Hao argues that the case of the sinophone is different from that of Western "-phone" literatures because unlike with these Western languages, the decision by local Chinese-descended writers to use Chinese for their works is not forced upon them by colonial conditions but remains a matter of choice. For Hao a more logical definition would include all works written in Chinese. Jing Tsu and David Der-wei Wang (2010) prefer the term "global Chinese literature." In her 2022 *Kingdom of Characters*, Tsu extends the idea of the sinosphere, the sinophone, and their attendant scriptworlds, to the digital age. She tracks how China over the twentieth century and down to the present has succeeded in accommodating Western word processing technologies such as the typewriter, telegraphy, card cataloguing, and the computer, to its own script traditions. In order to enable texts in the various scripts derived from ancient or traditional Chinese script forms to be digitally accessible in all countries using these scripts, IT engineers and linguists from these countries, along with US scientists, have worked out a uniform coding system. The result, according to Tsu (2022b: 279) is that China "is poised to create its own Han script sphere of influence, once again, in the current millennium," rivalling the Western script sphere. "China's domestic market," she argues, "can sustain its own internet sphere, even if decoupled from the alphabetic world." And, she continues,

> this time, the Han script sphere of influence would also mean much more than just a system of writing ideographic signs shared by regional neighbors ... the Chinese digital sphere of influence is not physically limited to the PRC or Chinese-speaking communities in the world; it can welcome

others into its fold, as long as they subscribe to China's digital technology and infrastructure, thereby multiplying its footprint.

(Tsu 2022b: 279)

Kuei-fen Chiu and Yingjin Zhang (2022) edited what is advertised as "a polemical intervention in the studies of world literature from the vantage point of Chinese-Sinophone literatures" – contributions are by a.o. Longxi Zhang, Shu-mei Shih, and Satoru Hashimoto. What is beyond dispute is that the idea of the sinophone has proved extremely productive over the last twenty years or so (Shih et al. 2004; Shih 2007 and 2012; Mather 2014; Tan 2016; Wu 2016; Wang 2017; Rojas 2018; Wong 2018; Fan 2019; Kuan 2019; Chia and Hoogervorst 2021; Shen 2022; Stenberg 2023).

Parallel to the emerging debate on the sinophone there has sprung up a debate on sinologism. Taking its cue from concepts and arguments laid out by Said in *Orientalism* (1979 [1978]), sinologism, with as main advocate Ming Dong Gu (2013, 2018), argues that Western scholarship about China, and Chinese scholarship in thrall to Western methods and theories, has consistently misinterpreted and misrepresented China, its history, its culture, and its literature. Sinologism has been avidly discussed and at times heavily criticized (Chen and Gong 2018; Gu and Zhou 2018; Zhou Ning 2018; Zhou Xian 2018; Zhou Yunlong 2018).

Obviously, it is not only Chinese or Chinese-descended scholars that over the past thirty years or so have discussed Chinese and/or East Asian literature in relation to world literature. A 2018 volume on world literature edited by Weigui Fang, with contributions by several of the best-known contemporary scholars of world literature such as Damrosch, Longxi Zhang, and Tihanov, contains, next to a very thorough introduction by Fang (2018), two articles by German scholars on Chinese literature (Kubin 2018; Pohl 2018) and another by a Chinese scholar (Liu Hongtao 2018). Another very wide-ranging collection with contributions by both Chinese and Western scholars is *A World History of Chinese Literature*, edited by Yingjin Zhang (2023). Its various sections, with contributions by David Der-wei Wang, Weigui Fang, Charles A. Laughlin, Barbara Mittler, Carlos Rojas, Jonathan Stalling, David Wang, Hu Ying, and Yingjin Zhang himself, next to many others, address Chinese historiography, the circulation and reception of China in world literature, literary genres, gender configurations, translation and transmediation, but also translingual authors and scholars, and sinophone worlds.

Jacob Edmond in *A Common Strangeness* (2012: 3) "triangulate(s) between Russian, Chinese, and US examples" to highlight how poets from these countries reacted to post-Cold War globalization. He notes (2012: 96) how the Chinese poet Bei Dao "has provoked one of the most extensive critical debates about translation, globalization, and national and world literature." The debate was sparked by Stephen Owen (1990) who, in Edmond's words,

> not only describes Bei Dao's work as a representative product of the transnational literary system – a new international poetry devoid of historical,

national, and linguistic tradition – but reads several poems as presenting metaphors or allegories of the global condition reflected in this new homogeneous, dislocated "world poetry."

Against Owen, Edmond (2012: 97) argues that

> Instead of fixing literature and history within a single story – a single world or world literature – or set of binaries (local/global or individual/collective), Bei Dao's use of allegory emphasizes the historical flux and contested readings that gave birth to our current era.

This is only one example how since the renewed interest in world literature from the late 1990s on, discussions of Chinese literature have moved from the periphery of the literary field to the center. Edmond at the 2006 ACLA annual congress organized a seminar on "global poetics," which led to articles on the topic by Romana Huk (2009 and 2019) and Edmond himself (2019). The 2019 articles by Huk and Edmond appeared in an issue of the *University of Toronto Quarterly* entirely devoted to world poetics and edited by Jonathan Locke Hart and Ming Xie, with attention paid to, next to Western poetry, also Persian (Ramazani 2019) and Kashmiri poetry (Kachru and Mikkelson 2019). Earlier, Ming Xie (2017: 504) had already argued that

> poetics, which is central to the idea of world poetry, has often been tied to Western theories; as far as the politics of canon formation is concerned, world poetry is usually used to mean poetry of the 'rest of the world' apart from Anglo-American or Euro-American poetry.

"What needs to be recognized," he insists, is "that world poetry does not merely supply raw untheorized material for a western-dominated poetics" but rather that "world poetry needs to be seen as an active mode or means of rethinking and expanding poetics that has been defined by any single or dominant literary tradition." Therefore (Xie 2017: 508), "world poetics should be driven by problems and problematics, and not only for the sake of inclusiveness and comparability." Longxi Zhang (2012c, 2022a) addresses the issue of "the poetics of world literature."

Earlier in this chapter, I referred to Thornber (2009) and Park (2016). Thornber (2014: 462) stresses that "some of the most sustained and vibrant twentieth- and early twenty-first century East Asian artistic relationships developed not within individual East Asian societies or between East Asian and Western literatures, but among the Chinese, Japanese, and Korean literary worlds." Along similar lines, but from a different perspective, Park (2013: 1) argues that "while there has been an increasing preoccupation with literary networks beyond the Western canon since the middle of the last century, the investigations have been restricted to the colonial world and the postcolonial states of the Western powers." At the same time, she notes, "the non-Western colonial field of the Pan-Asian Empire (1894–1945) – Imperial Japan, colonial Korea, semi-colonial China, and Taiwan – has been not so much relegated to the margins as just passed over." Park's aim, then, is to "recalibrate the dynamics of 'the West and the rest' and 'center/periphery' models of world literature by bringing an East Asian perspective to the discussion."

The increased interest in the literatures of East Asia has also yielded such boldly comparative studies as Alexander Beecroft's *Authorship and Cultural Identity in early Greece and China* (2010) or Wiebke Denecke's *Classical World Literatures: Sino-Japanese and Greco-Roman Comparisons* (2014). Denecke compares the relationship of the literatures of Japan and Rome in their formative stages to that of what she calls, after Longxi Zhang (2012b), their respective "reference cultures," the Chinese and the Greek or Hellenic. In her introduction she stresses that rather than privileging the chronologically earlier European case over the later East-Asian one, and discussing the latter from the ontological perspective of what it lacks in comparison with the former, she has "framed her comparison as a quadruple constellation, which, although it still consists of two binaries, avoids essentializing dichotomy and the creation of false ellipses" (Denecke 2014: 12–13). Instead, she considers China and Japan, and Greece and Rome, "as long-standing constellations of cultural reception processes, of cultural *translatio*," and "when we come to compare the four literary cultures of the Ancient Mediterranean and East Asia, we are not in fact comparing cultures, but reception processes" (Denecke 2014: 12). Likewise, Beecroft (2010) is not comparing cultures but how authorship functions in the two cultures concerned. Denecke (2014: 15) argues that her book "tries to make a seductive case for dialogue," and the same can be said of Beecroft's. Both Beecroft and Denecke, then, approach world literature from what Longxi Zhang has argued that "a comparative literature for our time should be – comparison not just within but beyond and across philologically linked language groups, across Romance and East Asian languages" (Zhang 2013: 59).

Although perhaps less often discussed in the context of world literature than Chinese literature, one of the earliest attempts to fruitfully compare Eastern and Western literary systems focused primarily on Japanese literature: Earl Miner's ground-breaking *Comparative Poetics* (1990). Victoria Young (2021) discusses the work of Yoko Tawada, who publishes in both Japanese and German, in the context of Japanese literature's shifting relationship to world literature. In passing she also mentions that the term "Japanophone" was already coined in 1972 by Kim Sokpom, but that it has undergone various shifts of meaning since then (Young 2021: 9–10).

Satoru Hashimoto (2022) underwrites Longxi Zhang's claim that nationalism, also in literary matters, led to the demise of the traditional East Asian Chinese scriptworld around the turn of the twentieth century. He sees such literary nationalism in Korean, Japanese, and Chinese literature as at least partially the result of writers from these countries being exposed to world literature, which in their case meant Western literature. In return, these writers saw a literature expressive of national character as the only way to make it into the ranks of world literature for themselves and their literature, with Hashimoto (2022: 426) quoting the Chinese writer Mao Dun in 1921 to this effect. Hashimoto then traces how the concept of world literature entered Chinese, Japanese, and Korean scholarship and developed over the twentieth century. He ends with a caveat at the tendency to talk of the sinosphere as constituted by several literatures on an equal footing. In fact, he argues, it was never a level playing field – works from China entered Japanese and Korean culture but the reverse direction was much harder, in fact almost unheard of. Here he sees an important task for world literature: "if encounters with classical East Asian literatures are charged with rescuing world literature from Eurocentrism, then encounters with world literature should similarly rescue classical East Asian literatures from Sinocentrism, revealing their marginalized formations, latent dynamics, and multidimensional structures" (Hashimoto 2022: 431).

Meera Lee and Edwin Van Bibber-Orr (2016: 109) in their introduction to a special issue of *Symposium* note that

> While the recognition of East Asian literature in both the global literary market and scholarly communities is unprecedented, its resulting canonization remains problematic. In *The Norton Anthology of World Literature, Shorter Third Edition* (2013), for example, Chinese and Japanese literatures feature heavily, yet Korean literature is almost entirely absent and there is no mention of any of the diasporic literatures of East Asia.

Hence, their special issue "seeks to illuminate the gap between the literary production of East Asia and the canon of world literature."

Satoru Hashimoto and Karen Thornber in 2019 edited a special issue of the *Journal of World Literature* (4.4) on "Trans-Regional Asia and Futures of World Literature." Haun Saussy (2018: 2) sketches a program for the Comparative History of Asian Literatures, a book series he heads for the International Comparative Literature Association and that is meant to complement that body's long-standing Comparative History of Literatures in European Languages series. Loosely taking his cue from Niklas Luhmann's concept that "a world is specified by the attainable horizon of communication for those who live in it," Saussy argues that "'World literature' is thus the literature of that world which is available to the persons who call it so," which for him is "the 'world' imagined by contemporary globalization narratives" and hence "a world whose history leads up to us, the audience for the product." As "an experimental corrective to several of the biases that inflect current conceptions of world literature," he proposes that "comparatists set themselves the task of considering the historical relationships among the languages, literatures and cultures of Asia before 1800." "A comparative literary history of Asia must reach far back in time, to a period before the nations of today originated" and "will demonstrate the cosmopolitan character of a single world region before the current dynamics of globalization got underway" (Saussy 2018: 2).

India, South Asia, and South-East Asia

Many of the most vocal scholars originating from the Indian subcontinent have reflected on the world literature debate from the perspective of postcolonialism and orientalism, for instance Gayatri Spivak and Homi Bhabha of an earlier generation and more recently Aamir Mufti, B. Venkat Mani, and Baidik Bhattacharya. Others, like Auritro Majumder (2021), explore South-South relations. Majumder discusses the shared sensibilities underlying Rabindranath Tagore's 1907 speech on world literature and Mao's Yenan talks on art comparison in the context of what he prefers to call "peripheral internationalism." He connects "India to 1920s and 1930s Mexico and the Soviet Union; 1960s and 1970s Vietnam, Cuba, and the Congo; and present-day China and the United States," discussing "how literary texts came to highlight marginalized groups across national boundaries, provincialize dominant histories, and articulate the distinctive yet interconnected problematic of peripheral literature." "What is significant here," he emphasizes, "is that an understudied constellation of writers outside the 'West' was drawing more on one another than on the imperial center when it came to their aesthetic sensibilities" (Majumder 2021: ix). The parallels with Thornber (2009, 2014) and Park (2013) are evident.

Orsini (2021: 411) spiritedly affirms that "to view India/South Asia as arriving on the world literary stage only with Tagore or with novel writing in English is to ignore its vast literary production over three millennia." This production draws not only on literature in Sanskrit, as in Pollock (2006), nor only in Hindi or Urdu, but also in Bengali, Tamil, and India's and South Asia's numerous other languages. The "spectacular critical and commercial success of Indian (and more recently Pakistani) literature in English … has dwarfed, and to a large extent made invisible writing in Indian languages," Orsini (2021: 424–425) argues. To counterbalance this, she reasons, "it is important to avoid equating English with world and to historicise its traffic through other literary traditions" and "to continue to explore plural forms of local worldmaking and the different circuits along which literature circulates" (Orsini 2021: 425). Orsini herself has conducted such explorations in the context of world literature (Orsini 2002, 2007, 2012, 2019; Orsini and Zecchini 2019), but she is not alone in this (Laachir, Marzagora, and Orsini 2018; Ebeling 2021). Orsini and Zecchini have also edited two special issues of the *Journal of World Literature* (4.1 and 4.2; 2019) on "The Locations of (World) Literature: Perspectives from Africa and South Asia." In 2017 Rosella Ciocca and Neelam Srivastava edited *Indian Literature and the World*, with contributions by a.o. Orsini and Rajeswari Sunder Rajan. In 2022 Bhavya Tiwari authored *Beyond English: World Literature and India* as a volume in Bloomsbury's "X as World Literature" series edited by Thomas Beebee. Adhira Mangalagiri (2023) explores the literary relations between India and China in the twentieth century.

Amelia Dina (2016) and Dewi Christa Kobis (2019) briefly situate Indonesian literature with respect to world literature. Much more substantial is an article by Tony Day (2007) that takes in the then still recent writings of Casanova (2004) and Moretti (2000) on world literature as well as Pollock's (2006) ideas on the Sanskrit cosmopolis for early Indonesian and particularly Javanese literature, and that further mainly focuses on the work of the Indonesian novelist Pramoedya Ananta Toer as a world author. Ronit Ricci (2010, 2011, 2019) in several monographs and articles has explored the interrelations between Islamicate literatures and cultures in South and South-East Asia, in particular in Malaysia, Indonesia, and Ceylon.

That the question of world literature and how their respective literatures relate to it moves scholars throughout South and South-East Asia shows from the *South Asian Review* soliciting contributions for a special issue on "Global Sri Lankan Literature and Culture" for December 2023, and from a conversation between Chamini Kulathunga and the Sri Lankan novelist Liyanage Amarakeerthi published online on the website of *Hopscotch Translation* in 2021. For Malaysian literature we may point to Liew (2021). If there are not already similar publications on the other South-East Asian literatures – from Laos, Cambodia, Myanmar, Singapore, Thailand, the Philippines – no doubt there soon will be. As Damrosch put it in a 2020 interview (Chen and Damrosch: 7): "Not enough Chinese or American scholars are working on Vietnamese literature or Thai literature or Indonesian. The world is full of great writers that we should get to know."

The World of Islam

Less often noticed than the work on Chinese and Indian literature in relation to world literature has been the contribution by scholars working on the so-called Middle East and the wider world of Islam. In Chapter 8 I already had occasion to refer to Waïl Hassan, but he is not the only one. In *Specters of World Literature: Orientalism, Modernity, and the Novel in the Middle East*, Karim Mattar (2020: xi) seeks "to demonstrate through a new reading of the Middle Eastern novel that world literature is always-already haunted by its others, the ghosts of modernity." Through a reading of texts by Abdel Rahman Munif, Naguib Mahfouz, Orhan Pamuk, Azar Nafisi, Yasmin Crowther, and Marjane Satrapi, "alongside classic statements of world literature from Johann Wolfgang von Goethe and Karl Marx to the present, the discourse of the modern novel as initiated by Miguel de Cervantes, and landmarks of Middle Eastern literary history such as the *Mu'allaqat* and *Alf Layla wa Layla* [the Arabian Nights, TD]," he intends to "show how the Middle Eastern novel traverses and reconfigures the aesthetic forms definitive of the modern novel – realism, modernism, postmodernism, postcolonialism, and cosmopolitanism – from the perspective of its others" (Mattar 2020: xi). Muhsin J. al-Musawi (2021) situates the *Arabian Nights* in contemporary world cultures and in the context of the culture industry.

In *Politicising World Literature: Egypt, Between Pedagogy and the Public*, May Hawas (2019: 1) "engages with Postcolonial and World Literature approaches to suggest a way that non-Western literature, here, literature about or from Egypt as a case in point, can be compared to European literature," but she is also strongly concerned with "the pedagogical or public objectives of teaching literature for the sake of prompting societal, political or academic reform." She pairs Waguih Ghali's *Beer in the Snooker Club* with Milan Kundera's *The Unbearable Lightness of Being*, Leila Ahmed's *A Border Passage* with Tsitsi Dangarembga's *Nervous Conditions*, a play of Tawfik al-Hakim with a Montalbano detective novel of Andrea Camilleri, and rounds off with an analysis of Amitav Ghosh's *In an Antique Land*. In her conclusion she recalls how the Egyptian critic Taha Hussein [Tāha Husayn] in a 1955 article, in English, laid out a theory of Arabic literature as world literature. He saw Arabic literature as qualifying as such because of what he called the two Arab Renaissances: the first covering the first four centuries of Islam, with the assimilation into Arabic literature of Greek, Indian, and Persian cultural elements, and the second, the "Modern Arabic Renaissance," the period from 1919 to 1950, with the assimilation of modern European culture. Hawas also edited a special issue of the *Journal of World Literature* (2.3; 2017) on "What is World Literature – of Arabic?" A survey article on "the world of Arabic literature" is Tarek El-Ariss (2022).

Michael Allan (2016) opens *In the Shadow of World Literature: Sites of Reading in Colonial Egypt* with a reference to a passage from Taha Hussein's autobiography *al-Ayyām* (The Days) where the latter describes how he acceded to literacy. However, Allan (2016: 2) argues, there is more to this than the simple autobiographical fact: "Beyond the pages of his life in letters, Hussein labored institutionally, serving as a professor, a dean, and a key figure in the crafting of literary curricula for the modern Egyptian state." In doing so, Hussein "helped to place Arabic literature … among the literary traditions of an emergent world literature …. To the literary models seen in Greek, Latin, French, English, and German, he added Arabic – a language he understood to embody a Mediterranean and cosmopolitan heritage" (Allan 2016: 2). Allan is concerned with how literary reading, as distinct from reading "based on memorization, embodiment, and recitation" as practiced in Qur'anic schools, marks one as being "recognizably educated in the modern state" (Allan 2016: 3). World literature, then, "is not the all-inclusive meeting place of national literary traditions, but the emergent distinction between those deemed literate, cosmopolitan, and modern, and those others who are not" (Allan 2016: 3).

Jahan Ramazani (2019: 210), known for his work on transnational poetics (2009), remarks that "although Goethe, who first propounded *Weltliteratur*, was inspired by Persian poetry, recent theorists of world literature have largely ignored it." Poised between those, with a nod to Damrosch, that advocate world literature as literature that gains in translation and those, with a nod to Apter, that argue poetry's untranslatability, Ramazani (2019: 210) proposes "a more nuanced position that allows for both losses and gains" and argues that "world literature must incorporate comparative literary specificity to be adequate to Persian and other varieties of lyric poetry." Omid Azadibougar (2020) situates the modernist Iranian author Sadegh Hedayat in the context of world literature. Hamid Dabashi authored *The Shahnameh: The Persian Epic as World Literature* (2019).

Africa

At present, most work on Africa and world literature largely limits itself to African literatures in European languages. This is the case, for instance with an article by Innocência Mata (2013) on African literatures in Portuguese. The same goes for a survey article by Helgesson (2022b). Helgesson (2018d) takes a closer look at South African literature under Apartheid. Uzoma Esonwanne (2021: 326) denounces that "world literature retains the view of Africa as a source of regional works that would supplement an already established archive of global cultural texts" and that to overcome this view "the relationship between Africa and world literature needs to be recalibrated by adopting strategies that recognize that Africa is an *agent* in the constitution and interpretation of the archive of global cultural texts we call world literature." To this end, he (2021: 340) contends, "legitimating African literary and oral texts is hardly all that world literature must now look into … it must also ask how we should read these texts as world literature." One of the rare attempts to do so is an article by Taban Lo Liyong (2018). Julien Jeusette and Silvia Riva edited a special issue of the *Journal of World Literature* (6.2; 2021) on "Contemporary Congolese Literature as World Literature." Riva (2020) also wrote on "Global Congo."

How Africa and its literature(s) figured in the very earliest world literature discussions, and particularly with Goethe and Henri Grégoire, is studied by Thomas Geider (2005). Jean-Marc Moura (2016) discusses Africa in the wider context of the Atlantic world. In a similarly Atlantic context, Jason Frydman (2014) looks at African American and Caribbean literatures as literatures of the African diaspora. In 2018 Russell West-Pavlov edited a volume on *The Global South and Literature* taking in transcontinental flows across Asia, Africa, and Latin America. Contributors are, among many others, Simon During, Thabish Khair, Vijay Mishra, and Isabel Hofmeyr. In an exercise in decolonizing literary space, Kyle Wanberg (2020) discusses works by writers issuing from Africa (Camara Laye, Yambo Ouologuem) and the Islamicate world (Imīl Habībī, Sadeq Hedayat) alongside the Native American Pima Ant Songs from Arizona in the present-day United States.

Oceanic and Antipodes

A very early instance of attention paid to Oceania in a world literature context is a very brief article by Bruno Lasker in 1944 that discusses writings about the region rather than its literature. One of the more recent developments in world literature studies is increasing attention to the maritime dimension (Ganguly 2021b; Frydman 2022). Ottmar Ette and Gesine Müller in 2012 edited a volume on archipelagos and islands, with contributions on literatures from the Pacific, the Indian ocean, the Caribbean, and French Polynesia, as well as on the concepts of "archipelago-ness" and insularity, including in a metaphorical sense. Stefan Helgesson, Birgit Neumann, and Gabriele Rippl, in 2020 edited a massive *Handbook of Anglophone World Literatures* with, next to chapters on theoretical issues related to world literature, contributions on the oceans (Meg Samuelson), and on specific countries or regions: Britain (Eva Ulrike Pirker), Ireland (Joakim Wrethed), the USA (David Watson), Canada (Katja Sarkowsky), The Caribbean (Sarah Phillips Casteel), Southern Africa (Stefan Helgesson), West Africa (Harry Garuba and Christopher E.W. Ouma), East Africa (Godwin Siundu), South Asia (Ragini Tharoor Srinivasan), Southeast Asia (Hong Kong and Singapore) (Kwok-kan Tam), Australia (Nicole Moore), and New Zealand (Andrew Dean).

In 2015 Brigid Rooney and Brigitta Olubas edited an issue of JASAL (Journal of the Association for the Study of Australian Literature) on Australian Literature / World Literature with contributions by a.o. Vilashini Cooppan, Sneja Gunew, Robert Dixon, and Paul Giles. Paul Giles (2021: 492) holds up Australia's otherness in terms of time and space – its antipodean relation to Western culture centered upon Europe and North America – as a productive ground for the "substantive reimagination of cultural relations between North and South, East and West, across an extensive global compass." Svend Erik Larsen (2017) eyes Australian literature from a world perspective as oscillating between whiteness and multiculturalism.

Conclusion

- Changing geopolitical conditions are accompanied by greater attention to non-European and non-North American literatures from the perspective of world literature.
- Increasingly, scholars from the countries from which these literatures originate enter the world literature debate.
- This is most notably the case with respect to East Asian literatures, and particularly in China and with respect to Chinese literature, but also when it comes to Japanese and Korean literature.
- Other literatures, such as Indian, Arabic, and Persian, are following suit, and, although at some greater distance, also African, Oceanic, and Australian literature, but much still remains to be done.

10 World Literature and Planetary Materialities

Overview

In earlier chapters I referred to Etiemble (1988) and Spivak (2003) calling for a "planetary" approach to world literature, by which they mainly meant including all writing beyond Euro- or Western-centrism, although with Spivak there are also intimations of wider concerns. Over the last two decades, however, the term "planetary" has received another dimension, linked to what I will call two kinds of "materiality." The first focuses on the material and particularly the environmental conditions of the planet itself, its ecology. Especially over the last decade-and-a-half, and mainly from a postcolonial perspective, this dimension has increasingly focused on the role of commodities. The second dimension concerns the material dimension of literature itself: the production, distribution, and marketing of texts, from books to digital texts. These developments are addressed in the present chapter.

Materialities of Nature

Ursula Heise (2022), summarizing her own earlier findings (Heise 2008, 2013 and 2017), sketches the evolution of ecocriticism since its beginnings in the 1980s and 1990s as follows: in its early days ecocriticism focused on depictions of environmental crises in English and American literature, as of approximately the turn of the millennium the field was enlarged to the rest of the world under the impulse of postcolonial and comparative studies, from around 2008 the Anthropocene became an important lens through which to look at literary works, while in its most recent developments the universalizing impetus of the Anthropocene approach is being replaced by an increasing emphasis on environmental justice. The latter shift is inspired by a growing awareness of how environmental issues such as climate change and ecological degradation affect different parts of the planet differently as the result of long-standing economic and political inequalities. For its theoretical frame the latter approach often draws upon insights borrowed from historical materialism, itself (sometimes loosely) inspired by Marxist theory. Of late, study of the material conditions of book production, distribution, and marketing have also sought inspiration from this approach.

As representative of the first phase of ecocriticism Heise (2022) points to Lawrence Buell's 1995 *The Environmental Imagination*. Markers for the second phase are Thornber (2012), focusing on East Asian literatures, and David V. Carruthers (2008), concentrating on Latin America. Thornber convincingly lays out how environmental concerns have long been part of East Asian literatures, while Carruthers shows how in Latin American literature they are routinely connected to economic, social, and political issues. As Heise (2022: 344) comments:

> reading environmental world literature entails reading for concerns with nature, specifically concerns over human damages to nature as they are framed by genres that range from political manifestoes and prose writings to science fiction and novels and performances, depending on the cultural context.

This also means "identifying the ways in which concerns with degraded nature are connected to other social struggles or indeed function as metaphors for them, and why they do so."

It is precisely the link between environmental and social concerns upon which postcolonial critical ecologist work has seized. Heise herself focuses on what she, after Alfred Crosby (2003 [1972]), calls the "Columbian Exchange" as a prime example of a "global upheaval of the biosphere" that was "in its own way no less consequential than climate change today" (Heise 2022: 345). However, and this has come increasingly to the fore in recent environmental ecocriticism, "beyond a fundamentally altered natural environment, postcolonial critics argue, the Columbian Exchange also instated a global socioeconomic system that is based on unequal economic exchange and perpetual radical inequality and injustice to this day" (Heise 2022: 345). In her 2022 survey article Heise nowhere mentions the work of the Warwick Research Collective, but her use of the terms "unequal economic exchange" and "inequality and injustice" clearly relate her views, and those of the postcolonial critics she refers to as working in a similar vein as herself (for instance Huggan and Tiffin 2010; Nixon 2011; DeLoughrey 2019; Wenzel 2020), to *Combined and Uneven Development: Towards a New Theory of World-Literature* (WReC 2015; also as Deckard et al. 2015). WReC proposes "to define 'world literature' as the literature of the world-system – of the modern capitalist world-system, that is." This system, which following Wallerstein (1974, 1980, 1989, 2011) they identify with the period that as of roughly 1500, at least from a European/Western perspective, has been customarily identified with "modernity," they see as marked by affecting the entire world – hence the use of the hyphenated "world-system," indicating that it is not simply "a" system existing "in the world," but precisely that it leaves no part of the world untouched. The point is that different parts of the world are affected differently, or, more precisely, unequally. "World-literature," then, is the label they ascribe to all literary works registering such unevenness, whether from the privileged site of the West or that of the underprivileged, disadvantaged, or outright oppressed non-West. In fact, it could be argued that all "modern" literary works in one way or another effect such registering, even works that at first sight would seem to have only local or immediately topical connections (D'haen 2017c). While the work of the WReC has mostly been concerned with the Global South, the issue of combined and uneven development can also be applied internally to "the West" or "Europe" itself, for instance with reference to the working classes and how they have been almost routinely neglected in discussions of world literature.

Like other postcolonial critics (Young 2012; Boehmer 2014 and 2018), postcolonial ecocritics routinely take world literature to task for glossing over the inequalities upon which they themselves focus. Heise here sees parallels with these same ecocritics' critiques of the use of the term "Anthropocene" for the period starting from either the end of the eighteenth century and the beginning of industrialization or 1492 and the start of the Columbian Exchange. In their view, the alternative term "Capitalocene" suggested by Jason Moore (2016) more accurately captures the causes that have led to the institution and continue the perpetuation of the inequalities mentioned. For ecocritics such as Jennifer Wenzel, it ultimately comes down to the "material foundations of markets, including literary ones" (Heise 2022: 349). Here, then, is where the material dimensions of the environment and of texts meet, with WReC or WReC-related approaches prominent in both.

Much postcolonial materialist ecocriticism picks up on some of the work done on the socio-economic impact of the circulation of commodities under colonialism, imperialism, and neo-liberalism. An early example is Ortiz (2002 [1940], 1995) on sugar and tobacco in Cuba. A very recent example is Sheldon Lu's article on how the eighteenth-century Chinese novel *Dream of the Red Chamber* (a.k.a. *The Story of the Stone*), while always maintaining a China-centered worldview, features "frequent appearances of foreign objects as well as glimpses of China's trade with the West," and evokes how the "encounter with foreign objects and material culture is a shocking and exciting discovery ... described in vivid details" (Lu: in press). Michael Niblett (2012: 16) explores "how world literature, understood as the literature of the capitalist world-system, registers the transformations in world ecology that have been both cause and consequence of the transition to, and subsequent reorganizations of the capitalist world-economy." Starting from Moore (2003), and analyzing how these transformations "imprint themselves on the aesthetics of texts from China, Nigeria, and the Caribbean," Niblett (2012: 16) seeks to propagate a "comparative model of literary study that holds out the possibility of detecting likenesses (and likenesses of the unlike) between peripheral literary forms as they respond to the same – yet differentially articulated – world-historical forces of capitalist modernity." Relating the emergence of magical realism in Latin American and Caribbean literature to "the imposition of latifundia and plantation monocultures" that "turned the region into an external nutrient supply for the core, its ecological resources leached away via the export of sugar-cane, coffee, rum, bananas, maize, and other commodities," he argues that "the combination of modern novelistic discourse with narrative forms inspired by Mayan sacred texts" in *Hombres de maíz* (1949; Men of Maize), by the Guatemalan Nobel Prize winner Miguel Ángel Asturias, "mediates a clash between the native Indian world and the forces of market capitalism that is at the same time a clash between different socio-ecologies" (Niblett 2012: 22). In China, Niblett (2012: 24) sees the work of Mao Dun, and especially a trilogy of stories he wrote in the 1930s, as documenting "the disintegration of China's rural economy under the combined pressures of imperialism and landlordism." And "the generic discontinuities generated by [Amos] Tutuola's combination of novel form and Yoruba narrative traditions" in *The Palm-Wine Drinkard* (1952) for Niblett (2012: 26) "can be interpreted ... as registering the ruptures in local socio-ecologies and nutrient cycles engendered by forcible integration into the capitalist world-ecology." Earlier, Wenzel (2006) had already related the occurrence of magic realism in Nigerian fiction to the disruption the coming of the oil industry caused there. In fact, fiction related to the oil industry earned itself the epithet "petro-fiction," coined by Amitav Ghosh (1992), and by now has attracted a considerable amount of ecocritical attention (Szeman 2012; Bergthaller 2017; Macdonald 2017; Tanak 2020; Balkan and Nandi 2021).

Oil is also one of the commodities Niblett focuses upon in his 2020 *World Literature and Ecology: The Aesthetics of Commodity Frontiers, 1890–1950*, where he elaborates upon the views put forward in his 2012 article, and in which he sketches out a thematic poetics centered upon how literary works and systems deal with, next to oil, other commodities such as sugar, coal, and cacao, in novels written in, respectively, Brazil, Britain, and Trinidad. His concern, Niblett says (2020: 3) is "with the way life- and environment-making processes have been registered not only at the level of content, but also at the levels of form, imagery, and style." Drawing on ideas developed by Raymond Williams (1977) and Roberto Schwarz (2001b), Niblett (2020: 5) sets out to "probe the myriad ways in which the ecological realities of the sugar, cacao, coal, and oil frontiers have been reconstituted as a force internal to literary forms" and to demonstrate that "the life- and environment-making dynamics of commodity frontiers provide fruitful grounds for a new form of world-literary comparativism." To elaborate such world-literary comparativism Niblett invokes work in the emergent field of the "energy humanities" as done by Yaeger (2011), Westall (2017), and others. He approvingly quotes Yaeger (2011: 305) asking what would happen if, instead of "divvying up literary works into hundred-year intervals (or elastic variants like the long eighteenth or twentieth century) or categories harnessing the history of ideas (Romanticism, Enlightenment)" we "sort texts according to the energy sources that made them possible?"

Niblett's focus on energy sources and commodities, and on the regions from which they originate and the impacts they have on the societies involved, has, from a world literature perspective, the added benefit of foregrounding texts that otherwise have often remained under the world literature scholarly radar. To be sure, some of the works that he analyses, and their authors, have received some international scholarly attention before – such is the case, for instance, with the Brazilian Jorge Amado, and to a lesser extent the Welshmen Gwyn Thomas and Rhys Davies, but most likely the names of Harold Heslop, José Américo de Almeida, Ellen Wilkinson, Ralph de Boissière, Stephen Cobham, Yseult Bridges, or José Lins do Rego will not ring a bell for most world literature scholars. Yet, Niblett's commodity-related focus allows him not only to demonstrate how these authors deserve our renewed attention, but also to link them to much better-known writers from sometimes unexpected angles. The Brazilian Lins do Rego, for example, used the Portuguese Eça de Queiroz's masterwork *Os Maias* (1880) as intertext for his 1934 novel *Banguë*, part of his sugar-cane cycle. De Queiroz worked on *Os Maias* while serving as Portuguese consul in Newcastle-upon-Tyne and Bristol, and the labor conflicts affecting the mining industry in England at the time, conflicts he commented upon in letters to the Portuguese foreign ministry, seeped into his views on social evolution speaking from his novel.

Niblett's commodity focus also allows him to draw attention to thematic relations linking interbellum writing across continents and languages, but hitherto little explored from a world literature perspective. He points, for instance, to the trope of the mangled body in British fiction about the coal mines, as in Heslop's *Last Cage Down*, Lewis Jones's *Cwnardy*, or J.C. Grant's *The Back-to-Backs*, but also in Trinidadian stories about cacao, as in Alfred Mendes's "One Day for John Small," or about oil, as in the same author's *Pitch Lake*, or about plantation workers in Brazil's North-East, as in Almeida's *A Bagaceira* (Trash). In 2016 Niblett, together with Chris Campbell, edited a volume concentrating on one region, the Caribbean, in terms of world-ecology, aesthetics, and politics, with contributions by several WReC members, next to others.

I have dwelled to considerable length on Niblett's work not because it is the only such around – far from it – but because it offers a handy shortcut to further recent work along the same lines, although of course each commentator has their own angle on things. Already in 2010 Laurenz Volkmann, Nancy Grimm, Ines Detmers, and Katrin Thomson edited a volume on *Local Natures, Global Responsibilities: Ecocritical Perspectives on the New English Literatures*. Energy resources and primarily petro-fiction are the subject of a special issue of the *Journal of Postcolonial Writing* (53.3; 2017) introduced by Westall (2017), and with contributions by Imre Szeman, Graeme Macdonald, Michael Niblett, Kerstin Oloff, Teresa DeLoughrey, Sharae Deckard, James Graham, and Anna Barnard, an interview of Jennifer Wenzel by Lucy Potter, and a review essay on work in hydropolitics by Hannah Boast. Alexandra Campbell and Michael Paye introduce a 2020 special issue of the journal

Humanities on "World Literature and the Blue Humanities" with an editorial on "Water Enclosure and World-Literature: New Perspectives on Hydro-Power and World-Ecology." The issue itself articulates "the commonalities and tensions between world literature, world-ecology, blue humanities, and hydrocultural approaches." Climate change informs Roman Bartosch's *Literature, Pedagogy, and Climate Change: Text Models for a Transcultural Ecology* (2019). Ganguly (2020) "explores the entanglement of radical humanisms and realist ontologies in theorizing catastrophe in the contemporary global novel," the catastrophe in question being climate collapse. Mary Louise Pratt (2022) discusses how 1990s Latin American fiction, in parallel with social movements, foregrounds the awareness of a similar catastrophic future brought on by the destructions wrought by neoliberalism, and proposes local forms of knowledge, rooted in indigeneity, as alternative modes of being.

Of course, there are also plenty of more general works on ecocriticism that touch on world literature issues. Hubert Zapf in 2016 edited a *Handbook of Ecocriticism and Cultural Ecology*. John Parham and Louise Westling in 2017 edited *A Global History of Literature and the Environment*. Vin Nardizzi and Tiffany Jo Werth (2019) edited a volume on *Premodern Ecologies in the Modern Literary Imagination*, with an "Afterword: Environmentalism, Eco-Cosmopolitanism, and Premodern Thought" by Heise (2019). Puchner (2022) tellingly titles the little volume resulting from his Oxford/Princeton joint lecture series *Literature for a Changing Planet*.

Materialities of the Text

Heise (2022) finds that at least some of the critiques especially postcolonial materialist ecocritics level at world literature is somewhat prejudiced or unwarranted when it comes to the latter's alleged neglect of market inequality issues, including literary markets. In her reading, the so-called foundational texts of the newer world literature approach (Moretti 2000 and 2003; Damrosch 2003; Casanova 2004) do pay attention to these issues, though admittedly without probing them to the depths postcolonial ecocriticism deems is called for. Moreover, she sees several more recent contributions to world literature as already mitigating these critiques. As examples she points to Helgesson and Vermeulen (2016), Müller, Locane, and Loy (2018), and Sánchez Prado (2018). And of course, there is the work of WReC itself.

Scholarly interest in the actual circulation of books arose only relatively recently, with the emergence of book history as a field of investigation in the second half of the twentieth century with the works of Lucien Febvre and Henri-Jean Martin (1958), Robert Escarpit (1958), Elisabeth Eisenstein (1979, 1983), Robert Darnton (1982), and Roger Chartier (1994). The institutionalization of the field is borne out by the creation of specialized societies, such as SHARP (Society for the History of Authorship, Reading and Publishing, Inc.), and journals, such as *Book History*, SHARP's official organ, which is devoted to every aspect of the history of the book, broadly defined as the history of the creation, dissemination, and reception of script and print. It publishes research on the social, economic, and cultural history of authorship, editing, printing, the book arts, publishing, the book trade, periodicals, newspapers, ephemera, copyright, censorship, literary agents, libraries, literary criticism, canon formation, literacy, literary education, reading habits, and reader response.[1]

SHARP was founded in 1992, at a time when, as the society's website recalls, "although questions that we now consider book historical had been active in the study of literature and history for some time, there was no interdisciplinary meeting place, no online discussion forum or website, no newsletter and no journal."[2] In 1995 the Center for the History of the Book was established at the University of Edinburgh. As is clear already from the mission statement of *Book History*, it was not only the production and circulation of books that became the subject of scholarly interest, but also related issues such as reading, with, next to works by the scholars already mentioned, a noted work by Alberto Manguel (1996). The role of libraries likewise received attention, with as some recent contributions Andrew Pettegree and Arthur der Weduwen (2019 and 2021). In world literature studies Moretti (1998) and B. Venkat Mani (2012, 2017, 2022) have ventured into this field, while Reingard Nethersole (2012 and 2022) offers a survey of the relation between world literature and the library, and Ann Steiner (2012 and 2022) looks at world literature and the book market. José Luís Jobim (2017) has edited two volumes on literary and cultural circulation, one in English and the other in Portuguese, but both comprising the same materials. A hitherto under-researched field remains that of periodical circulation and its actual readership, as argued by Luc Van Doorslaer (2011) also with respect to translations. Similarly, the role of reviews in world literature has been undervalued, as argued by Anita Traninger and Federica La Manna (2023).

Steiner (2012: 316 and 2022: 259) starts off with "In 2009, the most widespread books in the world were three crime novels by Swedish author Stieg Larsson and the four novels in American Stephenie Meyer's vampire series *Twilight*." With a clear reference to Damrosch's definition of world literature as literary works that travel beyond their cultures of origin either in the original or translation, she specifies that "these are examples of popular novels at the top of bestseller lists all over the globe – novels that travel across borders, cultures, and traditions – in translation as well as in the original language." From the perspective of many commentators on world literature, the rub here would be the "popular" in this last sentence. Indeed, earlier commentators usually sharply distinguished between works that continue to draw readers, and critical commentary, over successive generations and ideally continuously so – the world canonical or even "hypercanonical" (Damrosch 2006b) classics – and works or authors that at a given moment may have loomed very large but that quickly faded, never to return – the merely popular. At first sight both the canonicals and the popular might seem to fit what Damrosch (2003: 4) means when he says that "a work only has an effective life as world literature whenever, and wherever, it is actively present within a literary system beyond that of its original culture." However, Fritz Strich already in 1930 warned that "there is a ... deeper concept of world literature that comprises not just a spatial but also a temporal dimension" (Strich 2013, p. 41). World literature, he contends, "is precisely that literature that has not been forgotten and that has not sunk below the horizon, even if once it may have enjoyed the widest dissemination and influence" (Strich 2013: 41). Strich's own examples of the "sunk" are Augustus von Kotzebue, a German contemporary of Goethe's, the turn-of-the-twentieth-century German playwright and novelist Hermann Sudermann, and the prolific early twentieth-century English crime and adventure writer Edgar Wallace, all of whom in their own day enjoyed immense popularity also beyond their culture of origin because, Strich contends, they joined topical relevance to easily digestible form. To truly belong to world literature, what is needed beyond sheer reach of "dissemination" and "supranational importance" are "duration" and "lasting validity" (Strich 2013: 41), both of which devolve from a work's "eternal relevance" (Strich 2013: 40). A fortuitous example of a combination of topical with eternal relevance, dressed in a popular and easily digestible form (at least at its moment of publication), is Goethe's *Werther*. "It is quite possible," Strich admits,

> that there are breaks in the total period of time that a work or an author enjoys world literary status ... a work or a writer may become suppressed by a particular period movement, and temporarily forgotten ... but when the work or author really is of lasting value, it or he will always again, when its hour has struck, emerge from the river of forgetfulness, as happened with Shakespeare and Cervantes.
>
> (Strich 2013: 41)

Clearly, the criterion of quantity is here amplified with the criterion of quality; of those works, and their authors, that stand out because of their wide dissemination it is only those that also show the extra qualities enumerated by Strich that fit his conception of world literature, clearly favoring what these days we might call an "elite" canon for cultured readers with what at the time would still most probably have been a "classical" education comprising some Latin and perhaps (ancient) Greek, and with what in German is called *Bildung*.

Steiner sees a conception of world literature à la Strich even almost one hundred years later still influencing and even determining how world literature is approached. Over against such a notion, she proposes (2012: 316 and 2022: 259), in our time "world literature is defined and propelled by forces and structures of the book trade that are intersected by the media market." Obviously, one here has to consider that the entire context in which literature functions in the twenty-first century is radically different from that of Strich's

1930s, and this applies to education as well as to the mediascape, including the publishing industry. Yet, she notes (2012: 316 and 2022: 259), even under these changed conditions Damrosch's "works circulating beyond their culture of origin" has "been applied primarily to literarily valuable fiction." However, she maintains (2012: 316 and 2022: 259), "if we take the full meaning of the notion and relate it to the actual contemporary book trade, a different and conceivably disconcerting, image will emerge." Today, "world literature is conditioned by sale systems, publishing traditions, translations, government support, taxes, and everything else related to the economy of literature" and "local and transnational companies producing and selling books determine what can be accessed, how it is marketed, and what many people read" (Steiner 2012: 316 and 2022: 259). The spectacular development of the internet, mergers and acquisitions in the publishing and media industry creating media conglomerates with a worldwide reach, and the integration of spin-off and concept creation activities decisively influence what really circulates as "world" literature.

Here the issue of translation crops up once again: what is available in English, and to a lesser extent in other "world languages" such as Spanish, French, or German, whether in the original or in translation, is accessible to more people around the world and publications in these languages stock the catalogues of international media conglomerates such as Bertelsmann, Hachette, Reed Elsevier, or Pearson. Still, the internet also allows the dissemination of publications in other languages and by other, more local, publishers. For instance, Amazon offers access to many books in smaller languages and by small publishers, and via its links to second-hand booksellers also to out-of-print such books. Many publishers and booksellers around the world advertise on the internet and offer online purchase facilities, and this provides a viable alternative revenue model to the conglomerates' model of mass sales (Anderson 2006). Of course, simply availability via the internet does not guarantee a wide readership, let alone a readership beyond a book's culture of origin.

Undeniably, then, books only enter the market of mass circulation beyond their culture of origin in a world language, whether originally so or in translation. Jérôme David (2011) situates the beginning of his book *Spectres de Goethe* in an airport where he enters into a conversation about world literature with a fellow traveler. When he asks his interlocutor what works the latter finds in the airport bookshop (the locale is not specified but we assume it to be somewhere in Europe – David himself teaches in Geneva), the latter responds that he sees works translated from English, French, and Portuguese, and apparently from the entire world. David's I-narrator, presumably David himself, replies that there are no works by Ivorians, Nigerians, Japanese, or Chinese, but that over the last thirty years (that is to say since the 1980s) the circulation of books has indeed become internationalized because of the internationalization of the publishing industry. In fact, he remarks, some books are now available in translation simultaneously with or even before publication in the original. To the traveler's remark that surely these are purely commercial products David acknowledges that this is true for some, but he points out that in airport bookshops one also finds books by Salman Rushdie, Paulo Coelho, David Lodge, Umberto Eco, Günter Grass, and José Saramago.

Two remarks seem apt here: David's noting the absence of authors from certain origins may have been correct in 2011 (though even then I doubt that Haruki Murakami would not have been present in translation in airport bookshops) but certainly does not apply any more in 2023. Second, and before going into specifics about what his interlocutor may find in such bookshops, David has asked him to look around and note what people are actually reading. One person is reading "un polar scandinave," another "le roman d'une femme écrivain américaine, prix Nobel de littérature" (David 2011: 10). As to the second author, the American Nobel Prize winner, the impact of international prizes such as the Nobel, but also the Man Booker, when it comes to boosting the worldwide sales of particular books or oeuvres, is the subject of James F. English's *The Economy of Prestige* (2005). Earlier, Richard Todd (1996) already looked at the Booker Prize from this perspective. For a very recent example consider the case of Abdulrazak Gurnah, whose works, regardless of repeatedly having been long- and shortlisted for British and US literary prizes, were mostly out of print and had seldom been translated before he was awarded the Nobel Prize in 2021, after which his works everywhere soared to the top of the charts. The Scandinavian police procedural is another story, and it is not for nothing that Steiner opened her 2012 and 2022 survey articles on the world literature market with a reference to what arguably has been *the* bestselling Nordic Noir, Stieg Larsson's Millennium trilogy.

As Walkowitz (2015) has argued, many contemporary writers purposefully write with an eye on translation, that is to say for their works to be translated. This goes for writers in English – Walkowitz's examples are J.K. Rowling and J.M Coetzee – but even more so for writers in other languages, for whom translation into English opens the door to the world – Walkowitz mentions Orhan Pamuk and Roberto Bolaño. These same authors often appeal to their international readership by situating their works within a very local context via geographical and historical references and the evocation of local color and events. With respect to postcolonial fiction Graham Huggan already in 2001 spoke of "the post-colonial exotic." In the context of the present chapter, it is not without importance that the subtitle to his book is "marketing the margins." For Walkowitz, authors such as Pamuk and Bolaño in their work integrate the issue of translation itself, via intertextual references or otherwise. Beyond this, though, Pamuk and Bolaño also appeal to a wider readership by their drawing on popular genre conventions, and first and foremost that of crime writing. Bolaño gained fame with *Los detectives salvajes* (1998; The Savage Detectives), a title that speaks for itself. Pamuk's *Benim Adım Kırmızı* (My Name is Red), published in the same year as Bolaño's best-seller, also has some traits of a detective story. With both these authors the relationship to the established genre of the detective story is nuanced, but we see that other established writers of "literary" prose increasingly turn to generic crime fiction. This is the case, for instance with John Banville, an Irish author who for his literary work has won numerous prizes, among which the James Tait Black, the Booker, and the Prince of Asturias, but who after authoring a historical detective novel set in turn-of-the-seventeenth-century Prague, a Philip Marlowe novel à la Raymond Chandler, and a set of novels featuring the Irish pathologist Quirke under the penname of Benjamin Black, most recently has been publishing his Detective Inspector Strafford and Pathologist Quirke detectives under his own name. The Sudanese-British Jamal Mahjoub in the late 1980s started out with literary novels, but as of 2012 has been writing detective novels using the pseudonym Parker Bilal. Or take William Boyd, who made his mark in the early 1980s with "colonial" novels such as *A Good Man in Africa* and *The Ice-Cream War* and later turned to what he calls "whole-life" novels in which he follows one character's entire life course. *Any Human Heart* (2002) is an exercise in the latter genre but also features Ian Fleming as a character. In 2012 Boyd wrote a James Bond novel, and in 2006 he ventured into the spy-thriller genre with *Restless*. Julian Barnes, repeatedly shortlisted for the Man Booker Prize and winner in 2011 with *The Sense of an Ending*, wrote crime novels under the penname Dan Kavanagh.

While there are other popular genres that generate large circulations – science fiction, adult phantasy, chicklit (Folie 2022), modern romance, horror – none can match the general appeal of crime fiction. The phenomenon has attracted considerable attention. Nilsson, Damrosch, and D'haen in 2017 edited *Crime Fiction as World Literature*. Particularly active in the field are Jesper Gulddal, Stewart King, and Alistair Rolls. In their 2022 *Cambridge Companion to World Crime Fiction* they posit that contemporary crime fiction "is, emphatically, a *global* phenomenon," and "the production of world crime fiction is transnational in the sense of involving a merger between internationally circulating tropes and literary traditions, which leads to the creation of new formats." The genre

> travels across borders with great ease in the form of licensed editions and translations, and readerships across the world display little hesitation with reading foreign crime fiction; indeed, the combination of familiar forms and unfamiliar, "exotic" content has become one of the major selling points of global crime fiction.
>
> (Gulddal and King 2022: 1)

A particularly important development over the recent few decades has been a direction away from the earlier hegemonic Anglo-American orientation of the genre in favor of "reciprocal forms of interaction as well as independent exchanges between non-Western crime literatures" (Gulddal and King 2022: 2). Their prime exhibit in this respect is Scandinavian crime fiction or socalled "Nordic Noir," which since the 1990s has emerged as a rival model to the Anglo one. The latter, by the way, is not just true for crime fiction proper but also for media productions in the genre (D'haen 2022). Scandinavian crime fiction receives a chapter by itself in Gulddal, King, and Rolls's *Companion*, as do other national, regional, or linguistic traditions: East Asian, South Asian, Arab, Sub-Saharan African, European, Iberian and Latin American, French. There are also chapters on women in global crime fiction, translation and circulation, the publishing industry, international crime fiction collections, and regional crime fiction. Yet, Gulddal and King start off their 2022 contribution to the *Routledge Companion to World Literature*, "one could say that world literature scholars have tended to ignore crime fiction, while crime fiction scholars have tended to avoid the world" (Gulddal and King 2022: 285). The foundational texts of world literature studies, also in its more recent avatar, they claim, have "privileged elite literature," and near-excluded "popular fiction" (Gulddal and King 2022: 285). Yet, they imply, crime fiction exemplarily lends itself to a world literature approach.

In an earlier publication, King (2014) discussed what a world literature approach to crime fiction might entail. He singles out Damrosch's statement in *What Is World Literature* (2003) that one of the functions world literature may serve is that of a window on specific cultures and societies. As an example he cites Jean Anderson, Carolina Miranda, and Barbara Pezzotti's 2012 edited volume *The Foreign in International Crime Fiction: Transcultural Representations* as proposing that "the proliferation of crime novels around the globe means that crime fiction could be considered 'a new form of travel writing,' albeit to places and situations the reader may never wish to experience firsthand" (King 2014: 14). The latter would account for the popularity of the Erlendur novels of Arnaldur Indriðason, set in Iceland, or of John Banville's *Snow* (2020), a Strafford and Quirke novel set in rural Ireland. But it also explains at least some of the appeal of television crime series set in out-of-the-way but picturesque places such as *Shetland* (2013–2019), based on the novels of Ann Cleeves; the western reaches of Iceland in *Trapped* (2016–2019); the not so picturesque country backwaters of the Spanish/Galician *O sabor das margaridas* (2019–2021); or the French *La Forêt* (2017), set in the French/Belgian Ardennes border region. Andrew Pepper and David Schmid, in their edited volume *Globalization and the State in Contemporary Crime Fiction: A World of Crime*, cite Clive James in *The New Yorker* as commenting that "in most of the crime novels coming out now, it's a matter not of what happens but of where. Essentially, they are guidebooks" (Pepper and Schmid 2016: 2). In some English-language remakes (such as those of Scandinavian noir works), this aspect is even heightened, as in Kenneth Branagh's remakes of the original Swedish series after the Wallander novels of Henning Mankell that feature, sometimes ad nauseam, "typically Nordic" vistas of deserted roads stretching endlessly away, looming forests, and lonely dwellings. As Michel Viegnes, Sylvie Jeanneret, and Lora Traglia argue in the volume they edited in 2020, what in French is called the "polar," or crime fiction more in general, moves between the national and the global "entre cultures nationales et mondialisation" (between national cultures and globalization).

Works of crime fiction and serials can also function as windows on the past – as illustrated for instance in an issue of *Clues* (40.1) that focuses on historical mysteries from Ukraine, Mexico, and China. Some recent European examples are series such as *Babylon Berlin* (2017–2020) or *Peaky Blinders* (2013–2021). Barbara Pezzotti in her book on Italian crime fiction, film, and television series argues that "historical crime fiction has in fact developed into the fastest growing type of crime fiction" and that "the success of crime narratives set in the near past speaks rather of the interest in making sense of the present by returning to its roots" (Pezzotti 2016: 3). Her book, then, "intends to examine the ways in which historical *giallo* novels, television series, and films have become a means to comment on and intervene in the social and political changes of the country" (Pezzotti 2016: 1). It is no exaggeration to say that today social critique, whether overt or underlying, is the rule rather than the exception in much crime fiction, film, and television or streaming service series, especially so in Europe, following the tradition established in the 1960s and 70s by Maj Sjöwall and Per Wahlöö with their Martin Beckman novels. King (2014: 15–16) mentions, for instance, how Katharina Hall (2013) focuses on how crime novels in various languages engage with the aftermath of Nazism. He notes how "transitional justice in postdictatorial societies" is a leading topic in the Argentinian Eduardo Sacheri's *La pregunta de sus ojos* (2005), subsequently turned into the award-winning movie *El secreto de sus ojos* (2009) and its American remake *Secret in Their Eyes* (2015), but he also cites Spanish, Finnish/Estonian, and German examples. In recent Catalonian crime fiction such as that by Vázquez Montalbán, King (2017) argues that the story of the crime doubles an underlying story having to do with Catalonia's past and particularly the memory of the Spanish Civil War but also reaching back further into the history of Catalonia's repeated defeats and incorporations by Castile, or "Spain."

More immediately topical, King (2017) also links violence to women to criminals associated with repressive centrist (and historically falangist) regimes and institutions as expressive of overall suppression and repression. In Stieg Larsson's Millennium Trilogy (2005–2007) Lisbeth Salander, one of the two protagonists, is sexually abused by the man who is supposed to be her guardian and the root of all crime is traced to the Nazi sympathies of an aristocratic, entrepreneurial family during World War II. The legacy of Nazism also plays a determining role in Donna Leon's debut novel *Death at La Fenice* (1992), Robert C. Wilson's *A Small Death in Lisbon* (1992), and Philip Kerr's Bernie Gunther series (1989–2019).

Other topical interests addressed in global crime fiction are the legacy of colonialism and continental migration due to political upheavals such as the Balkan civil wars after the break-up of Yugoslavia, with Serbs, Croats, and Bosnians moving to Europe's northern countries, as well as labor migration from East and Central Europe to Western/Northern Europe, with arms, drug, and human trafficking, as in Henning Mankell's novel *Villospår* (1995; Sidetracked). The murderers in Mankell's *Mördare utan ansikte* (1991; Faceless

Killers) are Polish criminals active in Sweden, and organized crime along ethnic lines is frequently featured in Swedish crime series. In *Dossier K* (2002), the Flemish author Jef Geeraerts pits his Antwerp detective duo Vincke and Verstuyft against Albanese drugs gangs. A related yet even more contemporary theme is that of intercontinental migration in the form of political refugees and their involvement with crime, whether as subjects of human trafficking, or as often involuntary participants in criminal activities. Such is the case, for instance, with a Syrian refugee in the Swedish/British television series *Young Wallander* (2020), and with another Syrian refugee who is pressed to turn police informant in the Flemish series *De 13 Geboden* (2018; The 13 Commandments). In fact, the plight of refugees, especially as victims of human traffickers, has become one of the most common themes of contemporary European crime fiction and media productions. It also forms the subject of Donna Leon's 2021 *Transient Desires*. In the Flemish/Dutch series *Grenslanders* (2019; Border Dwellers) a number of these themes come together in the figure of an African girl who after making her way clandestinely to Europe is forced into prostitution. Following Andrew Pepper and David Schmid's argument in their volume cited earlier, we can see human trafficking, international drug trafficking, financial border-crossing crimes, and many other kinds of crime as proof of the interconnectedness of the local and the global under the aegis of neoliberalism and globalization, where a crime, although perpetrated in a specific locale, is linked to wider, often international, movements involving economic, social, and political developments transcending the nation. This is the point Andrew Nestingen (2016) makes with respect to Scandinavian or Nordic noir in his contribution to Pepper and Schmid's volume, and particularly of his discussion of Mankell's Wallander series and Larsson's Millennium Trilogy. In practice, issues such as foregrounded by Pepper, Schmid, and Nestingen today have assumed a planetary dimension.

Although I have dwelled in some detail only on crime fiction as a "world" genre, pretty much the same analysis could be made with respect to the other popular genres I listed earlier. Steiner (2012 and 2022) refers to Stephenie Meyers's vampire novels, but we here may also think of J.K. Rowling's Harry Potter novels, Philip Pullman's His Dark Materials trilogy, or Nora Roberts's or Lucinda Riley's romance novels – examples are legion. Something they all share is what Jan Baetens (2018, 2022) calls "remediation": the repeated cross-over between fiction, visualization, novelization, and the marketing of concept objects and events. Baetens (Baetens and Frey 2014; Baetens, Frey, and Tabachnick 2018) has also repeatedly written on another highly popular genre with global reach: the graphic novel. A major difference, and why crime fiction in my opinion merits closer study in the context of contemporary world literature studies, is that works in these other genres are usually much less concerned with "planetary" matters than crime fiction.

In Chapter 9 I referred to Tihanov's use (2019) of the term "regime of relevance." In "Epilogue: A Fast-Forward to 'World Literature'" from his 2019 book on literary theory, Tihanov (2019: 175) invokes as one of the reasons for what he calls "the death of theory" that "the patrimony of literary theory is currently active within a regime of relevance that thinks literature through its market and entertainment value, with only residual calls of its previously highly treasured autonomy." The "interpretative framework" this regime of relevance has engendered, Tihanov calls "world literature," a term he associates with "a particular liberal Anglo-Saxon discourse grounded in assumptions of mobility, transparency, and a recontextualizing (but also decontextualizing) circulation that supports the free consumption and unrestricted comparison of literary artifacts" (2019: 175). However, he adds, "like so many other discourses of liberal persuasion, the discourse on world literature, too, often passes over its own premises in silence, leaving them insufficiently reflected upon, and at times even naturalizing them" (2019: 181). In fact, Tihanov's contention is that "we need to begin to understand the current Anglo-Saxon discourse of world literature, in which the legitimization of reading and analyzing literature in and through translation plays a pivotal role, as an echo of, and a late intervention in, a debate that begins in the early days of modern literary theory" (2019: 180) and specifically with the Russian Formalists. According to Tihanov (2019: 176), Viktor Shlovsky and Mikhail Bakhtin already in the interbellum developed ideas that come close to what he calls the "the non-Eurocentric and translation-friendly thrust of today's Anglo-Saxon academic programs in world literature." Tihanov sees especially Damrosch as following Shlovsky's lineage by insisting on "the legitimacy of working in translation" (2019: 182) and by

> concluding that studying [a literary work] in the languages of its socialization is more important than studying it in the language of its production, not least because this new priority restricts and undermines the monopoly of methodological nationalism in literary studies.
> (Tihanov 2019: 182)

Sarah Brouillette (2016) takes issue with a view of world literature that she sees as propagated most vocally by Simon During (2009), Emily Apter (2013), and the editors of the journal *n+1* in their 2014 editorial "World Lite," but that according to her has become almost commonplace. This view posits world literature as "an elite commodity" (Brouillette 2016: 93) that

> today tends to entail the production of a writing that translates local particularities into sameness and homogeneity, whether this translation occurs during the writing process – when a writer knowingly presents a place as an exotic paradise, for example … or writes in such a way that her work will be easily translated into several languages … – or after the act of writing has been completed and the work is acquired, marketed, purchased, and read.
> (Brouillette 2016: 95)

World literature, she contends, by now has commonly come to be understood as a "niche commercial category serving relatively elite consumers' desires to be exposed to exotic or simply unusual experiences or even just to have their biases confirmed" as these

> privileged consumers either read world literature in such a way that its contrapuntal or oppositional tendencies are effectively muted, or the work is from the get-go written in a style that is meant to allow for the accumulation of acclaim and prestige and little else.
> (Brouillette 2016: 95–96)

The works that fall under Brouillette's view of world literature would be those routinely assumed under the postcolonial label. Following the Warwick Research Collective's insights, however, she argues that, rather than "endlessly recounting the story of the commodification of cultural difference for elite consumers," what really matters to a materialist critique of world literature is "the recognition of the division of labour under capitalism and of the iniquitous and uneven nature of literary production and reception" (Brouillette 2016: 93). What Brouillette (2016: 101) calls for, then, is "a contemporary sociology of world literary production." This would entail looking into the actual locales and processes of book production: editorial offices, literary agents, contract agreements, etc. – what Brouillette (2016: 102) calls "brand equity." It would also take into consideration issues of class as "a crucial restriction on access to literary experiences" (Brouillette 2016: 102). An autobiographical reflection on this is Mark Hodkinson (2022) who autobiographically reflects on how "literature" was an alien territory for an English working-class boy in the second half of the twentieth century. Re-iterating a point she earlier already made (2014), Brouillette (2016: 103) argues that contemporary literary authors are aware that their work, even if "highly critical of capitalism," is still subject to "consecration within the market." Therefore, Brouillette (2016: 104) concludes, "we might understand the contemporary moment of world literature" as "a moment of purportedly global circulation that is really a moment of uneven distribution of the agency and ability to author and of uneven access to reading materials and the means of publication."

A comparable critique of Apter is voiced by Pieter Vermeulen (2016: 80) when he says that

> with no Untranslatable to be invested with political power because it refuses to count, literary studies in the age of market saturation need to find ways to describe literature's engagement with – rather than celebrate its illusory disengagement from – the market.

Vermeulen (2016) and Brouillette (2016), then, both take issue with Apter's defense of untranslatability as resistance to the supposed homogenization of literary works as world literature through translation into English – instead, they argue, and especially Brouillette does so, Apter's complaint is simply part of established discourse in academic circles (and my argument would be especially so in US academic circles which often are far removed from reality – that is to say the economic reality of "the common man") and completely by-passes what is really at issue in talking about world literature: the uneven access to writing and authorship, and to reading, and I take it that this applies both to inequalities pertaining to Western and non-Western, "First" and "Third" World, but also to class differences in the Western world itself. In other words, their argument is that both the proponents of world literature and the opponents, but perhaps even more so the latter than the former, indulge in word games for their own elite circles, veiling or masking the underlying economic relations.

Christine Emmett (2022: 2) applies the Warwick Research Collective methodology to explain what she calls forms of "narratorial disidentification," in which "coldness and distance are encoded into the narration or focalisation of a novel, ultimately serving to undermine readerly identification," in South African fiction. This narratorial stance issues from the blatant inequality of South African society, where the privileged position of the writer as inevitably a member of the cultured elite leads to ambiguity as to their authority to legitimately represent her or his society. These "experiences of social bifurcation in semi-peripheral locations" then "are translated into this form of narrative coldness which seeks to undermine readerly identification and emphasize externality." While she specifically focuses on South African fiction, where she finds (Emmett 2022: 3) that "the form traverses both apartheid-era texts, such as Nadine Gordimer's *Late Bourgeois World* (1966), and postapartheid texts, such as Zoë Wicomb's *Playing in the Light* (2006) and Achmat Dangor's *Bitter Fruit* (2001), so that the apartheid-postapartheid distinction falls away with the form's diffusion," she also identifies this particular narratorial stance in Albert Camus' *L'Etranger* (The Stranger), and sees it as pertinent for other semi-peripheral literatures under comparable social conditions. "The point about narratorial disidentification," she insists, "is not that the characters who frame these narratives are particularly deficient, but rather that the realist form of the novel, with its normative structure of identification, cannot capture the contradictory and constrained agency which attends inequality" (Emmet 2022: 9).

Marko Juvan (2022: 5) also situates his approach to world literature in the context of the Warwick Research Collective's framework:

> The literary world-system, which arises from and is dependent on and responsive to the modern world-system of capitalism … channels inter-literary exchange in a way that is homologous to the economic inequality between the centers, which are capable of accumulating surplus value, and the peripheries, which enable the global dominance of the centers by providing the market, labor, and resources for the goods produced or distributed by the centers.

Further drawing on Said (1984 [1983]), Casanova (2005), Eric Hayot (2011, 2012a, 2012b), Moretti (2013a), and Cheah (2016), Juvan (2022: 20) arrives at the conclusion that in a world that is "one but unequal" or

> combined but unequal ... agencies of transnational literary circulation often do not perceive authors who appear universal from a particular internal perspective at all, unless the perspective in question is located in a dominant literary system or makes its way into it.

Liliana Weinberg (2016) makes a similar point when she discusses the situation of present-day Latin American literature in the world literary market.

Juvan's conclusion in the final analysis comes down to who has the authority to "make" world literature. For WReC and its sympathizers this clearly is the market, which is under the sway of unequal conditions in the literary as in all other fields. In their discussion of the institutions regulating the literary market, though, Juvan, WReC, and most other commentators on world literature are still sticking to the traditional agents or agencies: publishers, editors, translators, literary agents, anthologies, etc. A different perspective is offered by Sandra Ponzanesi (2021). For Ponzanesi,

> the making of world literature is not left only to the mechanisms of circulation, exchange, and reception but also entails the integration of a cosmopolitan dimension that aspires to a world without borders, which is both a part of new imaginaries and of a politics of contestation.
> (Ponzanesi 2021: 849)

The latter is particularly pertinent for Ponzanesi who is specifically interested in what she (2021: 848) calls the "postcolonial cultural industry." Here she sees an important role to play for "digital technologies that manage to compress space and time and create forms of connectivity which were not possible before, reconfiguring diasporas into virtual communities and offering new strategies for approaching mobility, migration, and networks," all aspects, she says, that "are also central to the debates of world literature" (Ponzanesi 2021: 849). Ponzanesi sees digital technology "not as a tool that facilitates or accelerates the making and distributing of literature but as a narrative strategy that can achieve a worlding effect across boundaries and genres" (Ponzanesi 2021: 860).

Amélie Hurkens (2022) directly invokes the authority of the internet. As her "abstract" reads:

> The marketing of world literature today is marked by the larger migration of literary culture to Web 2.0. This has gone hand in hand with a reconsignment of influence of orthodox authorities, from established reviewing organs to awards, to the amateur readers congregating on social media platforms, first and foremost on Goodreads, the world's

largest online community for circulating literary recommendations and socialization ... the reconsignment of influence is concluded to be regulated by the algorithmic rules of Goodreads and its proprietary platform, Amazon.com.

(Hurkens 2022: 449)

Hurkens (2022: 450) argues that the time when the reader played a passive role in "making a book" has passed, quoting Simone Murray (2019) that

> digital processes and platforms undeniably infiltrate the global book industry at every stage: from production (digital files, eBook rights, print-on-demand, online self-publishing, Wattpad, crowdfunded publishing), through circulation (online book retailing, authorial social media use, publisher search-engine optimisation, book trailers, blog tours, audiobooks), to consumption (reader reviews, fan fiction, bookish social networking, amateur booktubing, bookstagramming).

Instead, readers, or more generally "downstream" producers and consumers of literature now actively intervene in the market in a "massive multiplayer online role-playing game (MMORPG)." The most important and most recent development for Hurkens (2022: 451) is "the impingement of the reader on the most hallowed process of the 'making of world literature', that is, consecration." The latter happens through several online possibilities, but mostly through Goodreads, a social media platform on which readers can exchange commentaries, evaluations, and recommendations, and perhaps most importantly, rate books. At the same time, Goodreads gives its parent company Amazon unique insight into readers' preferences and tastes, and thus helps it become even more performant as an online seller of books (and much else!). For one thing, books can now be promoted with quotes from Goodreads evaluations appealing to readers probably or presumably sharing the same tastes in literature. But social media platforms such as Goodreads also offer opportunities for influencers to insert themselves into the conversation. If they grow a substantial following this in turn serves to promote books of their choice, which in turn provides valuable information for book-producing and selling companies, foremost again Amazon – and so the machine grinds on.

Conclusion

- Interest in the materialities of nature – ecocriticism – and of texts – the circulation of books, as material artefacts or generic, arose only fairly recently, actually more or less on a par with the renewed interest in world literature.
- Whereas the foundational texts of the renewed study of world literature focus almost exclusively on what are deemed to be texts of "literary" quality, more recent approaches emphasize other aspects, whether the

ecological interest vested in hitherto neglected works or the global reach of popular genres.
- Works foregrounding ecological issues and in popular genres are actually more "worldly" than literarily higher-appreciated works in that they either touch upon more immediately life-related concerns of humanity and the planet or circulate in greater numbers and reach more people, often via media spin-offs.
- Both materialist ecocriticism and ditto book or text history stress that world literature is not a level playing field.
- Digital technologies and changes in the cultural industries also affect world literature.

Notes

1 https://www.press.jhu.edu/journals/book-history; accessed 01 September 2023.
2 https://sharpweb.org/about/sharps-history/; accessed 01 September 2023.

Bibliography

Adam, Ian and Helen Tiffin (eds) (1991) *Past the Last Post: Theorizing Post-Colonialism and Post-Modernism*. London: Harvester/Wheatsheaf.
Adorno, Theodor W. (2003) [1966] *Negative Dialektik*. Frankfurt: Suhrkamp.
Adorno, Theodor W. (1974) "Ist die Kunst heiter?" In *Noten zur Literatur IV*. Frankfurt a.m.: Surhrkamp, 147–157.
Adorno, Theodor (1991a) "The Schema of Mass Culture." In *The Culture Industry: Selected Essays on Mass Culture*. London: Routledge, 61–97. (Originally "Das Schema der Massenkultur," in Theodor Adorno and Max Horkheimer [1944] *Dialektik der Aufklärung [Dialectic of Enlightenment]*.)
Adorno, Theodor (1991b) "Culture Industry Reconsidered." In *The Culture Industry: Selected Essays on Mass Culture*. London: Routledge, 98–106. (Originally transl. by Anson G. Rabinbach in *New German Critique* 6 [Fall 1975]: 12–19, from Theodor W. Adorno, *Ohne Leitbild*, Frankfurt am Main: Suhrkamp, 1967.)
Adorno, Theodor W. and Max Horkheimer (1988) [1944] *Dialektik der Aufklärung*. Frankfurt: Fischer.
Ahmad, Aijaz (1992) *In Theory: Classes, Nations, Literatures*. London: Verso.
Ahmed, Siraj (2018) *Archaeology of Babel: The Colonial Foundation of the Humanities*. Redwood City: Stanford University Press.
Albers, Frank (2019) "Orpheus in the Trenches: Modes of Translation in Stefan Hertmans' *War and Turpentine*." In Theo D'haen (ed.) *Dutch and Flemish Literature as World Literature*. New York, London, etc.: Bloomsbury Academic, 284–294.
Aldridge, Owen A. (1986) *The Reemergence of World Literature*. Cranbury, NJ: Associated University Presses.
Allan, Michael (2016) *In the Shadow of World Literature: Sites of Reading in Colonial Egypt*. Princeton: Princeton University Press.
Anderson, Benedict (1998) *The Spectre of Comparison: Nationalism, Southeast Asia, and the World*. London: Verso.
Anderson, Chris (2006) *The Long Tail: Why the Future of Business is Selling Less of More*. New York: Hyperion.
Andersen, Tore Rye (2011) *Den nye amerikanske roman* [The New American Novel]. Aarhus Universitetsforlag/Aarhus University Press.
Andreasen, B., M. Jørgensen, S.E. Larsen and D. Ringgaard (2009) *litteraturDK*. Copenhagen: Lindhardt & Ringhof.

Antonelli, Roberto, Maria Serena Sapegno, Gioia Paradisi and Tullio De Mauro (eds) (2012) *Letteratura europea. Il canone*. Rome: Sapienza Università di Roma Dipartimento di studi europei americani e interculturali.
Appiah, Kwame Anthony (1991) "Is the Post- in Postmodernism the Post- in Post-Colonial?" In *Critical Inquiry* 17. 2 (Winter): 336–357.
Appiah, Kwame Anthony (2006) *Cosmopolitanism: Ethics in a World of Strangers*. New York and London: W.W. Norton & Company.
Apter, Emily (1995) "Comparative Exile: Competing Margins in the History of Comparative Literature." In Charles Bernheimer (ed.) *Comparative Literature in the Age of Multiculturalism*. Baltimore and London: The Johns Hopkins University Press, 86–96.
Apter, Emily (2001) "On Translation in a Global Market." *Public Culture* 13. 1: 1–12.
Apter, Emily (2003) "Global *Translatio*: The 'Invention' of Comparative Literature, Istanbul, 1933." In *Critical Inquiry* 29: 253–281.
Apter, Emily (2006a) "'Je ne crois pas beaucoup a la littérature comparée'." In Haun Saussy (ed.) *Comparative Literature in an Age of Globalization*. Baltimore: Johns Hopkins University Press, 54–62.
Apter, Emily (2006b) *The Translation Zone: A New Comparative Literature*. Princeton and Oxford: Princeton University Press.
Apter, Emily (2008) "Untranslatables: A World System." In *New Literary History* 39. 3: 581–598.
Apter, Emily (2013) *Against World Literature: On the Politics of Untranslatability*. London and New York: Verso.
Arac, Jonathan (2002) "Anglo-Globalism?" In *New Left Review* 16 (July–August): 35–45.
Arac, Jonathan (2004) "Global and Babel: Two Perspectives on Language in American Literature." In *ESQ* 50. 1–3: 94–119.
Arac, Jonathan (2007) "Babel and Vernacular in an Empire of Immigrants: Howells and the Languages of American Fiction." In *boundary 2* 34. 2: 1–20.
Arac, Jonathan (2008) "Commentary: Literary History in a Global Age." In *New Literary History* 39. 3: 747–760.
Arbor Aldea, Mariña (ed.) (2012) *El canon de la literatura europea*. Santiago de Compostela: Servizo de Publicacións da Universidade de Santiago de Compostela.
Arnold, Matthew (1978) [1869] *Culture and Anarchy*. Cambridge: Cambridge University Press.
Assmann, Aleida (2010) "Re-Framing Memory: Between Individual and Collective Forms of Constructing the Past." In Karin Tilmans, Frank van Vree and Jay Winter (eds) *Performing the Past: Memory, History, and Identity in Modern Europe*. Amsterdam: Amsterdam University Press, 35–50.
Auerbach, Erich (1953) *Mimesis: The Representation of Reality in Western Literature*. Transl. Willard Trask. Princeton: Princeton University Press.
Auerbach, Erich (1969) [1952] "Philology and *Weltliteratur*." Transl. Maire and Edward Said. In *The Centennial Review* 13. 1: 1–17.
Auerbach, Erich (2009) [1952] "Philology and *Weltliteratur*." In David Damrosch, Natalie Melas and Mbongiseni Buthelezi (eds) *The Princeton Sourcebook in Comparative Literature*. Princeton: Princeton University Press, 125–138.
Azadibougar, Omid (2020) *World Literature and Hedayat's Poetics of Modernity*. Singapore: Palgrave Macmillan.
Bachner, Andrea (2021) "Transregional Critique and the Challenge of Comparison: Between Latin America and China." In Debjani Ganguly (ed.) *The Cambridge History of World Literature*, Volume II. Cambridge: Cambridge University Press, 789–803.

Baetens, Jan (2018) *Novelization: From Film to Novel.* Columbus: The Ohio State University Press.

Baetens, Jan (2022) "World Literature and Popular Literature: The Remediated Word." In Theo D'haen, David Damrosch and Djelal Kadir (eds) *The Routledge Companion to World Literature.* Second Edition. London and New York: Routledge, 277–284.

Baetens, Jan and Hugo Frey (2014) *The Graphic Novel.* Cambridge: Cambridge University Press.

Baetens, Jan, Hugo Frey and Stephen Ely Tabachnick (2018) *The Cambridge History of the Graphic Novel.* Cambridge: Cambridge University Press.

Baggesgaard, Mads Anders (2016) *Nye franske verdener* [French New Worlds]. Aarhus: Aarhus Universitetsforlag/Aarhus University Press.

Bahun, Sanja (2012) "The Politics of World Literature." In Theo D'haen, David Damrosch and Djelal Kadir (eds) *The Routledge Companion to World Literature.* London: Routledge, 373–382.

Bahun, Sanja (2022) "The Politics of World Literature." In Theo D'haen, David Damrosch and Djelal Kadir (eds) *The Routledge Companion to World Literature.* Second Edition. London: Routledge, 320–328.

Baldensperger, Fernand (1927) "Georg Brandes (1842–1927)." In *Revue de littérature comparée* 7: 368–371.

Balkan, Stacey and Swaralipi Nandi (2021) *Oil Fictions: World Literature and Our Contemporary Petrosphere.* University Park, Penn.: The Pennsylvania State University Press.

Bartosch, Roman (2019) *Literature, Pedagogy, and Climate Change: Text Models for a Transcultural Ecology.* Cham: Palgrave Macmillan.

Bassel, Naftoli and Ilana Gomel (1991) "National Literature and Interliterary System." In *Poetics Today* 12. 4: 773–779.

Bassnett-McGuire, Susan (1980) *Translation Studies.* London and New York: Methuen.

Bassnett, Susan (1993) *Comparative Literature: A Critical Introduction.* Oxford: Blackwell.

Bassnett, Susan (2006) "Reflections on Comparative Literature in the Twenty-First Century." In *Comparative Critical Studies* 3. 1–2: 3–11.

Bassnett, Susan and André Lefevere (1992) *Translation, History and Culture.* London: Pinter.

Bassnett, Susan and Harish Trivedi (eds) (1999) *Post-Colonial Translation: Theory and Practice.* London: Routledge.

Batts, Michael S. (1993) *A History of Histories of German Literature, 1835–1914.* Montreal: McGill-Queen's University Press.

Beck, Ulrich (2006) *Cosmopolitan Vision.* Cambridge: Polity Press.

Beebee, Thomas O. (2016) *German Literature as World Literature.* New York and London: Bloomsbury.

Beecroft, Alexander (2008) "World Literature Without a Hyphen: Towards a Typology of Literary Systems." In *New Left Review* 54: 87–100.

Beecroft, Alexander (2010) *Authorship and Cultural Identity in Early Greece and China: Patterns of Literary Circulation.* Cambridge and New York: Cambridge University Press.

Beecroft, Alexander (2015) *An Ecology of World Literature: From Antiquity to the Present Day.* London and New York: Verso.

Benjamin, Walter (1982) [1940] "Theses on the Philosophy of History." In *Illuminations*, edited and with an introduction by Hannah Arendt, translated by Harry Zohn. London: Fontana/Collins.

Benjamin, Walter (2000) [1968, 1923] "The Task of the Translator." Transl. Harry Zohn. In Lawrence Venuti (ed.) *The Translation Studies Reader*. London and New York: Routledge, 15–25.

Berczik, Árpád (1963) "Eine ungarische Konzeption der Weltliteratur. (Hugo v. Meltzls vergleichende Literaturtheorie)." In István Sőtér (ed.) *La Littérature comparée en Europe orientale*. Budapest: Akadémiai, 287–294.

Berczik, Árpád (1972) "Die ersten ungarischen Verkünder der Weltliteratur und der vergleichenden Literaturwissenschaft." In *Zagadnienia rodzajw literackich* 10. 112: 156–173.

Bergthaller, Hannes (2017) "Cli-Fi and Petrofiction: Questioning Genre in the Anthropocene." In *Amerikastudien / American Studies* 62. 1: 120–125.

Berman, Antoine (1984) *L'Épreuve de l'étranger: Culture et traduction dans l'Allemagne romantique*. Paris: Gallimard. (Engl. transl. S. Heyvaert. *The Experience of the Foreign: Culture and Translation in Romantic Germany*. Albany, NY: State University of New York Press, 1992.)

Bernheimer, Charles (ed.) (1995) *Comparative Literature in the Age of Multiculturalism*. Baltimore and London: The Johns Hopkins University Press.

Bertens, Hans (1986) "The Postmodern Weltanschauung and its Relation with Modernism: An Introductory Survey." In Douwe Fokkema and Hans Bertens (eds) *Approaching Postmodernism*. Amsterdam and Philadelphia: John Benjamins, 9–51.

Bertens, Hans (1991) "Postmodern Cultures." In Edmund J. Smyth (ed.) *Postmodernism and Contemporary Fiction*. London: Batsford, 123–137.

Bertens, Hans (1994) *The Idea of the Postmodern: A History*. London and New York: Routledge.

Bertens, Hans and Douwe Fokkema (eds) (1997) *International Postmodernism: Theory and Practice*. A Comparative History of Literatures in European Languages Sponsored by the International Comparative Literature Association, Vol. XI, Amsterdam and Philadelphia: John Benjamins.

Bessière, Jean and Jean-Marc Moura (eds) (1999) *Littératures postcoloniales et representations de l'ailleurs. Afrique, Caraïbes, Canada*. Paris: Honoré Champion.

Bessière, Jean and Jean-Marc Moura (eds) (2001) *Francophonie et postcolonialisme*. Paris: Honoré Champion.

Bhabha, Homi K. (1994a) "Introduction: Locations of Culture." In *The Location of Culture*. London and New York: Routledge, 1–18.

Bhabha, Homi K. (1994b) "The Postcolonial and the Postmodern: The Question of Agency." In *The Location of Culture*. London and New York: Routledge, 171–197.

Bhabha, Homi K. (1994c) "How Newness Enters the World: Postmodern Pace, Postcolonial Times and the Trials of Cultural Translation." In *The Location of Culture*. London and New York: Routledge, 212–235.

Bhattacharya, Baidik (2016) "On Comparatism in the Colony." In *Critical Inquiry* 42. 3: 677–711.

Bhattacharya, Baidik (2018) *Postcolonial Writing in the Era of World Literature: Texts, Territories, Globalizations*. London and New York: Routledge.

Bhattacharya, Baidik (2022) "Postcolonialism and World Literature." In Theo D'haen, David Damrosch and Djelal Kadir (eds) *The Routledge Companion to World Literature*. Second Edition. London and New York: Routledge, 165–175.

Birla, Ritu (2010) "Postcolonial Studies: Now That's History." In *Can the Subaltern Speak? Reflections on the History of an Idea*. New York: Columbia University Press, 87–99.

Birus, Hendrik (2000) "The Goethean Concept of World Literature and Comparative Literature." In *CLCWeb* 2. 4: Article 7. http://docs.lib.purdue.edu/clcweb/vol2/iss4/7 (accessed 3 January 2011).

Bleicher, Thomas (1979) "Novalis und die Idee der Weltliteratur." In *Arcadia* 14. 3: 254–270.

Bloom, Allan (1987) *The Closing of the American Mind: How Higher Education Has Failed Democracy and Impoverished the Souls of Today's Students*. New York: Simon and Schuster.

Boehmer, Elleke (2014) "The World and the Postcolonial." In *European Review* 22. 2: 299–308.

Boehmer, Elleke (2018) *Postcolonial Poetics: 21st-Century Critical Readings*. Cham, Switzerland: Springer International Publishing/Palgrave Macmillan.

Boldrini, Lucia (2006) "Comparative Literature in the Twenty-First Century: A View from Europe and the UK." In *Comparative Critical Studies* 3. 1–2: 13–23.

Bongie, Chris (2008) *Friends and Enemies: The Scribal Politics of Post/Colonial Literature*. Liverpool: Liverpool University Press.

Borges, Jorge Luis (2000) "The Argentine Writer and Tradition." In *Jorge Luis Borges: The Total Library – Non-Fiction, 1922–1986*. Edited by Eliot Weinberger. London: Allen Lane – The Penguin Press, 421–427.

Bourdieu, Pierre (1992) *Les règles de l'art*. Paris: Seuil.

Boyle, Nicholas (1991–2000) *Goethe*. 2 vols. Oxford: Oxford University Press.

Brandes, Georg (1899–1910) *Samlede Skrifter*. Copenhagen: Gyldendal.

Brandes, Georg (1902) [1899] "Verdenslitteratur." *Samlede Skrifter* 12. København: Gyldendal, 23–28. Engl. transl. http://global.wisc.edu/worldlit/readings/brandes-worldliteraturePdf (accessed 18 August 2010).

Brandes, Georg (2009) [1899] "World Literature." In David Damrosch, Natalie Melas and Mbongiseni Buthelezi (eds) *The Princeton Sourcebook in Comparative Literature*. Princeton: Princeton University Press, 61–66.

Braz, Albert (2016) "The Uneven World of Letters: Textual Migration, Translation, and World Literature." In *Neohelicon* 43: 577–589.

Brennan, Timothy (1997) *At Home in the World: Cosmopolitanism Now*. Cambridge MA and London: Harvard University Press.

Brennan, Timothy (2018) "Cosmopolitanism and World Literature." In Ben Etherington and Jarad Zimbler (eds) *The Cambridge Companion to World Literature*. Cambridge: Cambridge University Press, 23–36.

Brouillette, Sarah (2014) *Literature and the Creative Economy*. Redwood City: Stanford University Press.

Brouillette, Sarah (2016) "World Literature and Market Dynamics." In Stefan Helgesson and Pieter Vermeulen (eds) *Institutions of World Literature: Writing, Translation, Markets*. London and New York: Routledge, 93–106.

Brown, Calvin S. (1953) "Debased Standards in World Literature." In *Yearbook of Comparative and General Literature* 2: 10–14.

Brown, Nicholas (2001) "The Eidaesthetic Itinerary: Notes on the Geopolitical Movement of the Literary Absolute." In *The South Atlantic Quarterly* 100. 3: 829–851.

Brunetière, Ferdinand (1973) [1900] "European Literature." In Hans-Joachim Schulz and Philip H. Rhein (eds) *Comparative Literature: The Early Years*. Chapel Hill, NC: The University of North Carolina Press, 157–182.

Buck, Philo M., Jr (ed.) (1934) *An Anthology of World Literature*. New York: Macmillan.
Buell, Lawrence (1995) *The Environmental Imagination: Thoreau, Nature Writing, and the Formation of American Culture*. Cambridge, Mass.: Harvard University Press.
Buescu, Helena (2012) "The Republic of Letters and the World Republic of Letters." In Theo D'haen, David Damrosch and Djelal Kadir (eds) *The Routledge Companion to World Literature*. London: Routledge, 126–135.
Buescu, Helena (2013) *Experiência do Incomun e Boa Vizinhança. Literatura Comparada e Literatura-Mundo*. Porto: Porto Editora.
Buescu, Helena (2021) "Comparative World Literature and Worlds in Portuguese." In Debjani Ganguly (ed.) *The Cambridge History of World Literature* Volume I. Cambridge: Cambridge University Press, 310–325.
Buescu, Helena C. and João Ferreira Duarte (2007) "Communicating Voices: Herberto Helder's Experiments in Cross-Cultural Poetry." In *Forum for Modern Language Studies* 4. 3: 173–186.
Buescu, Helena Carvalhão and Simão Valente (2022) "Comparative World Literatures in Portuguese." In Theo D'haen, David Damrosch and Djelal Kadir (eds) *The Routledge Companion to World Literature*. Second Edition. London and New York: Routledge, 379–387.
Buescu, Helena Carvalhão, Cristina Almeida Ribeiro and Maria Graciete Silva (eds) (2012) *Un Cânone Literário para a Europa*. Lisbon: Centro de Estudos Comparatistas/Húmus.
Buescu, Helena Carvalhão, et al. (eds) (2018–2020) *Literatura-Mundo Comparada: Perspectivas em Português*. 6 vols. Lisbon: Tinta-de-China.
Bystrom, Kerry and Joseph R. Slaughter (eds) (2018) *The Global South Atlantic*. New York: Fordham University Press.
Campbell, Alexandra and Michael Paye (2020) "Water Enclosure and World-Literature: New Perspectives on Hydro-Power and World-Ecology." In *Humanities* 9: 106 (Web).
Campbell, Chris and Michael Niblett (eds) (2016) *The Caribbean: Aesthetics, World-Ecology, Politics*. Liverpool: Liverpool University Press.
Campos, Haroldo de (1981) *Deus e o Diabo no Fausto de Goethe*. São Paulo: Perspective.
Candido, Antonio (1965) *Literatura e sociedade: estudos de teoria e história literária*. São Paulo: Companhia Editora Nacional.
Candido, Antonio (1975) *Formação da literatura brasileira*. São Paulo: Editora da Universidade de São Paulo.
Candido, Antonio (1993) *O discurso e a cidade*. São Paulo: Duas Cidades.
Cao, Shunqing (2013) *The Variation Theory of Comparative Literature*. Heidelberg: Springer.
Carpentier, Alejo (1967) "De lo real maravilloso americano." In *Tientos y diferencias*. Montevideo: Arca, 102–120.
Carré, Jean-Marie (2009) [1951] "Preface to *La Littérature comparée*." In David Damrosch, Natalie Melas and Mbongiseni Buthelezi (eds) *The Princeton Sourcebook in Comparative Literature*. Princeton: Princeton University Press, 158–160.
Carrière, Moritz (1884) *Die Poesie. Ihr Wesen und ihre Formen mit Grundzügen der vergleichenden Literaturgeschichte*. Leipzig. (Second revised edition of *Das Wesen und die Formen der Poesie*, 1854.)
Carruthers, David V. (2008) "Introduction: Popular Environmentalism and Social Justice in Latin America." In David V. Carruthers (ed.) *Environmental Justice in Latin America: Problems, Promise, and Practice*. Cambridge, Mass.: MIT Press, 1–22.

Carvalhal, Tania Franco (ed.) (1997) *Comparative Literature Worldwide: Issues and Methods*. Porto Alegre: L&Pm Editores.
Casanova, Pascale (1999) *La République mondiale des lettres*. Paris: Seuil.
Casanova, Pascale (2004) *The World Republic of Letters*. Transl. M. DeBevoise. Cambridge, MA: Harvard University Press.
Casanova, Pascale (2005) "Literature as a World." In *New Left Review* 31: 71–90.
Cassin, Barbara (2004) *Vocabulaire européen des philosophies: Dictionnaire des intraduisibles*. Paris: Seuil.
Cassin, Barbara, Emily Apter, Jacques Lezra and Michael Wood (2014) *Dictionary of Untranslatables: A Philosophical Lexicon*. Princeton: Princeton University Press.
Catford, J.C. (1965) *A Linguistic Theory of Translation: An Essay in Applied Linguistics*. London: Oxford University Press.
Chakrabarty, Dipesh (2000) *Provincializing Europe: Postcolonial Thought and Historical Difference*. Princeton and Oxford: Princeton University Press.
Chartier, Roger (1994) *The Order of Books: Readers, Authors, and Libraries in Europe Between the 14th and 18th Centuries*. Redwood City: Stanford University Press.
Chasles, Philarète (1973) [1835] "Foreign Literature Compared." In Hans-Joachim Schulz and Philip H. Rhein (eds) *Comparative Literature: The Early Years*. Chapel Hill, NC: The University of North Carolina Press, 16–37.
Chaudhuri, Rosinka (2021) "Viśvasāhitya: Rabindranath Tagore's Idea of World Literature." In Debjani Ganguly (ed.) *The Cambridge History of World Literature*, Volume I. Cambridge: Cambridge University Press, 261–278.
Cheah, Pheng (2009) "The Material World of Comparison." In *New Literary History* 40. 3: 525–545.
Cheah, Pheng (2014) "World against Globe: Toward a Normative Conception of World Literature." In *New Literary History* 45. 3: 303–329.
Cheah, Pheng (2016) *What Is a World? On Postcolonial Literature as World Literature*. Durham: Duke University Press.
Cheah, Pheng and Bruce Robbins (eds) (1998) *Cosmopolitics: Thinking and Feeling beyond the Nation*. Minneapolis: University of Minnesota Press.
Chen, Lizhen and David Damrosch (2020) "Reconsidering Chinese Literature and World Literature: An Interview with David Damrosch." https://wgyxy.hznu.edu.cn/upload/resources/file/2020/09/25/7601479.pdf.
Chen, Xiaoming and Ziqiang Gong (2018) "Sinologism: A New Critical Perspective." In *Contemporary Chinese Thought* 49. 1: 27–35.
Chia, Caroline and Tom Hoogervorst (eds) (2021) *Sinophone Southeast Asia: Sinitic Voices across the Southern Seas*. Leiden and Boston: Brill.
Chinweizu, Ibekwe (1987) *Decolonizing the African Mind*. Lagos: Pero Press.
Chinweizu, Ibekwe, Onwuchekwa Jemie and Ihechukwu Madubuike (1980) *Toward the Decolonization of African Literature*. London and Boston: KPI Limited.
Chiu, Kuei-fen and Yingjin Zhang (eds) (2022) *The Making of Chinese-Sinophone Literatures as World Literature*. Hong Kong: Hong Kong University Press.
Chow, Rey (2004) "The Old/New Question of Comparison in Literary Studies: A Post-European Perspective." In *ELH* 71. 2: 289–311.
Christy, Arthur E. and Henry H. Wells (eds) (1947) *World Literature: An Anthology of Human Experience*. New York: American Book Company.
Ciocca, Rosella and Neelam Srivastava (eds) (2017) *Indian Literature and the World*. London: Palgrave Macmillan.

Clark, Katerina (2021) *Eurasia Without Borders: The Dream of a Leftist Literary Commons 1919–1943*. Cambridge, MA: Harvard University Press.
Clark, Kenneth (1972) [1953] *The Nude: A Study in Ideal Form*. Princeton: Princeton University Press.
Cleary, Joe (2021) *Modernism, Empire, World Literature*. Cambridge: Cambridge University Press.
Coletti, Vittorio (2011) *Romanzo mondo: La Letteratura nel villaggio globale*. Bologna: IL Mulino.
Combe, Dominique (2010) "Littératures francophones, littérature-monde en français." In *Modern & Contemporary France* 18. 2: 231–249.
Cooppan, Vilashini (2004) "Ghosts in The Disciplinary Machine: The Uncanny Life of World Literature." In *Comparative Literature Studies* 41. 1: 10–36.
Corstius, J.C. Brandt (1963) "Writing Histories of World Literature." In *Yearbook of Comparative and General Literature* 12: 5–14.
Coulombe, Diane and William L. Roberts (2001) "The French-as-a-Second-Language Learning Experience of Anglophone and Allophone University Students." In *Research on Immigration and Integration in the Metropolis Working Paper Series*01–02, Vancouver Centre of Excellence.
Coutinho, Eduardo (ed.) (2018) *Brazilian Literature as World Literature*. London: Bloomsbury.
Crosby, Alfred (2003) [1972] *The Columbian Exchange: Biological and Cultural Consequences of 1492*. Westport: Praeger.
Culler, Jonathan (2006) "Whither Comparative Literature?" In *Comparative Critical Studies* 3. 1–2: 85–97.
Culler, Jonathan (2007) *The Literary in Theory*. Redwood City: Stanford University Press.
Curtius, Ernst Robert (1948) *Europäische Literatur und Lateinisches Mittelalter*. Bern: A. Francke AG Verlag.
Curtius, Ernst Robert (1953) *European Literature and the Latin Middle Ages*. Transl. Willard Trask. Princeton: Princeton University Press.
Curtius, Ernst Robert (1973) *Essays on European Literature*. Transl. Michael Kowal. Princeton: Princeton University Press.
Dabashi, Hamid (2019) *The Shahnameh: The Persian Epic as World Literature*. New York: Columbia University Press.
Dainotto, Roberto (2007) *Europe (in Theory)*. Durham NC and London: Duke University Press.
Damrosch, David (2003) *What Is World Literature?* Princeton and Oxford: Princeton University Press.
Damrosch, David (2004) "From the Old World to the Whole World." In Jeffrey R. Di Leo (ed.) *On Anthologies: Politics and Pedagogy*. Lincoln and London: University of Nebraska Press, 31–46.
Damrosch, David (2006a) "Rebirth of a Discipline: The Global Origins of Comparative Studies." In *Comparative Critical Studies* 3. 1–2: 99–112.
Damrosch, David (2006b) "World Literature in a Postcanonical, Hypercanonical Age." In Haun Saussy (ed.) *Comparative Literature in an Age of Globalization*. Baltimore: John Hopkins University Press, 45–53.
Damrosch, David (2008) "Toward a History of World Literature." In *New Literary History* 39. 3: 481–495.

Damrosch, David (2009a) *Teaching World Literature*. New York: The Modern Language Association of America.
Damrosch, David (2009b) *How to Read World Literature*. Chichester: Wiley-Blackwell.
Damrosch, David (2012) "Hugo Meltzl and 'The Principle of Polyglottism'." In Theo D'haen, David Damrosch and Djelal Kadir (eds) *The Routledge Companion to World Literature*. London and New York: Routledge, 12–20.
Damrosch, David (2014) "Review: Against World Literature." In *Comparative Literature Studies* 51. 3: 504–508.
Damrosch, David (2016) "Scriptworlds Lost and Found." In *Journal of World Literature* 3. 2: 143–157.
Damrosch, David (2020) *Comparing the Literatures: Literary Studies in a Global Age*. Princeton: Princeton University Press.
Damrosch, David (2021) *Around the World in 80 Books*. A Pelican Book. Penguin Random House.
Damrosch, David (2022a) "Hugo Meltzl and 'The Principle of Polyglottism'." In Theo D'haen, David Damrosch and Djelal Kadir (eds) *The Routledge Companion to World Literature*. Second Edition. London and New York: Routledge.
Damrosch, David (2022b) "World Literature and Comparative Literature." In Theo D'haen, David Damrosch and Djelal Kadir (eds) *The Routledge Companion to World Literature*. Second Edition. London and New York: Routledge, 101–110.
Damrosch, David and David L. Pike (eds) (2004) *Longman Anthology of World Literature*. New York: Longman.
Damrosch, David and Gunilla Lindberg-Wada (eds) (2022) *Literature: A World History*. 4 vols. London: Wiley.
Damrosch, David, Haun Saussy and Jacob Edmond (2016) "Trying to Make It Real: An Exchange between Haun Saussy and David Damrosch." In *Comparative Literature Studies* 53. 4: 660–693.
Dantzig, Charles (2019) *Dictionnaire égoïste de la littérature mondiale*. Paris: Grasset.
Darnton, Robert (1982) "What is the History of Books?" In *Daedalus* 111. 3: 65–83.
David, Jérôme (2011) *Spectres de Goethe: Les métamorphoses de la "littérature mondiale"*. Paris: Les Prairies ordinaires.
David, Jérôme (2018) *Martin Bodmer et les promesses de la littérature mondiale*. Genève: Les Éditions d'Ithaque.
Davis, Paul, Gary Harrison, David M. Johnson and John F. Crawford (eds) (2003) *The Bedford Anthology of World Literature*. New York: Bedford/St. Martins.
Day, Tony (2007) "Locating Indonesian Literature in the World." In *Modern Language Quarterly* 68. 2: 173–193.
Deckard, Sharae, et al. (Warwick Research Collective) (2015) *Combined and Uneven Development: Towards a New Theory of World-Literature*. Liverpool: Liverpool University Press.
Deeney, John J. (1981) "Chinese Literature from Comparative Perspectives." In *Chinese Literature: Essays, Articles, Reviews (CLEAR)* 3. 1: 130–136.
Deeney, John J. (1990) *Comparative Literature from Chinese Perspectives*. Shenyang: Liaoning University Press.
Delanty, Gerard and David Inglis (2011) *Cosmopolitanism*. 4 vols. London: Routledge.
DeLoughrey, Elizabeth (2019) *Allegories of the Anthropocene*. Durham, NC: Duke University Press.

Denecke, Wiebke (2014) *Classical World Literatures: Sino-Japanese and Greco-Roman Comparisons.* Oxford: Oxford University Press.

D'haen, Theo (1990) "The Dutch Byron: Byron in Dutch Translation." In C.C. Barfoot and Theo D'haen (eds) *Centennial Hauntings: Pope, Byron and Eliot in the Year 88.* Amsterdam and Atlanta: Rodopi, 232–251.

D'haen, Theo (1991) "W.B. Yeats and A. Roland Holst: (S)Elective Affinities." In *Yeats: An Annual of Critical and Textual Studies* 8. Ann Arbor: The University of Michigan Press, 49–70.

D'haen, Theo (1994) "Countering Postmodernism." In *REAL* (Yearbook of Research in English and American Literature) 10. Tübingen: Gunter Narr Verlag, 49–64.

D'haen, Theo (1995) "Magic Realism and Postmodernism: Decentering Privileged Centers." In Lois Parkinson Zamora and Wendy B. Faris (eds) *Magical Realism: Theory, History, Community.* Durham and London: Duke University Press, 191–208.

D'haen, Theo (1997) "Postmodernisms: from Fantastic to Magic Realist." In Hans Bertens and Douwe Fokkema (eds) *International Postmodernism: Theory and Practice*, A Comparative History of Literatures in European Languages Sponsored by the International Comparative Literature Association, Vol. XI. Amsterdam and Philadelphia: John Benjamins, 283–293.

D'haen, Theo (gen. ed.) (2000) *Proceedings of the XVth ICLA Congress, Leiden 1997*, 9 vols. Amsterdam and Atlanta: Rodopi.

D'haen, Theo (2005) "'A Splenetic Englishman': The Dutch Byron." In Richard A. Cardwell, ed., *The Reception of Byron in Europe, Volume II: Northern, Central and Eastern Europe*, London and New York: Thoemmes Continuum, 269–282.

D'haen, Theo (2006) "Yeats in the Dutch-Language Low Countries." In Klaus Peter Jochum (ed.) *The Reception of W.B. Yeats in Europe.* London and New York: Continuum, 12–24.

D'haen, Theo (2009) "Mapping Modernism: Gaining in Translation – Martinus Nijhoff and T.S. Eliot." In *Comparative Critical Studies* 6. 1: 21–41.

D'haen, Theo (2013) "Major Languages, Minor Literatures, Multiple Legacies." In Tim Parks and Edoardo Zuccato (eds) *Towards a Global Literature/Verso una letteratura globalizzata.* Milan: Marcos y Marcos, 11–22.

D'haen, Theo (2014) "Major Histories, Minor Literatures, and World Authors." In *CLCWeb: Comparative Literature and Culture* 15. 5. http://dx.doi.org/10.7771/1481-4374.2342.

D'haen, Theo (2016) "Major/Minor in World Literature." In *Journal of World Literature* 1. 1: 29–38.

D'haen, Theo (2017a) "Anthologizing World Literature in Translation: Global/Local/Glocal." In *Forum for World Literature Studies* 9. 4: 539–557.

D'haen, Theo (2017b) "Capitalizing (on) World Literature: Brussels as Shadow Capital of Modernism/Modernity." In Richard Hibbitt (ed.) *Other Capitals of the Nineteenth Century: An Alternative Mapping of Literary and Cultural Space.* New York: Palgrave Macmillan, 111–127. (Also as "Capitalizing (on) World Literature," in Laura Mesina, et al. [eds] [2014] *Echilibrul între Antiteze*, Bucharest: University of Bucharest Press, 11–26.)

D'haen, Theo (2017c) "For 'Global Literature', Anglo-Phone." In *Anglia* 135. 1: 35–50.

D'haen, Theo (2020) "Magic Realism: The European Trajectory." In Kim Anderson Sasser and Christopher Warnes (eds) *Magic Realism and Literature.* Cambridge: Cambridge University Press, 117–130.

D'haen, Theo (2021a) "Worlding European Literature." In *CompLit: Journal of European Literature, Arts and Society* 1. 1: 193–207.
D'haen, Theo (2021b) "Saving Europe through *Weltliteratur*: The Case of Victor Klemperer." In Debjani Ganguly (ed.) *The Cambridge History of World Literature*. Vol. 1. Cambridge: Cambridge UP, 240–260.
D'haen, Theo (2022) "Contemporary European Crime Narratives: 'Euro-Glocal?'" In *Clues: A Journal of Detection* 40. 2: 29–38.
D'haen, Theo (2023a) "Flemish Literature and World Literature." In *Canadian Review of Comparative Literature*, 50. 1: 15–33.
D'haen, Theo (2023b) *Dutch Interbellum Canons and World Literature: A. Roland Holst, M. Nijhoff, J. Slauerhoff*. Singapore: Palgrave Macmillan.
D'haen, Theo, David Damrosch and Djelal Kadir (eds) (2012) *The Routledge Companion to World Literature*. London: Routledge.
D'haen, Theo, David Damrosch and Djelal Kadir (eds) (2022) *The Routledge Companion to World Literature*. Second Edition. London: Routledge.
Dharwadker, Vinay (ed.) (2001) *Cosmopolitan Geographies: New Locations in Literature and Culture*. New York and London: Routledge.
Dimock, Wai Chee (2006a) "Genre as World System: Epic and Novel on Four Continents." In *Narrative* 14. 1: 85–101.
Dimock, Wai Chee (2006b) *Through Other Continents: American Literature Across Deep Time*. Princeton: Princeton University Press.
Dimock, Wai Chee and Lawrence Buell (eds) (2007) *Shades of the Planet: American Literature as World Literature*. Princeton and Oxford: Princeton University Press.
Dina, Amelia (2016) "Indonesian Literature's Position in World Literature." In *Teknosastik* 14. 2: 1–5.
Dirlik, Arif (1994) "The Postcolonial Aura: Third World Criticism in the Age of Global Capitalism." In *Critical Inquiry* 20. 2: 328–356.
Domínguez, César (2012a) "Dionýz Ďurišin and a Systemic Theory of World Literature." In Theo D'haen, David Damrosch and Djelal Kadir (eds) *The Routledge Companion to World Literature*. London: Routledge, 99–107.
Domínguez, César (2012b) "World Literature and Cosmopolitanism." In Theo D'haen, David Damrosch and Djelal Kadir (eds) *The Routledge Companion to World Literature*. London: Routledge, 242–252.
Domínguez, César (2013) "Juan Andrés: On the Origin, Progress and Present State of Literature (Excerpts)." In Theo D'haen, César Domínguez and Mads Rosendahl Thomsen (eds) *World Literature: A Reader*. London: Routledge, 1–8.
Domínguez, César (2022a) "Dionýz Ďurišin and a Systemic Theory of World Literature." In Theo D'haen, David Damrosch and Djelal Kadir (eds) *The Routledge Companion to World Literature*. Second Edition. London: Routledge, 61–68.
Domínguez, César (2022b) "World Literature and Cosmopolitanism." In Theo D'haen, David Damrosch and Djelal Kadir (eds) *The Routledge Companion to World Literature*. Second Edition. London: Routledge, 185–193.
Drinkwater, John (1923–1924) *The Outline of Literature*. New York, London: G.P. Putnam's Sons.
During, Simon (2004) "Comparative Literature." In *ELH* 71: 313–322.
During, Simon (2009) *Exit Capitalism: Literary Culture, Theory and Post-Secular Modernity*. London: Routledge.
Ďurišin, Dionýsz (1992) *Čo je svetová literatúra?* (What Is World Literature?). Bratislava: Vydavateľstvo Obzor.

Ďurišin, Dionýsz and Armando Gnisci (eds) (2000) *Il Mediterraneo: una rete interletteraria*. Roma: Bulzoni.
Ebeling, Sascha (2021) "From Diasporic Tamil Literature to Global Tamil Literature." In Debjani Ganguly (ed.) *The Cambridge History of World Literature*, Volume I. Cambridge: Cambridge University Press, 393–407.
Edmond, Jacob (2012) *A Common Strangeness*. New York: Fordham University Press.
Edmond, Jacob (2019) "Global Rhythms: Setting the Stage for World Poetry in 1960s London." In *University of Toronto Quarterly* 88. 2: 263–276.
Eisenstein, Elisabeth (1979) *The Printing Press as an Agent of Change*. 2 vols. Cambridge: Cambridge University Press.
Eisenstein, Elisabeth (1983) *The Printing Revolution in Early Modern Europe*. Cambridge: Cambridge University Press.
Eisler, Rudolf (1930) *Kant-Lexicon*. http://www.textlog.de/32413.html (accessed 23 July 2010).
El-Ariss, Tarek (2022) "The World of Arabic Literature." In Theo D'haen, David Damrosch and Djelal Kadir (eds) *The Routledge Companion to World Literature*. Second Edition. London and New York: Routledge, 407–415.
Elias, Amy J. (2008) "Interactive Cosmopolitanism and Collaborative Technologies: New Foundations for Global Literary History." In *New Literary History* 39. 3: 705–725.
Emmer, Pieter (2022) "Decoloniality in the Netherlands." In *European Review* 30. S1: 59–64.
Emmett, Christine (2022) "Inequality, Legitimacy and Disidentification: From South African to Global Modernism." In *Literature Compass* 9: e12680.
Engdahl, Horace (2008) "Canonization and World Literature: The Nobel Experience." In Karen-Margrethe Simonsen and Jakob Stougaard-Nielsen (eds) *World Literature, World Culture: History, Theory, Analysis*. Aarhus: Aarhus University Press, 195–214.
English, James (2005) *The Economy of Prestige: Prizes, Awards, and the Circulation of Cultural Value*. Cambridge, Mass.: Harvard University Press.
Escarpit, Robert (1958) *Sociologie de la littérature*. Paris: Presses Universitaires de France.
Escobar, Arturo (2007) "Worlds and Knowledges Otherwise: The Latin American modernity/coloniality research program." In *Cultural Studies* 21. 2–3: 179–210.
Esonwanne, Uzoma (2021) "Africa and World Literature." In Debjani Ganguly (ed.) *The Cambridge History of World Literature*, Volume I. Cambridge: Cambridge University Press, 326–342.
Etiemble, René (1966) *The Crisis in Comparative Literature*. Transl. and with a Foreword by Herbert Weisinger and Georges Joyaux. East Lansing, MI: Michigan State University Press. (Translation of *Comparaison n'est pas raison*, 1963.)
Etiemble, René (1977) [1963] *Comparaison n'est pas raison*. Paris: Gallimard.
Etiemble, René (1975) [1964, 1966] "Faut-il réviser la notion de *Weltliteratur*?" In *Essais de littérature (vraiment) générale*. Paris: Gallimard.
Etiemble, René (1988) *Ouverture(s) sur un comparatisme planétaire*. Paris: Christian Bourgois.
Ette, Ottmar (2016a) *Writing – Between – Worlds: TransArea Studies and the Literatures-Without-A-Fixed Abode*. Transl. Vera Kutzinski. Berlin and Boston: De Gruyter.
Ette, Ottmar (2016b) *TransArea: A Literary History of Globalization*. Transl. Mark W. Person. Berlin and Boston: De Gruyter.
Ette, Ottmar (2016c) "Toward a Polylogical Philology of the Literatures of the World." In *Modern Language Quarterly: A Journal of Literary History* 77. 2: 143–173.

Ette, Ottmar (2021) *Literatures of the World: Beyond World Literature*. Transl. Mark W. Person. Leiden and Boston: Brill.

Ette, Ottmar Ette and Gesine Müller (2012) *Worldwide: Archipels de la mondialisation / Archipiélagos de la globalización. Contribuciones en español, francés, inglés y alemán*. Frankfurt: Vervuert Verlagsgesellschaft.

Even-Zohar, Itamar (2000) [1978/1990] "The Position of Translated Literature within the Literary Polysystem." In Lawrence Venuti (ed.) *The Translation Studies Reader*. London and New York: Routledge, 193–197.

Ezli, Özkan, Dorothee Kimmich and Annette Werberger (eds) (2009) *Wider den Kulturenzwang: Migration, Kulturalisierung und Weltliteratur*. Bielefeld: Transcript Verlag.

Fan, Victor (2019) "Rethinking the Sinophone." In *Monde Chinois* 57. 1: 13–24.

Fang, Weigui (2018) "Introduction: What Is World Literature?" in Weigui Fang (ed.) *Tensions in World Literature: Between the Local and the Universal*. Singapore: Palgrave Macmillan, 1–64.

Fanon, Frantz (1952) *Peau noire, masques blancs*. Paris: Editions du Seuil.

Fanon, Frantz (1961) *Les damnés de la terre*. Paris: Maspero.

Fanon, Frantz (1963) *The Wretched of the Earth*. Transl. Constance Farrington. New York: Grove Weidenfeld.

Fanon, Frantz (1967) *Black Skin, White Masks*. Transl. Charles Lam Markmann. New York: Grove Weidenfeld.

Farn, Regelind (2005) *Colonial and Postcolonial Rewritings of "Heart of Darkness": A Century of Dialogue with Jospeh Conrad*. Boca Raton, FL: Dissertation.com.

Febvre, Lucien and Henri-Jean Martin. 1958. *L'apparition du livre*. Paris: Albin Michel.

Ferguson, Frances (2008) "Planetary Literary History: The Place of the Text." In *New Literary History* 39: 657–684.

Figlerowicz, Matylda and Lucas Mertehikian (2023) "An Ever-Expanding World Literary Genre: Defining Magic Realism on Wikipedia." In *Journal of Cultural Analytics* 8. 2: 1–27.

Figueira, Dorothy (2008) *Otherwise Occupied: Pedagogies of Alterity and the Brahminization of Theory*. Albany: State University of New York Press.

Figueira, Dorothy (2010) "Comparative Literature versus World Literature." *The Comparatist* 34: 29–36.

Fischer, Frank, Jacob Blakesley, Paula Wojcik and Robert Jäschke (2023) "Preface: World Literature in an Expanding Digital Space." In *Journal of Cultural Analytics* 8. 2: 1–14.

Fitz, Earl (2002) "Internationalizing the Literature of the Portuguese-Speaking World." In *Hispania* 85. 3: 439–448.

Fogel, Joshua (2009) *Articulating the Sinosphere: Sino-Japanese Relations in Space and Time*. Cambridge, Mass.: Harvard University Press.

Fokkema, Douwe (1984) *Literary History, Modernism, and Postmodernism*. Amsterdam and Philadelphia: John Benjamins.

Fokkema, Douwe (1986) "The Semantic and Syntactic Organization of Postmodernist Texts." In Douwe Fokkema and Hans Bertens (eds) *Approaching Postmodernism*. Amsterdam and Philadelphia: John Benjamins, 81–98.

Fokkema, Douwe and Hans Bertens (eds) (1986) *Approaching Postmodernism*. Amsterdam and Philadelphia: John Benjamins.

Folie, Sandra (2022) *Beyond "Ethnic Chick Lit" – Labelingpraktiken neuer Welt-Frauen-Literaturen im transkontinentalen Vergleich*. Bielefeld: Transcript Verlag.

Forsdick, Charles (2010a) "World Literature, Littérature-Monde: Which Literature? Whose World?" In *Paragraph* 33. 1: 125–143.
Forsdick, Charles (2010b) "Late Glissant: History, 'World Literature,' and the Persistence of the Political." In *Small Axe* 33. 14: 121–134.
Forsdick, Charles and David Murphy (eds) (2003) *Francophone Postcolonialism: A Critical Introduction*. London: Arnold.
Fotache, Oana and Liviu Papadima (eds) (2012) *Ghid de Literatură europeană*, CD. Bucharest: University of Bucharest.
Freudiger, Reynald (2019) *Une brève histoire de la littérature mondiale*. Vevey: Editions de l'Aire.
Friederich, Werner, with the collaboration of David Henry Malone (1954) *Outline of Comparative Literature; from Dante Alighieri to Eugene O'Neill*. Chapel Hill: University of North Carolina Press.
Friederich, Werner P. (1960) "On the Integrity of Our Planning." In *The Teaching of World Literature*, ed. Haskell M. Block. UNC Studies in Comparative Literature 28. Chapel Hill, N.C.: The University of North Carolina Press, 9–22.
Friederich, Werner P. (1970) "Great Books Versus 'World Literature'." In *The Challenge of Comparative Literature and Other Addresses*. Chapel Hill, N.C.: The University of North Carolina Press, 25–35.
Friedman, Susan Stanford (2018) "Conjunctures of the 'New' World Literature and Migration Studies." In *Journal of World Literature* 3. 3: 267–289.
Frydman, Jason (2014) *Sounding the Break: African American and Caribbean Routes of World Literature*. Charlottesville and London: University of Virginia Press.
Frydman, Jason (2022) "Oceans, Archipelagoes, and World Literature." In Theo D'haen, David Damrosch and Djelal Kadir (eds) *The Routledge Companion to World Literature*. Second Edition. London and New York: Routledge, 442–451.
Fuller, Margaret (1839) *Conversations with Goethe in the Last Years of his Life, Translated from the German of Eckermann*. Specimens of Foreign Standard Literature Vol. IV. Edited by George Ripley. Boston: Hilliard, Gray, and Company.
Gallagher, Mary (2010) "Connection Failures: Discourse on Contemporary European and Caribbean Writing in French." In *Small Axe* 33. 14 (November): 21–32.
Gane, Gillian (2002) "Migrancy, the Cosmopolitan Intellectual, and the Global City in *The Satanic Verses*." In *MFS Modern Fiction Studies* 48. 1: 18–49.
Ganguly, Debjani (2008) "Global Literary Refractions: Reading Pascale Casanova's *The World Republic of Letters* in the Post-Cold War Era." In *English Academy Review* 25. 1: 4–19.
Ganguly, Debjani (2016) *This Thing Called the World.: The Contemporary Novel as Global Form*. Durham, NC: Duke University Press.
Ganguly, Debjani (2020) "Catastrophic Form and Planetary Realism." In *New Literary History* 51. 2: 419–453.
Ganguly, Debjani (ed.) (2021a) *The Cambridge History of World Literature*. 2 vols. Cambridge: Cambridge University Press.
Ganguly, Debjani (2021b) "Oceanic Comparativism and World Literature." In Debjani Ganguly (ed.) *The Cambridge History of World Literature*, Volume I. Cambridge: Cambridge University Press, 429–457.
Ganguly, Debjani (2023) "Angloglobalism, Multilingualism and World Literature." In *interventions* 25. 5: 601–618.
Gasché, Rodolphe (2009) *Europe, or the Infinite Task: A Study of a Philosophical Concept*. Redwood City: Stanford University Press.

Gayley, Charles Mills (1973) [1903] "What is Comparative Literature?" In Hans-Joachim Schulz and Philip H. Rhein (eds) *Comparative Literature: The Early Years*. Chapel Hill, NC: The University of North Carolina Press, 85–103.

Geider, Thomas (2005) "Afrika im Umkreis der frühen Weltliteraturdiskussion: Goethe und Henri Grégoire." In *Revue de littérature comparée* 314: 241–260.

Gentzler, Edwin (2017) *Translation and Re-Writing in the Age of Post-Translation Studies*. London and New York: Routledge.

Ghosh, Amitav (1992) "Petrofiction: The Oil Encounter and the Novel." In *The New Republic* 12: 29–34.

Gikandi, Simon (1992) *Writing in Limbo: Modernism and Caribbean Literature*. Ithaca: Cornell University Press.

Gikandi, Simon (2001) "Globalization and the Claims of Postcoloniality." In *The South Atlantic Quarterly* 100. 3: 627–658.

Giles, Paul (2021) "Antipodal Turns: Antipodean Americas and the Hemispheric Shift." In Debjani Ganguly (ed.) *The Cambridge History of World Literature*, Volume I, Cambridge: Cambridge University Press, 477–494.

Giles, Paul (2022) "World Literature and Global English." In Theo D'haen, David Damrosch and Djelal Kadir (eds) *The Routledge Companion to World Literature*. Second Edition. London and New York: Routledge, 388–397.

Gillespie, Gerald (2013) "Comparative Literature in the United States." In Steven Tötösy de Zepetnek and Tutun Mukherjee (eds). *Companion to Comparative Literature, World Literatures, and Comparative Cultural Studies*. Foundation Books. New Delhi: Cambridge University Press India, 352–367.

Glissant, Edouard (1981) *Le discours antillais*. Paris: Seuil. (Transl. J. Michael Dash [1989] *Caribbean Discourse*. CARAF Books. Charlottesville, NC and London: University Press of Virginia.)

Glissant, Edouard (1993) *Tout-monde*. Paris: Gallimard.

Glissant, Edouard (1997) *Traité du tout-monde*. Paris: Gallimard.

Gnisci, Armando, Franca Sinopoli and Nora Moll (2010) *La letteratura del mondo nel XXI secolo*. Milano: Bruno Mondadori.

Goethe, Johann Wolfgang von (1819) *West-östlicher Diwan*. Stuttgart: in der Cottaischen Buchhandlung. http://www.deutschestextarchiv.de/goethe/divan/1819/viewer/image/9 (accessed 20 December 2010).

Goethe, Johann Wolfgang von (1970) *Italian Journey*. Transl. By W.H. Auden and Elizabeth Mayer. London: Penguin.

Goethe, Johann Wolfgang von (1986) *Essays on Art and Literature*. John Gearey (ed.). *Goethe's Collected Works*, Vol. 3. New York: Suhrkamp.

Goethe, Johann Wolfgang von (2007) *Italienische Reise*. Jubilaeumsausgabe. Munich: C.H. Beck.

Goldmann, Lucien (1955) *Le Dieu caché; étude sur la vision tragique dans les* Pensées *de Pascal et dans le théâtre de Racine*. Paris: Gallimard.

Goldmann, Lucien (1964) *Pour une sociologie du roman*. Paris: Gallimard.

Gómez-Montero, Javier (2013) "Europäische Lektüren jenseits von Europa: Weltliteratur, literarischer Kanon und die Bildung in Europa." *Interlitteraria* 18. 2: 289–308.

Gorky, Maxim (1969) [1919] "Weltliteratur." In *Maxim Gorki. Über Weltliteratur*. Leipzig: Philipp Reclam, 31–40.

Gossens, Peter (2010) "Weltliteratur: eine historische Perspektive." In *ide: informationen zur deutschdidaktik: Zeitschrift für den Deutschunterricht in Wissenschaft und Schule* 34. 1: 9–28.

Gossens, Peter (2011) *Weltliteratur: Modelle transnationaler Literaturwahrnehmung im 19. Jahrhundert*. Stuttgart-Weimar: Verlag J.B. Metzler.

Graff, Gerald (1987) *Professing Literature: An Institutional History*. Chicago: The University of Chicago Press.

Gu, Ming Dong (2013) *Sinologism: An Alternative to Orientalism and Postcolonialism*. London and New York: Routledge.

Gu, Ming Dong (2018) "The Theoretical Debate on 'Sinologism': A Rejoinder to Mr. Zhang Xiping." In *Contemporary Chinese Thought* 49. 1: 55–70.

Gu, Ming Dong and Xian Zhou (2018) "Sinology, Sinologism, and New Sinology." In *Contemporary Chinese Thought* 49. 1: 1–6.

Guérard, Albert (1940) *Preface to World Literature*. New York: Henry Holt and Company.

Guha, Ranajit (1982) *Subaltern Studies*. Delhi: Oxford University Press.

Guillén, Claudio (1993) [1985] *The Challenge of Comparative Literature*. Transl. Cola Franzen. Cambridge, Mass: Harvard University Press.

Guillory, John (1993) *Cultural Capital: The Problem of Literary Canon Formation*. Chicago: The University of Chicago Press.

Gulddal, Jesper and Stewart King (2022) "World Crime Fiction." In Theo D'haen, David Damrosch and Djelal Kadir (eds) *The Routledge Companion to World Literature*. Second Edition. London and New York: Routledge, 285–293.

Gulddal, Jesper, Stewart King and Alistair Rolls (eds) (2022) *The Cambridge Companion to World Crime Fiction*. Cambridge: Cambridge University Press.

Gumbrecht, Hans Ulrich (2002) *Vom Leben und Sterben der grossen Romanisten*. Munich: Carl Hanser Verlag.

Gutzkow, Karl (1836) *Über Goethe. Im Wendepunkt zweier Jahrhunderte*. Berlin: Verlag der Plan'schen Buchhandlung (L. Nitse). http://books.google.be/books?id=unsuAAAAYAAJ&printsec=frontcover&dq=Karl+Gutzkow+Ueber+Goethe&source=bl&ots=nrsHycGrSr&sig=mwzFajj7jtjS6mJJHtW5hni20W0&hl=en&ei=y0h5Td7PGIaWhQe0hoj4Bg&sa=X&oi=book_result&ct=result&resnum=4&ved=0CCwQ6AEwAw#v=onepage&q&f=false (accessed 9 March 2011).

Habermas, Jürgen (1992) [1980] "Modernity – An Incomplete Project." In Peter Brooker (ed.) *Modernism/Postmodernism*. London: Longman, 125–138.

Hall, Katharina (2013) "The 'Nazi Detective' as Provider of Justice in Post-1990 British and German Crime Fiction: Philip Kerr's *The Pale Criminal*, Robert Harris's *Fatherland*, and Richard Birkefeld and Göran Hachmeister's *Wer übrig bleibt, hat recht*." In *Comparative Literature Studies* 50. 2: 288–313.

Hallward, Peter (1998) "Edouard Glissant between the Singular and the Specific." In *The Yale Journal of Criticism* 11. 2: 441–464.

Hao, Yucong (2017) "The Sinophone." In Ursula K. Heise, Dudley Andrew, Alexander Beecroft, Jessica Berman, David Damrosch, Guillermina De Ferrari, César Domínguez, Barbara Harlow and Eric Hayot (eds) *Futures of Comparative Literature. ACLA State of the Discipline Report*. London and New York: Routledge, 228–229.

Hashimoto, Satoru (2022) "World Literature and East Asian Literatures." In Theo D'haen, David Damrosch and Djelal Kadir (eds) *The Routledge Companion to World Literature*. Second Edition. London and New York: Routledge, 425–433.

Hassan, Ihab (1975) *Paracriticisms: Seven Speculations of the Times*. Urbana: University of Illinois Press.

Hassan, Ihab (1980) *The Right Promethean Fire: Imagination, Science, and Cultural Change*. Urbana: University of Illinois Press.

Hassan, Ihab (1982) [1971] *The Dismemberment of Orpheus: Toward a Postmodern Literature.* New York: Oxford University Press.

Hassan, Ihab (1987) *The Postmodern Turn: Essays in Postmodern Theory and Culture.* Ohio State University Press.

Hassan, Waïl S. (2000) "World Literature in the Age of Globalization: Reflections on an Anthology." In *College English* 63. 1 (September): 38–47.

Hassan, Waïl S. (2002) "Postcolonial Theory and Modern Arabic Literature: Horizons of Application." In *Journal of Arabic Literature* 33. 1: 45–64.

Hassan, Waïl S. (2017) "Arabic and the Paradigms of Comparison." In Ursula K. Heise, Dudley Andrew, Alexander Beecroft, Jessica Berman, David Damrosch, Guillermina De Ferrari, César Domínguez, Barbara Harlow and Eric Hayot (eds) *Futures of Comparative Literature. ACLA State of the Discipline Report.* London and New York: Routledge, 187–194.

Hassan, Waïl S. (2018) "Postcolonialism and Modern Arabic Literature: Twenty-First Century Horizons." In *Interventions* 20. 2: 157–173.

Hassan, Waïl S. (2019) "Arabs and the Americas: A Multilingual and Multigenerational Legacy." In *Review: Literature and Arts of the Americas* 52. 2: 166–169.

Hawas, May (2019) *Politicising World Literature: Egypt, Between Pedagogy and the Public.* New York and London: Routledge.

Hayot, Eric (2011) "On Literary Worlds." In *Modern Language Quarterly* 72. 2: 129–161.

Hayot, Eric (2012a) *On Literary Worlds.* Oxford: Oxford University Press.

Hayot, Eric (2012b) "World Literature and Globalization." In Theo D'haen, David Damrosch and Djelal Kadir (eds). *The Routledge Companion to World Literature.* London and New York: Routledge, 223–231.

Heilbron, Johan (1995) "Nederlandse vertalingen wereldwijd: Kleine landen en culturele mondialisering." In Johan Heilbron, et al. (eds) *Waarin een klein Land: Nederlandse Cultuur in Internationaal Verband.* Amsterdam: Prometheus, 206–252.

Heilbron, Johan (1999) "Towards a Sociology of Translation: Books Translations as a Cultural World System." In *European Journal of Social Theory* 2. 4: 429–444.

Heilbron, Johan (2008) "L'évolution des échanges culturels entre la France et les Pays-Bas à l'hégémonie de l'anglais." In Gisèle Sapiro (ed.) *Translatio: Le marché de la traduction en France à l'heure de la mondialisation.* Paris: CNRS, 311–331.

Heilbron, Johan and G. Sapiro (2007) "Outline for a Sociology of Translation. Current Issues and Future Prospects." In M. Wolf and A. Fukari (eds) *Constructing a Sociology of Translation.* Amsterdam: John Benjamins, 96–97.

Heise, Ursula K. (2008) *Sense of Place and Sense of Planet: The Environmental Imagination of the Global.* Oxford: Oxford University Press.

Heise, Ursula (2013) "Globality, Difference, and the International Turn in Ecocriticism." In *PMLA* 123. 3: 636–643.

Heise, Ursula (2017) "Comparative Literature and the Environmental Humanities." In *Futures of Comparative Literature.* New York: Routledge, 293–301.

Heise, Ursula K. (2019) "Environmentalism, Eco-Cosmopolitanism, and Premodern Thought." In Vin Nardizzi and Tiffany Jo Werth (eds) *Premodern Ecologies in the Modern Literary Imagination.* Toronto: University of Toronto Press, 282–288.

Heise, Ursula (2022) "World Literature and Cultures of the Environment." In Theo D'haen, David Damrosch and Djelal Kadir (eds) *The Routledge Companion to World Literature.* Second Edition. London and New York: Routledge, 340–351.

Helgesson, Stefan (2014) "Postcolonialism and World Literature: Rethinking the Boundaries." In *interventions* 16. 4: 483–500.

Helgesson, Stefan (2017) "Ngugi wa Thiong'o and the Conceptual Worlding of Literature." In *Anglia* 135. 1: 105–121.

Helgesson, Stefan (2018a) "'Literature,' Theory from the South and the Case of the São Paulo School." In *Cambridge Journal of Postcolonial Literary Inquiry* 5. 2: 141–157.

Helgesson, Stefan (2018b) "The World-Literary Formation of Antonio Candido." In Gesine Müller, Jorge J. Locane and Benjamin Loy (eds) *Re-mapping World Literature: Writing, Book Markets and Epistemologies between Latin America and the Global South/Escrituras, mercados y epistemologías entre América Latina y el Sur Global*. Berlin and Boston: De Gruyter, 225–235.

Helgesson, Stefan (2018c) "Translation and the Circuits of World Literature." in Ben Etherington and Jarad Zimbler (eds) *The Cambridge Companion to World Literature*. Cambridge: Cambridge University Press, 85–99.

Helgesson, Stefan (2018d) "Literary World-Making under Apartheid: *Staffrider* and the Location of Print Culture." In S. Helgesson, A. Alling, Y. Lindqvist and H. Wulff (eds). *World Literature: Exploring the Cosmopolitan-Vernacular Exchange*. Stockholm: Stockholm University Press, 171–184.

Helgesson, Stefan (2022a) *Decolonisations of Literature: Critical Practice in Africa and Brazil After 1945*. Liverpool: Liverpool University Press.

Helgesson, Stefan (2022b) "African Angles on World Literature." In Theo D'haen, David Damrosch and Djelal Kadir (eds) *The Routledge Companion to World Literature*. Second Edition. London and New York: Routledge, 416–424.

Helgesson, Stefan and Pieter Vermeulen (eds) (2016) *Institutions of World Literature: Writing, Translation, Markets*. London and New York: Routledge.

Helgesson, Stefan, Annika Mörte Alling, Yvonne Lindqvist and Helena Wulff (eds) (2018) *World Literatures: Exploring the Cosmopolitan-Vernacular Exchange*. Stockholm: Stockholm University Press.

Helgesson, Stefan, Birgit Neumann and Gabrielle Rippl (eds) (2020) *Handbook of Anglophone World Literatures*. Berlin and Boston: De Gruyter.

Henighan, Stephen (2008) "The Translation Gap." In *A report on the afterlife of culture*. Emeryville: Biblioasis, 125–139.

Henighan, Stephen (2012) "The Fall of Translation." In *Translation: A Transdisciplinary Journal* 4. biblioasistranslation.blogspot.ca/2012/03/on-october-27–2011-writer-clarkblaise.html (accessed 26 November 2012).

Henitiuk, Valerie (2012) "The Single, Shared Text? Translation and World Literature." In *World Literature Today* 86. 1: 30–34.

Henrion, Matthieu-Richard-Auguste (1827) *Histoire littéraire de la France*. Paris: J.J. Blaise. http://books.google.be/books?id=pj_Is1MkThoC&printsec=frontcover&dq=Matthieu+Richard+Auguste+Henrion&source=bl&ots=30gsYMBqOg&sig=Sb4C76gK6T1fP3aGmN_ZNpXCQFs&hl=en&ei=E80pTZzsJYOAhAe838nlAQ&sa=X&oi=book_result&ct=result&resnum=1&ved=0CBkQ6AEwADgK#v=onepage&q&f=false (accessed 9 January 2011).

Hensbroek, P.A.M. Boele van (1911) *Der Wereld Letterkunde voor Nederlanders bewerkt*. Leiden and Antwerp: A. W. Sijthoff's Uitgeversmaatschappij and De Nederlandsche Boekhandel.

Hermans, Theo (1985) *The Manipulation of Literature: Studies in Literary Translation*. London: Croom Helm.

Hertel, Hans (ed.) (1985–1994) *Gyldendals Verdens litteraturhistorie*. 7 vols. Copenhagen: Gyldendal.

Hesse, Herman (2008) [1929, 1953, 1978] *Eine Bibliothek der Weltliteratur.* Stuttgart: Reclam.

Hightower, James Robert (1953) "Chinese Literature in the Context of World Literature." In *Comparative Literature* 5. 2: 117–124.

Hitchcock, Peter (2009) *The Long Space: Transnationalism and Postcolonial Form.* Redwood City: Stanford University Press.

Hitchcock, Peter (2012) "The Ethics of World Literature." In Theo D'haen, David Damrosch and Djelal Kadir (eds) *The Routledge Companion to World Literature*, London and New York: Routledge, 365–372.

Hitchcock, Peter (2022) "The Ethics of World Literature." In Theo D'haen, David Damrosch and Djelal Kadir (eds) *The Routledge Companion to World Literature.* Second Edition. London and New York: Routledge, 313–319.

Hodkinson, Mark (2022) *No One Round Here Reads Tolstoy: Memoirs of a Working-Class Reader.* Edinburgh and London: Canongate.

Hoesel-Uhlig, Stefan (2004) "Changing Fields: The Directions of Goethe's *Weltliteratur.*" In Christopher Prendergast (ed.) *Debating World Literature*, London: Verso, 26–53.

Hoffmann, Gerhard (1982) "The Fantastic in Fiction: Its 'Reality' Status, Its Historical Development and Its Transformation in Postmodern Narrative." in *REAL (Yearbook of Research in English and American Literature)* 1: 267–364.

Holmes, James S. (2000) [1972] "The Name and Nature of Translation Studies." In Lawrence Venuti (ed.) *The Translation Studies Reader.* London and New York: Routledge, 172–185.

Hoyos, Hector (2016) *Beyond Bolaño: The Global Latin American Novel.* New York: Columbia University Press.

Huggan, Graham (2001) *The Post-Colonial Exotic: Marketing the Margins.* London and New York: Routledge.

Huggan, Graham and Helen Tiffin (2010) *Postcolonial Ecocriticism: Literature, Animals, Environment.* Abingdon: Routledge.

Huk, Romana (2009) "A New Global Poetics?" In *Literature Compass* 6. 3: 758–784.

Huk, Romana (2019) "A New Global Poetics? Revisited, Ten Years on: Coming to Terms." In *University of Toronto Quarterly* 88. 2: 292–306.

Hurkens, Amélie (2022) "Worldlit as MMORPG? Wholesaling World Literature in the Age of Amazon." In *Journal of World Literature* 7. 2: 449–469.

Hutcheon, Linda (1984) *Narcissistic Narrative: The Metafictional Paradox.* New York and London: Methuen.

Hutcheon, Linda (1985) *A Theory of Parody: The Teachings of Twentieth-Century Art Forms.* New York and London: Methuen.

Hutcheon, Linda (1988) *A Poetics of Postmodernism: History, Theory, Fiction.* New York and London: Routledge.

Hutcheon, Linda (1989) *The Politics of Postmodernism.* London and New York: Routledge.

Hutcheon, Linda (1991) "'Circling the Downspout of Empire'." In Ian Adam and Helen Tiffin (eds) *Past the Last Post: Theorizing Post-Colonialism and Post-Modernism.* London: Harvester/Wheatsheaf, 167–189.

Huyssen, Andreas (1986) *After the Great Divide: Modernism, Mass Culture, Postmodernism.* Bloomington and Indianapolis: Indiana University Press.

Hwa, Yol Jung (2015) "Zhang Longxi's Contribution to World Literature in the Globalizing World of Multiculturalism: A Tribute." In Suoqiao Qian (ed.) *Cross-cultural*

Studies: China and the World. A Festschrift in Honor of Professor Zhang Longxi. Leiden and Boston: Brill, 209–239.

Jameson, Fredric (1984) "Postmodernism, or the Cultural Logic of Late Capitalism." In *New Left Review* 146: 59–92.

Jameson, Fredric (1991) *Postmodernism, or, The Cultural Logic of Late Capitalism*. Durham, NC: Duke University Press.

Jameson, Fredric (2000) *The Jameson Reader*. Edited by Michael Hardt and Kathi Weeks. Oxford: Blackwell.

Jobim, José Luís (ed.) (2017) *A circulação literária e cultural*. Oxford: Peter Lang.

Jobim, José Luís (ed.) (2017) *Literary and Cultural Circulation*. Oxford: Peter Lang.

Jørgensen, Steen Bille and Mads Anders Baggesgaard (eds) (2015) *Verden på fransk* [The World in French]. Aarhus: Aarhus Universitetsforlag/Aarhus University Press.

Jost, François (1974) *Introduction to Comparative Literature*. Indianapolis: Pegasus.

Juvan, Marko (2022) "Wordliness, Worlds, and Worlding of Literature." In *Metacritic Journal for Comparative Studies and Theory* 8. 1: 5–22.

Kachru, Sonam and Jane Mikkelson (2019) "The Mind Is Its Own Place: Of Lalla's Comparative Poetics." In *University of Toronto Quarterly* 88. 2: 125–141.

Kadir, Djelal (2004) "To World, to Globalize – Comparative Literature's Crossroads." In *Comparative Literature Studies* 41. 1: 1–9.

Kadir, Djelal (2006) "Comparative Literature in a World Become Tlön." In *Comparative Critical Studies* 3. 1–2: 125–138.

Kadir, Djelal (2011) *Memos from the Besieged City: Lifelines for Cultural Sustainability*. Redwood City: Stanford University Press.

Kalliney, Peter J. (2022) *The Aesthetic Cold War: Decolonization and Global Literature*. Princeton: Princeton University Press.

Kant, Immanuel (1971) [1790] *Kritik der praktischen Vernunft. Kritik der Urteilskraft*. Berlin: De Gruyter. (*Critique of the Power of Judgment* [2000], edited by Paul Guyer, translated by Paul Guyer and Eric Mathews, Cambridge and New York: Cambridge University Press.)

Kant, Immanuel (1795) *Zum ewigen Frieden*. Königsberg: Friedrich Nicolovius. (*Perpetual Peace and Other Essays* [1983], Cambridge, MA: Hacket.)

Keen, Ruth (1988) "Information Is All That Counts: An Introduction to Chinese Women's Writing in German Translation." In *Modern Chinese Literature* 4. 2: 225–234.

King, Stewart (2014) "Crime Fiction as World Literature." In *Clues: A Journal of Detection* 32. 2: 8–19.

King, Stewart (2017) "The Palimpsestic Past: Crime Fiction, Cultural Memory and Catalonia." In *Bulletin of Hispanic Studies* 94. 8: 817–830.

Klemperer, Victor (1956) *vor 33 / nach 45: Gesammelte Aufsätze*. Berlin: Akademie-Verlag.

Kliger, Ilya (2010) "World Literature Beyond Hegemony in Yuri M. Lotman's Cultural Semiotics." In *Comparative Critical Studies* 7. 2–3: 257–274.

Klobucka, Anna (1997) "Theorizing the European Periphery." In *symploke* 5. 1: 119–135.

Kobis, Dewi Christa (2019) "Indonesian Literature Position in World Literature." In *Lingua Jurnal Ilmiah* 15. 1: 28–39.

Koch, Max (1973) [1877] "Introduction." In Hans-Joachim Schulz and Philip H. Rhein (eds) *Comparative Literature: The Early Years*. Chapel Hill, NC: The University of North Carolina Press, 67–77. ("Zur Einführung," in *Zeitschrift für vergleichende Litteraturgeschichte* 1: 1–12.)

Koch, Manfred (2002) *Weimaraner Weltbewohner. Zur Genese von Goethes "Weltliteratur"*. Tübingen: Niemeyer.
Kristal, Efraín (2002) "Considering Coldly … A Response to Franco Moretti." In *New Left Review* 15: 61–74.
Kristmannsson, Gauti (2014) "Die Entdeckung der Weltliteratur." In Andreas F. Kelletat and Aleksey Tashinskiy (eds) *Übersetzer als Entdecker: Ihr Leben und Werk als Gegenstand translationswissenschaftlicher und literaturgeschichtlicher Forschung*. Berlin: Frank & Timme.
Kuan, Chee Wah (2019) "The Articulation of Anti-China-Centrism in Sinophone Malaysian Films." In *Popular Communication* 17. 3: 219–232.
Kubin, Wolfgang (2018) "World Literature from and in China." In Weigui Fang (ed.) *Tensions in World Literature: Between the Local and the Universal*. Singapore: Palgrave Macmillan, 301–310.
Kulathunga, Chamini and Liyanage Amarakeerthi (2021) "Mapping the World in Sinhalese: Chamini Kulathunga in Conversation with Liyanage Amarakeerthi." In *Hopscotch Translation* (Tuesday, February 9). https://hopscotchtranslation.com/2021/02/04/kulathunga-amarakeerthi/.
Kumar, Amitava (ed.) (2003) *World Bank Literature*. Foreword by John Berger; afterword by Bruce Robbins. Minneapolis: University of Minnesota Press.
Laachir, Karima, Sara Marzagora and Francesca Orsini (2018) "Significant Geographies in lieu of World Literature." In *Journal of World Literature* 3. 3: 290–310.
Labelle, Maurice Jr M. (2020) "On the Decolonial Beginnings of Edward Said." In *Modern Intellectual History* 19: 600–624.
Laclau, Ernesto and Chantal Mouffe (1987) *Hegemony and Socialist Strategy: Towards a Radical Democratic Politics*. London: Verso.
Lambert, José (1987) "Un modèle descriptif pour l'étude de la littérature: la littérature comme polysystème." *Contextos* 9. 5: 47–67.
Lamping, Dieter (2010) *Die Idee der Weltliteratur: Ein Konzept Goethes und seine Karriere*. Stuttgart: Kröner.
Lamping, Dieter (ed.) (2015) *Meilensteine der Weltliteratur: Von der Aufklärung bis in die Gegenwart*. Stuttgart: Kröner.
Landrin, Xavier (2010) "La sémantique historique de la *Weltliteratur*: genèse conceptuelle et usages savants." In Anna Boschetti (ed.) *L'Espace culturel transnational*. Paris: Nouveau Monde.
Large, Duncan, Moroko Akashi, Wanda Józwickowska and Emily Rose (eds) (2018) *Untranslatability: Interdisciplinary Perspectives*. London: Routledge.
Larsen, Neil (2022) "The Jargon of Decoloniality." In *Catalyst: A Journal of Theory & Strategy* 6. 2: 52–77.
Larsen, Svend Erik (2010) "Local Literatures, Global Perspectives: On Writing a Literary History for Secondary Schools." In *Otherness: Essays and Studies* 1. 1: 1–30. http://www.otherness.dk/journal/ (accessed 29 November 2010).
Larsen, Svend Erik (2012) "Georg Brandes: The Telescope of Comparative Literature." In Theo D'haen, David Damrosch and Djelal Kadir (eds) *The Routledge Companion to World Literature*. London: Routledge, 21–31.
Larsen, Svend Erik (2017) "Australia between White Australia and Multiculturalism: A World Literature Perspective." In *Comparative Literature: East & West* 1. 1: 74–95.
Larsen, Svend Erik (2022) "Georg Brandes: The Telescope of Comparative Literature." In Theo D'haen, David Damrosch and Djelal Kadir (eds) *The Routledge Companion to World Literature*. Second Edition. London: Routledge, 19–28.

Lasker, Bruno (1944) "Oceania in World Literature." In *Far Eastern Survey* 13. 8: 72–73.

Lawall, Sarah (1968) *Critics of Consciousness: The Existential Structures of Literature.* Cambridge, MA: Harvard University Press.

Lawall, Sarah (1988.) "The Alternate World of World Literature." In *ADE Bulletin* 90: 53–58.

Lawall, Sarah (ed.) (1994) *Reading World Literature: Theory, History, Practice.* Austin, TX: Texas University Press.

Lawall, Sarah (1996) "Richard Moulton and the Idea of World Literature." In Michael Thomas Carroll (ed.) *No Small World: Visions and Revisions of World Literature.* Urbana, Illinois: National Council of Teachers of English, 3–19.

Lawall, Sarah (2004) "Anthologizing 'World Literature'." In Jeffrey R. Di Leo (ed.) *On Anthologies: Politics and Pedagogy.* Edited and with an introduction by Jeffrey R. Di Leo. Lincoln and London: University of Nebraska Press, 47–89.

Lawall, Sarah (2009) "The West and the Rest: Frames for World Literature." In David Damrosch (ed.) *Teaching World Literature.* New York: The Modern Language Association of America, 17–33.

Lazarus, Neil (1999) *Nationalism and Cultural Practice in the Postcolonial World.* Cambridge: Cambridge University Press.

Le Bris, Michel and Jean Rouaud (eds) (2007) *Pour une littérature-monde.* Paris: Gallimard.

Lee, Meera and Edwin Van Bibber-Orr (2016) "Reshaping East Asia, Rethinking-World Literature." In *SYMPOSIUM* 70. 3: 109–111.

Lefevere, André (ed.) (1992) *Translation/History/Culture: A Sourcebook.* London: Routledge.

Lefevere, André (2000) [1982] "Mother Courage's Cucumbers: Text, System and Refraction in a Theory of Literature." In Lawrence Venuti (ed.) *The Translation Studies Reader.* London and New York: Routledge, 233–249.

Lernout, Geert (2006) "Comparative Literature in the Low Countries." In *Comparative Critical Studies* 3. 1–2: 37–46.

Levie, Sophie and Maarten De Pourcq (eds) (2018) *European Literary History: An Introduction.* London: Routledge.

Liew, Brandon K. (2021) "The Unquiet Dreams of Lesser Malaysian Writers: Tradition and the Global Malaysian Novel." In *Archiv Orientalni* 89. 2: 283–310.

Lima, Luiz Costa (1980) *Mimesis e Modernidade.* Rio de Janeiro: Graal.

Lima, Luiz Costa (2003) *O Redemunho do Horror: As Margens do Ocidente.* São Paulo: Editora Planeta.

Lima, Luiz Costa (2009) *O controle do imaginário & a afirmação do romance.* São Paulo: Companhia das letras.

Lima, Thayse Leal (2017) "Translation and World Literature: The Perspective of the 'Ex-Centric'." In *Journal of Latin American Cultural Studies* 26. 3: 461–481.

Lindenberger, Herbert (1990) "On the Sacrality of Reading Lists: The Western Culture Debate at Stanford University." In Herbert Lindenberger. *The History in Literature: On Value, Genre, Institutions.* New York: Columbia University Press. http://www.pbs.org/shattering/lindenberger.html (accessed 29 October 2010).

Lionnet, Françoise (2012) "World Literature, Francophonie, and Creole Cosmopolitics." In Theo D'haen, David Damrosch and Djelal Kadir (eds) *The Routledge Companion to World Literature.* London: Routledge, 325–335.

Lionnet, Françoise (2022) "World Literature, Francophonie, and Creole Cosmopolitics." In Theo D'haen, David Damrosch and Djelal Kadir (eds) *The Routledge Companion to World Literature*. Second Edition. London: Routledge, 267–276.

Liu, Hongtao (2018) "How to Become World Literature: Chinese Literature's Aspiration and Way to 'Step into the World'." In Weigui Fang (ed.) *Tensions in World Literature: Between the Local and the Universal*. Singapore: Palgrave Macmillan, 287–299.

Liyong, Taban Lo (2018) "Indigenous African Literary Forms May Determine the Future Course of World Literature." In *English in Africa* 45. 2: 17–28.

Llovet, Jordi (ed.) (2003) *Lecciones de literatura universal: siglos XII a XX*. Madrid: Cátedra.

Löffler, Sigrid (2013) *Die neue Weltliteratur und ihre großen Erzähler*. München: C.H. Beck.

Loliée, Frédéric (1906) [1903] *A Short History of Comparative Literature from the Earliest Times to the Present Day*, translated by M. Douglas Power. London: Hodder and Stoughton.

Lu, Sheldon (in press) "The Early Modern Period, Dream of the Red Chamber, and World Literature." In *JWL (Journal of World Literature)*.

Luhmann, Niklas (1989) *Ecological Communication*. Cambridge: Polity Press.

Lukács, Geörgy (1974) [1916] *The Theory of the Novel*. Cambridge, Mass.: MIT Press.

Lukács, Geörgy (1983) [1937] *The Historical Novel*. Omaha: University of Nebraska Press.

Lukács, Geörgy (2001) [1938] "Realism in the Balance." In Vincent B. Leitch (ed.) *The Norton Anthology of Theory and Criticism*. New York: Norton, 1033–1058.

Lund, Joshua (2001) "Barbarian Theorizing and the Limits of Latin American Exceptionalism." In *Cultural Critique* 47: 54–90.

Ma, Sheng-mei (2017) *Sinophone-Anglophone Cultural Duet*. Cham: Palgrave Macmillan.

Macaulay, Thomas Babington (2011) [1835] *Minute on Indian Education*. http://www.columbia.edu/itc/mealac/pritchett/00generallinks/macaulay/txt_minute_educa-tion_1835.html (accessed 8 February 2011).

Macdonald, Graeme (2017) "'Monstrous Transformer': Petrofiction and World Literature." In *Journal of Postcolonial Writing* 53. 3: 289–302.

Macy, John Albert (1925) *The Story of the World's Literature*. Garden City, NY: Garden City Publishing Co.

Majumder, Auritro (2021) *Insurgent Imaginations: World Literature and the Periphery*. Cambridge: Cambridge University Press.

Maldonado-Torres, Nelson (2006) "Césaire's Gift and the Decolonial Turn." In *Radical Philosophy Review* 9. 2: 114.

Maldonado-Torres, Nelson (2007) "On Coloniality of Being: Contributions to the Development of a Concept." In *Cultural Studies* 21. 2–3: 240–270.

Maldonado-Torres, Nelson (2011) "Thinking Through the Decolonial Turn: Postcontinental Interventions in Theory, Philosophy, and Critique – An Introduction." In *Transmodernity: Journal of Peripheral Cultural Production of Luso-Hispanic World* 1. 2: 1–15.

Mangalagiri, Adhira (2023) *States of Disconnect: The China-India Literary Relation in the Twentieth Century*. New York: Columbia University Press.

Manguel, Alberto (1996) *A History of Reading*. New York: HarperCollins.

Mani, B. Venkat (2012) "Bibliomigrancy: Book Series and the Making of World Literature." In Theo D'haen, David Damrosch and Djelal Kadir (eds) *The Routledge Companion to World Literature*. London: Routledge, 283–296.

Mani, B. Venkat (2017) *Recoding World Literature: Libraries, Print Culture, and Germany's Pact with Books.* New York: Fordham University Press.

Mani, B. Venkat (2021) "The Indian Republic, Reading Publics, and World Literary Catalogues." In Debjani Ganguli (ed.) *The Cambridge History of World Literature. Volume*II. Cambridge: Cambridge University Press, 821–841.

Mani, B. Venkat (2022) "Canons and Caravans of Bibliomigrancy: Creating World Literary Readerships." In Theo D'haen, David Damrosch and Djelal Kadir (eds) *The Routledge Companion to World Literature.* Second Edition. London and New York: Routledge, 234–242.

Marno, David (2008) "The Monstrosity of Literature: Hugo Meltzl's World Literature and its Legacies." In Karen-Margrethe Simonsen and Jakob Stougaard-Nielsen (eds) *World Literature, World Culture: History, Theory, Analysis.* Aarhus: Aarhus University Press, 37–50.

Marx, Karl and Friedrich Engels (2010) [1848] *Communist Manifesto.* http://www.marxists.org/archive/marx/works/download/pdf/Manifesto.pdf (accessed 14 December 2010).

Marx, William (2020) *Vivre dans la bibliothèque du monde.* Paris: Collège de France/Fayard.

Mata, Inocência (2013) "Literatura-Mundo em português: encruzilhadas em África – World Literature in Portuguese: Intersections in Africa." In *1616: Anuario de Literatura Comparada* 3: 107–122.

Mather, Jeffrey (2014) "Sinophone Studies: A Critical Reader." In *Journal of Postcolonial Writing* 50. 3: 373–374.

Mattar, Karim (2020) *Specters of World Literature: Orientalism, Modernity, and the Novel in the Middle East.* Edinburgh: Edinburg University Press.

McDonald, Christie and Susan Rubin Suleiman (eds) (2010) *Global French: A New Approach to Literary History.* New York: Columbia University Press.

McGann, Jerome (2008) "Pseudodoxia Academica." In *New Literary History* 39. 3: 645–656.

McHale, Brian (1987) *Postmodernist Fiction.* New York and London: Methuen.

McHale, Brian (1992) *Constructing Postmodernism.* New York, London: Routledge.

McMartin, Jack (2019a) *Book to Book: Flanders in the Transnational Literary Field.* PhD Dissertation University of Leuven.

McMartin, Jack (2019b) "'Our Catalogue is our National Literature': State Agents and Target(ed) Publisher Outreach in the World Market for Book Translations." In Beatriz Martínez Ojeda and María Luisa Rodríguez Muñoz (eds) *Translation in and for Society: Sociological and Cultural Approaches in Translation.* Córboba: Editorial Universidad de Córdoba, 23–40.

McMartin, Jack (2019c) "A Small, Stateless Nation in the World Market for Book Translations: The Politics and Policies of the Flemish Literature Fund." In *TTR: Traduction, terminologie, rédaction* 32. 1: 145–175.

McMartin, Jack (2020) "Dutch Literature in Translation: A Global View." In *Dutch Crossing: A Journal of Low Country Studies* 44. 2: 145–164.

McMartin, Jack (2021) "The International Circulation of Dutch Literature from Flanders." In *Canadian Journal of Netherlandic Studies/Revue canadienne d'études néerlandaises* 41. 2: 17–32.

McMartin, Jack and Paola Gentile (2020) "The Transnational Production and Reception of 'a Future Classic': Stefan Hertmans's *War and Turpentine* in Thirty Languages." In *Translation Studies* 13. 3: 271–290.

Meltzl de Lomnitz, Hugo (1973) [1877] "Present Tasks of Comparative Literature, Parts I and II." In Hans-Joachim Schulz and Philip H. Rhein (eds) *Comparative Literature: The Early Years.* Chapel Hill, NC: The University of North Carolina Press, 56–62. ("Vorläufige Aufgaben der vergleichenden Literatur", *Acta comparationis litterarum universarum* 1 [January 1877]: 179–182 and 2 [October 1877]: 307–315.)

Menand, Louis (2005) "All That Glitters: Literature's Global Economy." In *The New Yorker* (December 26).

Mignolo, Walter (1988) "Globalization, Civilization Processes, and the Relocation of Languages and Cultures." In Fredric Jameson and Masao Miyoshi (eds) *The Cultures of Globalization.* Durham and London: Duke University Press, 32–53.

Mignolo, Walter (1995) *The Darker Side of the Renaissance: Literacy, Territoriality, and Colonization.* Ann Arbor: The University of Michigan Press.

Mignolo, Walter (2000) *Local Histories/Global Designs: Coloniality, Subaltern Knowledges, and Border Thinking.* Princeton: Princeton University Press.

Mignolo, Walter (2007a) "Introduction: Coloniality of Power and De-Colonial Thinking." In *Cultural Studies* 21. 2–3: 155–167.

Mignolo, Walter (2007b) "Delinking: The Rhetoric of Modernity, the Logic of Coloniality and the Grammar of Decoloniality." In *Cultural Studies* 21. 2–3: 449–514.

Mignolo, Walter (2011) *The Darker Side of Western Modernity: Global Futures, Decolonial Options.* Durham and London: Duke University Press.

Mignolo, Walter (2021) *The Politics of Decolonial Investigations.* Durham and London: Duke University Press.

Mignolo, Walter and Arturo Escobar (eds) (2010) *Globalization and the Decolonial Option.* London: Routledge.

Min, Eric (2013) *De eeuw van Brussel: Biografie van een wereldstad 1850–1914.* Antwerpen: De Bezige Bij.

Miner, Earl (1990) *Comparative Poetics: An Intercultural Essay on Theories of Literature.* Princeton: Princeton University Press.

Mishra, Vijay and Bob Hodge (1991) "What is Post(-)Colonialism?" In *Textual Practice* 5. 3: 399–414.

Møller, Peter Ulf (1989) "Writing the History of World Literature in the USSR." In *Culture and History* 5: 19–37.

Moore, Jason (2003) "The Modern World-System as Environmental History? Ecology and the Rise of Capitalism." in *Theory and Society* 32: 307–377.

Moore, Jason W. (2016) "Introduction: Anthropocene or Capitalocene? Nature, History, and the Crisis of Capitalism." In Jason W. Moore (ed.) *Anthropocene or Capitalocene? Nature, History, and the Crisis of Capitalism.* Oakland: P M Press, 1–11.

Moretti, Franco (1998) *Atlas of the European Novel, 1800–1900.* London: Verso.

Moretti, Franco (2000) "The Slaughterhouse of Literature." In *Modern Language Quarterly* (March): 207–227.

Moretti, Franco (2003) "More Conjectures." In *New Left Review* 20: 73–81.

Moretti, Franco (2004) [2000] "Conjectures on World Literature." In Christopher Prendergast (ed.) *Debating World Literature.* London: Verso, 148–162. (Originally in *New Left Review* 1 [January-February 2000]: 54–68.)

Moretti, Franco (2005) *Graphs, Maps, Trees: Abstract Models for Literary Study.* London: Verso.

Moretti, Franco (2009a) [2006] "*Evolution, World-System, Weltliteratur.*" In David Damrosch, Natalie Melas and Mbongiseni Buthelezi (eds) *The Princeton Sourcebook in Comparative Literature.* Princeton: Princeton University Press, 399–408.

(Originally in *Studying Transcultural Literary History*, ed. Gunilla Lindberg-Wada, Berlin: De Gruyter, 113–121.)

Moretti, Franco (2009b) "Style, Inc. Reflections on Seven Thousand Titles (British Novels, 1740–1850)." In *Critical Inquiry* 36: 134–158.

Moretti, Franco (2010) "History of the Novel, Theory of the Novel." In *Novel* 43. 1: 1–10.

Moretti, Franco (2011) "Network Theory, Plot Analysis." In *New Left Review* 68: 80–102.

Moretti, Franco (2013a) *Distant Reading*. London and New York: Verso.

Moretti, Franco (2013b) "'Operationalizing' or, the Function of Measurement in Literary Theory." In *New Left Review* 84: 103–119.

Moretti, Franco (2017) *Canon/Archive: Studies in Quantitative Formalism*. n+1 Foundation.

Moretti, Franco (2022) *Falsche Bewegung: Die digitale Wende in den Literatur- und Kulturwissenschaften*. Transl. Bettina Engels. Konstanz: Konstanz University Press.

Moser, Christian and Linda Simonis (eds) (2014) *Figuren des Globalen: Weltbezug und Welterzeugung in Literatur, Kunst und Medien*. Bonn: Bonn University Press.

Moulton, Richard Green (1921) [1911] *World Literature and Its Place in General Culture*. New York: The Macmillan Company.

Moulton, Richard Green (1915) *The Modern Study of Literature: An Introduction to Literary Theory and Interpretation*. Chicago: University of Chicago Press.

Moura, Jean-Marc (1999) *Littératures francophones et théorie postcoloniale*. Paris: Puf (Presses universitaires de France).

Moura, Jean-Marc (2016) "D'un sous-ensemble de la littérature mondiale: Les lettres transatlantiques." In *Canadian Review of Comparative Literature / Revue Canadienne de Littérature Comparée* 43. 3: 406–413.

Moura, Jean-Marc (2023) *Totalité littéraire: Théorie et enjeux de la littérature mondiale*. Paris: Presses Universitaires de France.

Mouré, Erin [Eirin Moure] (2001) *Sheep's Vigil by a Fervent Person: A Transelation of Alberto Caeiro/Fernando Pessoa's O guardador de rebanhos*. Toronto: Anansi.

Mufti, Aamir R. (2016) *Forget English! Orientalisms and World Literatures*. Cambridge, Mass: Harvard University Press.

Müller, Gesinne, Jorge L. Locane and Benjamin Loy (eds) (2018) *Re-Mapping World Literature: Writing, Book Markets, and Epistemologies between Latin America and the Global South*. Berlin: De Gruyter.

Murray, Simone (2019) "Secret Agents: Algorithmic Culture, Goodreads and Datafication of the Contemporary Book World." In *European Journal of Cultural Studies* 24. 4: 970–989.

al-Musawi, Muhsin J. (2021) *The Arabian Nights in Contemporary World Cultures: Global Commodification, Translation, and the Culture Industry*. Cambridge: Cambridge University Press.

Nakai, Asako (2000) *The English Book and Its Marginalia: Colonial/Postcolonial Literature after Heart of Darkness*. Amsterdam and New York: Rodopi.

Nardizzi, Vin and Tiffany Jo Werth (eds) (2019) *Premodern Ecologies in the Modern Literary Imagination*. Toronto: University of Toronto Press.

Ndlovu-Gatshen, Sabelo J. (2015) "Decoloniality as the Future of Africa." In *History Compass* 13. 10: 485–496.

Nestingen, Andrew (2016) "Scandinavian Crime Fiction and the Facts: Social Criticism, Epistemology, and Globalization." In Andrew Pepper and David Schmid (eds) *Globalization and the State in Contemporary Crime Fiction: A World of Crime*. London: Palgrave Macmillan, 159–177.

Nethersole, Reingard (2012) "World Literature and the Library." In Theo D'haen, David Damrosch and Djelal Kadir (eds) *The Routledge Companion to World Literature*. London and New York: Routledge, 307–315.

Nethersole, Reingard (2022) "World Literature and the Library." In Theo D'haen, David Damrosch and Djelal Kadir (eds) *The Routledge Companion to World Literature*. Second Edition. London and New York: Routledge, 250–258.

Niblett, Michael (2012) "World-Economy, World-Ecology, World Literature." In *Green Letters* 16. 1: 15–30.

Niblett, Michael (2020) *World Literature and Ecology: The Aesthetics of Commodity Frontiers, 1890–1945*. Cham: Palgrave Macmillan.

Nilsson, Louise, David Damrosch and Theo D'haen (eds) (2017) *Crime Fiction as World Literature*. New York, London, etc.: Bloomsbury.

Nixon, Rob (2011) *Slow Violence and the Environmentalism of the Poor*. Cambridge, Mass.: Harvard University Press.

Nussbaum, Martha C. (1997) *Cultivating Humanity: A Classical Defense of Reform in Liberal Education*. Cambridge, Mass.: Harvard University Press.

Nussbaum, Martha C. (2019) *The Cosmopolitan Tradition: A Noble but Flawed Ideal*. Cambridge, Mass.: The Belknap Press of Harvard University Press.

Orsini, Francesca (2002) "Maps of Indian Writing." In *New Left Review* 13: 75–88.

Orsini, Francesca (2007) "India in the Mirror of World Fiction." In *New Left Review* 12. 1: 75–88.

Orsini, Francesca (2012) "How to Do Multilingual Literary History? Lessons from Fifteenth- and Sixteenth-Century North India." In *Indian Economic and Social History Review* 49. 2: 225–246.

Orsini, Francesca (2019) "World Literature, Indian Views, 1920s-1940s." In *Journal of World Literature* 4. 1: 46–81.

Orsini, Francesca (2021) "The Multilingual Local: Worlding Literature in India." In Dejani Ganguly (ed.) *The Cambridge History of World Literature*, Volume I. Cambridge: Cambridge University Press, 411–428.

Orsini, Francesca (2023) *East of Delhi: Multilingual Literary Culture and World Literature*. Oxford: Oxford University Press.

Orsini, Francesca and Laetitia Zecchini (2019) "The Locations of (World) Literature: Perspectives from Africa and South Asia." In *Journal of World Literature* 4. 1: 1–12.

Ortiz, Fernando (2002) [1940] *Contrapunteo cubano del tabaco y el azúcar*. Edición de Enrico Mario Santí. Madrid: Catedra.

Ortiz, Fernando (1995) *Cuban Counterpoint: Tobacco and Sugar*. Durham and London: Duke University Press.

Owen, Stephen (1990) "What Is World Poetry?" In *The New Republic* (November 19): 28–32.

Parham, John and Louise Westling (eds) (2017) *A Global History of Literature and the Environment*. Cambridge: Cambridge University Press.

Park, Sowon (2013) "The Pan-Asian Empire and World Literatures." In *CLCWeb: Comparative Literature and Culture* 15. 5, article 15. docs.lib.purdue.edu/clcweb/vol15/iss5/15/.

Park, Sowon (2016) "Introduction: Transnational Scriptworlds." In *Journal of World Literature* 1. 2: 275–293.

Park, Sowon (2018) "Scriptworlds." In Ben Etherington and Jarad Zimbler (eds) *The Cambridge Companion to World Literature*. Cambridge: Cambridge University Press, 100–115.

Pepper, Andrew and David Schmid (eds) (2016) *Globalization and the State in Contemporary Crime Fiction: A World of Crime*. London: Palgrave Macmillan.

Perloff, Marjorie (1995) "'Literature' in the Expanded Field." In Charles Bernheimer (ed.) *Comparative Literature in the Age of Multiculturalism*. Baltimore and London: The Johns Hopkins University Press, 175–186.

Pettegree, Andrew and Arthur der Weduwen (2019) *The Bookshop of the World: Making and Trading Books in the Dutch Golden Age*. New Haven, Conn.: Yale University Press.

Pettegree, Andrew and Arthur der Weduwen (2021) *The Library: A Fragile History*. London: Profile Books.

Pettersson, Anders (2005) "The Possibility of Global Literary History." In Suthira Duangsamosorn, et al. (eds) *Re-Imagining Language and Literature for the 21st Century*. Amsterdam and New York: Rodopi, 55–66.

Pettersson, Anders (2008) "Transcultural Literary History: Beyond Constricting Notions of World Literature." In *New Literary History* 39: 463–479.

Pezzotti, Barbara (2016) *Investigating Italy's Past through Historical Crime Fiction, Films, and TV Series: Murder in the Age of Chaos*. New York: Palgrave Macmillan.

Pichois, Claude and A.M. Rousseau (1967) *La littérature comparée*. Paris: Armand Colin.

Pizer, John (2006) *The Idea of World Literature: History and Pedagogical Practice*. Baton Rouge, LA: Louisiana State University Press.

Pohl, Karl Heinz (2018) "Chinese Literature as Part of World Literature." In Weigui Fang (ed.) *Tensions in World Literature: Between the Local and the Universal*. Singapore: Palgrave Macmillan, 265–286.

Pollock, Sheldon (1996) "The Sanskrit Cosmopolis, 300–1300: Transculturation, Vernacularization and the Question of Ideology." In Jan Houben (ed.) *Ideology and Status of Sanskrit: Contributions to the History of the Sanskrit Language*. Leiden: Brill, 197–249.

Pollock, Sheldon (2006). *The Language of the Gods: Sanskrit, Culture, and Power in Premodern India*. Berkeley, Los Angeles, London: University of California Press.

Ponzanesi, Sandra (2021) "The Cultural Industry and Digital World Making." In Debjani Ganguly (ed.) *The Cambridge History of World Literature*, Volume II. Cambridge: Cambridge University Press, 842–863.

"Pour une 'littérature-monde' en français." *Le Monde* 16 mars 2007.

Posnett, Hutcheson Macaulay (1886) *Comparative Literature*. London: Kegan Paul, Trench & Co.

Posnett, Hutcheson Macaulay (2009) [1886] "The Comparative Method and Literature." In David Damrosch, Natalie Melas and Mbongiseni Buthelezi (eds) *The Princeton Sourcebook in Comparative Literature*. Princeton: Princeton University Press, 50–60.

Posnett, Hutcheson Macaulay (1973) [1901] "The Science of Comparative Literature." In Hans-Joachim Schulz and Philip H. Rhein (eds) *Comparative Literature: The Early Years*. Chapel Hill, NC: The University of North Carolina Press, 186–206.

Pradeau, Christophe and Tiphaine Samoyault (eds) (2005) *Où est la littérature mondiale?*Vincennes: Presses universitaires de Vincennes.

Pratt, Mary Louise (1991) "Arts of the Contact Zone." In *Profession*: 33–40.

Pratt, Mary Louise (2022) *Planetary Longings*. Durham and London: Duke University Press.

Prawer, Siegbert S. (1976) *Karl Marx and World Literature*. Oxford: Oxford University Press.
Prendergast, Christopher (ed.) (2004a) *Debating World Literature*. London and New York: Verso.
Prendergast, Christopher (2004b) [2001] "The World Republic of Letters." In Christopher Prendergast (ed.) *Debating World Literature*. London: Verso, 1–25. (Originally as "Negotiating World Literature," in *New Left Review*, second series, *8*, March/April 2001.)
Puchner, Martin (2017) *The Written World: The Power of Stories to Shape People, History, Civilization*. New York: Random House.
Puchner, Martin (2022) *Literature for a Changing Planet*. Princeton: Princeton University Press.
Puchner, Martin, et al. (eds) (2012–2018) *The Norton Anthology of World Literature*. 6 vols New York and London: W.W. Norton & Company.
Quayson, Ato (2021) "Reading World Literature through the Postcolonial and Diasporic Lens." In Debjani Ganguly (ed.) *The Cambridge History of World Literature*, Volume II. Cambridge: Cambridge University Press, 804–820.
Querrien, Anne (1986) "The Metropolis and the Capital." In *Zone* 1–2: 219–221.
Quijano, Anibal (1991) "Colonialidad y Modernidad/Racionalidad." In *Perú Indígena* 13. 29: 11–20. Lima: Instituto Indigenista Peruano.
Quijano, Anibal (1999) "Coloniality and Modernity/Rationality." In Goran Therborn (ed.) *Globalizations and Modernities*. Stockholm: FRN.
Quijano, Anibal (2000a) "Coloniality of Power and Social Classification." In *Journal of World Systems* 6. 2: 342–386.
Quijano, Anibal (2000b) "Coloniality of Power, Eurocentrism and Latin America." In *Nepantla: Views from the South* 1. 3: 533–579.
Quijano, Anibal (2007) "Coloniality and Modernity/Rationality." In *Cultural Studies* 21. 2–3: 168–178.
Rama, Ángel (2008) [1982] *Transculturación narrativa en América Latina*. Buenos Aires: El Andariego.
Rama, Ángel (2012) *Writing across Cultures: Narrative Transculturation in Latin America*. Edited and translated by David Frye. Durham and London: Duke University Press.
Ramazani, Jahan (2009) *A Transnational Poetics*. Chicago: University of Chicago Press.
Ramazani, Jahan (2019) "Persian Poetry, World Poetry, and Translatability." In *University of Toronto Quarterly* 88. 2: 210–228.
Remak, H.H. (1961) "Comparative Literature: Its Definition and Function." In Newton P. Stallknecht and Horst Frenz (eds) *Comparative Literature: Method and Perspective*. Carbondale and Edwardsville and London: Southern Illinois University Press, 1–57.
Ribeiro, Darcy (2000) *The Brazilian People: Formation and Meaning of Brazil*. Transl. Gregory Rabassa. Gainesville: UP of Florida.
Ricci, Ronit (2010) "Islamic Literary Networks in South and Southeast Asia." In *Journal of Islamic Studies* 21. 1: 1–28.
Ricci, Ronit (2011) *Islam Translated: Literature, Conversion, and the Arabic Cosmopolis of South and Southeast Asia*. Chicago: Chicago University Press.
Ricci, Ronit (2012) "World Literature and Muslim Southeast Asia." In Theo D'haen, David Damrosch and Djelal Kadir (eds) *The Routledge Companion to World Literature*. London and New York: Routledge, 497–506.

Ricci, Ronit (2019) *Banishment and Belonging: Exile and Diaspora in Sarandib, Lanka and Ceylon*. Cambridge: Cambridge University Press.

Ricci, Ronit (2022) "World Literature and Muslim Southeast Asia." In Theo D'haen, David Damrosch and Djelal Kadir (eds) *The Routledge Companion to World Literature*. Second Edition. London and New York: Routledge, 434–441.

Riddle, Amy (2018) "Petrofiction and Political Economy in the Age of Late Fossil Capital." In *Mediations: Journal of the Marxist Literary Group* 31. 2: s.l. (Web).

Ringgaard, Dan and Mads Rosendahl Thomsen (eds) (2010) *Verdenslitteratur i bevægelse: Nye tilgange til verdenslitteratur* [World Literature on the Move: New Approaches to World Literature]. Aarhus: Aarhus Universitetsforlag/Aarhus University Press.

Ringgaard, Dan and Mads Rosendahl Thomsen (eds) (2018) *Danish Literature as World Literature*. London and New York: Bloomsbury.

Riquer, Martín de and José María Valverde (2010) *Historia de la literatura universal*. 2 Vols. Madrid: Gredos.

Riva, Silvia (2020) "Global Congo." In *Continents Manuscrits* 15. Web.

Robbins, Bruce (1999) *Feeling Global: Internationalism in Distress*. New York and London: New York University Press.

Robbins, Bruce and Paulo Lemos Horta (2017) *Cosmopolitanisms*. New York: New York University Press.

Rojas, Carlos (2018) "A World Republic of Southern [Sinophone] Letters." In *Modern Chinese Literature and Culture* 30. 1: 42–62.

Rooney, Brigid and Brigita Olubas (eds) (2015) *Australian Literature / World Literature: borders, skins, mappings. JASAL* 15. 3.

Said, Edward (1979) [1978] *Orientalism*. New York: Random House.

Said, Edward (1984) [1983] "The World, The Text, and the Critic." In *The World, the Text, and the Critic*. London: Faber and Faber, 31–53.

Said, Edward (1993) *Culture and Imperialism*. London: Chatto and Windus.

Said, Edward (2003) "*Orientalism* 25 Years Later: Worldly Humanism v. the Empire-Builders." In *CounterPunch* (August 4). http://www.counterpunch.org/said08052003.html (accessed 1 March 2011).

Said, Edward (2004) *Humanism and Democratic Criticism*. New York: Columbia University Press.

Sakai, Cécile and Nao Sawada (eds) (2021) *Pour une autre littérature mondiale: La traduction franco-japonaise en perspective*. Arles: Editions Picquier.

Sánchez Prado, Ignacio (2018) *Strategic Occidentalism: On Mexican Fiction, the Neoliberal Book Market, and the Question of World Literature*. Chicago: Northwestern University Press.

Sangari, Kumkum (1990) "The Politics of the Possible." In Abdul R. JanMohamed and David Lloyd (eds) *The Nature and Context of Minority Discourse*. New York and Oxford: Oxford University Press, 216–245.

Sapiro, Gisèle and Delia Ungureanu (eds) (2022) *Pascale Casanova's World of Letters and Its Legacies*. Leiden and Boston: Brill.

Saussy, Haun (ed.) (2006a) *Comparative Literature in an Age of Globalization*. Baltimore: The Johns Hopkins University Press.

Saussy, Haun (2006b) "Exquisite Cadavers Stitched from Fresh Nightmares: Of Memes, Hives, and Selfish Genes." In Haun Saussy (ed.) *Comparative Literature in an Age of Globalization*. Baltimore: The Johns Hopkins University Press, 3–42.

268 Bibliography

Saussy, Haun (2018) "The Comparative History of East Asian Literatures: A Sort of Manifesto." In *Modern Languages Open* 1: 1–6.
Schamoni, Wolfgang (2008) "'Weltliteratur' zuerst 1773 bei August Ludwig Schlözer." In *Arcadia* 43: 288–298.
Scherr, Johannes (1848) *Bildersaal der Weltliteratur*. Stuttgart: Ad. Becher.
Scherr, Johannes (1851) *Allgemeine Geschichte der Literatur von den ältesten Zeiten bis auf die Gegenwart. Ein handbuch für alle Gebildeten*. Stuttgart: Franck'sche Buchhandlung.
Scherr, Johannes (1895) *Illustrierte Geschichte der Weltliteratur. Ein Handbuch in zwei Bänden*. Neunte Auflage. Durchgesehen und bis auf die neueste Zeit ergänzt von Otto Haggenmeister. Stuttgart: Franck'sche Verlagsbuchhandlung.
Schlözer, August Ludwig von (1773) *Isländische Literatur und Geschichte*. Göttingen and Gotha: Joh. Christian Dieterich.
Schlözer, August Ludwig von (1792–1801) *Weltgeschichte nach ihren Haupttheilen im Auszug und Zusammenhange*. 2 vols. Göttingen.
Schmeling, Manfred (ed.) (1995) *Weltliteratur heute: Konzepte und Perspektiven*. Würzburg: Königshausen & Neumann.
Schmeling, Manfred, Monika Schmitz-Emans and Kerst Walstra (eds) (2000) *Literatur im Zeitalter der Globalisierung*. Würzburg: Königshausen & Neumann.
Schneider, Jost (2004) "Psychische Globalisierung? Vom Projekt einer Weltliteratur zur Realität des Weltunterhaltungskultur." In *TRANS: Internet-Zeitschrift für Kulturwissenschaften* 15 (April).
Schrimpf, Hans Joachim (1968) *Goethes Begriff der Weltliteratur*. Stuttgart: Metzler.
Schulz, Hans-Joachim and Philip H. Rhein (eds) (1973) *Comparative Literature: The Early Years*. Chapel Hill: The University of North Carolina Press.
Schwarz, Roberto (1970) *Um Mestre na Periferia do Capitalismo: Machado de Assis*. São Paulo: Duas Cidades.
Schwarz, Roberto (1992) *Misplaced Ideas: Essays on Brazilian Culture*. Edited and with an Introduction by John Gledson. London and New York: Verso.
Schwarz, Roberto (2001a) *A Master on the Periphery of Capitalism: Machado de Assis*. Translated and with an Introduction by John Gledson. Durham and London: Duke University Press.
Schwarz, Roberto (2001b) "National Adequation and Critical Originality." In *Cultural Critique* 49. 1: 18–42.
Seeba, Hinrich C. (2003) "Ernst Robert Curtius: Zur Kulturkritik eines Klassikers in der Wisschenschaftsgeschichte." In *Monatshefte* 95. 4: 532–540.
Shackford, Charles Chauncey (1973) (1871) "Comparative Literature." In Hans-Joachim Schulz and Philip H. Rhein (eds) *Comparative Literature: The Early Years*. Chapel Hill: The University of North Carolina Press, 42–51.
Shen, Shuang (2022) "Rethinking the History of Chinese Empires from the Sinophone South." In *Comparative Literature Studies* 59. 1: 123–141.
Shepard, Todd (2006) *The Invention of Decolonization: The Algerian War and the Remaking of France*. Ithaca: Cornell University Press.
Shi, Flair Donglai (2021) "Reconsidering Sinophone Studies: The Chinese Cold War, Multiple Sinocentrisms, and Theoretical Generalisation." In *International Journal of Taiwan Studies* 4: 311–344.
Shih, Shu-mei (2004) "Against Diaspora." In Shu-mei Shih, Chien-hsin Tsai and Brian Bernards (eds) *Sinophone Studies: A Critical Reader*. New York: Columbia University Press, 25–42.

Shih, Shu-mei (2007) *Visuality and Identity: Sinophone Articulations across the Pacific.* Berkeley and Los Angeles: University of California Press.
Shih, Shu-mei (2010) "Theory, Asia, and the Sinophone." In *Postcolonial Studies* 13. 4: 465–484.
Shih, Shu-mei (2011) "The Concept of the Sinophone." In *PMLA* 126. 3: 709–718.
Shih, Shu-mei (2012) "Foreword: The Sinophone as History and the Sinophone as Theory." In *Journal of Chinese Cinemas* 6. 1: 5–8.
Shih, Shu-mei, Chien-hsin Tsai and Brian Bernards (eds) (2012) *Sinophone Studies: A Critical Reader.* New York: Columbia University Press.
Shlovsky, Viktor (1970) *A Sentimental Journey: Memoirs, 1917–1922.* Transl. Richard Sheldon. Ithaca, NY: Cornell University Press. (Originally *Sentimental'noe puteshestvie: Vospominaniia, 1917–1922.* Moscow and Berlin: Gelikon, 1923.)
Shohat, Ella (1992) "Notes on the Post-Colonial." In *Social Text* 31–32: 93–111.
Shurtleff, Oliver (1947) "World Literature." In *The Clearing House* 21. 9: 575.
Simonsen, Karen-Margrethe and Jakob Stougaard-Nielsen (eds) (2008) *World Literature, World Culture: History, Theory, Analysis.* Aarhus: Aarhus University Press.
Sinopoli, Franca (2022) "Traiettorie della mondialità letteraria contemporanea in Europa. La letteratura transnazionale e la politica culturale europea." In *Le forme e la storia* 15. 1–2: 265–277.
Siskind, Mariano (2012) "The Genres of World Literature: The Case of Magical Realism." In Theo D'haen, David Damrosch and Djelal Kadir (eds) *The Routledge Companion to World Literature.* London: Routledge, 345–355.
Siskind, Mariano (2014) *Cosmopolitan Desires: Global Modernity and World Literature in Latin America.* Evanston: Northwestern University Press.
Siskind, Mariano (2022) "The Genres of World Literature: The Case of Magical Realism." In Theo D'haen, David Damrosch and Djelal Kadir (eds) *The Routledge Companion to World Literature.* Second Edition. London: Routledge, 294–304.
Slemon, Stephen (1991) "Modernism's Last Post." In Ian Adam and Helen Tiffin (eds) *Past the Last Post: Theorizing Post-Colonialism and Post-Modernism.* London: Harvester/Wheatsheaf, 1–11.
Sontag, Susan (1964) "Against Interpretation." In *Evergreen Review* 8. 34; also in Sontag 1966: 13–23.
Sontag, Susan (1966) *Against Interpretation and Other Essays.* New York: Dell.
Spivak, Gayatri (1988) "Can the Subaltern Speak?" In Cary Nelson and Lawrence Grossberg (eds) *Marxism and the Interpretation of Culture.* Basingstoke: Macmillan, 271–313.
Spivak, Gayatri (1999) *A Critique of Postcolonial Reason: Toward a History of the Vanishing Present.* Cambridge, Mass.: Harvard University Press.
Spivak, Gayatri (2000a) [1992] "The Politics of Translation." In Lawrence Venuti (ed.) *The Translation Studies Reader.* London and New York: Routledge, 397–416.
Spivak, Gayatri (2000b) "Translation as Culture." In *Parallax* 6. 1: 13–24.
Spivak, Gayatri (2003) *Death of a Discipline.* New York: Columbia University Press.
Spivak, Gayatri (2010) "Can the Subaltern Speak?" revised edition, from the "History" chapter of "Critique of Postcolonial Reason." In Rosalind C. Morris (ed.) *Can the Subaltern Speak? Reflections on the History of an Idea.* New York: Columbia University Press, 21–78.
Spoiden, Stéphane (1997) "The Treachery of Art: This Is Not Belgium." In *symplokē* 5. 1–2 (Special Issue: Refiguring Europe): 137–152.

Steiner, Ann (2012) "World Literature and the Market." In Theo D'haen, David Damrosch and Djelal Kadir (eds) *The Routledge Companion to World Literature*. London: Routledge, 316–324.

Steiner, Ann (2022) "World Literature and the Market." In Theo D'haen, David Damrosch and Djelal Kadir (eds) *The Routledge Companion to World Literature*. Second Edition. London: Routledge, 259–266.

Steinmetz, Horst (1985) "Weltliteratur: Umriss eines literaturgeschichtlichen Konzepts." In *Arcadia* 20. 1: 2–19. (Also in Horst Steinmetz [1988] *Literatur und Geschichte*. Munich: Iudicium Verlag, 103–126.)

Steinmetz, Horst (1988) *Literatur und Geschichte*. Munich: Iudicium Verlag.

Stenberg, Josh (2023) "Diverse Fragility, Fragile Diversity: Sinophone Writing in the Philippines and Indonesia." In *Asian Ethnicity* 24. 1: 59–77.

Stern, Adolf (1888) *Geschichte der Weltliteratur in übersichtlicher Darstellung*. Stuttgart: Rieger'sche Verlagsbuchhandlung.

Strich, Fritz (2013) [1930]. "World Literature and Comparative Literary History." In Theo D'haen, César Domínguez and Mads Rosendahl Thomsen (eds) *World Literature: A Reader*. London and New York: Routledge, 36–49. (Originally as "Weltliteratur und Vergleichende Literaturgeschichte" in Emil Ermatinger (ed.) [1930] *Philosophie der Literaturwissenschaft*, Berlin: Junker and Dünnhaupt, 422–441.)

Strich, Fritz (1957) [1946] *Goethe und die Weltliteratur*. Bern: Francke Verlag.

Strich, Fritz (1949) *Goethe and World Literature*. Transl. C.A.M. Sym. New York: Hafner Publishing Company.

Sturm-Trigonakis, Elke (2007) *Global playing in der Literatur: Ein Versuch über die Neue Weltliteratur*. Würzburg: Königshausen & Neumann.

SubStance (2009) "Editors' Preface." 11938.2: 3–7.

Swiggers, Pierre (1982) "A New Paradigm for Comparative Literature." In *Poetics Today* 3. 1: 181–184.

Szeman, Imre (2012) "Introduction to Focus: Petrofictions." In *American Book Review* 33. 3: 3.

Tagore, Rabindranath (2001) "World Literature." In *Rabindranath Tagore: Selected Writings on Literature and Language*, ed. Sukanta Chaudhuri. New Delhi: Oxford University Press, 138–150.

Tan, E.K. (2016) "In Search of New Forms: The Impact of Bilingual Policy and the 'Speak Mandarin' Campaign on Sinophone Singapore Poetry." In *interventions* 18. 4: 526–542.

Tanaka, Shouhei (2020) "The Great Arrangement: Planetary Petrofiction and Novel Futures." In *MFS Modern Fiction Studies* 66. 1: 190–215.

Tanoukhi, Nirvana (2008) "The Scale of World Literature." In *New Literary History* 39: 599–617.

Taylor, Byron (2022) "Untranslatability: The Rebirth of Theory?" In *Journal of Comparative Literature and Aesthetics* 45. 1: 25–39.

Texte, Joseph (1898) "L'histoire comparée des littératures." In *Etudes de littérature européenne*. Paris: Colin, 1–24.

Thiong'o, Ngugi wa (1986) *Decolonising the Mind: The Politics of Language in African Literatures*. London: James Currey Ltd/Heinemann.

Thomsen, Mads Rosendahl (2008a) *Mapping World Literature: International Canonization and Transnational Literatures*. London and New York: Continuum.

Thomsen, Mads Rosendahl (ed.) (2008b) *Verdenslitterær kritik og teori* [World Literature: Theory and Criticism]. Aarhus: Aarhus Universitetsforlag/Aarhus University Press.

Thornber, Karen (2009) *Empire of Texts in Motion: Chinese, Korean, and Taiwanese Transculturations of Japanese Literature*. Cambridge, Mass: Harvard.

Thornber, Karen (2012) *Ecoambiguity: Environmental Crises and East Asian Literatures*. Ann Arbor: Michigan.

Thornber, Karen (2014) "Rethinking the World in World Literature: East Asia and Literary Contact Nebulae." In David Damrosch (ed.) *World Literature in Theory*. London: Wiley Blackwell, 460–479.

Thornber, Karen (2020) *Global Healing: Literature, Advocacy, Care*. Leiden: Brill.

Tiffin, Helen (1991) "Introduction." In Ian Adam and Helen Tiffin (eds) *Past the Last Post: Theorizing Post-Colonialism and Post-Modernism*. London: Harvester/Wheatsheaf, vii–xvi.

Tihanov, Galin (2011) "Cosmopolitanism in the Discursive Landscape of Modernity: Two Enlightenment Articulations." In David Adams and Galin Tihanov (eds) *Enlightenment Cosmopolitanism*. London: Legenda, 133–152.

Tihanov, Galin (2017) "The Location of World Literature." In *Canadian Review of Comparative Literature / Revue Canadienne de Littérature Comparée* 44. 3: 468–481.

Tihanov, Galin (2019) *The Birth and Death of Literary Theory*. Redwood City: Stanford University Press. Kindle edition.

Tiwari, Bhavya (2022) *Beyond English: World Literature and India*. London and New York: Bloomsbury.

Tiwari, Bhavya and David Damrosch (eds) (2023) *World Literature and Postcolonial Studies*. Leiden and Boston: Brill.

Todd, Richard (1996) *Consuming Fictions: The Booker Prize and Fiction in Britain Today*. London: Bloomsbury.

Torre, Guillermo de (1956) "Goethe y la literatura universal." In *Las Metamórfosis de Proteo*. Buenos Aires: Losada, 278–289.

Tötösy de Zepetnek, Steven and Tutun Mukherjee (eds) (2013) *Companion to Comparative Literature, World Literatures, and Comparative Cultural Studies*. Foundation Books. New Delhi: Cambridge University Press India.

Toury, Gideon (1995) *Descriptive Translation Studies – and Beyond*. Amsterdam: John Benjamins.

"Toward a 'World-Literature' in French." Transl. Daniel Simon. 2009. In *World Literature Today* 8. 2: 54–56. ("Pour une 'littérature-monde' en français," *Le Monde* 16 mars 2007.)

Traninger, Anita and Federica La Manna (eds) (2023) *Die Rezension als Medium der Weltliteratur*. Berlin: De Gruyter.

Tsu, Jing (2010) "Getting Ideas about World Literature in China." In *Comparative Literature Studies* 47. 3: 290–317.

Tsu, Jing (2012) "World Literature and National Literature(s)." In Theo D'haen, David Damrosch and Djelal Kadir (eds) *The Routledge Companion to World Literature*. London: Routledge, 158–168.

Tsu, Jing (2022a) "World Literature and National Literature(s)." In Theo D'haen, David Damrosch and Djelal Kadir (eds) *The Routledge Companion to World Literature*. Second Edition. London: Routledge, 120–128.

Tsu, Jing (2022b) *Kingdom of Characters: A Tale of Language, Obsession, and Genius in Modern China*. London: Allen Lane.

Tsu, Jing and David Der-wei Wang (2010) "Introduction: Global Chinese Literature." In Jing Tsu and David Der-wei Wang (eds) *Global Chinese Literature: Critical Essays*. Leiden: Brill, 1–13.

Bibliography

Valentin, Jean-Marie (2007) "La *'Weltliteratur'* selon Goethe. Réalité et projet." In *Minerve et les muses. Essais de littérature allemande*. Paris: Presses de l'Université Paris-Sorbonne, 231–249.
Valéry, Paul (1960) [1939] "La liberté de l'esprit." In *Oeuvres*, Vol. II. Bibliothèque de la Pléiade. Paris: Gallimard.
Van Doorslaer, Luc (2011) "The Relative Neglect of Newspapers in Translation Studies Research." In Antoine Chalvin (ed.) *Between Cultures and Texts: Itineraries in Translation History*. Peter Lang, 25–33.
Van Tieghem, Paul (1931) *La littérature comparée*. Paris: Colin.
Venuti, Lawrence (ed.) (2000) *The Translation Studies Reader*. London: Routledge.
Venuti, Lawrence (2008) *The Translator's Invisibility: A History of Translation*. Second Edition. London: Routledge.
Venuti, Lawrence (2012) "Translation Studies and World Literature." In Theo D'haen, David Damrosch and Djelal Kadir (eds) *The Routledge Companion to World Literature*. London: Routledge, 180–193.
Venuti, Lawrence (2019) *Contra Instrumentalism*. Nebraska: Nebraska University Press.
Venuti, Lawrence (2022) "Translation Studies and World Literature." In Theo D'haen, David Damrosch and Djelal Kadir (eds) *The Routledge Companion to World Literature*. Second Edition. London: Routledge, 129–139.
Vermeulen, Pieter (2016) "On World Literary Reading: Literature, the Market, and the Antinomies of Mobility." In Stefan Helgesson and Pieter Vermeulen (eds) (2016) *Institutions of World Literature: Writing, Translation, Markets*. London and New York: Routledge, 79–92.
Vertovec, Steven and Robin Cohen (eds) (2002) *Conceiving Cosmopolitanism: Theory, Context, and Practice*. Oxford: Oxford University Press.
Viegnes, Michel, Sylvie Jeanneret and Lora Traglia (eds) (2020) *Les lieux du polar: Entre cultures nationales et mondialisation*. Neuchâtel: Editions Livreo-Alphi.
Viswanathan, Gauri (1989) *The Masks of Conquest: Literary Study and British Rule in India*. New York: Columbia University Press.
Vlasta, Sandra (2022) "World Literature and Migration Literature." In Theo D'haen, David Damrosch and Djelal Kadir (eds) *The Routledge Companion to World Literature*. Second Edition. London: Routledge, 176–184.
Volkmann, Laurenz, Nancy Grimm, Ines Detmers and Katrin Thomson (eds) (2010) *Local Natures, Global Responsibilities: Ecocritical Perspectives on the New English Literatures*. Amsterdam and New York: Rodopi.
Walkowitz, Rebecca L. (2006) *Cosmopolitan Style: Modernism Beyond the Nation*. New York: Columbia University Press.
Walkowitz, Rebecca L. (2015) *Born Translated: The Contemporary Novel in an Age of World Literature*. New York: Columbia University Press.
Wallerstein, Immanuel (1974, 1980, 1989, 2011) *The Modern World-System* I, II, III and IV. Berkeley: University of California Press.
Wanberg, Kyle (2020) *Maps of Empire: A Topography of World Literature*. Toronto: University of Toronto Press.
Wang, Bing (2017) "Classical Chinese Poetry in Singapore: A Perspective of Sinophone Literature." In *Monumenta Serica* 65. 2: 421–444,
Wang, Ning (1993a) "Constructing Postmodernism: The Chinese Case and Its Different Versions." In *Canadian Review of Comparative Literature/Revue canadienne de littérature comparée* 20. 1–2: 49–61.

Wang, Ning (1993b) "Confronting Western Influence: Rethinking Chinese Literature of the New Period." In *New Literary History* 24. 4: 905–926.

Wang, Ning (1996a) "Toward a Translation Study in the Context of Chinese-Western Comparative Culture Studies." In *Perspectives: Studies in Translatology* 4: 43–52.

Wang, Ning (1996b) "Toward a New Framework of Comparative Literature." In *Canadian Review of Comparative Literature/Revue canadienne de littérature comparée* 23. 1: 91–100.

Wang, Ning (1997) "'Decolonizing' Chinese Culture in a Post-Colonial Era?" In *Canadian Review of Comparative Literature/Revue canadienne de littérature comparée* 24. 4: 999–1006.

Wang, Ning (2005) "Translating Journals into Chinese: Toward a Theoretical (Re)Construction of Chinese Critical Discourse." In *New Literary History* 36. 4: 649–659.

Wang, Ning (2006) "'Death of a Discipline?' Toward a Global/Local Orientation of Comparative Literature in China." In *Neohelicon* 23. 1: 149–163.

Wang, Ning (2010a) "Global English(es) and Global Chinese(s): Toward Rewriting a New Literary History in Chinese." In *Journal of Contemporary China* 19. 63: 159–174.

Wang, Ning (2010b) "World Literature and the Dynamic Function of Translation." In *Modern Language Quarterly* 71. 1: 2–14.

Wang, Ning (2013) "Variation Theory and Comparative Literature: A Book Review Article about Cao's Work." In *CLCWeb: Comparative Literature and Culture* 15. 6, Article 19.

Wang, Ning (2015) "On the Construction of World Poetics." In *Social Sciences in China* 36. 3: 186–196.

Ward, Stuart (2016) "The European Provenance of Decolonization." In *Past & Present* 230: 227–260.

Weinberg, Liliana (2016) "The Oblivion We Will Be: The Latin American Literary Field after Autonomy." In Stefan Helgesson and Pieter Vermeulen (eds) *Institutions of World Literature: Writing, Translation, Markets*. London and New York: Routledge, 67–78.

Weisgerber, Jean (1987) "La locution et le concept." In Jean Weisgerber (ed.) *Le réalisme magique: roman - peinture - cinéma*. Genève: l'Age d'Homme, 11–32.

Weitz, Hans J. (1987) "Weltliteratur zuerst bei Wieland." In *Arcadia* 22: 206–208.

Wellek, René (2009) [1959] "The Crisis of Comparative Literature." In David Damrosch, Natalie Melas and Mbongiseni Buthelezi (eds) *The Princeton Sourcebook in Comparative Literature*. Princeton: Princeton University Press, 162–172.

Wenzel, Jennifer (2006) "Petro-Magic-Realism: Toward a Political Ecology of Nigerian Literature." In *Postcolonial Studies* 9. 4: 449–464.

Wenzel, Jennifer (2020) *The Disposition of Nature: Environmental Crisis and World Literature*. New York: Fordham University Press.

West-Pavlov, Russell (2018) *The Global South and Literature*. Cambridge: Cambridge University Press.

Westall, Claire (2017) "World-Literary Resources and Energetic Materialism." In *Journal of Postcolonial Writing* 53. 3: 265–276.

Wienbarg, Ludolf (1982) [1835] "Goethe und die Weltliteratur." In *Literaturkritik des Jungen Deustchlands: Entwicklungen – Tendenzen – Texte*. Ed. Hartmut Steinecke. Berlin: Erich Schmidt, 155–164.

Williams, Raymond (1977) *Marxism and Literature*. Oxford: Oxford University Press.

274 *Bibliography*

Wong, Alvin K. (2018) "Including China? Postcolonial Hong Kong, Sinophone Studies, and the Gendered Geopolitics of China-centrism." In *Interventions* 20. 8: 1101–1120.

Woodberry, George (1973) [1903] "Editorial." In Hans-Joachim Schulz and Philip H. Rhein (eds) *Comparative Literature: The Early Years*. Chapel Hill, NC: The University of North Carolina Press, 211–214.

"World Lite" (2014) *Editorial n+1* 17 (Web).

WReC (Warwick Research Collective) (2015) *Combined and Uneven Development: Towards a New Theory of World-Literature*. Liverpool: Liverpool University Press.

Wu, Guanjun (2016) "Narrating a Fantasmatic Unity: On the Contemporary Sinophone Discourse of China's Civilizational Subjectivity." In *Frontiers of Philosophy in China* 11. 4: 633–651.

Xie, Ming (2017) "World Poetry, without Baedeker: The Very Idea." In *Canadian Review of Comparative Literature / Revue Canadienne de Littérature Comparée* 44. 3: 501–509.

Xie, Shaobo (2020) "World Literature, Translation, Untranslatability." In *Asia Pacific Translation and Intercultural Studies* 7. 2: 151–163, doi:10.1080/23306343.2020.1801555.

Yaeger, Patricia (2011) "Editor's Column." In *PMLA* 126. 2: 305–310.

Young, Robert J.C. (1995) *Colonial Desire: Hybridity in Theory, Culture and Race*. London and New York: Routledge.

Young, Robert J.C. (2010) "The Legacies of Edward W. Said in Comparative Literature." In *Comparative Critical Studies* 7. 2–3: 357–366.

Young, Robert J.C. (2012) "World Literature and Postcolonialism." In Theo D'haen, David Damrosch and Djelal Kadir (eds) *The Routledge Companion to World Literature*. London and New York: Routledge, 213–222.

Young, Victoria (2021) "Beyond 'Transborder'." In *Japanese Language and Literature* 55. 1: 1–34.

Zabus, Chantal (2002) *Tempests after Shakespeare*. London: Palgrave Macmillan.

Zapf, Hubert (ed.) (2016) *Handbook of Ecocriticism and Cultural Ecology*. Berlin: De Gruyter.

Zelenka, Miloš (2022) "The Concept of World Literature in Czech and Slovak Comparative Literary Studies." In *World Literature Studies* 14. 2: 5–30.

Zhang, Longxi (1992) *The Tao and the Logos: Literary Hermeneutics, East and West*. Durham: Duke University Press.

Zhang, Longxi (1999) *Mighty Opposites: From Dichotomies to Differences in the Comparative Study of China*. Redwood City: Stanford University Press.

Zhang, Longxi (2005) *Allegoresis: Reading Canonical Literature East and West*. Ithaca, NY: Cornell University Press.

Zhang, Longxi (2012a) "Qian Zhongshu as Comparatist." In Theo D'haen, David Damrosch and Djelal Kadir (eds) *The Routledge Companion to World Literature*. London: Routledge, 81–88.

Zhang, Longxi (2012b) "Divine Authority, Reference Culture, and the Concept of Translation." In *Taiwan Journal of East Asian Studies* 9. 1: 1–23.

Zhang, Longxi (2012c) "The Poetics of World Literature." In Theo D'haen, David Damrosch and Djelal Kadir (eds) *The Routledge Companion to World Literature*. London and New York: Routledge, 356–364.

Zhang, Longxi (2013) "Crossroads, Distant Killing, and Translation: On the Ethics and Politics of Comparison." In Rita Felski and Susan Stanford Friedman (eds) *Comparison: Theories, Approaches, Uses*. Baltimore: The Johns Hopkins University

Press, 46–63. (Also in Longxi Zhang [2015] *From Comparison to World Literature*. Albany: State University of New York Press, 11–29.)

Zhang, Longxi (2015) *From Comparison to World Literature*. (SUNY series in Chinese Philosophy and Culture). Albany, NY: SUNY Press.

Zhang, Longxi (2021) "East Asia as Comparative Paradigm." In Debjani Ganguly (ed.) *The Cambridge History of World Literature* Volume I. Cambridge: Cambridge University Press, 281–294.

Zhang, Longxi (2022a) "The Poetics of World Literature." In Theo D'haen, David Damrosch and Djelal Kadir (eds) *The Routledge Companion to World Literature*. Second Edition. London and New York: Routledge, 305–312.

Zhang, Longxi (2022b) "Qian Zhongshu as Comparatist." In Theo D'haen, David Damrosch and Djelal Kadir (eds) *The Routledge Companion to World Literature*. Second Edition. London: Routledge, 45–52.

Zhang, Longxi (2023a) *World Literature as Discovery: Expanding the World Literary Canon*. London and New York: Routledge.

Zhang, Longxi (2023b) *A History of Chinese Literature*. London and New York: Routledge.

Zhang, Yingjin (ed.) (2023) *A World History of Chinese Literature*. London and New York: Routledge.

Zhao, Xifang (2018) "A Critical Review of Sinologism." In *Contemporary Chinese Thought* 49. 1: 20–26.

Zhou, Ning (2018) "'Sinologism': Rethinking the Legitimacy of Sinology as Knowledge." In *Contemporary Chinese Thought* 49. 1: 7–12.

Zhou, Xian (2018) "The Problems of Sinologism and Strategies to Cope with Them." In *Contemporary Chinese Thought* 49. 1: 71–80.

Zhou, Xiaoyi and Q.S. Tong (2009) [2000] "Comparative Literature in China." In David Damrosch, Natalie Melas and Mbongiseni Buthelezi (eds) *The Princeton Sourcebook in Comparative Literature*. Princeton: Princeton University Press, 341–357.

Zhou, Yunlong (2018) "'Sinologism,' or Anxiety of the Thinking Subject." In *Contemporary Chinese Thought* 49. 1: 13–19.

Index

Abrahams, Peter 23
Achebe, Chinua 183
Adam, Ian 174
Adichie, Chimamanda Ngozi 183
Adorno, Theodor 8, 125–126, 173
Aeschylus 89, 92
Aesop 99
Ahmad, Aijaz 172
Ahmed, Leila 215
Ahmed, Siraj 182
Albers, Frank 163
Aldridge, A. Owen 20, 199; *The Reemergence of World Literature* 82, 199
Alexis, Willibald 29
al-Hakim, Tawfik 215
Allan, Michael 215
Amado, Jorge 222
Amarakeerthi, Liyanage 214
American Comparative Literature Association 2, 57, 78, 81, 118
American pedagogical construct 81–103
"American" school 3, 66–67, 75
Ampère, Jean-Jacques 52–53
Anaxagoras 99
Andersen, Hans Christian 109
Anderson, Benedict 174, 194
Anderson, Jean 229
Anderson, Perry 134
Andrés, Juan 49; *Dell'origine dei progressi e dello stato attuale d'ogni letteratura* 116–117
Andrews, John 49
Angenot, Marc 68
anglophony 184–187
Ansatzpunkt 45, 126, 128
antropofagismo 153, 157
Appiah, Kwame Anthony 176

Apter, Emily 28, 45–47, 77, 126, 138, 158–160, 164–165, 168–169, 171, 191–192, 215, 232–234; ACLA report 2; Bernheimer report 169; *The Translation Zone: A New Comparative Literature* 2, 26, 37, 45–46, 70
Aquinas, Thomas 95
Arac, Jonathan 1, 123–124, 137–138, 140, 182, 184
Arendt, Hannah 148, 181
Aristophanes 88
Arnold, Matthew 18, 86–87; *Culture and Anarchy* 35, 86
Assmann, Aleida 11
Asturias, Miguel Ángel 221, 228
Atwood, Margaret 154
Auden, W.H. 33
Auerbach, Erich 28, 36–37, 39, 40–47, 66, 70, 77–78, 126, 160, 168–169; *Mimesis* 37, 40, 42, 45; "Philologie der Weltliteratur" 36, 46, 126, 158; Woolf's novel 43–44
Augustine 89, 95
Aurélio, Diogo Pires 118
Austen, Jane 86
Azadibougar, Omid 216

Babits, Mihály 75–76
Bachner, Andrea 196
Bacon, Francis 88
Baetens, Jan 231
Bakhtin, Mikhail 68, 138, 160, 232
Baldensperger, Fernand 20, 61–62, 66, 107
Balzac, Honoré 88, 125
Banville, John 228, 229
Barenboim, Daniel 45
Barnard, Anna 222
Barnes, Julian 228
Bartosch, Roman 223

Bartsch, Karl 11
Bassnett, Susan 151, 153–154, 157, 164; *Comparative Literature: A Critical Introduction* 153–154, 157; *Translation Studies* 151
Batts, Michael S. 10–11; *A History of Histories of German Literature* 11
Baudelaire 148
Beebee, Thomas O. 213
Beecroft, Alexander 50, 65, 123, 128, 141–3
Bei Dao 209–210
"belles-lettres" 15, 50, 85, 109, 131
Benjamin, Walter 27, 113, 145, 148–150, 164; "Six Theses on History" 126
Bennett, William 95
Berczik, Árpád 48, 54, 149
Berman, Antoine 128
Bernabé, Jean 188, 190
Bernal, Martin 34
Bernheimer report 168–169
Bertens, Hans 172–173, 175–176
Bessière, Jean 185
Beyer, Edvard 24
Bhabha, Homi 151, 156, 159, 164, 165, 167–169, 171–172, 175, 178, 192, 196, 213
Bhattacharya, Baidik 180, 183–184, 213
Bible 87–88, 89, 95, 99, 148, 161
Bildung 34–35, 147, 225
Birla, Ritu 186–187
Birus, Hendrik 6, 149–150
Bleicher, Thomas 5
Bloom, Allen 95
Boccacio, Giovanni 130
Boehmer, Elleke 179–181, 183
Bolaño, Roberto 227
Boldrini, Lucia 78–79
Bologna reform 83–84
Bongie, Chris 190
Borges, Jorge Luis 113, 157, 165
Bourdieu, Pierre 26, 128–30
Bouterwek, Friedrich 52
Boyd, William 228
Boyle, Nicholas 32
Branagh, Kenneth 229
Brandes, Georg 53, 107–109, 111–112, 115, 161, 194
Brassai, Samuel 54
Braudel, Fernand 128
Braz, Albert 163–164
Brecht, Bertolt 23, 152
Bridges, Yseult 222
Brontë, Charlotte 156

Brontë, Emily 156
Brossard, Nicole 154
Brouillette, Sarah 232–234
Brown, Nicholas 184
Brunel, Pierre 68
Brunetière, Ferdinand 60–61, 66, 107
Buck, Philo 90–92, 94, 96; *Anthology of World Literature* 90–91
Buell, Lawrence 187, 219
Buescu, Helena 79, 118–121, 131, 163
Bull, Francis 20
Byron, George 51, 88, 155–156, 160
Bystrom, Kerry 196

Cabo, Fernando 117
Camilleri, Andrea 215
Campbell, Alexandra 222–223
Campbell, Chris 222
Camus, Albert 234
Candido, Antonio 195–196
Canetti, Elias 76
Cao, Shunqing 204
Cao Yu 203
Carlyle, Thomas: *German Romance* 59, 149; *Life of Schiller* 8–9, 123–4, 168
Carpentier, Alejo 193–194
Carré, Jean-Marie 62, 66
Carrière, Moritz 60
Carruthers, David V. 219
Carvalhal, Tania Franco 75
Casanova, Pascale 26, 65, 75–76, 106, 109, 113, 114, 123, 128, 137, 139–143, 160–162, 178, 180, 184, 214, 235; criticism of 131–135; *République mondiale des lettres* 1–2, 128–131
Cassin, Barbara 159
Casteel, Sarah Phillips 217
Catford, J.C. 152
Catullus 99
Caws, Mary Ann 97
Cervantes, Miguel de 15, 88, 151, 157, 214, 225
Chaitanya, Krisha 21
Chakrabarty, Dipesh 47, 186
Chakravorty, Gayatri 134
Chamoiseau, Patrick 188, 190
Chartier, Roger 223
Chasles, Philarète 13–15, 17, 52–3
Chateaubriand, René de 10
Chatterjee, Partha 186
Chaucer, Geoffrey 88, 92
Chaudhuri, Amit 170
Cheah, Pheng 179–183, 194, 235
Chen Jitong 200–201

Chevrel, Yves 68
Chinweizu, Ibekwe 192
Chiu, Kuei-fen 209
Chow, Rey 176, 205
Christy, Arthur E. 201
Ciocca, Rosella 213
Clark, Katerina 23–24
Clark, Kenneth 46
classicism 32, 58
Cleary, Joe 182
Cleeves, Ann 229
Cliff, Michelle 180
Cobham, Stephen 222
Coelho, Paulo 227
Coetzee, J.M. 156, 163, 183, 227
Combe, Dominique 190
commodity fetishism 126
Communist Manifesto 8, 95, 123–124, 127, 184
comparative literature 1–3, 48–80; crisis 66–69; origins 56
comparative method 14, 63, 65
comparative morphology 72, 136
Comte, August 60
Condé, Maryse 156, 188
Confiant, Raphaël 188, 190
Congress of Natural Scientists, Goethe's address 7–8, 28–29
Conley, Tom 192
Conley, Verena Andermatt 192
Conrad, Joseph 86, 156
Constant, Benjamin 51
Cooppan, Vilashini 169–171, 217
Corstius, J.C. Brandt 17–21
cosmopolitan literary system 142
cosmopolitanism 13, 17, 51, 56–58, 61, 64, 108–109, 159, 194, 207, 214, 223
Coulombe, Diane 207
counter-postmodernism 174–175
Coutinho, Eduardo 194
Couto, Mia 196
Craveirinha, José 163
creolization theories 73
Crescimbeni, Giovanni Mario 49
Creuzer, Georg Friedrich 40
Crosby, Alfred 219
Crowther, Yasmin 214
Culler, Jonathan 2, 82, 100, 194
Cultural China 203–204
cultural semiotics 127, 140
"culture wars" 81, 90, 94
Curtius, Ernst Robert 28, 37–42, 46–47, 76–78
Cuvier, Georges 52

Daeninckx, Didier 188
D'Aguiar, Fred 183
Dainotto, Roberto 117
Damrosch, David 2, 25–27, 56–60, 71, 73–76, 91, 97–99, 102, 113, 119, 126, 143, 148, 160, 164, 178, 180–181, 183–184, 206, 209, 214–215, 224–225, 228, 232; ACLA report 2; criticism of Casanova 132–135; *How to Read World Literature* 2; *Teaching World Literature* 2; *What is World Literature?* 2, 26, 70–71, 98, 132, 154, 229
Dangarembga, Tsitsi 215
Dangor, Achmat 234
Dante Alighieri 38, 40, 47, 52, 87, 89, 93, 95, 130
Darnton, Robert 223
Darwin, Charles 14, 95
David, Jérôme 226–227
Davis, Paul 98
Davis, Rhys 156
Day, Tony 214
de Almeida, José Américo 222
de Andrade, Oswald 153
de Assis, Machado 153
de Boissière, Ralph 222
de Campos, Haroldo and Augusto 153, 165, 195
de la Barca, Pedro Calderón 87
de Man, Paul 94
de Queiroz, Eça 222
de Sanctis, Francesco 53
de Sena, Jorge 118
De Staël, Mme 12, 51–52; *De la littérature considérée dans ses rapports avec les institutions sociales* 51; *De l'Allemagne* 12, 51
de Staël-Holstein, Anne Louise Germaine 12
de Torre, Guillermo 115
de Troyes, Chrétien 88
Dean, Andrew 217
Deckard, Sharae 222
deconstructionism 94
Deeney, John J. 199
Defoe, Daniel 156
Deism 30
Dekker, Eduard Douwes *see* Multatuli
Deleuze, Gilles 25, 158, 177–178, 183
DeLillo, Don 181
DeLoughrey, Teresa 222
Denby, David 90
Denecke, Wiebke 101, 211
Denina, Carlo 49

der Weduwen, Arthur 224
Derrida, Jacques 35, 94, 158, 181
Detmers, Ines 222
Dharwadker, Vinay 101
Di Leo, Jeffrey R. 97
Dickens, Charles 86, 88
Dickinson, Emily 84
diffusionist models 106, 117, 195
Dimock, Wai-Chee 126, 138–139, 187
Dina, Amelia 214
Diouf, Abdou 189
Dirlik, Arif 176
"distant reading" 72, 135, 138–139
Dixon, Robert 217
Djebar, Assia 196
Docherty, Tomas 2
Domínguez, César 2, 116–117, 121, 127, 194
Dostoevsky, Fyodor 88, 92
Drinkwater, John 21, 201
Dryden, John 49, 146
Du Bellay, Joachim 130
Duarte, João Ferreira 118
During, Simon 65
Ďurišin, Dionýsz 69, 76–77, 117, 122, 123, 127–128; *Èo je svetová literatúra?* 127
Dussel, Enrique 192
Dyserinck, Hugo 68

Eagleton, Terry 134
Eastman, Max 23
Eckermann, Johann Peter 6, 34, 51, 84, 123
Eco, Umberto 227
Edmond, Jacob 209–210
Eikhenbaum, Boris 76
Eisenstein, Elisabeth 223
El-Ariss, Tarek 215
Elias, Amy J. 71
Eliot, George 86
Eliot, T.S. 38, 47, 86, 155–156
elliptical approach 98
Emerson, Ralph Waldo 15, 34, 84, 146
Emmett, Christine 234
Empedocles 99
Engels, Friedrich 8, 95, 123–125, 127, 184
English, James 134
Enlightenment 16, 30, 35, 51, 176, 200, 221
Eötvös, József 58
epichoric mode 141, 143
Erasmus, Desiderius 30, 88
Erskine, John 89, 91
Escarpit, Robert 223

Esonwanne, Uzoma 216
Estrada, Ezequiel Martínez 20
Etiemble, René 25, 69–70, 72–73, 93, 119, 187, 199, 218; *Comparaison n'est pas raison* 69, 187; *Essais de littérature (vraiment) générale* 69
Ette, Ottmar 217
Euripides 88
Eurocentrism 3, 22, 24–26, 28–29, 36, 42, 45–47, 74, 95, 100, 105, 169, 173, 177, 179, 187, 192–195, 200, 204, 206–208, 212, 232
Even-Zohar, Itamar 127–128, 135, 145, 151–154
evolution theory 135–136

factualism 60–61, 67
Fang, Weigui 209
Fanon, Frantz 184, 192
Farah, Nuruddin 180
Febvre, Lucien 223
feminism 84, 95, 153–154, 156–157, 171, 174
Ferguson, Frances 134, 139
Fielding, Henry 137
Figlerowicz, Matylda 194
Figueira, Dorothy 74
Fitz, Earl 114, 118–119, 195
Fogel, Joshua 206
Fokkema, Douwe 68, 173, 176
folk literature/poetry 31, 55
folk-culture 12
folklore 59
Forsdick, Charles 189–191
Foscarini, Marco 10
Foucault, Michel 25, 158, 177–178
Frankfurt School 8, 126, 173
"free trade" of literature 123–127
"French" school 3, 48, 60–62, 66–67, 93
Frenz, Horst 67
Freud, Sigmund 95
Friederich, Werner 92–93, 102, 105–106, 198
Friedman, Susan Stanford 196
Froissart, Jean 88
Frydman, Jason 216–217
Fuller, Margaret 34–35

Galileo Galilei 95
Gallagher, Mary 190–191
Gallant, Mavis 154
Gane, Gillian 186
Ganguly, Debjani 131, 138, 179–181, 223
Garibaldi, Giuseppe 38

Garuba, Harry 217
Gasché, Rodolphe 34–35
Gayley, Charles Mills 66
Gearey, John 8
Geeraerts, Jef 231
Geider, Thomas 216
Geneva School 93–94
Gentile, Paola 163
Gentzler, Edwin 154
"Germanistik" 11, 58
Gervinus, Georg Gottfried 10–11, 13, 55, 58
Ghali, Waguih 215
Ghosh, Amitav 180, 215
Gibson, Helen 160
Gikandi, Simon 175–177, 185–186
Giles, Paul 181, 217
Gillespie, Gerald 74
Gimma, Giaconto 10
Glissant, Edouard 73, 188–191
global literature 142
glocalization 177, 194
Gnisci, Armando 117, 121
Godbout, Jacques 188
Goethe, Johann Wolfgang von 5–9, 31–32, 35–38, 54, 59, 63–64, 87–88, 98, 123–124; Congress of Natural Scientists 7, 28; cosmopolitanism 13; *Gespräche mit Goethe* 6; humanism 28–31; *Italienische Reise* 32; in Italy 31–35; *The Sorrows of Young Werther* 5; *Sturm und Drang* 31–32, 41; *Über Kunst und Altertum* 6, 28–29, 59; *Werther* 31, 95, 225; *West-östlicher Diwan* 5, 44, 149–150
Goldmann, Lucien 167
Gordimer, Nadine 234
Gorky, Maxim 21–24, 125, 160
Gorter, Herman 155
Gossens, Peter 13, 16–17, 124–125
Graça-Moura, Vasco 118
Graff, Gerald 85
Graham, James 222
Gramsci, Antonio 185
Grant, J.C. 222
Grass, Günter 25
Grierson, George Abraham 184
Grimm, Nancy 222
Grimm brothers 11, 31
Gu, Ming Dong 209
Guattari, Félix 25, 183
Guérard, Albert 19–20, 35–36, 69–70, 88, 94, 119, 145
Guerra, Nina e Filipe 118

Guha, Ranajit 186
Guillén, Claudio 10, 19–20, 49–52, 59–62, 66–67, 116–117
Guillory, John 162
Gulddal, Jesper 228–229
Gumbrecht, Hans Ulrich 37–39, 45; *Vom Leben und Sterben der grossen Romanisten* 37
Gunew, Sneja 217
Guo Moruo 203
Gurnah, Abdulrazak 227
Gutzkow, Karl 13
Guyard, Marius-François 62

Habermas, Jürgen 126
Habīb, Imīl 216
Hafez 5
Hall, Katharina 230
Hallward, Peter 190
Hao, Yucong 207–208
Haring, Georg Wilhelm Heinrich *see* Alexis, Willibald
Harrison, Gary 98
Hart, Jonathan Locke 210
Hashimoto, Satoru 209, 211–212
Hassan, Ihab 172–173
Hassan, Waïl 118, 134, 184–185, 196, 214
Hauptmann, Gerhart 88
Hawas, May 215
Hayot, Eric 235
Hazard, Paul 61
Hébert, Anne 154
Hedayat, Sadegh 216
Heerikhuizen, F.W. van 20
Hegel, G.W.F. 13, 107
Heidegger, Martin 35, 180
Heilbron, Johan 161–163
Heine, Heinrich 12–13, 54
Heise, Ursula 218–220
Helder, Herberto 118
Helgesson, Stefan 163, 194, 196, 216–217, 223
Hellenism 34
Hemingway, Ernest 23
Henighan, Stephen 164
Henitiuk, Valerie 164
Henrion, Matthieu Richard Auguste 10
Heraclitus 99
Herbst, Josephine 23
Herder, Johann Gottfried 11, 13, 29–31, 182
Hermans, Theo 152, 160

Hertel, Hans 25
Hesiod 99
Heslop, Harold 222
Hesse, Herman 118, 147–148
Hettner, Hermann 16; *Geschichte der Weltliteratur in übersichtlicher Darstellung* 16
Higginson, Thomas Wentworth 84–85, 91
Hillis-Miller, J. 94
Hitchcock, Peter 179
Hobbes, Thomas 95
Hodge, Bob 176
Hodkinson, Mark 233
Hoesel-Uhlig, Stefan 9
Hoffmann, Gerhard 173
Hofmeyr, Isabel 216
Holmes, James S. 151
Holst, Adrian Roland 155–156
Homer 38, 40, 64, 89, 98, 156; *Iliad* 89, 95, 99; *Odyssey* 98, 147
Horkheimer, Max 126
Hospital, Janet Turner 181
Howells, William Dean 138
Hoyos, Hector 194
Hrushovski, Benjamin 151
Hu Ying 209
Huggan, Graham 219, 227
Hugo, Victor 88
Huk, Romana 210
humanist ideal 28–47
Hurkens, Amélie 235–236
Hussein, Taha 215
Husserl, Edmund 35
Huston, Nancy 188
Hutcheon, Linda 2, 173–174
Huxley, Aldous 88
Huyssen, Andreas 173
Hwa Yol Jung 207

"imagined community" 171
Indian National Council of Education 21
Indriðason, Arnaldur 229
industrialization 11, 220
"influence studies" 61
Institut de France 10
interliterary processes 127, 234
International Comparative Literature Association 56, 67, 69, 71, 75, 78, 199, 212
Iraq War 70, 73
Irele, F. Abiola 192
Iser, Wolfgang 68
Ishiguro, Kazuo 189

Jakobson, Roman 160
James, Henry 86
Jameson, Fredric 8, 125–126, 169–171, 173, 176
Jansen, F.J. Billeskov 24
Jauss, Hans Robert 68
Jeanneret, Sylvie 229
Jelloun, Tahar Ben 187–188
Jeusette, Julien 216
Jobim, José Luís 224
Jockers, Matthew 139
Jonckbloet, W.J.A 11
Jones, Lewis 222
Jones, William 52, 182, 184
Jost, François 49, 52–53, 68–9; *Introduction to Comparative Literature* 49
Joyaux, Georges 69
Joyce, James 38, 131
Juvan, Marko 234–235

Kadir, Djelal 2, 42, 72–73, 100, 102, 107, 126, 180
Kafka, Franz 98, 131, 133–134
Kalidasa 98
Kalliney, Peter J. 24
Kant, Immanuel 9, 14, 29, 31, 50, 110
Keen, Ruth 207
Kerr, Philip 230
Kesteloot, Lylian 189
Khair, Thabish 216
Khayyam, Omar 87–88
Kierkegaard, Søren 109
King, Stewart 228–230
Klemperer, Victor 77
Kliger, Ilya 128, 140–1
Klobucka, Anna 105, 120–121, 177
Kobis, Dewi Christa 214
Koch, Max 58–60, 104
Konrad, Nikolai 75
Krauss, Karl 37
Kristal, Efraín 138, 195
Kristmannsson, Gauti 161
Kulathunga, Chamini 214
Kumar, Amitava 170–171
Kundera, Milan 215
Kuntaka 98
Kureishi, Hanif 189

La Manna, Federica 224
Laath, Erwin 21
Labelle, Maurice 192
Laclau, Ernesto 175–176
Laferrière, Dany 188
Lahiri, Jhumpa 170–171

282 *Index*

Lambert, José 127
Lamine Sall, Amadou 189
Larsen, Niel 193
Larsen, Svend Erik 107–108, 111–112, 217
Larsson, Stieg 224, 227, 230
Lasker, Bruno 216
Laughlin, Charles A. 209
Laurence, Margaret 154
Lavalette, Robert 20
Lawall, Sarah 1, 70, 82, 90, 92–93, 96–97, 99–101, 104
Laye, Camara 216
Lazarus, Neil 178
Le Bris, Michel 189, 191
Le Clézio, J.M.G. 188, 191
Le Monde manifesto 187–190
Leavis, F.R. 86, 177
Lee, Meera 212
Leerssen, Joep 68
Lefevere, André 152, 154, 156, 160
Leon, Donna 230–231
Lernout, Geert 68
"letters" 7–9, 50, 130–131
Levinas, Emmanuel 186
Lezra, Jacques 159
Li Bai 156
Liew, Brandon K. 214
Lima, Luiz Costa 196
Lima, Thayse Leal 165
Lindberg-Wada, Gunilla 2, 25
Lindenberger, Herbert 89, 95
Lionnet, Françoise 2, 53, 192
Li-Po 156
"littérature universelle" 19
"litteraturvetenskap" 110
Liyong, Taban Lo 216
Llosa, Mario Vargas 194–195
Llovet, Jordi 116
Locane, Jorge J. 223
Lodge, David 227
Loliée, Fréderic 18, 115
London, Jack 23
Longfellow, Henry Wadsworth 82
Longxi Zhang 200, 205, 209–211
Lotman, Yuri 68, 127–128, 140–1
Louandre, Charles 53
Loy, Benjamin 223
Lu, Sheldon 220
Lu Xun 107, 147, 201–203, 220
Lubbock, Sir John 70
Lucretius 88, 99
Luhmann, Niklas 128, 141, 212
Lukács, Geörgy 125–126

Lund, Joshua 195
Luther, Martin 14, 95, 148

Maalouf, Amin 188
Macaulay, Thomas Babington 86
Macdonald, Graeme 222
Machiavelli, Niccolo 95
Mack, Maynard 94, 97
Macy, John Albert 201–202
Magdeburg, Mechtild von 133
Mahfouz, Naguib 214
Mahjoub, Jamal 228
Majumder, Auritro 213
Maldonado-Torres, Nelson 192
Malone, David Henry 93
Malory, Thomas 88
Mangalagiri, Adhira 213
Manguel, Alberto 224
Mani, B. Venkat 180, 213, 224
Mankell, Henning 229–230, 231
Mann, Thomas 23, 41, 125
Mao Dun 212, 221
Marlowe, Christopher 87, 108
Marno, David 57–58
Marseilles *Athénée* discourses 52
Martin, Henri-Jean 223
Marx, Karl 8–9, 95, 123–128, 184, 214
Marxism 23, 72, 125–127, 134, 135, 144, 173, 185, 218
Mata, Inocência 216
Mattar, Karim 214
Mayer, Elizabeth 33
Mayr, Ernst 72
McDonald, Christie 191
McGann, Jerome 132
McHale, Brian 173
McMartin, Jack 162–163
McPherson, James 31, 87
Meltzl, Hugo 53–59, 71, 108
Memmi, Albert 184
"men of letters" 7–8, 34, 50
Menand, Louis 134
Menchú, Rigoberta 133
Mendes, Alfred 222
Menzel, Wolfgang 54
Mertehikian, Lucas 194
Meyers, Stephenie 231
Michelangelo 33
Mignolo, Walter 192–193, 195
Miller, Christopher L. 192
Miner, Earl 211
Miranda, Carolina 229
Mirizio, Annalisa 196
Mishra, Pankaj 170

Mishra, Vijay 176, 216
Mitchell, David 181
Mittler, Barbara 209
Mohamed, Nadifa 183
Molière 88, 92
Møller, Peter Ulf 20, 24
monolingualism 70, 73
Montaigne, Michel de 10, 15, 89
Montalbán, Vázquez 230
Moore, Jason 220
Moore, Nicole 217
More, Thomas 30
Moretti, Franco 1–2, 26, 65, 72, 75–76, 104, 106, 113–114, 123, 128, 135–143, 159–160, 178, 180, 184, 195, 214, 223–224, 235; *Atlas of the European Novel 1800–1900* 26, 135; "Conjectures on World Literature" 1, 26, 72, 137; "Evolution, World Systems, *Weltliteratur*" 2; *Graphs, Maps, Trees* 2, 26, 72; *Modern Epic* 136; "More Conjectures on World Literature" 1
Mouffe, Chantal 175
Moulton, Richard 19–20, 35–36, 62, 85–91, 94, 134, 146, 201; *World Literature and Its Place in General Culture* 19, 62, 85, 201
Mouré, Erin 163–164
Mufti, Aamir 180, 182, 213
Müller, Gesinne 217, 223
Multatuli 162
multiculturalism 25, 70, 73, 94–95, 167–168, 172, 176, 185–6, 196, 217
Mundt, Theodor 13, 15
Munif, Abdel Rahman 214
Munro, Alice 154
Murakami, Haruki 227
Murphy, David 191
Murray, Simone 236

Nafisi, Azar 214
Naipaul, V.S. 183
Nair, K.K. *see* Chaitanya, Krisha
naming world literature 5–27
Nardizzi, Vin 223
national context 142
national literature 9–12, 130
NATO literature 92, 198
Ndlovu-Gatshen, Sabelo J. 192
neo-Marxism 126, 134, 144, 173
Nestingen, Andrew 231
Nethersole, Reingard 224
Neuhumanismus 30

Neumann, Birgit 217
"New Criticism" 66, 91, 94, 127, 134
Ngal, Mwbil, Giambatista Viko 133
Niblett, Michael 220–222
Niethammer, Friedrich Immanuel 29
Nijhoff, Martinus 155–156
Nilsson, Louise 228
Ning, Wang 202
Noël, Jean-François-Michel 52

Okri, Ben 183, 189
Oloff, Kerstin 222
Olubas, Brigitta 217
Ondaatje, Michael 181
Orsenna, Eric 188
Orsini, Francesca 138, 185, 213
Ortíz, Fernando 195, 220
Ouma, Christopher E.W. 217
Ouologuem, Yambo 216
Ovid 99
Owen, Stephen 209

Palladio, Andrea 32–34
Pamuk, Orhan 214, 227
panchoric system 50, 141–3
Pannwitz, Rudof 149–151
Parham, John 223
Parisian *Athénée* lectures 14, 53
Park, Sowon 206
Patočka, Jan 35
Pavič, Milorad 133
Paye, Michael 222
Penguin Classics 147
Pepper, Andrew 229, 231
Perloff, Marjori 186
Peshkov, Aleksey Maximovich *see* Gorky, Maxim
Pessoa, Fernando 163–164
Petöfi, János 68
Petöfi, Sándor 58
Petrarch, Francesco 92, 130
Pettegree, Andrew 224
Pettersson, Anders 15–17, 110, 200
Pezzotti, Barbara 229–230
Philip, NourbeSe 183
philology 14, 30–31, 35–41, 44, 46–47, 52, 57, 66, 126, 158, 182
Pichois, Claude 18–19, 53; *La Littérature comparée* 68
Pima Ant Songs 216
Pineau, Gisèle 188
Pirker, Eva Ulrike 217
Pizer, John 13, 84–85, 90, 102–103, 164; *The Idea of World Literature* 2, 12

planetary materialities 218–237
Plantin, Christoffel 30
Plato 40, 88, 95, 98–99
Pléiade 21
Poirier, Richard 43
Pollock, Sheldon 50, 143, 213–214
polyglottism 54–56, 58–59, 71
polysystem theory 127, 136, 145, 151, 154
Ponzanesi, Sandra 235
Pope, Alexander 146
popular literature 8
Poquelin, Jean-Baptiste *see* Molière
positivism 59–60, 64, 107
Posnett, Hutcheson Macaulay 20, 76, 82, 143, 146; *Comparative Literature* 18, 63–65
postcolonialism 4, 25, 153–154, 171–175; and translation 153–154; as Western projection 175–184
postmodernism 171–175
postnationalism 159
Potter, Lucy 222
Poulet, Georges 94
Pound, Ezra 149
Prakash, Gyan 186
Prampolino, G. 21
Pratt, Mary Louise 206, 223
Prendergast, Christopher 1, 97, 131, 133–134; *Debating World Literature* 1
provincializing 47
Puchner, Martin 99, 101, 223
Pullman, Philip 231
Puxan-Oliva, Marta 196

Qian Zhongshu 200
Quadrio, Francesco Saverio 49
Quayson, Ato 183
Queneau, Raymond 21
Querrien, Anne 133
Quijano, Anibal 192

Rabelais, François 15, 88
Racine, Jean Baptiste 88
Rajan, Rajeswari Sunder 213
Rama, Ángel 194–195
Ramazani, Jahan 215
Raphaël 33
reader reception theories 68
Reclam Verlag 147–148
Rego, José Lins do 222
Remak, H.H. 67–68
Renaissance 28, 30, 32–35, 39, 46–47, 51, 75, 87–88, 92, 123, 215

"Republic of Letters" 7–8, 50–51, 130–131
Rhein, Philip H. 15, 58, 60, 62, 64
Rhys, Jean 156
Ribeiro, Darcy 195
Ricci, Ronit 214
Riley, Lucinda 231
Ringgaard, Dan 113
Rippl, Gabrielle 217
Riquer, Martín de 21, 116
Riva, Silvia 216
Roberts, Nora 231
Roberts, William L. 207
Robinet, Jean-Baptiste-René 49
Robinson, Edwin Arlington 88
Roh, Franz 193
Rojas, Carlos 209
Rolls, Alistair 228–229
Romanticism 9, 11, 30–31, 92, 221
Rooney, Brigid 217
Rosenkranz, Karl 16
Rouaud, Jean 188–189, 191
Rousseau, André-M. 18–19; *La Littérature comparée* 68
Rowling, J.K. 227, 231
Roy, Arundhati 170
Rushdie, Salman 174, 181, 183, 185–186, 189, 227
"Russian" school 68

Sacheri, Eduardo 230
Said, Edward 4, 25, 28, 36–37, 39, 41–47, 70, 77, 79, 117, 138, 155, 158, 168–169, 180–182, 184, 192, 209, 235; *Culture and Imperialism* 42–43; *Humanism and Democratic Criticism* 37, 39, 41–42, 45–46, 70; *Orientalism* 36, 44, 46, 117, 209; *The World, The Text, and the Critic* 42, 46, 180
Said, Maire 36, 46
Saint Maur monks 10
Sainte-Beuve, Charles-Augustin 53, 107
Saint-Simonism 54
Salih, Tayeb 183
Samarin, R.M. 24
Samoyault, Tiphaine 135
Samuelson, Meg 217
Sánchez Prado, Ignacio 223
Sangari, Kumkum 173, 176
Sapiro, Gisèle 135, 161, 163, 192
Sappho 99
Saramago, José 120, 227
Sarkozy, Nicolas 189, 217
Sarraute, Nathalie 188
Sartre, Jean-Paul 70

Satrapi, Marjane 214
Saussy, Haun 2, 56–58, 74, 81, 212
Schamoni, Wolfgang 5
Scherr, Johannes 16, 18; *Allgemeine Geschichte der Literatur von den ältesten Zeiten bis auf die Gegenwart* 16; *Bildersaal der Weltliteratur* 16; *Illustrierte Geschichte der Weltliteratur* 16
Schiller, Friedrich 41; Carlyle's biography of 8–9, 123–124, 168
Schlegel, August Wilhelm von 51–52; *Comparaison entre Phèdre de Racine et celle d'Euripide* 52
Schlegel brothers 11, 31
Schlözer, August Ludwig von 5; *Isländische Literatur und Geschichte* 5
Schmid, David 229, 231
Schmidt, S.J. 68
Schneider, Jost 8
Schubert, Franz 12
Schulz, Hans-Joachim 15, 58, 60, 62, 64
Schumann, Robert 12
Schwarz, Roberto 196, 221
scientism 60, 67
Scott, Walter 88, 125
Scottish Antiquaries 31
Seeba, Hinrich 78
Seferis, George 98
September 11th terrorist attack 26, 36, 37, 45, 70, 73
Shackford, Charles Chauncey 18–19, 62–63
Shakespeare, William 40, 87, 89, 108, 156, 161, 225
Shelley, Percy Bysshe 146
Shields, Carol 154
shifts in translation 152
Shikibu, Murasaki 116
Shlovsky, Viktor 76, 160, 232
Shohat, Ella 176
Shurtleff, Oliver 91
Sienkiewicz, Henryk 88
Sinclair, Upton 23
Sinopoli, Franca 121
Siskind, Mariano 194
Sismondi, Jean-Charles Léonard Simonde de 51–52; *Littérature du midi de l'Europe* 51
Siundu, Godwin 217
Sjöwall, Maj 230
Slauerhoff, J.J. 156
Slaughter, Joseph R. 196
Slemon, Stephen 174, 179

Smith, Zadie 189
Societas Comparationis Litterarum Universarum 56
Society of Comparative Literature 66
Sokpom, Kim 211
Solon 98
Sontag, Susan 160
Sophocles 89
Spenser, Edmund 88
Spiegelman, Art 181
Spingarn, Joel 168
Spitzer, Leo 28, 36–37, 43, 45–47, 66, 70, 77–78, 158; "Linguistics and Literary History" 45–46
Spivak, Gayatri 79, 134, 138, 157–159, 164, 168, 177–178, 184–187, 192, 204, 213, 218; *Death of a Discipline* 70, 101, 186–7
Srinivasan, Ragini Tharoor 217
Srivastava, Neelam 213
Stakhanov, Alexei 23
Stalling, Jonathan 209
Stallknecht, Newton P. 67
Stangerup, Hakon 24
Steinbeck, John 88
Steiner, Ann 161, 224–227, 231
Steinmetz, Horst 177, 180
Stern, Adolf 16–17
Strich, Fritz 6–8, 28–29, 132, 225; *Goethe and World Literature* 29
structuralism 69, 94, 151
subaltern studies 25–26, 75, 185–186
Sudermann, Hermann 225
Suleiman, Rubin 191
supranationality 117
Symposium 212
systems, world literature as 123–144
Szeman, Imre 222
Szerb, Antal 76

Tagore, Rabindranath 21–23, 213; "Shakuntala: Its Inner Meaning" 98
Taine, Hippolyte 60, 107
Tam, Kwok-kan 217
Tamen, Pedro 118
Tanoukhi, Nirvana 139
Tawada, Yoko 211
Taylor, Byron 160
Tennyson, Alfred 88
terrorism, 9/11 26, 36, 37, 45, 70, 73
Texte, Joseph 50, 53, 61
Thales 99
Thiong'o, Ngugi wa 183, 192, 196
Thomas, Gwyn 222

Index

Thomsen, Mads Rosendahl 2, 113, 132, 135, 169
Thomson, Katrin 222
Thornber, Karen 123, 206, 210, 212–213, 219
Thucydides 98
Tiffin, Helen 174, 176
Tihanov, Galin 75–77, 128, 160, 207, 209, 231–232
Tito, Josip Broz 122
Tiwari, Bhavya 183, 213
Todd, Richard 227
Toer, Pramoedya Ananta 214
Tolstoy, Leo 88
Tong, Q.S. 199–200
Toury, Gideon 151–152
Traglia, Lora 229
Traninger, Anita 224
Transcendentalist Circle 84
translation 145–166; and "new" comparative literature 157–165; postcolonialism and feminism 153–154; rise of translation studies 151–153
Traube, Kimi 100
Traustedt, P.H. 24
Trilling, Lionel 89
Tsu, Jing 135, 200–202, 208–209
Tu Wei-ming 203
Tynianov, Yury 76

Ungureanu, Delia 135
"universal literature" 18–20, 22, 61–62, 87
universalism 34–35
utopianism 124, 189

Valenta, Simão 121
Valéry, Paul 128–129
Valverde, José María 21, 116
Van Bibber-Orr, Edwin 212
van Dijk, Teun A. 68
Van Doorslaer, Luc 224
van Hensbroek, P.A.M. Boele 17
van Tieghem, Paul 20, 51, 62, 67; *La Littérature comparée* 62
Venuti, Lawrence 160–161, 163–164
"Verkehr" 123, 127
Vermeulen, Pieter 223, 233
vernacular mode 108, 130–131, 142–143, 182
Vico, Giambattista 42
Viegnes, Michel 229
Villanueva, Dario 117
Villemain, Abel-François 52
Virgil 38, 40, 92, 99

Viswanathan, Gauri 86
Vlasta, Sandra 196
Volkmann, Laurenz 222
Volpe, Galvano della 72, 135
Voltaire 49, 95
von Kotzebue, Augustus 225
Von Leixner, Otto 17
von Tunk, Eduard 20
Vossler, Karl 37

Wahlöö, Per 230
Walcott, Derek 98, 156
Waley, Arthur 156
Wallace, Edgar 225
Wallerstein, Immanuel 26, 105, 135, 137, 142, 162, 219
Wang, David Der-wei 209
Ward, Stuart 192
Warren, Austin 66–67
Warwick Research Collective 219, 233–234
Watson, David 217
Weimar classicism 32
Weinberg, Liliana 235
Weisgerber, Jean 193
Weisinger, Herbert 69
Weisstein, Ulrich 68
Wellek, René 60, 66–69, 78, 93–94, 168; "The Crisis of Comparative Literature" 68; *Discriminations* 60; *Norton Anthology of World Masterpieces* 92, 94, 96–97
Wells, Henry H. 201
Wenzel, Jennifer 220–221
Werth, Tiffany Jo 223
Westall, Claire 221–222
Westling, Louise 223
West-Pavlov, Russell 216
Wicomb, Zoë 234
Wiegler, Paul 17
Wieland, Christoph Martin, Horace's letters 5
Wienbarg, Ludolf 12
Wilkinson, Ellen 222
Williams, Raymond 221
Wilson, Emily 100, 100–101
Wilson, Robert C. 230
Winchester, Caleb Thomas 201
Winckelmann, Johann Joachim 30, 32, 34
Wodehouse, P.G. 133
Wood, Michael 159
Woodberry, George Edward 65–66; *Great Writers* 15
Woolf, Virginia 89; *To the Lighthouse* 43
Wordsworth, William 88

world systems theory 105, 135–136, 162
"worlding" 4, 26, 42, 72–73, 79, 100–103, 180, 235
WReC 219–220, 222–223, 235
Wrethed, Joakim 217

Xie, Shaobo 164–165
Xie Liu 204
Xit, Ming 210

Yeats, W.B. 155–156
Young, Robert 44, 60, 178–179, 183
Young, Victoria 211

Young Germany movement 12, 54
Yue Daiyun 200

Zapf, Hubert 223
Zecchini, Laetitia 185, 213
Zelenka, Milo 127
Zeng Pu 200
Zhang, Yingjin 209
Zheng Zhenduo 201–202
Zhirmunsky, V.M. 117
Zhou Xiaoyi 199–200
Zhou Zuoren 147, 200–202
Zola, Emile 88

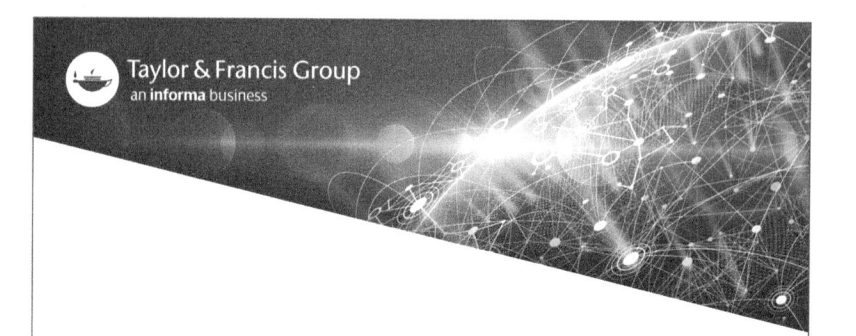